WORK MOTIVATION
IN THE CONTEXT OF A
GLOBALIZING ECONOMY

WORK MOTIVATION
IN THE CONTEXT OF A
GLOBALIZING ECONOMY

Edited by

Miriam Erez
University of Haifa

Uwe Kleinbeck
University of Dortmund

Henk Thierry
University of Tilburg

Routledge
Taylor & Francis Group

LONDON AND NEW YORK

First published in 2001 by Lawrence Erlbaum Associates, Inc.

Published 2017 by Routledge
2 Park Square, Milton Park, Abingdon, Oxon OX14 4RN
711 Third Avenue, New York, NY 10017, USA

Routledge is an imprint of the Taylor & Francis Group, an informa business

Copyright © 2001 by Taylor & Francis.

Cover Design:	Kathryn Houghtaling Lacey
Textbook Production Manager:	Paul Smolenski

This book was typeset in 10/12 pt. Times Roman, Bold, and Italic.
The heads were typeset in Americana and Americana Bold.

Library of Congress Cataloging-in-Publication Data

Work motivation in the context of a globalizing economy / edited by M. Erez, U. Kleinbeck, H. Thierry.
    p. cm.
    Includes bibliographical references and index.
    ISBN 0-8058-2814-1 (cloth : alk. paper) – ISBN 0-8058-2815-X (pbk. : alk. paper)
    1. Employee motivation.   2. Organizational commitment.   3. Globalization. I. Erez, Miriam. II. Kleinbeck, Uwe. III. Thierry, Henk.

HF5549.5.M63 W3728   2001
658.3'14—dc21

2001023196

ISBN 13: 978-0-8058-2815-3 (pbk)

Contents

v

     of Organizational Withdrawal Models   293
     Kathy A. Hanisch, Charles L. Hulin, and Steven T. Seitz

21   Some New Organizational Perspectives on Moderators
     and Mediators in the Stress–Strain Process: Time Urgency,
     Management, and Worker Control   313
     Meni Koslowsky

IV   THE CULTURAL LEVEL
     Introduction—Miriam Erez

22   Different Carrots for Different Rabbits: Effects of
     Individualism–Collectivism and Power Distance
     on Work Motivation   329
     Kwok Leung

23   Self-actualization versus Collectualization: Implications
     for Motivation Theories   341
     Simcha Ronen

24   Understanding Social Motivation From an Interpersonal
     Perspective: Organizational Face Theory   369
     P. Christopher Earley

25   An Evolutionary Perspective on Change and Stability
     in Personality, Culture and Organization   381
     Nigel Nicholson

26   Surveying the Foundations: Approaches to Measuring Group,
     Organizational, and National Variation   395
     Michael Harris Bond

     Author Index   413
     Subject Index   427

Preface

In the winter of 1996 an internationally renowned group of scholars met together in *Ein Gedi, near* the Dead Sea in Israel for a conference on work motivation. These scholars were given the charge of creating a vision of motivation research for the 21st century. Coming from different parts of the world they represented a wide range of perspectives from the very micro focus on the individual level of motivation, through the meso-levels of groups and organizations, and up to the macro level of culture. *The book is organized in line with these four levels.* In the *introductory chapter* that follows we provide an entry to the book by summarizing several mega-trends manifest across all of the chapters, and identifying several emerging trends that are left for future research.

ACKNOWLEDGEMENTS

We would also like to gratefully acknowledge the support of a number of people and institutions for their help that made the conference possible and thus, this volume as well. Special thank is given to Michael Strub, and the U.S. Army Research, Development and Standardization Group—UK, as well as to the Technion—Israel

ix

Institute of Technology, for their generous support of the conference. In addition, we also want to thank The Israel Academy of Sciences and Humanities, The S. Neaman Institute for Advanced Studies in Sciences and Technology, and Professor Bilha Mannheim—The Yigal Alon Chair in the Sciences of Man at Work, for their support of the conference. The warm hospitality of Eitan Verdesheim, Amichai Elbar, and the Ein-Gedi Guesthouse is highly appreciated. Special thanks to Gilad Paz for coordinating the conference and the publication material for this book, and to Anne Duffy, our Editor in LEA who did not stop believing that this book would get to press.

Miriam Erez
Haifa, Israel

Uwe Kleinbeck
Dortmund, Germany

Henk Thierry
Tilburg, the Netherlands

1

Introduction—Trends Reflected in Work Motivation

Miriam Erez and Dov Eden

THE MEANING OF WORK MOTIVATION

It is no coincidence that, as we enter the new millennium, questions regarding the meaning of human life and self-identity, the impact of the changing environment, and the role of work in these issues are arousing intense discussion. The first issue of the *American Psychologist* in the year 2000 was dedicated to "Happiness, Excellence, and Optimal Human Functioning." Twentieth-century psychology was focused mainly on healing illness and repairing dysfunction, based on a disease model of human behavior (Seligman & Csikszentmihalyi, 2000). Much less attention was given to understanding human life in normal, everyday circumstances. Seligman and Csikszentmihalyi have proposed a major shift of attention toward "positive psychology" in order to learn more about happiness, excellence, and ordinary human functioning.

Work motivation, on the other hand, is perhaps one of the few areas in psychology that has always been driven by the positive approach of humanizing the workplace and finding ways to help working people satisfy their needs for self-worth and well-being. Theories of motivation explore the sources of pleasure that people experience when they maintain equilibrium and preserve homeostasis by avoiding pain and overstimulation. Other motivational theories focus on the enjoyment people experience when they break through the boundaries of homeostasis and stretch their limits. The sources of pleasure and enjoyment are seen as residing in the individual, in the work environment, and in the fit between the two.

As we enter the 21st century such theories are being expanded to incorporate changes occurring in work tasks, in organizations, and in the globe at large. First, task design is shifting from the individual to teams. Consequently, the impact of teams on work motivation at both the individual and team level is coming under more scrutiny. Second, organizations are becoming less centralistic, more diffuse, and more multinational as they globalize. These changes have implications for the levels of autonomy and responsibility vested in employees, as well as for leadership. Finally, multinational corporations, international mergers and acquisitions, and international joint ventures and alliances are becoming the rule rather than the exception, infusing cultural pluralism into the workplace. Clearly, all these trends reflect an enormous amount of change occurring in today's workplace.

The dynamic process of change in and of itself has important implications for employees in modern organizations. In particular, it affects their basic need to know who they are as a secure anchor amid incessant change. Frequent changes in organizations and in technology influence the power structure, the skills needed to excel on the job, an organization's values, and its managerial philosophy. More people are encountering new cultures as multinational firms span geographical, political, and cultural boundaries. In response to such changes, the authors of the first issue of the *Academy of Management Review* in the year 2000 struggled with the need to redefine the meaning of one's identity. Among the many creative ideas proposed were for the individual to develop multiple identities (Pratt & Foreman, 2000) or to keep one's identity more fluid to help adapt it to the changing work environment (Gioia, Schultz, & Corley, 2000).

This volume reflects these changes in the work environment and integrates them into the new models of work motivation. The organization of the book represents the multilevel approach, and its chapters are integrated accordingly into four parts that present the individual, group, organizational, and cultural levels.

FROM THE INDIVIDUAL TO THE GLOBAL CONTEXT

Work motivation research began, as did the psychology of motivation in general, as a branch of individual psychology. However, more than theories of personality and human abilities, theories of work motivation traditionally have encompassed both individual and situational characteristics. Among the individual-based theories are Maslow's need hierarchy, Atkinson and McClelland's needs for achievement, affiliation, and power, Vroom's Expectancy–Valence theory, Locke's goal-setting theory, Higgins's theory of prevention–promotion motivation, and Dweck's theory of goal orientation. Part 1 of this book represents this approach. Furthermore, other theories of work motivation have brought contextual factors into focus. These are instantiated by Herzberg's Hygiene–Motivation theory, which postulated differential effects of extrinsic and intrinsic factors on work motivation, Hackman and Oldham's job-design model, Adams' equity theory, and theories that examined the effects of the social environment, including groups and organizations. Other theories advocated person–situation fit as the determinant of employee work behavior and satisfaction (Schneider, 1975). However, these theories were still mostly explicated at the individual level of analysis.

Only recently have cross-level and multiple-level theories begun to analyze work motivation at the meso- and macro-levels of groups, organizations, and cultures. If in the past a researcher who had sampled, say, 100 workers in each of 30 factories in each of 10 countries had to decide whether to regard this as a sample of 10 countries, of 300 factories, or of 3,000 workers, the dilemma no longer exists; the data can be analyzed simultaneously as originating from 3,000 workers grouped into 30 factories and further grouped into 10 countries without violating the integrity of any of the three levels. We thus gain the added knowledge of how country- and organization-level variables influence individuals as well as how individuals influence higher-level variables, and begin to achieve understanding of phenomena that are emergent at the group, organization, and country levels, an impossible mission a few years ago. Indeed, this shift towards cross-level analysis is beginning to be evident in numerous areas of organizational psychology (e.g., leadership; see Dansereau & Yammarino, 1998).

The trend toward higher levels of analysis is reflected in the ordering of the parts of this volume as well as in its title. The chapters are arranged in a progression from the individual level through the group and organizational levels, culminating in the cross-cultural level. The individual level still gets the largest number of chapters— 10—in the book. Moreover, although the chapters devoted to higher levels of theory and analysis together outnumber these, most of the "higher-level" chapters are still focused on the effect of the higher-level context on individual motivation. Only a few chapters focus on a higher level entity per se. We believe that this reflects where the field is moving, gradually supplementing the individual level with higher levels of theory and analysis as researchers contemplate why people exert effort at work from ever-broader perspectives. This process is facilitated by the emergence of more elaborate cross-level theoretical frameworks (e.g., Klein & Kozlowsky, 2000) and the recent development of cross-level analytical tools such as hierarchical linear modeling. The various contributions display some of the new insights gained by recent use of new cross-level tools. This broad vista is likely to continue, as a retreat to an exclusive—or even dominant—focus on the individual appears unlikely due to inexorable processes set in motion by globalization, requiring a broader perspective to understand the forces impinging upon individuals at work and affecting their motivation.

FROM MONOCULTURAL
TO MULTICULTURAL
MOTIVATION RESEARCH

The apex of levels originating with the individual and extending through the group and the organization is the cultural level. In the past, motivation was studied at the individual level and within one cultural milieu. As this was expanding to the group level and then to the organizational level, other branches of psychology were exploring cross-cultural issues. Organizational psychology became cross-cultural as business began to globalize. We now live in a cross-cultural age dominated by a cross-cultural Zeitgeist. We witness Europe's Gastarbeiter taking advantage of higher-paying industrial production jobs than those available back in their native countries, as well as expatriate executives sent all over the world to manage their multinational concerns' overseas subsidiaries. If in the past it was relatively rare in most countries for indigenous employees to work alongside "foreigners," the phenomenon has become so commonplace and normative that the very words "foreigner" and "alien" have assumed pejorative meaning. The global movement of workers has become so massive that it is not only the individual crossing into a new culture that must adapt to unfamiliar customs and mores, but also the indigenous workers who must accommodate large numbers of new managers and coworkers, who bring with them unfamiliar ways of doing things.

Thus, globalization has brought with it mass movement of workers and unprecedented cross mingling of persons from different cultures. Unlike residential neighborhoods, which usually are ethnically and culturally segregated, the workplace is the meeting ground of these diverse cultures, and management has to see to their smooth meshing. When successful, the synergistic outcome can be extraordinarily productive and profitable. The cross-cultural perspective is reflected in the varied countries of origin of the authors of this volume, as well as in its contents.

Cross-cultural theory and research are the productive academic response to this aspect of globalization. Erez and Earley (1993) incorporated culture and organizational behavior into their model of cultural self-representation. Their model bridges culture—a macro-level factor—managerial practices in organizations at the meso level, and the individual self and behavior—micro-level factors. According to this model, cultural values are represented in the self. These values serve as criteria for evaluating the meaning of management practices for a person's self-worth and well-being. Positive evaluations result in positive work attitudes and high performance, whereas negative evaluations lead to negative attitudes and low performance.

The cross-level perspective dominates this volume. Reading through the book from chapter to chapter reveals a progression leading up to a cross-cultural pinnacle that is based on everything that preceded it. So long as globalization and international open-borders policies prevail, the cross-cultural perspective will be indispensable for understanding work motivation at *any* level.

TRENDS NOT REFLECTED
IN THIS VOLUME

No work is complete. There are important repercussions of globalization and modernization that are not discussed in this collection. We mention them briefly in the hope that they get addressed in future work.

Stretching Beyond Sensible Limits— Is There a Dark Side of Motivation?

The notion of "super motivation" has become a popular topic in recent years. The mass media (e.g., Tolson, 2000) and best-selling trade books (e.g., Loehr, 1998) have popularized motivational concepts taken from sports psychology and applied them to life in general, and to work and management in particular. Readers are advised how to enter an "ideal performance state," to develop "mental toughness," to "focus," to put themselves in a state of "flow," and to be "in the zone," all in order to achieve "learned effectiveness." The aim is to become a champion and achieve supreme success in whatever realm of endeavor the individual is pursuing.

Our chapters do not deal with super motivation. Many of these concepts have a folkloric flavor, and as of yet, lack sound scientific basis. To be sure, there are people who push themselves beyond reasonable limits and achieve great things. Yet, many others end up paying a tragic toll in terms of health and well-being. Job stress and the work-family interface are beyond the scope of the present volume. However, as a counterweight to the potential payoff that may be reaped by exerting superhuman effort at work, the inevitable costs that must be factored in make may render the outcome of dubious value. It seems likely that the inverted-U-shaped relationship between stress and performance proved valid also for motivation and performance, for we should then find ourselves advising management how to reduce overmotivation among those afflicted by it. To the extent that globalization of high-tech industries is enticing greater numbers of workers into super motivation, the process and its results are worthy of future research attention.

Money—The Prime Mover

Nations rich and poor are witnessing escalation of the number of new millionaires. The high-tech industry worldwide is attracting growing numbers of ambitious entrepreneurs who have the dream of being successful and getting rich fast. Seeing the increasing number of individuals who have succeeded in this race energizes newcomers to take the risk and intensify their efforts. The media bombard the public with colorful stories of young people working 80- and 90-hour weeks for months and years in the hope of breaking through to the ranks of the mega-wealthy.

It is as though "economic man," the straw man of work-motivation theory of the 1950s and 1960s, is resurrected.

As industrial psychology and social psychology were hybridizing into social-industrial and organizational psychology, work motivation theory abandoned economic need as the sole or even major source of employees' willingness to exert effort and embraced the higher motives postulated by Maslow's need. The result was a new genre of work motivation theories emphasizing "higher" ego needs and intrinsic motivation over economic drive. This tradition of minimizing money as an important motivator is clearly reflected in this collection of papers. The only chapter devoted to a new way of thinking about compensation is Thierry's, in which he identifies four meanings of money and discusses how they relate to the individual's self-identity. We hope future volumes expand our understanding of the complexity of money as a motivator. For example, one interesting question is how the meaning of money may differ across cultures. To what extent does globalization create clash or convergence of values in regard to money?

Left Out—The Uneducated Masses

Largely ignored in this volume, as well as in work motivation research in general, are the countless millions who toil in return for subsistence wages to make the products we consume. The flow of capital to the less developed parts of the globe, where abundant uneducated masses make labor "competitive" (i.e., cheap), has accelerated to the point that few of the manufactured products purchased and consumed in the industrialized countries are made domestically. International tensions are rising in face of the uneasy contrast between the small proportion of wealthy nations and wealthy individuals within those nations, who are high up on the need hierarchy, and the toiling millions who are barely subsisting. This stark reality is all around us to see, and is constantly exposed in the media. Its threatening implications make it easy to ignore or to relegate to that pile of "facts of life" that are immutable. Moreover, international and intranational inequality is increasing, not decreasing.

As these words are being written, memories are still fresh of the thousands who took to the streets recently in violent protest against the globalization policies embodied in the General Agreement on Tariffs and Trade (GATT) during the meeting of the World Trade Organization in Seattle in 1999, during the meeting of the Joint Development Committee of the International Monetary Fund (IMF) and the World Bank in Washington, D.C., and again on the occasion of the annual meeting of the World Bank and the IMF in Prague, in 2000. Obviously, globalization is not universally regarded as a blessing, and it may be implicated in exacerbating inequality. International bodies could doubtless do more to promote faster mobility and less inequality in and between the countries in which they operate.

The work motivational implications are unclear. Those at the very top, the affluent in the middle clawing to advance toward the top, and those at the bottom struggling to avoid hunger, are all motivated to earn more money. But is it the same? Saying that everybody wants a bigger piece of the pie does not illuminate the motivational differences between the have-nots who want more and the haves who also want more. Viewed globally, the distinction between the motivation of the rich and the motivation of the poor is confounded with cross-cultural differences due to the concentration of wealth in a few countries and profound, widespread poverty in others. How does the interplay of national culture and wealth or poverty translate into motivational forces in the workplace? Has the accumulation of material rewards lessened the economic motivation of individuals who should by all accounts be motivated by higher-level needs? Can we learn anything about this from analyzing change in countries such as India and the People's Republic of China, in which rapidly growing middle classes provide a living laboratory where informative contrasts can be made, holding national culture constant? The present volume says little about this issue, though the enduring divide between haves and have-nots shows no sign of abating. This issue will not recede in the near future, and it is worthy of research attention.

Genes and Motives

As psychologists, we have expanded our perspective beyond the individual to the group, organization, and society, that is, to macro levels. However, we have not looked in the other direction: inward to the cellular and genetic levels where the biochemical determinants of human behavior are being rapidly unveiled. In his popularized account of the current mapping of the human genome, Ridley (1999) tells of the marvels of the gene *D4DR*, which lies on the short arm of chromosome 11. This gene determines how receptive neurons are to dopamine, which in turn controls neural electrical discharge and, ultimately, regulates the flow of blood through the brain. Via these mechanisms, dopamine determines a person's activity level. In Ridley's words, "to simplify grossly, dopamine is perhaps the brain's motivation chemical. Too little and the person lacks initiative and motivation. Too much and the person is easily bored and frequently seeks new adventures. Here perhaps lies the root of a difference in personality" (p. 163).

Although for us as psychologists the jump from chemicals to motivation to personality is a bit abrupt, the trend is clear: We are drawing nearer to the dream—or nightmare—of chemistry-based motivation. Self-imposed "substance abuse" for quick energy among the overworked is widely reported. Sports practitioners have advanced chemical arousal with the aim of marshalling the body's resources for supreme exertion to the point where competitors are routinely monitored—and disqualified—for illegal drug use by means considered unacceptably invasive only a few years ago. The chemical future is approaching. It would be naive to rule out use of chemical substances by repressive regimes to keep the toiling masses working, and perhaps enjoying their toil, too.

Our volume is silent on these genetic advances. Although there is some attention to these issues in the organizational literature (i.e., Arvey's study of monozygotic twins and work satisfaction), they should exert an impact on work motivation theory and practice in the future. We predict a future of work motivation research delving down into the microbiological depths of the chemistry within the individual in parallel to the current ascent to the group, organization, and society that surround the individual. Exploration of the internal environment will complement the recent expansion of work motivation research out into the individual's external environment. We foresee a future motivational analysis in which the individual's work motivation will be understood in the dual context of ever larger layers of the surrounding social milieu and ever more microscopic constituents of his or her internal chemistry. This is the complete picture that awaits the next generation of work-motivation theorists and researchers.

We hope that this volume will illuminate the multidimensional levels of work motivation, and will open up new research avenues. The book is organized into four sections that span the level of analysis discussed above: the individual, the group, the organization, and the cultural levels. Each section is preceded by a short introduction.

REFERENCES

Arvey, R. D., Bouchard T. J., Jr., Segal, N. L., and Abraham, L. M. (1989). Job satisfaction: Environmental and genetic components. *Journal of Applied Psychology, 74,* 187–192.

Dansereau, F., & Yammarino, F. J. (1998). (Eds.). *Leadership: The multiple level approaches: Classical and new wave.* Greenwich, CT: JAI Press.

Erez, M., & Earley, P. C., (1993). *Culture, self-identity, and work.* New York: Oxford University Press.

Gioia, D. A., Schultz, M., & Corley, K. G. (2000). Organizational identity, image and adaptive instability. *Academy of Management Review, 25,* 63–81.

Loehr, J. E. (1998). *Stress for success.* New York: Times Books.

Pratt, M., & Foreman, P. A. (2000). Classifying managerial responses to multiple organizational identities. *Academy of Management Review, 25,* 18–42.

Ridley, M. (1999). *Genome: The autobiography of a species in 23 chapters.* New York: HarperCollins.

Schneider, B. (1975). Organizational Climate: An essay. *Personnel Psychology, 28,* 447–479.

Seligman, E. P., & Csikszentmihalyi, M. (2000). Positive psychology: An introduction. *American Psychologist, 55,* 5–14.

Tolson, J. (2000, July 3). Into the zone: The kind of mental conditioning that makes athletes into superstars also helps ordinary folks become extraordinary. *U.S. News & World Report.*

I
Work Motivation—
The Individual Level

INTRODUCTION—UWE KLEINBECK AND MIRIAM EREZ

The first part of this book consists of ten chapters, focusing on work motivation at the individual level. The chapters offer a new twist on the motivational concepts of goal setting, self-efficacy, feedback, expectancies, compensation, and personal dispositions.

The first three chapters focus on the goal-setting theory of motivation. Chapters 4 and 5 further illuminate the concept of efficacy and its practical application. Chapter 6 examines personal initiation as a form of self-set goals, and elaborates on its theoretical and practical implications. Chapters 7 and 8 examine positive and negative motivational forces, and their effect on behavior. Chapter 9 empirically tests the expectancy model of motivation. Finally, Chapter 10 proposes a conceptual framework for understanding the meaning of compensation.

The chapter by **Ed Locke**, entitled *"Self-set Goals and Self-efficacy as Mediators of Incentives and Personality,"* examines the mediating effect of the "motivation hub" (see Locke, 1991) on the relationship between incentives and personality, and performance. The motivational hub consists of personal goals, goal commitment, and self-efficacy. One interesting finding is that personal goals and self-efficacy did not predict performance when neither assigned goals nor feedback were present. This finding needs to be further explored in order to clarify what *was* regulating performance in such cases.

Robert Wood, Jane George-Falvy, and Shelda Debowski, in their chapter, *"Motivation and Information Search on Complex Tasks,"* examined task complexity as the boundary condition of the goal-setting model. More specifically, they studied the effects of complexity and motivational states on searches in databases. They measured search effort, search scope, and search sequencing, plus the effects of one core motivational state, self-efficacy, on search behavior. The results indicated that self-efficacy, one of the core motivational states from social cognitive theory, predicts several dimensions of search behavior and performance. The ecological validity of the task and future research possibilities are discussed.

The study by **Jürgen Wegge, Uwe Kleinbeck, and Klaus-Helmut Schmidt,** *"Goal Setting and Performance in Working Memory and Short-Term Memory Tasks,"* examined the effect of difficult versus do best goals on two different memory tasks: The first task was a reading span test and the second task was a traditional memory span test with lists of one-syllable words. The time of day for performing these tasks was controlled. The results demonstrate that high work motivation induced by goal setting facilitated short-term retention of information mainly for subtasks with high memory load and around midday, when short-term storage of information is usually impaired due to circadian performance rhythms. The authors concluded that goal setting leads to a temporary increase in cognitive arousal (working memory capacity), especially around midday.

Dov Eden, in his chapter *"Means Efficacy: External Source of General and Specific Subjective Efficacy,"* further advances the efficacy theory by conceptualizing previously undefined dimensions and sources of efficacy beliefs. Eden introduces the concept of means efficacy, which is the individual's belief in the utility of the means available for performing the job. Means efficacy reflects the individual's beliefs in (a) the quality of the organization's internal services, and available tools for facilitating his or her particular job performance, (b) the expertise of his or her immediate supervisor, and (c) the competence of his or her teammates. The role of the leaders in organizations is to lead employees to believe in their own competence, general and specific, as well as to be confident in the efficaciousness of the general and specific means available to them.

Zeeva Milman and Gary Latham, in their chapter *"Increased Reemployment Through Training in Verbal Self-guidance,"* examine the effect of training on self-persuasion, self-efficacy, and its consequent behavior. Their study showed that training in verbal self-guidance is an effective method of self-persuasion. Managers who were unemployed but had the benefit of the training exhibited stronger self-efficacy than did those in the control group and hence were more successful in attaining their goal to be reemployed. The findings suggest that people who find employment are those who have high self-efficacy created by positive self-guidance. They tell themselves that success is the result of their own efforts.

Michael Frese focuses on personal initiative and relatively unexplored motivational characteristics in *"Personal Initiative (PI): The Theoretical Concept and Empirical Findings."* Personal Initiative is a behavioral syndrome resulting in an individual's taking a self-starting, active, and persistent approach to work. This behavior should also be consistent with the organization's mission. Self-starting implies that the goals are not given by somebody else but that the person develops those goals him/herself. Frese developed a theoretical model that explains the effect of personal dispositions, and situational factors on personal initiation, and its relationship to performance. The model is supported by empirical evidence. The practical implications of personal initiation are further discussed.

   Avi Kluger examined the effect of *feedback–expectation discrepancy, arousal and locus of cognition.* His study was stimulated by the finding that approximately one-third of all feedback interventions reduces performance. Furthermore, both negative and positive feedback messages yield similar performance. To explain these counterintuitive findings, Kluger proposes that feedback sign activates two regulation systems. One system operates with asymmetric rules: the more *positive* the feedback-standard discrepancy, the happier and the less task-focused is the recipient. The other system operates with symmetric rules: the more *extreme* is the feedback-standard discrepancy, the more aroused and the more task-focused is the recipient, irrespective of the feedback sign. The present study examines these two hypotheses and raises questions about the complexity of the motivational processes activated by feedback interventions. The proposed mechanisms may help to generate hypotheses about the conditions that lead to a negative effect of feedback.

   Abraham Korman, in his chapter *"Self-enhancement and Self-protection: Toward a Theory of Work Motivation,"* proposes a theoretical model in which work motivation can be generated by two independent processes: the desire for self-enhancement and the desire for self-protection. Self-enhancement and self-protective motivation occurs as a function of both personal dispositions and situational factors. Furthermore, Korman proposes that the likelihood of occurrence of either of these forms of behavior is a function of the relative strength at the time of the personal dispositions, and situational factors, which generate these patterns. The chapter elaborates on the meaning of self-enhancement and self-protective motivation. It discusses how personal and situational factors generate each one of the two motivational processes.

   Wendelien Van Eerde and Henk Thierry explored the effects of *VIE functions, self-set goals, and performance.* Their experiment examined the effects of the expectancy theory on self-set goals and performance. Valence, instrumentality, and expectancy were manipulated in a between-subjects experimental design to establish effects on self-set goals and performance. The results showed that there was only one significant effect of expectancy on the self-set goals. However, apart from gender differences, some interesting differences between subjects were discovered in the rating of the variables. The authors proposed that motivation theories might be differentially valid for different persons.

   Henk Thierry proposes a theoretical framework for understanding the motivational effect of compensation. His paper on *the reflection theory of compensation* summarized his model. The reflection on pay theory proposes that pay has no informational value and meaning "in itself"; pay gets significance, since it *refers to* other domains, which are important to the individual person at work. Pay "reflects" information about what is happening in other fields, the meaning of which connects to the person's self-identity. Pay does this through its amount, its composition, its differentials, and its procedures. This chapter presents the theory's core characteristics. Then, four meanings of pay are highlighted. Finally, some moderating variables of the effect of pay on both performance and satisfaction are discussed.

2

Self-set Goals and Self-efficacy as Mediators of Incentives and Personality

Edwin A. Locke

College of Business and Management
University of Maryland, College Park, MD

In a provocative report published in 1935, C. A. Mace made the following obser-vation:

> So, generally, whatever incentive or incentive conditions may be employed, the per-formance of any task is throughout controlled by some specific intention. . . . Super-vision, verbal encouragement or reproof, the prescription of standards and so forth, are of value, just in so far as, directly or indirectly, they control the specific intention which is operative in the performance of the given task. (Mace, 1935, p. 2)

It has taken more than 50 years for Mace's idea to be taken seriously enough to be systematically tested. Based on Mace, as well as on Ryan (1970), I hypothesized the role of goals and intentions as causal mediators of incentives in Locke (1968b). More recently (Locke, 1991), I proposed an enlarged mediation model focused around the concept of the "motivation hub." A hub is a "center of activity." In the context of motivation theory it refers to the place where the action is, or, more precisely, that part of the motivation sequence that is closest to action. By closest I mean closest in time and in causal influence. The hub in Locke (1991) was part of a proposed "motivation sequence" model that started with needs and values and ended with rewards and satisfaction. My focus here is on the first several links

13

of the model—those going from needs and incentives to action. This part of the model (which is modified slightly from Locke, 1991) is shown below.

THE MEDIATION-LINKING MODEL

Motivation Hub

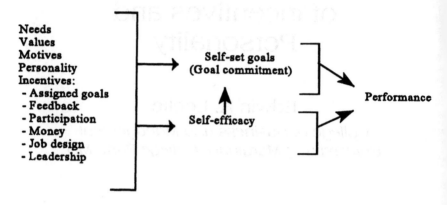

This model asserts that self-set or personal goals (which is what Mace meant by intentions) and self-efficacy (which refers to task-specific self-confidence) are the most immediate, motivational determinants of action (Bandura, 1986; Locke & Latham, 1990), and that they mediate or link the effects of other motivators. For the purpose of this paper, I am treating goal commitment as part of the motivation hub. (It is true, of course, that goals themselves are mediated by various mechanisms [attention, effort, and persistence], but these core mechanisms are activated relatively automatically in response to goals.) Previously (Locke, 1991), I discussed two motivational elements hypothesized to be mediated by goals and self-efficacy: needs and values (or motives), both of which are internal factors. Here I have added two more elements to the model: personality, which reflects values and motives as well as personal style, and incentives, which are external inducements to action (e.g., feedback, participation, job characteristics, leadership, and money incentives).

The basic assumption of the hub model is that self-set goals and self-efficacy, which are task and situationally-specific, take into account or reflect the other motivational elements in the context of the specific situation at hand. Consider, for example, values. Values may affect how individuals choose and "frame" situations. Individuals who highly value achievement, for example, should be more likely to: look for situations in which they can achieve, conclude that tasks and situations they encounter are pertinent to achievement or opportunities for achievement, look for ways to measure their accomplishments, set high achievement goals, and be highly committed to these goals as compared to individuals who do not value achievement highly. What goals are set also will be affected by the individual's perceived self-efficacy for the task at hand. The principle is the same for external incentives; they can also help to frame situations. For example, individuals who value money highly should be more likely to look for money-making opportunities, think of ways to turn situations into opportunities for making money, set higher goals for money and for achievements that will gain money (depending again on their self-efficacy) and be more committed to such goals than individuals who do not value it. (Observe here that, to be effective, external incentives must appeal to values.) Leaders can motivate followers through framing. By communicating an inspiring vision that appeals to their values and expressing high confidence in followers, leaders can convince them that high performance is important and that they are capable of achieving it (Kirkpatrick & Locke, 1996).

As shown in the hub model, goals and goal commitment will be affected not only by values and incentives, but by the individual's degree of self-efficacy for the specific task involved (Bandura, 1986). Self-efficacy may also be affected by external factors (e.g., participation; Latham, Winters, & Locke, 1994) and, like goals, has a direct effect on performance.

Several limitations of the proposed model must be noted. An obvious limitation is that the model does not explicitly include cognition (e.g., knowledge, skills, task strategies). Knowledge and skill, of course, are known to affect action over and above the effects of motivational variables—assuming some motivation is present. The hub model in no way denies such factors, but, because of its focus on motivation, it does not specify them. Self-efficacy, of course, is a cognitive judgment, an estimate of capacity for performing, but it functions as a motivator of action (Bandura, 1986). A related cognitive element is volition, the choice to think or not to think (Binswanger, 1991). How and if a person thinks can affect every part of the model (Locke, 1991).

A second limitation of the model is that it does not take into account subconscious motivation, that is, motives that affect action independent of conscious awareness, including conscious goal setting and self-efficacy. In other words, subconscious motivation may bypass the hub altogether. For example, it may affect arousal or direction of attention without affecting conscious goals. Another alternative is possible, however. A person might be unaware of certain subconsciously held values and yet these values still might affect the person's conscious goals or self-efficacy beliefs. The precondition of relevant studies on the topic of subconscious motivation is the measurement of such motives in task-performance settings—a very difficult undertaking.

A third limitation of the model is that it does not address emotions as direct determinants of action. The full causal sequence model (Locke, 1991) places emotions at the end of the causal sequence, as consequences of value appraisals of events and situations, including one's own performance and the rewards that it produces. This, however, does not preclude the possibility that emotions, once experienced, can affect subsequent performance. Whether these operate through or around the hub is an interesting research question. Similarly, the model does not incorporate moods, which are enduring emotional states.

Thus the model is best viewed as a working hypothesis with obvious limitations. The model does not specify whether goals or self-efficacy will be the more critical link in a given case. Despite being conceptually distinct, the two concepts represent two complimentary aspects of motivation: what individuals are trying to accomplish and the confidence that they can accomplish it. These are often highly correlated. In this chapter I will summarize studies that have tested the basic mediation idea. This will give some indication of its basic viability.

Based on Guzzo's and Hanges' (1997) recent paper, we make no distinction between causal linking models in which A → B → C but A is not related to C and traditional mediation models in which A → C but is mediated by B. Guzzo and Hanges (1997) argue that both are properly called mediation meodels. Thus far, there are seven categories of studies that have tested the mediation-linking model. Six categories pertain to incentives (defined broadly) and one to personality.

Assigned Goals

Locke and Latham (1990) argue that assigned goals affect performance through their effects on personal goals and on self-efficacy. Although assigned and self-set goals are typically correlated, there may be discrepancies between them because individuals are not always fully committed to what others ask them to accomplish. Assigned goals can also affect self-efficacy, for example, because assigning difficult goals is an expression of confidence and may constitute a form of Pygmalion effect (Eden, 1990) or persuasion (Bandura, 1986). Self-efficacy may affect performance both directly and through its effects on personal goals.

Meyer and Gellatly (1988) found that assigned goals also supply to subjects normative information that they use when setting their own goals. In two laboratory studies they found that the effects of assigned goal difficulty on performance were fully mediated: by personal goals, and by performance expectancies (efficacy) via a path from perceived norms. Another laboratory study, by Meyer, Schact-Cole, and Gellatly (1988), also found a mediation effect. Two of the laboratory studies reported by Earley and Lituchy (1991) found that personal goals and self-efficacy substantially, but not totally, mediated the significant effects of experimenter-assigned goal difficulty on performance.

In quite a different type of study, conducted in a field setting, Zimmerman, Bandura, and Martinez-Pons (1992) found that 9th- and 10th-grade students' personal grade goals fully mediated the effects of their parents' grade goals (that is, the grades their parents wanted them to get) on actual grade performance. Although self-efficacy also affected grade performance, it did not mediate the effects of the parents' goals.

Feedback

Feedback, by which I mean here, knowledge of results (KR)—that is, knowledge of how you are doing on a task—was the most studied incentive with respect to the issue of mediation at the time Locke and Latham (1990) published their integration of the goal-setting literature. Locke and Bryan (1966) found no effect of degree of KR on the performance of subjects working on a complex computation task, but when the subjects were resorted according to the level of the performance goals they reported trying for, there was a significant relationship between goal level and performance.

A better-designed study by Locke and Bryan (1968) found a significant main effect of KR (versus no KR) using the same computation task. However, subjects in the KR condition set significantly harder goals than those in the no-KR condition. When goal difficulty was partialed out the KR effect was vitiated, thus indicating complete mediation of the KR effect by goals.

A third study (Locke, 1968a) replicated this finding using a reaction-time task. Both degree of KR and goal difficulty were varied. These variables were highly correlated with each other and with performance when one experimental group given full KR and low (easy) goals was excluded from the analysis. When this group was included, it had the effect of partialing out a high, preexisting (and artifactual) correlation between degree of KR and goal level among subjects in the remaining conditions. When this was done, the effect of KR was eliminated, whereas the goal effect remained highly significant.

A number of studies gave subjects feedback on two or more performance dimensions but assigned goals for only one dimension or outcome or measured what outcomes subjects set goals for. In all cases performance improved only on the dimensions for which goals were set (e.g., Locke & Bryan, 1969; see Locke & Latham, 1990, for a summary). These studies show that KR only improves performance to the extent that goals single out which performance dimension requires improvement.

Some feedback, of course, is necessary for goal setting to be effective (Locke & Latham, 1990), but the key finding here is that KR alone does not directly cause better performance. KR, of course, must be distinguished from task knowledge (knowledge of how to perform the task effectively), which does have a direct effect on performance.

A recently published study by Prussia and Kinicki (1996) examined the mediators of positive and negative feedback given to groups of subjects who worked on a brainstorming task. Following performance, the groups were given bogus, normative feedback indicating that they had performed better or worse than the average group, and then were given another brainstorming task. Group goals and group efficacy were very highly correlated (.80) but were kept separate in the LISREL analysis. The feedback effects on performance were mediated through self-efficacy in this case, but would have been equally well mediated through goals if the efficacy variable had been excluded.

Participation

The topic of participation in decision-making, or pdm, has a long a contentious history (e.g., see Locke & Latham, 1990, and Locke, Alavi, & Wagner, 1997, for a summaries). I will only be concerned here with the small portion of it relevant to goal mediation. Erez, Earley, and Hulin (1985) varied both degree of pdm and whether the subjects set or did not set personal goals in a laboratory study involving making up class schedules. Pdm subjects significantly outperformed those given assigned goals in Phase 1 of the study. However, this effect was mediated by degree of goal acceptance (commitment). Acceptance was significantly related to performance and, when entered before pdm in the regression, vitiated its effects. This could be considered a weak mediation finding, however, in that the R^2 reduction was very small and was not tested for significance.

The other study relevant to pdm is Study 3 of Latham, Erez, and Locke (1988), which used the same task as Erez, Earley, and Hulin (1985). There were three goal conditions: tell, tell and sell, and participative. For low-ability subjects, there was a significant effect of goal condition, with pdm leading to higher performance than telling the subjects what goal to aim for. This effect, however, was fully mediated by goal commitment and self-efficacy, which were higher in the pdm condition.

The two studies above suggest that to the extent that pdm does motivate higher performance, it may do so partly through its effects on goal commitment and self-efficacy. This does not preclude pdm effects on goal level as well. Latham and Yukl (1975) found that uneducated woods workers set higher goals in a pdm than in an assigned goal condition and that the pdm workers showed higher productivity, but they did not conduct a formal mediation analysis.

Recent research suggests that there are strong (though contingent—Scully, Kirkpatrick, & Locke, 1995) cognitive benefits of pdm (Locke, Alavi, & Wagner, 1997). These cognitive effects of pdm, which also raise self-efficacy (e.g., Latham, Winters, & Locke, 1994), may be more significant and reliable than its motivational effects. It is intriguing to consider the probability that self-efficacy may help mediate both the motivational and cognitive benefits of pdm.

Money Incentives

A number of studies have examined the role of goals and goal commitment in mediating the effects of money incentives, but the results have been inconsistent. On the negative side, Latham, Mitchell, and Dossett (1978), Pritchard and Curtis (1973) and Reidel, Nebeker, and Cooper (1988) all found that incentives affected performance even when goal level and goal commitment were controlled or partialed out. Furthermore, the first two studies did not even find an effect of incentives on commitment. Reidel, Nebekar, and Cooper (1988) did find an effect of incentives on both goal level and commitment, but, as noted, these did not fully mediate the incentive effect. None of these studies used a validated measure of goal commitment, and none used self-efficacy as a mediator.

On the positive side, Wright (1989) found evidence for mediation in which incentives affected personal goals and commitment, which in turn affected performance. However, there was no initial effect of incentives on performance. In a later study, Wright (1992) found that an interactive goal-incentive effect on performance was mediated by goal commitment.

One factor to consider about the above studies is that no one of them met the following four criteria: (a) significant incentive effects or goal-incentive interactions were obtained; (b) a validated commitment measure was used (e.g., the Hollenbeck scale); (c) personal goals were measured after the experimental inductions were made; (d) self-efficacy was measured. Although (a) is not obligatory according to Guzzo's and Hanges' (1997) definition of mediation, (b), (c), and (d) are needed in order to include all the potential mediators that constitute the motivation hub. The inclusion of self-efficacy is especially critical, because Bandura (1986) has found consistently that incentives are not effective unless people believe they have the capacity to take the actions required to earn them.

A recent study by Lee, Locke, and Phan (1997), however, did meet these four criteria. Three types of incentives (piece rate, bonus, and hourly) were crossed with three levels of assigned goals. A significant interaction in the second trial following performance feedback (given after the first trial) was found in line with an earlier study by Mowen, Middlemist, and Luther (1981): Under piece-rate pay, performance was higher with hard than with medium assigned goals, but under bonus pay performance was higher with medium than with hard goals. Although commitment was not significantly affected by the experimental treatments, personal (self-set) goals and self-efficacy (which were significantly correlated with commitment) were. Furthermore, goals and self-efficacy completely mediated the interaction effect. For example, when subjects tried to attain hard to impossible assigned goals, personal goals and self-efficacy dropped or failed to increase under bonus pay but increased under piece-rate pay. These results indicate that with a proper design, mediation effects for money incentives can be obtained.

Job Design

Job design, especially job enrichment, has been studied for several decades (Hackman & Oldham, 1980). The results indicate that enriched jobs characteristically raise the level of job satisfaction (Oldham, 1996), but their effect on performance is more problematic, especially when actual productivity rather than satisfaction-related actions such as absenteeism and turnover are considered (Kirkpatrick, 1992). Kirkpatrick conducted a laboratory study using a proofreading task in an attempt to isolate the performance-enhancing elements of job design. Both autonomy and responsibility were manipulated. Manipulated responsibility enhanced the level of personal goals (measured directly and in terms of anticipated satisfaction with various levels of performance) and goal commitment. Personal goals, in turn, enhanced performance. Goal commitment was only related to satisfaction. Although manipulated responsibility strongly affected experienced responsibility, the latter was unrelated to performance. These results suggest that it may be motivation hub variables (goals this case) rather than critical intervening states (Hackman & Oldham, 1980) that link job redesign to motivational performance improvements.

Charismatic Leadership

Charismatic or transformational leadership is a hot topic in the leadership literature today, but most relevant studies have been correlational in design. There is some question as to the mechanisms by which this style produces beneficial organizational outcomes, if it does. Kirkpatrick and Locke (1996) designed a laboratory study, using a clerical task used by a real organization, that isolated three elements of this leadership style: vision, charismatic personality style (divorced from vision content), and task information (which is akin to intellectual stimulation). They found that vision was the most potent of the three components. Vision (which stressed quality) significantly affected both personal goal level for quality and self-efficacy for quality, which in turn significantly affected quality of task performance. Goal commitment was not related to performance. Task strategy information, a cognitive variable, followed a partial mediation model; it affected performance quantity through its effects on quantity goals and efficacy, and also directly. Vision had the most potent effects on a variety of attitude measures, e.g., trust in the leader, congruence between own beliefs and vision, inspiration, and perceived charisma. Charismatic personality style had few effects of any kind. These results, shown in Fig. 2.1, suggest that, in leadership, substance (vision content) counts more than style and that vision operates, in part, through it effects on goals and self-efficacy.

Of course, there are other mediators of leadership that must be considered, e.g., communication, reward system, selection, training, team building, structuring, etc. Many of these are highly cognitive, but even these, as we found was the case with task strategy information, may operate in part through the hub variables.

Personality

Whereas there are relatively few relevant studies, and sometimes only one, relevant to the previous six categories, there have been at least eight studies of hub variables as mediators of personality effects. The first of these was a laboratory study

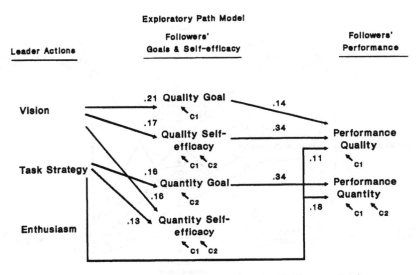

FIG. 2.1. Exploratory path diagram showing linking model from leader vision to performance (from Kirkpatrick & Locke, 1996). Copyright by American Psychological Association, reprinted by permission of author.

conducted by Matsui, Okada, and Kakuyama (1982), who found that a self-report measure of achievement motivation was significantly related to performance on a perceptual speed task. This effect was fully mediated by the difficulty or level of the goals the subjects set for themselves on the task.

Taylor, Locke, Lee, and Gist (1984) examined the relationship between the Type A personality style and the scholarly productivity of university faculty. The significant association between Type A scores and productivity was fully mediated by three variables: productivity goals, self-efficacy, and one task strategy—working on multiple projects rather than completing them one at a time. The Type A subscale that was mainly responsible for the results entailed job involvement. (In recent years, the definition of the Type A syndrome has changed to emphasize hostility or anger as the core component).

In a set of three studies conducted by Earley and Lituchy (1991), they found that trait efficacy was significantly associated with personal goals and task-specific self-efficacy, which in turn were related to performance.

Johnson and Perlow (1992) found that need for mastery, a component of self-reported need for achievement, was significantly related to goal commitment, which, in turn, was significantly related to performance on a complex laboratory task. Personal goals and self-efficacy were not measured.

Barrick, Mount, and Strauss (1993) conducted a field study using sales personnel. They found that conscientiousness (one of the "big five" personality dimensions) was associated with both sales volume and performance ratings by

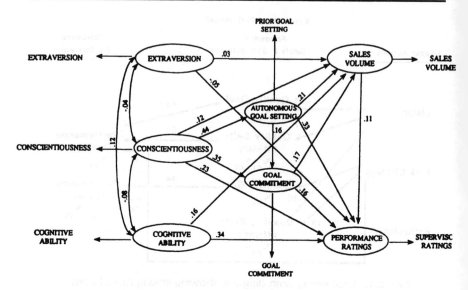

FIG. 2.2. LISREL model showing mediation of conscientiousness effect on sales volume and performance rating (from Barrick,
Mount, & Strauss, 1993). Copyright by American Psychological Association, reprinted by permission of author.

supervisors (see Fig. 2.2). The association of conscientiousness with sales volume
was partly mediated by autonomous goal setting (setting goals on one's own), and
the association with performance ratings was partially mediated by goal commitment. Since mediation was not complete, obviously other causal variables must
have been involved, including ability. Notably, self-efficacy was not measured in
this study.

Mone, Baker, and Jeffries (1995) found that college students' self-esteem, although unrelated to grades, was significantly associated with personal (grade) goals
and self-efficacy, which in turn predicted course performance.

Lerner's and Locke's (1995) study occurred in a sports-exercise context. Students in P.E. classes were given hard or easy goals to meet on a sit-up task. Half
the subjects competed with a standard (assigned goal) and half competed with a
"stooge" who performed at the level of the assigned goal. The students' scores
on a previously validated sports orientation questionnaire, which measured traits
such as competitiveness and goal orientation, was significantly associated with sit-
up performance. This association was completely mediated by personal (self-set)
goals and self-efficacy. Goal commitment was significantly related to performance,
self-set goals, and self-efficacy, but did not explain any performance variance beyond that attributable to the other two mediators.

The final study (Gellatly, 1996) was a laboratory investigation using a simple arithmetic task. A Conscientiousness factor was significantly related to performance.

This effect was completely mediated by expectancy (which was actually a measure of self-efficacy) and two personal goal measures. One was a direct goal item and the other was a measure of expected satisfaction with various levels of performance (valence). Notably, of the six Conscientiousness subscales, only three were significantly associated with performance and with the mediators: cognitive structure, order, and impulsiveness (−). The subscales were not defined.

SUBCONSCIOUS MOTIVATION

Only one study to date has examined both conscious goals and subconscious motives as predictors of performance. Howard and Bray, (personal communication), based on reanalyses of the data in their 25-year longitudinal study of AT&T managers (Howard & Bray, 1988), found that a one-item interview question in year 1, which asked the hirees how many levels they wanted to progress in the company, was strongly related to subsequent promotion over the next 25 years. In contrast, McClelland s managerial TAT measures were unrelated to promotion except for one subscale (need for affiliation), which predicted promotion weakly (and negatively) for nontechnical managers only. There was no interaction between the conscious and the subconscious measures. Obviously, further studies of this type would be useful, but the problem will be finding subconscious measures that are valid predictors.

CONCLUSION

Although only a limited number of relevant studies have been done to date, there is considerable support for the thesis that the effects of incentives and personality affect performance at least partly through "hub" variables, i.e., personal goals or goal commitment, and self-efficacy.

To our surprise, in those studies in which goal commitment was measured along with personal goals and self-efficacy, commitment does not explain any performance variance over and above that attributable to personal goals and self-efficacy. Typically, commitment is significantly related to goals and efficacy, indicating that they may act as a proxy for commitment. More committed people set higher goals and have higher self-efficacy than less committed people (or vice versa).

A qualification to the hub model that will need exploration is that it may not operate effectively in certain conditions. For example, Cervone and Wood (1995) found that when neither assigned goals nor feedback were present, personal goals and self-efficacy did not predict performance. Cervone, Jiwani, and Wood (1991) found that even when feedback was given but assigned goals were not, personal goals and self-efficacy did not predict performance. These results are somewhat puzzling in that one wonders what *was* regulating performance in such cases. Obviously this issue needs to be explored further.

Finally, as our knowledge develops, it will be necessary to bring relevant cognitive variables (knowledge, skill) into the model in order to provide a more comprehensive explanatory framework. However, since I am a believer in grounded (i.e., inductively developed) theory (Locke, 1996), I prefer to postpone this task until we have more data.

ACKNOWLEDGEMENTS

The author is indebted to Chris Earley and Robert Wood for their helpful comments on this chapter.

REFERENCES

Bandura, A. (1986). *Social foundations of thought and action.* Englewood Cliffs, NJ: Prentice-Hall.
Barrick, M. R., Mount, M. K., & Strauss, J. P. (1993). Conscientiousness and performance of sales representatives: Test of the mediating effects of goal setting. *Journal of Applied Psychology, 78,* 715–722.
Binswanger, H. (1991). Volition as cognitive self-regulation. *Organizational Behavior & Human Decision Processes, 50,* 154–178.
Cervone, D., Jiwani, N., & Wood, R. (1991). Goal setting and the differential influence of self-regulatory processes on complex decision-making performance. *Journal of Personality and Social Psychology, 61,* 257–266.
Cervone, D., & Wood, R. (1995). Goals, feedback, and the differential influence of self-regulatory processes on cognitively complex performance. *Cognitive Therapy and Research, 19,* 519–545.
Earley, P. C., & Lituchy, T. R. (1991). Delineating goal and efficacy effects: A test of three models. *Journal of Applied Psychology, 76,* 81–98.
Eden, D. (1990). *Pygmalion in management.* Lexington, MA: Lexington Books.
Erez, M., Earley, P. C., & Hulin, C. L. (1985). The impact of participation on goal acceptance and performance: A two-step model. *Academy of Management Journal, 28,* 50–66.
Gellatly, I. (1996). Conscientiousness and task performance: Test of a cognitive process model. *Journal of Applied Psychology, 81,* 474–482.
Guzzo, R. A., & Hanges, P. J. (1997). *Reconsidering the traditional criteria for establishing mediator variables.* Unpublished Manuscript, Department of Psychology, University of Maryland.
Hackman, J. R., & Oldham, G. R. (1980). *Work redesign.* Reading, MA: Addison-Wesley.
Howard, A., & Bray, D. (1988). *Managerial lives in transition.* New York: Guilford Press.
Johnson, D. S., & Perlow, R. (1992). The impact of need for achievement components on goal commitment and performance. *Journal of Applied Social Psychology, 22,* 1711–1720.
Kirkpatrick, S. A. (1992). *The effect of psychological variables on the job characteristics–work outcomes relations.* Paper presented at Eastern Academy of Management.
Kirkpatrick, S. A., & Locke, E. A. (1996). Direct and indirect effects of three core charismatic leadership components on performance and attitudes. *Journal of Applied Psychology, 81,* 36–51.
Latham, G. P., Erez, M., & Locke, E. A. (1988). Resolving scientific disputes by the joint design of crucial experiments: Applications to the Erez-Latham dispute regarding participation in goal setting. *Journal of Applied Psychology, 73,* 753–772.

Latham, G. P., Mitchell, T. R., & Dossett, D. L. (1978). Importance of participative goal setting and anticipated rewards on goal difficulty and job performance. *Journal of Applied Psychology, 63*, 163–171.

Latham, G. P., Winters, D. C., & Locke, E. A. (1994). Cognitive and motivational effects of participation: A mediator study. *Journal of Organizational Behavior, 15*, 49–63.

Latham, G. P., & Yukl, G. A. (1975). Assigned versus participative goal setting with educated and uneducated woods workers. *Journal of Applied Psychology, 60*, 299–302.

Lee, T. W., Locke, E. A., & Phan, S. H. (1997). Explaining the assigned goal-incentive interaction: The role of self-efficacy and personal goals. *Journal of Management, 23*, 541–559.

Lerner, B. S., & Locke, E. A. (1995). The effects of goal setting, self-efficacy, competition, and personal traits on the performance of an endurance task. *Journal of Sport and Exercise Psychology, 17*, 138–152.

Locke, E. A. (1968a). Effects of knowledge of results, feedback in relation to standards and goals on reaction-time performance. *American Journal of Psychology, 81*, 566–574.

Locke, E. A. (1968b). Toward a theory of task motivation and incentives. *Organizational Behavior and Human Performance, 3*, 157–189.

Locke, E. A. (1991). The motivation sequence, the motivation hub and the motivation core. *Organizational Behavior and Human Decision Processes, 50*, 288–299.

Locke, E. A. (1996). Using programmatic research to build a grounded theory. In P. Frost & S. Taylor (Ed.), *Rhythms of academic life*. Thousand Oaks, CA: Sage.

Locke, E. A., Alavi, M., & Wagner, J. (1997). Participation in decision-making: An information exchange approach. In G. R. Ferris (Ed.), *Research in Personnel and Human Resource Management* (Vol. 15). Greenwich, CT: JAI Press.

Locke, E. A., & Bryan, J. F. (1966). The effects of goal setting, rule-learning and knowledge of score on performance. *American Journal of Psychology, 79*, 451–457.

Locke, E. A., & Bryan, J. F. (1968). Goal setting as a determinant of the effect of knowledge of score on performance. *American Journal of Psychology, 81*, 398–406.

Locke, E. A., & Bryan, J. F. (1969). The directing function of goals in task performance. *Organizational Behavior & Human Performance, 4*, 35–42.

Locke, E. A., & Latham, G. P. (1990). *A theory of goal setting and task performance*. Englewood Cliffs, NJ: Prentice-Hall.

Mace, C. A. (1935). Incentives—Some experimental studies. *Industrial Health Research Report No. 72* (Great Britain).

Matsui, T., Okada, A., & Kakuyama, T. (1982). Influence of achievement need on goal setting, performance, and feedback effectiveness. *Journal of Applied Psychology, 67*, 645–648.

Meyer, J. P., & Gellatly, I. R. (1988). Perceived performance norm as a mediator in the effect of assigned goal on personal goal and task performance. *Journal of Applied Psychology, 73*, 410–420.

Meyer, J. P., Schacht-Cole, B., & Gellatly, I. R. (1988). An examination of the cognitive mechanisms by which assigned goals affect task performance and reactions to performance. *Journal of Applied Social Psychology, 18*, 390–408.

Mone, M. A., Baker, D. D., & Jeffries, F. (1995). Predictive validity and time dependency of self-efficacy, self-esteem, personal goals and academic performance. *Educational and Psychological Measurement, 55*, 716–727.

Mowen, J. C., Middlemist, R. D., & Luther, D. (1981). Joint effects of assigned goal level and incentive structure on task performance: A laboratory study. *Journal of Applied Psychology, 66*, 598–603.

Oldham, G. (1996). Job design. In C. Cooper & I. Robertson (Eds.), *International review of industrial and organizational psychology*. Chichester, UK: Wiley.

Pritchard, R. D., & Curtis, M. I. (1973). The influence of goal setting and financial incentives on task performance. *Organizational Behavior and Human Performance, 10*, 175–183.

Prussia, G. E., & Kinicki, A. J. (1996). A motivational investigation of group effectiveness using social-cognitive theory. *Journal of Applied Psychology, 81*, 187–198.

Reidel, J. A., Nebeker, D. M., & Cooper, B. L. (1988). The influence of monetary incentives on goal choice, goal commitment, and task performance. *Organizational Behavior and Human Decision Processes, 42*, 155–180.

Ryan, T. A. (1970). *Intentional behavior.* New York: Ronald Press.

Scully, J. A., Kirkpatrick, S. A., & Locke, E. A. (1995). Locus of knowledge as a determinant of the effects of participation on performance, affect and perceptions. *Organizational Behavior and Human Decision Processes, 61*, 276–288.

Taylor, M. S., Locke, E. A., Lee, C., & Gist, M. E. (1984). Type A behavior and faculty productivity: What are the mechanisms? *Organizational Behavior and Human Performance, 34*, 402–418.

Wright, P. M. (1989). Test of the mediating role of goals in the incentive-performance relationship. *Journal of Applied Psychology, 74*, 699–705.

Wright, P. M. (1992). An examination of the relationships among monetary incentives, goal level, goal commitment and performance. *Journal of Management, 18*, 677–693.

Zimmerman, B., Bandura, A., & Martinez-Pons, M. (1992). Self-motivation for academic attainment: The role of self-efficacy beliefs and personal goal setting. *American Educational Research Journal, 29*, 663–676.

3

Motivation and Information Search on Complex Tasks

Robert E. Wood
Australian Graduate School of Management

Jane George-Falvy
University of Washington

Shelda Debowski
Murdoch University

Search behaviors are an important but neglected component in the study of effort on complex tasks in which strategy development has a significant influence on performance. On many tasks in organizations, the effort devoted to the acquisition of information will exceed the effort spent processing the information obtained. An understanding of search behaviors is also important to the generalization of results from laboratory studies of motivation on complex tasks to work settings where task environments are more dynamic and less well defined for the task performer. In this chapter, the motivational dynamics of external search behavior on complex tasks are considered within a social cognitive framework (Bandura, 1986, 1997).

MOTIVATIONAL EFFECTS
ON COMPLEX TASKS

Studies of motivational processes on complex decision-making tasks have identified several effects that, on the surface, appear inconsistent with motivational effects observed on simpler tasks in which behavioral effort is more directly related to performance. There is a large body of evidence that, for simple tasks, behavioral effort and the resulting performance are positively related to the self-regulatory processes of (a) negative self-evaluative reactions, such as dissatisfaction with past performance, (b) commitment to specific, challenging goals, and (c) strength of self-efficacy beliefs (for reviews, see Bandura, 1986, 1997) . All three motivational states have been shown to have consistent, positive effects on performance in the presence of relevant feedback for simple effort-to-performance tasks, such as ergometers (e.g., Bandura & Cervone, 1986), where the strategy development and information processing requirements are quite limited by the task or study setting. The explanations for these effects are the arousal, focusing, and persistence mechanisms commonly used in motivational theories (e.g., Kanfer, 1990; Locke & Latham, 1990).

A growing body of evidence has shown that these three core motivational states from social cognitive theory also predict strategies and performance on complex tasks (e.g., Earley, Connolly, & Ekegren, 1989; Wood & Bandura, 1990). However, the relationships between self-efficacy, self-evaluative reactions, goals, and performance have often been found to differ from those identified in the study of simple tasks. These differences, discussed later, indicate a need for a closer consideration of motivational dynamics on complex tasks.

Self-efficacy

In concert with goal setting and self-evaluative reactions, self-efficacy judgments have been shown to be a significant predictor of performance on both simple and complex tasks. However, studies have shown that the mediational processes for self-efficacy differ between simple and complex tasks. On tasks where effort is directly related to performance, people with high self-efficacy tend to work harder (Bandura & Cervone, 1983, 1986). On tasks where memory and strategy development are required, individuals with a stronger sense of efficacy often display lower levels of decision effort but still manage to outperform their less efficacious colleagues who exert much greater decision effort, but become erratic in their analytical thinking and are more likely to make poor strategic choices (Cervone, Jiwani, & Wood, 1991; Wood & Bandura, 1989). Therefore, it appears that people with high self-efficacy work harder on tasks with simple effort-to-performance relationships but work smarter, or more strategically, than their less efficacious colleagues on more complex tasks. Perceived self-efficacy determines both the level of effort expenditure and how productively that effort is deployed on a task.

The impact of initial, preperformance self-efficacy estimates on task performance also differs between simple and complex tasks. On simple tasks, high initial efficacy estimates generally enhance task persistence and motivation (e.g., Cervone & Peake, 1986). Cervone and Wood (1994) found a negative relationship between initial strength of self-efficacy and performance on a complex decision task. High-efficacy individuals tended to overestimate their capabilities, which results in marked discrepancies between expectations and attainments.

Goals

Several studies have found that challenging goals either do not affect the mean levels of performance on complex tasks (Wood, Bandura, & Bailey, 1989) or have significantly less impact than on simple tasks (Wood, Mento, & Locke, 1987). The differential performance effects of specific challenging goals for simple and complex tasks have been attributed to the different processes by which goals regulate performance on the two types of tasks (Wood & Locke, 1990). Goals influence behavior through their effects on the level of individual resources (i.e., attention and effort) devoted to a task and through their cuing effects in the focusing of attention and allocation of effort to specific acts. On complex tasks, the performance effects of these processes are mediated by strategies whose selection is determined in part by the properties of the goals and partly by the available cognitive capacity of the individual. When the information-processing requirements of a task consume all the attentional resources of an individual, the arousal produced by challenging goals can interfere with the cognitive processes involved in the selection and development of strategies (Kanfer & Ackerman, 1989), leading to the misdirection of attention and effort (e.g., Huber, 1985).

Self-evaluative Reactions

On cognitively complex tasks, the impact of affective reactions has also been found to differ from the effects observed on simpler tasks where dissatisfaction with performance is positively related to performance (Bandura & Cervone, 1983, 1986). On complex decision tasks, dissatisfaction with one's failure to achieve a goal has been shown to cause performance to deteriorate (Bandura & Jourdan, 1991; Cervone et al., 1991; Cervone & Wood, 1994). Those who are dissatisfied with their goal-directed progress after initial performance assessments do worse on subsequent attempts.

Studies of affective reactions to performance on complex decision tasks have also revealed that subjects who are in a more positive mood perform at higher levels in subsequent blocks of trials (Cervone et al., 1991; Cervone & Wood, 1994). This finding is consistent with research indicating that positive mood enhances the speed and efficiency of decision making (Forgas, 1989), whereas negative mood states can deleteriously affect short-term-memory functions (Humphreys & Revelle, 1984) or bias the recall of previously encoded information (Isen, Shalker, Clark, & Karp, 1978).

In summary, existing research suggests that the paths by which self-regulatory processes influence performance may differ between simple tasks and more complex tasks that require higher levels of cognitive effort. However, what is not fully evident from the available evidence is the nature of the causal pathways between the motivational states and the observed performance effects. A fuller description of the mediating motivational dynamics first requires some further description of the meaning of cognitive effort and of the relationships between effort and task complexity.

COMPLEXITY AND EFFORT

Effort on complex tasks frequently includes both information acquisition and information processing, and these two processes are often closely related to one another. According to Newell and Simon (1972), the process of search in problem solving is the defining feature of decision strategies. In this section we discuss alternative views on the concept of cognitive effort and then outline some ideas on how complexity influences the levels of effort required for task performance.

Defining Cognitive Effort

Definitions of effort level typically refer to the expenditure of energy over time. Naylor, Pritchard, and Ilgen (1980), for example, identify time and energy as the two primary resources that are under individual control and available for allocation to different behaviors. They then define effort as "... the amount of energy spent on [an] act per unit time" (1980, p. 8). Their examples of effort devoted to a task include concentration while reading a book and the energy expended on physical activities, such as riding a bicycle. There is widespread understanding of the meaning of physical or behavioral effort; however, theories of work motivation have tended to be less specific about the meaning of effort that is involved in the performance of complex tasks. This is an important oversight, because there is evidence that for much of the work that occurs in organizations cognitive effort is more important than physical effort.

Recent discussions of effort on complex tasks have taken a strictly information-processing view of effort which, as we will argue later, may have limited applicability for the study of motivation on many complex tasks in organizations and other natural settings. Kanfer and Ackerman (1989; Kanfer, 1987, 1990), for example, have presented a resource allocation model of motivation that builds on earlier theories of information processing (Kahneman, 1973; Navon & Gopher, 1979; Norman & Bobrow, 1975). In this model, cognitive effort is defined as the level of attentional resources allocated to different activities, including self-regulatory activities and other off-task as well as on-task activities. Such models have been most useful for the study of skill acquisition on complex tasks where data to be processed is perceptually available across repeated trials, and there is a high level of consistency in the data available and in the judgments to be made. They describe the processes by which responses become automatic over time (Fitts & Posner, 1967; Kahneman, 1973; Kanfer & Ackerman, 1989).

However, the conceptualization of cognitive effort in resource allocation models has limited application in the study of many complex tasks in organizations for two reasons. First, there is the evidence that learning processes may be different and not well described by proceduralization on tasks that require problem solving. Studies have shown that learning may progress from the use of implicit knowledge to identify responses, to specific surface features of a task, to declarative knowledge of the task structure (Novick, 1988; Stanley et al., 1989). The development of explicit mental models of tasks that can be verbally described has been shown to be important to the transfer of skills from one task to the next (e.g., Novick, 1988) but is also of obvious importance in organization settings where problem solving typically involves many people and is facilitated by a common understanding of the structure of problems.

A second potential limitation of resource attention models for the study of complex tasks in organizations is their lack of attention to the off-task activities by which individuals acquire information. In resource allocation models, off-task attention is considered to be detrimental in the early stages of learning when task performance is resource-dependent (Norman & Bobrow, 1975). Kanfer and Ackerman (1989), for example, argue that self-regulatory processes, an off-task demand on attentional resources, are detrimental to learning in early stages when performance is governed by controlled processes and is highly demanding of attentional capacity. However, self-regulatory processes and other off-task activities will often be deliberately undertaken to acquire the information needed to perform a task. Therefore, on many tasks, off-task activities may have a positive effect on performance in the early stages of learning, when acquisition of information is most important.

The cognitive effort associated with different decision strategies has also been described in terms of the numbers and mix of elementary information processes required for each strategy (Bettman, Johnson, & Payne, 1990). The elementary information processes used in the cognitive effort calculations include a range of mental operations such as reading a piece of information into short-term memory, multiplying two or more values, comparing different values, and so forth.[1] However, like the resource allocation model discussed earlier, the Bettman et al. (1990) model provides a perspective on problem-solving effort that may be of limited applicability to the study of search in organizational problems. First, elementary information processes operate at a subconscious level and, therefore, do not allow us to examine the human–environment interaction that is the focus of search behavior. Second, the eight elementary information processes described focus mainly on information processing. Only one process, Read, deals directly with information acquisition.

On many naturally occurring complex tasks, individuals must constantly acquire and process new information (Simon, 1976; Wood & Locke, 1990). Often, the acquisition of information will consume much more time and effort than the processing of the information acquired (Janis & Mann, 1977). The acquisition of

---

[1]Bettman et al. (1990) describe eight elementary information processes (EIPs) used to transform an initial problem state of knowledge into the final goal state of knowledge. The levels of cognitive effort for each of the EIPs were found to be independent of the decision strategies in which they were used but were expected to vary as a function of task variables such as information format.

information will require active search of off-task sources and often may yield no return for the effort invested. For example, when working on a crossword puzzle an individual may consult a dictionary, a thesaurus, an atlas, or any number of reference books. He or she may even ask another person for an answer to a given clue. If none of these interrogations of the external environment yield an appropriate answer, as they often don't, the individual may complete other sections of the puzzle and return to the unyielding clue at a later time. The order in which an individual considers clues and the level of effort devoted to search on each clue will determine the overall effort required to complete the puzzle.

Search strategies may also be used to regulate the information processing demands of a task. As Shiffrin and Schneider note, the process of controlled search is "... usually serial in nature with a limited comparison rate, is easily established, altered, and even reversed by the subject, and is strongly dependent upon load" (1977, p. 127). In most real-world decision tasks, individuals regulate cognitive load or task demands through selective interrogation of the task and sequential processing of the information presented. This external search runs in parallel with short-term memory searches.

Task Complexity

The cognitive effort required in the performance of a task is intricately bound up with the level and the nature of the task's complexity. Despite several conceptualizations of the complexity construct that emphasize information-processing demands of performance (e.g., Campbell, 1988; Wood, 1986; Wood & Locke, 1990), the features that distinguish tasks of differing complexity and their impacts on performance are not well understood (Kanfer, 1990). The impacts of complexity on performance are further confounded by the effects of practice and learning on cognitive effort required for performance of a task.

On some tasks, practice leads to the proceduralization of knowledge and the consequential reduction in the demand for cognitive resources, even though the objective complexity of the task remains constant (Norman & Bobrow, 1975). A novice air traffic controller, for example, requires much more cognitive effort to prevent planes from crashing than an expert who has been working at the job for many years. Other tasks require continuing problem solving, including the deliberate acquisition and processing of information, such that practice does not lead to the same level of proceduralization and related reduction in the demands of cognitive effort. Practice at managerial tasks, for example, may lead to the establishment of behavioral routines and understanding of problems that differentiate the expert manager from the novice. However, the dynamic and social nature of organizational problems often means that the cognitive effort required for complex managerial tasks remains high even for very experienced managers.

The proceduralization of knowledge that leads to the reduction in cognitive demands requires a high degree of consistency in the information-processing demands (Fisk, Ackerman, & Schneider, 1987). Variations in the information-processing demands of a task are one aspect of the dynamic complexity described in Wood (1986). When task stimuli are encountered in the same format over multiple trials and stimulus–response relationships are relatively stable, the demand on cognitive resources will diminish with practice and learning. The process of skill development that leads to this reduction in the cognitive effort requirements for a given level of performance is typically described as shift from the effortful application of declarative knowledge to the automatic application of procedural knowledge (Anderson, 1993; Fitts & Posner, 1967; Kanfer & Ackerman, 1989). The proceduralization of knowledge and skill development can take place on tasks that vary quite widely in their levels of component and coordinative complexity (Wood, 1986). For example, Kanfer and Ackerman (1989) demonstrate proceduralization on the ATC task at quite high levels of component and coordinative complexity.[2]

However, this process of proceduralization only describes routine skill acquisition and does not adequately account for the cognitive effort required to handle novel situations or to reason about and understand the principles and underlying structures of tasks (Ackerman, 1992; Holyoak & Spellman, 1993). On problem-solving tasks, individuals may rely on automatic, nonconscious access to information in the early stages of learning and then progress to more conscious, declarative models of the task structure (Broadbent, Fitzgerald, & Broadbent, 1986; Stanley, Mathews, Buss, & Kotler-Cope, 1989). Although not the reverse of proceduralization, this is a different process of skill development. Furthermore, in organizations, where tasks often require cooperation and communication, the development of mental models is an important input to the effective coordination of work.

A second aspect of complexity that is relevant to the cognitive effort requirements of a task, particularly the nature and levels of information search, is the mapping of the relationships between the surface features and the structure of the task. A surface feature is a readily observable feature of a problem that may or may not be relevant to the identification of the correct responses. Structural features may be less obvious but describe the cause–effect relationships that are relevant for identifying correct responses.[3] Numerous studies have shown that

---

[2]ATC is an air traffic control task in which individuals must monitor many planes at different stages of approach to an airport and land them on different runways. The high-component complexity in this task is a function of the many cues that must be monitored and processed when making landing and plane-movement decisions. The coordinative complexity is a function of the different rules that must be learned to land planes correctly. For example, a rule might be that planes can only land on an east–west runway when the wind is in an easterly direction and above 20 knots.

[3]The distinction between surface features and structure of a task is illustrated by the sugar production tasks and person interaction tasks used by Berry and Broadbent (1984, 1988) in studies of implicit memory. Both tasks have the same structure defined by a mathematical function in which output is a function of the individual's response, previous output, and a random noise factor. The cues, or surface features, that the indiviudal observes for each task are quite different.

novices use surface features when attempting to solve problems, whereas experts also consider structural features (e.g., Chi, Feltovich, & Glaser, 1981; Novick, 1988). The structures of tasks can of course be represented as rules that are presented to individuals along with other surface features. This is what is done in the ATC task. However, when individuals have to discover the rules that describe the structure of a task, then the search process and associated problem solving becomes more important. The less obvious the mapping between the surface features and the structure of the task, the greater the required search. In general, we would expect the dissociation between the surface features and the structure of a task to increase as the coordinative and dynamic complexity of a task increases. Search, often including experimentation or hypotheses testing (Wood & Bandura, 1989), will be required to discover the structures that underpin novel tasks that have high levels of coordinative and dynamic complexity. However, where tasks are well understood, explicit statements of the rules governing coordinative and dynamic complexity can influence their impacts on requirements of cognitive effort.

In summary, dynamic complexity and forms of coordinative complexity that are not obvious from the surface features of a task will require external search processes. Understanding the nature of search is therefore important to our understanding of motivation and learning on complex tasks.

SEARCH BEHAVIOR

Information useful for self-regulation and task performance may be obtained from internal memory or from perceptually available external data, including feedback on the consequences of one's actions. When neither of these two sources provides needed information, it must be actively sought from external data sources. External search refers to behaviours undertaken to interrogate the environment and obtain information that is not readily accessible from either memory or a perceptually available external source of data. External sources of information can include other people, written records, electronic databases, and others. The methods of obtaining information from different external sources will vary depending on the data source and the level of processing required to convert the data into useful information. Search behaviors might include asking questions, consulting a reference book or some other records, or analyzing a database.

Whenever a person is confronted with a problem state and the need to "know something," they are immediately faced with deciding what information they need and where and in what order to make their inquiries (Bruner, Goodnow, & Austin, 1956). They must also consider the amount of time and effort they will devote to search relative to the processing of information and the execution of the task. Decisions regarding the amount of effort to devote to search behavior, the order of search, and the focus of the search are themselves often the product of dynamic decision processes. For example, a person may investigate a source and find that the information they were seeking is not available and that they have to adjust their search strategy. Alternatively, information may be obtained that leads to a redefining of the problem state that motivated the original search. This may then lead to a revision of the search strategy before seeking further information to solve the problem for which the search is being undertaken.

External search is typically a conscious goal-directed behavior (Newell & Simon, 1972) that can be undertaken for a range of different purposes, however it is not always the case that the information obtained serves the intended purpose. Examples of serendipity and incidental noticing are frequently mentioned in descriptions of discovery processes (e.g., Harre, 1981). The information obtained through search processes might be used to firm up goals and commitment to those goals; for selecting appropriate actions and developing plans to achieve goals; to guide the implementation of actions through a process of comparison with models; or for self-evaluations. The purposes of search behavior may change at different stages of a task. For example, in the predecisional activity leading to a goal choice (Kanfer & Ackerman, 1989), search could be directed at information relating to the difficulty of the goal, likely obstacles, and competing task demands. This information would then be combined with self-evaluations in reaching a decision regarding commitment to a goal. Once a goal is accepted, information might be sought on alternative actions for achieving the goal.

Search behaviours can influence performance on complex tasks through several different paths (Bruner et al., 1956). First, they provide information that is relevant to the objectives of the inquiry, which might be to solve a problem or to obtain a self-assessment. Second, search strategies influence the cognitive effort needed to process the information obtained in attempts to solve problems. Effective problem solving requires being able to keep track of what has been found and integrating that information into the knowledge used to reach the goal state. Third, search strategies can influence the degree of risk involved in attempts to solve a problem within a defined set of constraints. Individuals may systematically investigate, evaluate, and select alternatives, or they may take a chance on an alternative and see what happens.

Dimensions of Search Behavior

Descriptions of search behaviors have often focused on strategy types that fit with the specific tasks being studied but do not easily generalize to ill-structured, problem-solving tasks (e.g., Bruner, Goodnow, & Austin, 1956; Payne, Bettman, & Johnson, 1993). The highly structured nature of the problems often used in the identification of strategies also means that search is limited to information that is immediately available, either from memory or the immediate perceptual field of the individual. There is no requirement or opportunity for open search of the environment, as is typically required in organizational problem solving. Others have described search strategies in more general terms and have applied them to problem solving and decision making in naturalistic settings (e.g., Janis & Mann, 1977).

We take a different approach and focus on the analytical dimensions that can be used to describe search behavior rather than strategy types. This approach is taken for two reasons. First, descriptions of strategy types mix a range of external search, information processing, and choice processes in ways that make it difficult to differentiate the effects of motivation on various components of the strategy. Second, studies often show that individuals shift between strategy types during problem solving and decision making (Payne et al., 1993). In our model, search behavior and the associated strategies are described in terms of total effort, wasted effort, search sequencing, and search scope. Search scope is further broken down into breadth and depth of search.

The *total effort* expended in search strategies will include both cognitive and physical resources expended acquiring information on a task. The behavioral component of search effort includes time and energy spent interacting with the environment acquiring the information to be processed. The cognitive effort is a function of the perceptual and higher-level processing required during the actual information acquisition process and can include a range of elementary information processes. In practice, it is often difficult to separate the effort spent on acquiring information from the effort spent on processing it, as the two will often occur simultaneously. For example, a person will compare words with a crossword clue as they read the reference source they have consulted.

However, the nature of link between external search and computational effort will vary as a function of the time constraints and available computational support mechanisms. In the ATC task used in the Kanfer and Ackerman (1989) studies, for example, there is a direct link between the information available on the screen and the computational load. This relationship is quite unlike that which exists when a manager must make, say, an investment decision. The manager may use a calculator or computer to support the required calculations, read from a range of sources, and discuss different aspects of the decision with colleagues before deciding. The time available for the decision enables a sequential process of search–process–search–process, and so on, in which the computational load is spread over the available time.

Indicators of the total effort spent on search will include time spent on the activity and the numbers of steps or other activities, such as questions asked or sources consulted. For the crossword example, this could include numbers of references to the dictionary, thesaurus, or other sources of information and the time spent on each activity. The total number of interactions with the environment weighted by the effort or time spent on each interaction will capture both the physical and cognitive effort of search. Each time a question is asked or a source is consulted, elementary information processes will occur as the individual compares words with clues and spaces and identifies matches or mismatches.

The total effort devoted to search may not be necessarily productive. On complex tasks, search is often an iterative process that includes trial and error and testing of options that are later discarded. *Wasted effort* is a natural by-product of this process. As tasks become more complex, people also often forget what they have done, repeat previous steps, make irrelevant inquiries, and persist in strategies that have previously failed to yield the required information. Slips and other errors may also lead to wasted effort. Misspelling of a word or an incorrectly worded question, for example, may invalidate the information obtained from a given step in the search process and, if not detected, may lead a subsequent search in the wrong direction. Effort wasted on redundant activities and correcting errors may have deleterious effects on task performance in a variety of ways, including: violations of time or other resource constraints; fatigue and quitting; poor task knowledge; and poor learning. Of course, errors may also be a source of learning and stimulate search in new directions. This point is taken up in the concluding discussion.

Scope of search can be described in terms of breadth and depth (e.g., Payne et al., 1993). *Search breadth* refers to the coverage of the different elements of a problems space, such as the range of options considered in a preferential choice task (Payne et al., 1993) or the number of sources tapped in a concept development task (Bruner et al., 1956). Individuals often reduce the breadth of their search in order to reduce the information-processing demands. Narrowing the scope of the search in this way often leads to a less comprehensive but more manageable search process.

The degree to which each element of the problem space is searched in detail defines the *search depth*, the second component of search scope. In the preferential choice literature reviewed by Payne et al. (1993) depth refers to the level of investigation focused on "... factors associated with the particular values of the objects in the specific decision set under consideration, including the similarity and the overall attractiveness of alternatives" (1993, p. 22). As tasks become more complex, the scope of search required to effectively cover the breadth and depth of the associated problem space will increase (Newell & Simon, 1972). At the same time, the information-processing demands associated with the scope of the search will increase and may quickly exceed the capacities of the individual.

Another dimension of search behavior is the *search sequence*, or the order in which information is obtained about the problem space. For many tasks, effective search strategies require some systematic sequencing of steps that balances the comprehensiveness of the search against the information-processing load generated by the successive steps. Bruner et al. (1956), for example, described their different strategies in terms of sequencing and associated processing loads. In the preferential choice literature, information search and processing sequences have been described in terms of alternative-based versus attribute-based, and consistent versus selective (Payne et al., 1993). Later, we will present an operationalization of search sequencing that is believed by experts to provide a manageable, comprehensive search of CD-ROM databases. This process is fairly equivalent to an alternative-based search followed by an attribute-based search, with consistent processing across both phases, which has been shown to lead to accurate judgments on preferential choice tasks (Payne et al., 1993). However, ideal search sequences will vary as a function of task complexity and other characteristics, such as time constraints and computational support.

Several different methods have been used to collect data on search behavior and strategies, including self-reports in the form of either ratings or verbal protocols, and process-tracing techniques (Carrol & Johnson, 1990).[4] The data base search task employed in the research presented below was selected for the opportunity it provided to obtain an objective measure of the dimensions of search strategies on complex, relatively ill-structured and dynamic tasks. Descriptions of the task and the measures of search behavior are presented in the next section. Discussion of the ecological validity of the task is presented in the concluding section.

STUDIES OF SEARCH BEHAVIOR

A program of research has been commenced in which we are examining the impacts of motivational states on the effort, scope, and quality of search activities and the resulting learning and performance on a complex database retrieval task. In the initial studies, the focus has been on the effects of self-efficacy on the different dimensions of search behavior (Debowski, 1997). The results of one these studies will be described shortly, but first we will (a) describe the database search task and the related measures of effort, search scope, sequencing, learning and performance, and (b) briefly describe some of our expectations for the relationships between self-efficacy and search for the study reported. The results of other studies conducted will be briefly mentioned in the conclusion.

The Task

The task requires the search of a CD-ROM databse to identify library records for an assigned problem. Records stored on the database included published journal articles, unpublished papers, books, and technical reports. Subjects are assigned problems containing a set of concepts for which they have to find a set of relevant records from the database. For example, on one task subjects were asked to search for database records relating to the problem, "What impact has technology has on managerial job satisfaction?" This problem requires a search of three concepts—technology, manager, and job satisfaction.

---

[4]Self-reports and process traces can provide valid data when collected under optimal conditions (Ericsson & Simon, 1984) but have been criticized for their intrusiveness, their representation of the processes being measured, and confounds due to their ex post nature.

For their interrogations of the database, subjects construct search statements containing terms and connectors. The terms used to define the concepts in a search statement can be obtained from memory or from two external sources of information: a key word index and a thesaurus. Each library record is indexed under a range of key words. The number of key words for a concept will depend on the number of subconcepts and indicators covered by the concept. A search that incorporates key words from the index is more likely to retrieve relevant records, but human judgment in the indexing process often provides an unpredictable element in the relevance of search outcomes. A thesaurus contains lists of related key words and can be used to focus the search of a database into related areas outside the list of key words provided under the concept headings in the key-word index. There are both potential benefits and risks associated with the use of a thesaurus to identify alternative lists of key words. It can also be used to reconceptualize the problem being searched and may open the searcher up to new records. However, the records obtained from the related areas can be irrelevant and overwhelming in number.

The key words or other terms included in a search statement are linked together with Boolean Connectors, including the words *and* and *or*. Use of the "and" connector narrows the scope to those records that are indexed under all of the terms connected. The more key words connected by *and*, the more focussed the search and the fewer records likely to be retrieved. Use of the *or* connector broadens the focus of the search to retrieve all records that are indexed under any of the key words connected. Depending upon the diversity of concepts connected, the use of *or* to connect two or more key words can very quickly lead to the retrieval of large numbers of records.

The database search process is both dynamic and interactive. Each search statement retrieves a certain number of records from the database. These can be inspected by the searcher, on the computer screen, and their relevance assessed. Based on these assessments, the searcher can then modify the search statement and interrogate the database further in an attempt to increase the number of relevant records and decrease the number of irrelevant records on the search outcome. For example, the *or* connector can be used to open up possibilities that can then be searched in more detail by varying the number and scope of key words and by use of the *and* connector. However, changing the connectors and terms in a search statement can either increase or decrease the numbers of relevant and irrelevant records retrieved in subsequent search outcomes, depending upon the quality and scope of the search statements used. The search process can proceed through a number of iterations until the searcher retrieves an acceptable list of relevant library records in his or her search outcome.

The cognitive effort required to assess and interpret lists of records will depend on the number and variety of records retrieved by a search statement. A search statement that retrieves hundreds of records, for example, will typically overwhelm the individual, who will then seek to refine the search statement so as to limit the number of records retrieved in subsequent rounds of interrogation. Alternatively, a search statement that retrieves only a few records will typically be adjusted to increase the number of records retrieved by subsequent interrogations of the database.

The Measures

Total search effort was a count of the total number of terms and connectors used across all search statements. The identification of key-word terms and the choice of connectors in the creation of search statements requires considerable cognitive effort. A second indicator of total effort is the total number of search statements created by an individual. Each search statement is a continuation of the search process and, therefore, requires the expenditure of further effort. A final indicator of total effort is the time spent on the search task. Subjects were allocated a maximum of 30 minutes but could take less time if they wished. Effort intensity scores were also calculated by dividing total search effort by the number of search trials and by the total time spent on the search task.

Wasted effort was calculated using counts of the number of errors, the number of lines of search statements rejected, and the number of redundant lines in the search statements used. Errors included counts of terms used that were unrelated to any of the concepts in the search statement, misspellings of terms, and misuses of connectors. For presentation purposes, the error and redundancy scores were standardized and combined to give a single score for wasted effort.

Search breadth was the sum of three factors: the number of times the search-expanding "or" connector was used, the number of times the thesaurus was used, and the number of different concepts linked in search statements. Each of these broaden the search to a more inclusive set of options. Narrow searches are those that cover few concepts from the problem set and constrain the search through the use of "and" rather than "or" connectors. *Search depth* was the number of different keywords used to define each search concept and the number of times these intraconcept searches were linked by the "or" connector. Without the use of *or*, the different terms are not treated as alternatives in the search process and do not provide any depth in the search for records containing references to the specific concept. *Search sequencing* was a rating based on the degree to which the search steps used were matched to the recommended search sequence for effective database searching. The sequence ratings were conducted by two expert searchers (librarians) using a key (Debowski, 1997). Scores were based on the match of the actual search sequence with those identified by experts and supported as most effective by research (e.g., Michel, 1994; Quint, 1991).

Learning was indexed by a count of the number of correct usages of connectors and terms on the final two search statements. *Performance* was the number of relevant library records identified with the final search statement. Several librarians who were expert users of the CD-ROM database conducted searches for the assigned search problems and then identified a list of all relevant records on the database. Subjects received one point for each records retrieved that matched a record on the experts' list.

The Hypotheses

Several possible processes by which self-efficacy could regulate search efforts on dynamic decision tasks suggest themselves. First, people with high self-efficacy may have greater control of their cognitive processes and, therefore, be less prone to the errors and redundancies that result from memory and processing lapses and waste effort in search. Analyses of the cognitive mediators of self-efficacy have shown that people who feel more efficacious demonstrate superior performance on memory tasks (Berry, 1987). Bouffard-Bouchard (1990) has shown that students whose sense of efficacy was raised through comparisons with fictitious peer norms made more accurate evaluations of their performance than peers of equal ability who felt less efficacious. Self-efficacy, therefore, may lead to a more effective mobilization of attention and memory resources in repeated interrogations of a task environment. Based on this reasoning, we would expect individuals who feel more efficacious about their capacity to perform dynamically complex tasks will conduct higher-quality searches (i.e., fewer errors and redundancies) than those who feel less efficacious.

A second possibility is that high self-efficacy leads to a greater willingness to explore the environment for new information, and this behaviour is bolstered by a greater capacity to process the information acquired and to learn from errors and other setbacks. Individuals who doubt their capacity to perform a complex task are more likely to rely on fewer, more predictable sources of information to protect themselves from the information overload, uncertainty, and negative feedback that can result from broader search activities. Research on complex decision tasks has shown that people with a robust sense of efficacy do take a more systematic and deliberate approach in their use of options, suggesting that they are using task behavior as an opportunity to test options and acquire more task information (Wood & Bandura, 1989). This is consistent with the finding that individuals with high self-efficacy are less prone to negative self-evaluations following failure experiences (Bandura & Wood, 1989). Those who lack efficacy for a task are, therefore, expected to employ searches that are more narrow in scope than the search processes of those who are more confident of their capabilities.

The Sample

Subjects were undergraduate students from different discipline areas who had either little or no previous experience with the CD-ROM searching task. In the study discussed here, subjects were randomly assigned to one of two groups: an experimental group ($N = 26$) that received a self-efficacy boosting manipulation at the end of training session, described below, and a control group ($N = 24$).

Self-efficacy Manipulation

Subjects were first trained in the use of the CD-ROM equipment and the conduct of searches. The training program was followed by a practice session in which the self-efficacy manipulation was introduced. Subjects in the experimental, high-efficacy condition worked on the practice search problems in a set order, starting with the easiest problem first and then working on problems of increasing difficulty. At set points in the practice session, subjects in the experimental condition also received positive statements from the trainer that emphasized the subject's performance achievements on the practice tasks, such as "You are completing these practice problems much quicker than nearly all the students who have done the training." Subjects in the low-efficacy, control condition were left to work on the practice problems in any order and were not given any encouragement regarding their progress. Completing the practice problems in the assigned order and the encouragement were intended to create a feeling of progressive mastery and thus boost the self-efficacy of subjects in the experimental group relative to their counterparts in the control group (Bandura, 1997).

Self-efficacy was measured with a 21-item scale that asked subjects for their confidence in the conduct of search activities such as using the CD-ROM equipment, preparing search statements, and identifying records (alpha coeff. $= .98$). Measures were collected before training and again after completion of the practice session in which the self-efficacy manipulation was introduced. The average strength of the confidence ratings for all 21 items in the scale was used in the analyses. The self-efficacy manipulation was effective. The initial levels of self-efficacy for subjects assigned to the experimental ($X = 4.13$) and control conditions ($X = 4.11$) were nearly identical. Changes in the pre- to posttraining self-efficacy levels showed a significantly greater increase for subjects in the experimental group compared to control subjects, $F(1, 47) = 4.62$, $p < .05$. There was no difference in the practice performance levels of subjects in the two conditions, indicating that the skill levels developed in the training and practice sessions did not differ between the two groups. For the performance task which followed the training program, subjects were given 30 minutes to identify at least 10 relevant records for the assigned search problem.

Results

Levels of total effort by subjects in the high- and low-self-efficacy group are shown in Fig. 3.1. There were no differences in the total search effort of subjects in the two conditions, $F(1, 47) = 0.4$, n.s., and none of the individual indicators of total effort differed between the low- and high-self-efficacy groups. However, the high self-efficacy subjects wasted much less effort than the low-efficacy group, $F(1, 47) = 3.69$, $p < .06$. Subjects who emerged from the training program with

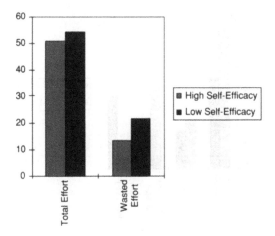

FIG. 3.1. Effort levels.

stronger self-efficacy were much more efficient in their search than their less efficacious counterparts in the control group. High-efficacy subjects made fewer errors in the use of keywords and connectors and the inputting of search statements, $F(1, 47) = 5.49$, $p < .05$. Low-efficacy subjects also used more redundant search statements than the high-efficacy subjects, but the difference was not significant. Therefore, there was support for the argument that stronger self-efficacy makes individuals less prone to memory lapses and other errors due to cognitive strain when acquiring information on a complex decision task.

The breadth and depth of searches conducted by subjects in the high- and low-efficacy groups are shown in Fig. 3.2. As expected, the high-self-efficacy subjects conducted more broadly focused searches, $F(1, 47) = 3.75$, $p < .06$. They also searched individual concepts in greater depth, but the difference between the two groups did not reach significance. Analyses of the different components included in the search breadth score revealed two significant differences between the high- and low-efficacy groups (Fig. 3.2). Subjects in the high-self-efficacy condition used the search expanding thesaurus as their primary external source of terms for identifying concepts in their search statements, $F(1, 47) = 9.53$, $p < .01$. Subjects in the control condition used the more narrowly focused Key-word index as their primary source of terms, $F(1, 47) = 7.17$, $p < .01$.

Subjects who were more confident in their capabilities for the task ignored the more detailed but more narrowly focused listing of terms for concepts in the key-word index. They chose instead to use the thesaurus almost exclusively to fashion more wide-ranging search statements. As a consequence of their use of related terms in place of those that were linked only to the concept being searched, subjects in the high-efficacy group received many more records in response to their early

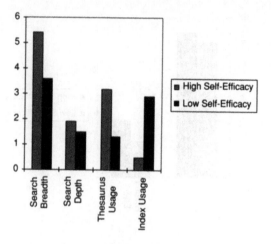

FIG. 3.2. Scope of search.

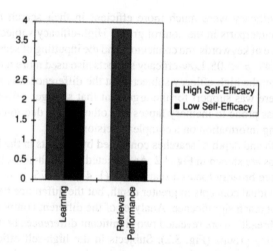

FIG. 3.3. Learning and performance.

search statements. Therefore, they had to process greater amounts of information than subjects in the low-efficacy group, including significant numbers of irrelevant records, in order to refine and focus their search process. The more efficient, more broadly focused search by subjects in the high self-efficacy condition was translated into superior performance (Fig. 3.3). They identified significantly more relevant library records than the less efficacious subjects in the control condition, $F(1, 47) = 10.78$, $p < .01$. The expected differences in learning did not reach significance.

DISCUSSION AND CONCLUSIONS

From our earlier review of existing research, we believe that there is sufficient evidence to argue that the processes by which goals, self-efficacy, and affect influence performance differ between simple effort-to-performance tasks and more complex tasks that require information acquisition and problem-solving. Learning and skill development processes also differ as tasks become more complex and dynamic in ways that require information acquisition and problem solving. The properties of complexity that shape the pathways to performance on different tasks have not been fully described; however, it is clear that a critical characteristic of performance on complex tasks is the search process. The results of the reported study indicate that self-efficacy, one of the core motivational states from social cognitive theory, predicts several dimensions of search behavior and performance on the database searching task.

Additional studies have replicated the finding that self-efficacy predicts wasted effort, search behavior, and performance and, in addition, have shown that self-efficacy mediates the relationship between training and search strategies (Debowski & Wood, 1997). In a study of the effects of positive versus negative feedback, positive feedback produced greater search effort, but this effect diminished across repeated search tasks. The sign of the feedback received had no impact on the search behavior, learning, or performance for this dynamically complex task (Wood & Debowski, 1997). In a further study that compared the effects of strategy and performance feedback with a control group, we found no feedback effects on self-efficacy, performance, or goals; however, strategy feedback did result in search strategies of greater breadth and depth (Wood & Debowski, 1997).

Future Research

The studies conducted to this point have indicated that the database searching task offers considerable potential for the continued study of the motivation and search on complex tasks. Future studies can easily consider the impact of goals on search, learning, and performance. The complexity of the task can also be easily manipulated at several levels to test for the impact of complexity on search behavior. The complexity of the assigned search problem will vary with the number of concepts included in the problem statement. An extension of the earlier three concept problems to include a fourth concept, say, performance, can be introduced simply by rewording the problem as follows: "What impact has technology had on managerial job satisfaction and managerial performance?" The individual concepts included in a problem statement can also vary in their component complexity, depending on the number of related concepts and associated key words. The complexity of a search task is also partly contingent on the context in which a concept is used and, therefore, involves a coordinative form of complexity (Wood, 1986). For example, if the earlier problem was restated as: "What impact has technology had on the performance of manufacturing companies and the satisfaction of production line workers?" different key words would be chosen from the list of options for technology in the key word index. Future research to examine the impacts of variations in complexity on search behavior, learning, and performance will help to fill some of the current gaps in our knowledge identified by Kanfer(1990).

Ecological Validity Considerations

In conclusion, we would like to relate our arguments more closely to work in modern organizations that must compete in the global economy. It is predicted that, by 1998, 80% of the world's information will be held electronically and that approximately half of that information will only be available electronically (Cook, 1995). Computerized databases and the Internet are becoming increasingly important sources of information for a wide range of work tasks. Searches to identify and evaluate options for the purchase of a car, a new appraisal system, capital investments, and potential new employees can all be conducted electronically. These searches can be international in breadth and of great depth. Electronic search is now a critical behavior in many jobs. Understanding the motivational processes that enable individuals to search electronic data sources efficiently and effectively is an important practical problem. Of practical and theoretical interest is the question of whether or not the motivational dynamics of electronic search behavior generalize to other forms of organizational search, such as asking questions.

REFERENCES

Ackerman, P. L. (1992). Predicting individual differences in complex skill acquisition: Dynamics of ability determinants. *Journal of Applied Psychology, 77*(5), 598–614.

Anderson, J. R. (1993). *Rules of the mind.* Hillsdale, NJ: Erlbaum.

Bandura, A. (1986). *Social foundations of thought and action: A social cognitive theory.* Englewood Cliffs, NJ: Prentice-Hall.

Bandura, A. (1997). *Self-efficacy: The exercise of control.* New York: W. H. Freeman and Company.

Bandura, A., & Cervone, D. (1983). Self-evaluative and self-efficacy mechanisms governing the motivational effects of goal systems. *Journal of Personality and Social Psychology, 45,* 1017–1028.

Bandura, A., & Cervone, D. (1986). Differential engagement of self-reactive influences on cognitive motivation. *Organizational Behavior and Human Decision Processes, 38,* 92–113.

Bandura, A., & Jourdan, F. J. (1991). Self-regulatory mechanisms governing the impact of social comparison on complex decision making. *Journal of Personality and Social Psychology, 60,* 941–951.

Bandura, A., & Wood, R. E. (1989). Effect of perceived controllability and performance standards on self-regulation of complex decision making. *Journal of Personality and Social Psychology, 56*(5), 805–814.

Berry, J. M. (1987). *A self-efficacy model of memory performance.* Paper presented at the American Psychological Association Meetings, September, New York.

Berry, D. C., & Broadbent, D. E. (1984). On the relationship between task performance and associated verbalizable knowledge. *Quarterly Journal of Experimental Psychology, 36A*(2), 209–231.

Berry, D. C., & Broadbent, D. E. (1988). Interactive tasks and the implicit-explicit distinction. *British Journal of Psychology, 79*(2), 251–272.

Bettman, J. R., Johnson, E. J. A., & Payne, J. W. (1990). A componential analysis of cognitive effort in choice. *Organizational Behaviour and Human Decision Processes, 45,* 111–139.

Bouffard-Bouchard, T. (1990). Influence of self-efficacy in performance on a complex task. *Journal of Social Psychology, 130,* 353–363.

Broadbent, D. E., Fitzgerald, P., & Broadbent, M. H. (1986). Implicit and explicit knowledge in the control of complex systems. *British Journal of Psychology, 77*(1), 33–50.

Bruner, J. S., Goodnow, J., & Austin, G. A. (1956). *A study of thinking.* New York: Wiley.

Campbell, D. J. (1988). Task complexity: A review and analysis. *Academy of Management Review, 13*(1): 40–52.

Carroll, J. S., & Johnson, E. J. (1990). *Decision research: A field guide.* Newbury Park, CA: Sage.

Cervone, D., Jiwani, N., & Wood, R. E. (1991). Goal setting and the differential influence of self-regulatory processes on complex decision-making performance. *Journal of Personality and Social Psychology, 61,* 257–266.

Cervone, D., & Peake, P. K. (1986). Anchoring, efficacy, and action: The influence of judgmental heuristics on self-efficacy judgments and behavior. *Journal of Personality and Social Psychology, 50,* 492–501.

Cervone, D., & Wood, R. E. (1994). Goals, feedback and the differential influence of self-regulatory processes on cognitively complex performance. *Cognitive Therapy and Research, 19,* 521–547.

Chi, M. T. H., Feltovich, P. J., & Glaser, R. (1981). Categorization and representation of physics problems by experts and novices. *Cognitive Science, 5,* 121–152.

Cook, B. (1995). Managing for effective delivery of information services in the 1990s: The integration of computing, educational and library services. In *The Virtual Information Experience: Proceedings of the Seventh Australasian Information Online and On Disc Conference and Exhibition* (pp. 1–19). Sydney.

Debowski, S. (1997). *The impacts of guided mastery training, self-efficacy and feedback on effort, search strategy and performance while conducting complex information search tasks.* Unpublished doctoral dissertation, University of Western Australia.

Debowski, S., & Wood, R. E. (1997). *The impacts of guided mastery versus exploratory self management training on errors and other forms of wasted effort.* Industrial and Organisational Psychology Conference, Melbourne, Australia.

Earley, P. C., Connolly, T., & Ekegren, G. (1989). Goals, strategy development, and task performance: Some limits on the efficacy of goal setting. *Journal of Applied Psychology, 74,* 24–33.

Ericsson, K. A., & Simon, H. A. (1984). *Protocol analysis: Verbal reports as data.* Cambridge, MA: MIT Press.

Fisk, A. D., Ackerman, P. L., & Schneider, W. (1987). Automatic and controlled processing theory and its application to human factors problems. In P. A. Hancock (Ed.), *Human factors psychology* (pp. 159–197). Amsterdam: North-Holland.

Fitts, P., & Posner, M. I. (1967). *Human Performance.* Belmont, CA: Brooks/Cole.

Forgas, J. P. (1989). Mood effects on decision making strategies. *Australian Journal of Psychology, 41,* 197–214.

Harre, R. (1981). *Great scientific experiments: Twenty experiments that changed our view of the world.* Oxford: Phaidon Press.

Holyoak, K. J., & Spellman, B. A. (1993). Thinking. *Annual Review of Psychology, 44,* 265–315.

Huber, V. L. (1985). Effects of task difficulty, goal-setting and strategy on performance of a heuristic task. *Journal of Applied Psychology, 70,* 492–504.

Humphreys, M. S., & Revelle, W. (1984). Personality, motivation and performance: A theory of the relationship between individual differences and information processing. *Psychological Review, 91,* 153–184.

Isen, A. M., Shalker, T. E., Clark, M., & Karp, L. (1978). Affect, accessibility of material in memory, and behavior: A cognitive loop? *Journal of Personality and Social Psychology, 36,* 1–12.

Janis, I. L., & Mann, L. (1977). *Decision making.* New York: Free Press.

Kahneman, D. (1973). *Attention and Effort.* Englewood Cliffs, NJ: Prentice-Hall.

Kanfer, R. (1987). Task specific motivation: an integrative approach to issues of measure, mechanisms, processes and determinants. *Journal of Social and Clinical Psychology, 5,* 237–264.

Kanfer, R. (1990). Motivation theory and industrial and organisational psychology. In M. D. Dunnette & L. M. Hough (Eds.), *Handbook of Industrial and Organisational Psychology* (pp. 75–170). Palo Alto: Consulting Psychologists Press.

Kanfer, R., & Ackerman, P. L. (1989). Motivation and cognitive abilities: An integrative/aptitude-treatment interaction approach to skill aquisition. *Journal of Applied Psychology, 74,* 657–690.

Locke, E. A., & Latham, G. P. (1990). *A theory of goal setting and task performance.* Englewood Cliffs, NJ: Prentice-Hall.

Michel, D. A. (1994). What is used during cognitive processing in information and retrieval and library searching? Eleven sources of search information. *Journal of the American Society for Information Science, 45*(7), 498–514.

Navon, D., & Gopher, D. (1979). On the economy of the human processing system. *Psychological Review, 86,* 214–255.

Naylor, J. C., Pritchard, R. D., & Ilgen, D. R. (1980). *A theory of behaviour in organizations.* New York: Academic Press.

Newell, A., & Simon, H. A. (1972). *Human problem solving.* Englewood Cliffs, NJ: Prentice-Hall.

Norman, D. A., & Bobrow, D. B. (1975). On data limited and resource-limited processes. *Cognitive Psychology, 7,* 44–64.

Novick, L. R. (1988). Analogical transfer, problem similarity, and expertise. *Journal of Experimental Psychology: Learning, Memory & Cognition, 14*(3), 510–520.

Payne, J. W., Bettman, J. R., & Johnson, E. J. (1993). *The adaptive decision maker.* Cambridge Press.

Quint, B. (1991). Inside a searcher's mind: The seven stages of an online search—Part 2. *Online,* July, 28–34.

Shiffrin, R. M., & Schneider, W. (1977). Controlled and automatic human information processing: II. Perceptual learning, automatic attending, and a general theory. *Psychological Review,* 127–190.

Simon, H. A. (1976). Discussion: Cognition and social behavior. In J. S. Carroll & J. W. Payne (Eds.), *Cognition and social behavior.* Hillsdale, NJ: Erlbaum.

Stanley, W. B., Mathews, R. C., Buss, R. R., & Kotler-Cope, S. (1989). Insight without awareness: On the interaction of verbalization, instruction and practice in a simulated process control task. *Quarterly Journal of Experimental Psychology Human Experimental Psychology, 41*(3-A), 553–577.

Wood, R. E. (1986). Task complexity: Definition of the construct. *Organizational Behavior and Human Decision Processes, 37,* 60–82.

Wood, R. E., & Bandura, A. (1989). Social cognitive theory of organizational management. *Academy of Management Review, 14,* 361–384.

Wood, R. E., Bandura, A., & Bailey, T. (1990). Mechanisms governing organizational productivity in complex decision-making environments. *Organizational Behavior and Human Decision Processes, 46,* 181–201.

Wood, R. E., & Debowski, S. (1997, June). *Learning from errors and feedback.* Paper presented at Industrial and Organisational Psychology Conference, Melbourne, Australia.

Wood, R. E., & Locke, E. A. (1990). Goal-setting and strategy effects on complex tasks. In B. M. Staw & L. L. Cummings (Eds.), *Research in organizational behavior* (Vol. 12). Greenwich, CT: JAI Press.

Wood, R. E., Mento, A. J., & Locke, E. A. (1987). Task complexity as a moderator of goal effects: A meta-analysis. *Journal of Applied Psychology, 72,* 416–425.

4

Goal Setting and Performance in Working Memory and Short-Term-Memory Tasks

Jürgen Wegge and Uwe Kleinbeck
Universität Dortmund, Organisationspsychologie

Klaus-Helmut Schmidt
Institute of Work-Physiology, Dortmund

In this chapter, the results of three experiments on the impact of goal setting on short-term retention of verbal information are reported. Participants were asked to work on two different memory tasks under two goal-setting conditions (do your best vs. specific and difficult goals). The first task was a reading span test that required (a) to read out sets of sentences without pausing during reading and (b) to recall the terminal words of each sentence, each time all sentences of a set were processed. The second task was a traditional memory span test with lists of one-syllable words. Time of day for performing these tasks was controlled. The results demonstrate that high work motivation induced by goal-setting facilitates short-term retention of information mainly for subtasks with high memory load and around midday, when short-term storage of information is usually impaired due to circadian performance rhythms. Furthermore, goal setting induced improvements in short-term retention of information seem to be restricted to conditions in which the use of a rehearsal strategy is impeded. Finally, results indicate that performance-enhancing effects of goal setting on memory performance are probably not caused by different encoding or recall strategies. Hence, it is concluded that goal setting leads to a temporary increase in cognitive arousal (working memory capacity), especially around midday. At other times of the day, no substantial changes in memory performance due to goal setting were observed.

Goal-setting theory is one of the best-established theories of human motivation and task performance (Ford, 1992; Kanfer, 1992). The fundamental idea of this theory is that performance goals are the most powerful determinants of task behavior. Based on the results of more than 400 studies (Locke & Latham, 1990), it can be concluded that striving for *difficult and specific* performance goals results in *higher* performance than striving for easy or nonspecific goals (e.g., "do your best" goals). When certain boundary conditions are met, such as feedback during task performance, high goal commitment and low to medium task complexity, challenging goals will lead to an increase in performance of up to 16%.

How does the theory explain this very robust phenomenon? The accumulated evidence in recent years has shown that there are at least four *mediating mechanisms* that are responsible for performance facilitating effects of difficult and specific goals. These goals motivate people to (a) exert more effort during task performance, (b) continue working on the task until the performance goal is reached, (c) direct their actions and attention to those behaviors and outcomes that are relevant for goal attainment, and (d) use or develop appropriate task strategies and plans (Wood & Locke, 1990). However, with the exception of strategy development, this list of mechanisms represents nothing more than a description of those attributes that are commonly ascribed to motivated behavior in general (intensity, persistence, and direction of behavior; see Kanfer, 1992). Therefore, it does not offer a detailed understanding of how goals actually determine performance outcomes on various tasks (Schmidt & Kleinbeck, 1990; for a similar view see also Wood et al., this volume). In order to give such an explanation, one has to find out which *micro*-processes that are necessarily involved in performing tasks are under motivational control and can therefore be modulated (e.g., accelerated, increased, or extended) in accordance with actual goal requirements. These processes might include, for example, the encoding of new information, specific comprehension processes, the comparison of information in working memory, short-term retention of information, or various motor processes, such as the planning and preparation of movements (Audia, Kristof-Brown, Brown, & Locke, 1996; Kanfer & Ackermann, 1989; Revelle, 1989; Schmidt & Kleinbeck, 1990; Wegge, 1998).

Let us illustrate this thesis with the findings of a recent study in which performance on an arithmetic task was analyzed (Wegge, 1998). Participants were asked to solve arithmetic equations. Each equation consisted of two simple rows of digits (e.g., $3 + 5 - 7 = ?$ and $8 - 2 + 5 = ?$) that were written one beneath the other on a sheet of paper. This is a rather simple task that was developed by Düker (1949) to measure individual differences in the ability to concentrate over time. Solving this task affords one to (a) calculate the results of both rows, (b) combine the two provisional results in one solution (if the result of the first row is larger than the result of the second row, the second must be subtracted from the first one, if this is not the case, the solution is the sum of both results), and (c) write down the solution. However, it was not allowed to take any notes while solving the task.

Hence, (d) task solution required short-term retention of information because it was necessary to remember the result of the first row while calculating the result of the second one. In the experiment, 44 university students served as participants. To make them familiar with the task and to collect a measure of individual ability, they had to solve some practice trials (of 2 minutes) first. After finishing these practice trials, participants were randomly assigned to one of two experimental conditions. Participants in the "do your best" condition were asked to solve as many equations as possible in the next 5 minutes without making errors. In the goal-setting condition, participants were instructed to solve at least 30 equations in 5 minutes without making errors. This goal level was determined on the basis of pilot testing, and it can be characterized as a difficult goal (only 2 of 10 pilot subjects reached this performance level). Task performance was measured by the number of solved equations (performance quantity) and by the number of errors (performance quality).

The results support the basic goal-setting hypothesis. Participants in the goal-setting condition solved more equations ($M = 26.3$; s $= 10.9$) in the same time than participants in the "do your best" (DYB) condition, $M = 18.9$; s $= 7.2$; $F(1, 42) = 6.9$; $p \leq .02$; Eta$^2 = .14$. In addition, there were no significant differences with respect to performance quality ($M = 3.7$; s $= 2.3$ and $M = 2.8$; s $= 2.5$ errors for the goal-setting and DYB conditions, respectively). The main effect of goal setting was still significant, $F(1, 42) = 4.7$; $p \leq .04$; Eta$^2 = .10$, when the number of correct solutions (solved equations minus errors) was considered the dependent variable. Furthermore, there were no significant differences between both groups regarding performance in practice trials.[1] Finally, the correlations between performance quantity and performance quality were not significant in eithr condition ($r = .10$ for DYB and $r = -.19$ for the goal-setting condition), and they did not differ substantially from each other.

Let us see how the performance-facilitating effect of goal setting can be explained in view of these results. We can exclude the possibility that variations in *persistence, ability,* or a *speed–accuracy tradeoff* are responsible for the findings. Moreover, it is not very plausible that the use of different *task strategies* can explain the main effect of goal setting, because participants were assigned to both experimental conditions randomly, and the task required well-learned, easy operations that can hardly be optimized by strategies.[2] In addition, the use of some performance-enhancing strategies (e.g., note taking, loud rehearsing of provisional results) was not allowed, and participants had only limited time to develop new strategies. Apart from this, one has to consider the possibility that the search for and

---

[1]The main effect of goal setting remains significant even when performance in practice trials is controlled as a covariate: $F(1, 41) = 7.3$; $p \leq .01$; Eta$^2 = .15$ for performance quantity and $F(1, 41) = 3.9$; $p \leq .06$; Eta$^2 = .09$ for the number of correct solutions.

[2]Some cognitive strategies that can be employed in this task were recently examined by Schütte and Jordan (1996).

the development of task strategies can hinder smooth task performance (Kanfer & Ackermann, 1989; Kluger & DeNisi, 1996). Therefore, we have to assume that participants in the goal-setting condition (a) directed their attention more on task-relevant stimuli and (b) invested more effort in solving the equations. However, based on observations of the experimenter and self-report measures, all participants were equally concentrating on the task. Thus, it is not plausible that the main effect of goal setting is completely due to variations with respect to *on-task attention*, and finally, we have to conclude that subjects striving for difficult and specific performance goals invested more *effort* during task solution.

How is it possible to invest more effort in solving arithmetic equations? There is no simple answer because, at this point, we have to examine on a micro-level what people really do when they solve such a task. This analysis will show that there are many different mental operations involved in task solution, such as detecting and reading the digits, finding out their meaning, calculating preliminary solutions according to the rules, remembering the first result while the second one is computed, and calculating and writing down the solution (see also Audia, Kristof-Brown, Brown, & Locke, 1996; Bettman, Johnson, & Payne, 1990; Sanders, 1990 for similar lists of elementary processes involved in other tasks). Any of these mental operations and processes might be accelerated or otherwise supported by the decision to invest more effort in solving the task. However, the most crucial feature for smooth performance of the arithmetic task is its working memory load. Several participants reported that they forgot the first result while computing the second one. If higher motivation induced by goal setting improves short-term retention of information (e.g., recalling the first result correctly after computation of the second one), these time-consuming errors would occur less often and, as a consequence, better performance in this condition could easily be understood. Of course, we cannot rule out completely the possibility that the main effect of goal setting previously documented is caused by some other factors as well. However, in view of these findings it seems reasonable to derive the hypothesis that *goal setting* can improve working memory or short-term memory capacity *during goal striving*. So far, this assumption has never been examined empirically. However, consistent with this idea, Heckhausen and Gollwitzer (1987) reported that other motivational processes can enhance short-term memory, and Goschke and Kuhl (1993) found that intentions had a higher level of activation in long-term memory. Hence, we decided to test this assumption in a series of experiments. In view of the well-known fact that time of day can have a strong impact on short-term retention of information (Revelle, 1989), we also controlled this factor in each experiment.

OVERVIEW OF EXPERIMENTS

To examine the effects of goal setting on short-term retention of information, three experiments were conducted. In each experiment, participants were randomly assigned to two different goal-setting conditions ("do your best" vs. difficult and specific performance goals). Participants had to solve two memory tasks. The first one was a reading span task that involves both the short-term storage and the simultaneous processing of verbal information (working-memory task). This task was used in all three experiments. The second task, a traditional memory-span test, was employed only in experiments 2 and 3. More detailed information regarding experimental designs is offered together with the results for each experiment. The sample, general experimental procedures, both memory tasks, and some previous findings with respect to the influence of time of day (circadian rhythms) on memory performance are briefly described below (for more information, see Wegge, 1998).

Sample

Fourty-four students participated in experiment 1 (23 women and 21 men), 42 students in experiment 2 (20 women and 22 men), and 100 students (43 women and 57 men) in experiment 3. All participants were enrolled at the University of Dortmund. They had an average age of 25 years (ranging from 19–38) and studied various majors (e.g., computer science, mathematics, statistics, and psychology excluded). All students were tested individually and received remuneration for participation (10 DM). Furthermore, in experiments 2 and 3 a financial incentive (5 DM) was offered for attaining the goals.[3]

Procedure

The general procedure for conducting the experiments can be sketched as follows. Upon arrival at the laboratory, the experimenter stated that the aim of the study was to collect normative data for a new task battery that will be used for assessment of stress in the workplace. The experimenter emphasized that only maximum task performance is useful for this purpose. After participants had filled out some questionnaires that measured several biographical and personality variables, they received instructions for solving the memory task to be completed next. Depending on the experimental condition, the experimenter asked participants to achieve a difficult and specific performance goal (see below) or to "do their best" in solving the task. The order of both memory tasks in experiments 2 and 3 was counterbalanced so that half of the students performed the working-memory task first and the other half the short-term memory task first (each participant was assigned only once to a goal-setting condition in these experiments).

---

[3]Participants knew this before performing the tasks. There was no partial payment for partial goal attainment.

Working-Memory Task

The working-memory task was adopted from Daneman and Carpenter (1980, 1983). Participants were asked to read out sets with phrases and to recall the last words of these sentences. A set consisted of three, four, or five sentences. Each sentence comprised 13 to 17 words and ended with a noun (sentences were taken from newspapers). The sentences and their last words had no obvious semantic relation to each other. Six sets of sentences were presented in experiment 1 (two sets each of three, four, and five sentences) and nine sets of sentences in experiments 2 and 3 (three sets each of three, four, and five sentences). Before participants started to read, they were instructed to recall the last word of each sentence in the correct order, each time they had finished reading one set of sentences. Moreover, they were instructed not to pause while reading the sentences of a set. According to Baddeley (1986, 1996), this task can be described as a working-memory task because it stresses both *processing* and *storage* functions at the same time (for other versions of this task, see Hacker, Sieler, & Pietzcker, 2000; Waters & Caplan, 1996).

Presentation of the working-memory task varied in the three experiments. In the first experiment, sentences were written on cards. The experimenter showed participants one card at a time, and as soon as the sentence was read, the next card was placed on the top of the previous one (a blank card indicated that a set was complete and participants should start recalling the words). Subjects were asked to recall the words orally, and all interactions between subjects and experimenters were recorded on tape to measure reading times and recall times. In experiments 2 and 3, all sentences were presented on a computer screen, one sentence at a time, to measure reading times and recall times more accurately. Participants had to press a button on the keyboard after reading each sentence and after recalling the words. To recall the words in these experiments, participants were asked to write down the words on a sheet of paper in the correct order. Memory performance was measured by the number of correctly recalled words. Furthermore, we calculated again how many words were reproduced on the right and on the wrong position of the list and how many errors participants made (number of "recalled" words that had not been presented[4]). Finally, in experiments 2 and 3 we also counted the number of correctly recalled words that were presented in the first sentence to be read (first words) and those that were presented in the last sentence to be read (last words) to have an indicator for primacy and recency effects. According to Parkin (1996), in a free-recall test the primacy effect is mainly based on (covert) rehearsal during stimulus presentation. In contrast, the recency effect is due to the availability of activated information in short-term memory at the beginning of the memory test. The effect is observed when a free recall test is administered immediately after

---

[4]The number of errors for both tasks in experiment 2 and 3 was very low (in the range of 0.4 to 1.1), and there was no significant difference between groups. Thus, no futher data will be reported for these variables.

the presentation of items (this procedure was used in all experiments reported here[5]).

Participants in goal setting conditions were instructed to recall at least 18 out of the 24 words in experiment 1 and 27 out of 36 words in experiments 2 and 3. When setting the goals, the experimenter explained that achieving this goal affords to recall at least three words in each set. Participants got immediate oral feedback about their performance after each set in the first experiment. To ensure that participants could see how they were doing in experiments 2 and 3, answer sheets with blank, numbered lines were used to collect responses.

Short-Term-Memory Task

We used a traditional word-span test with one-syllable words to measure short-term memory performance in experiments 2 and 3. The stimulus material was identical to that of Heckhausen and Gollwitzer (1987). However, we presented all lists of words on a computer screen. The subjects saw 18 lists of words (six lists with 5, six with 6, and six with 7 words). Each word was shown for one second on the screen. Inter-stimulus-interval was one second in experiment 2 and 0.5 seconds in experiment 3. The interval was shortend in experiment 3 to increase task difficulty. After a list of words was presented, subjects were asked to write down all words of the list in the correct order on a sheet of paper, and recall times were again recorded by the computer. Memory performance in this task was measured by the number of correctly recalled words. In addition, we calculated how many words were reproduced on the right (wrong) position of the list. Finally, we counted again the number of correctly recalled words that were presented first in a list of words (first words) and those that were presented last in a list of words (last words) to have indicators for primacy and recency effects.

In goal-setting conditions, participants were instructed to recall at least 90 out of the 108 words presented. To help participants in getting constant feedback regarding their performance, the experimenter explained that achieving this goal affords to recall at least five words from each of the 18 lists. In addition, we again used answer sheets with blank, numbered lines to collect responses. Therefore, even for this long-term goal, participants were able to determine constantly whether they were recalling enough words to reach the goal. At the end of the task, all participants knew perfectly whether they had achieved or missed the goal. The following table gives a summary of experimental variables and their variations across the three experiments.

The various times of the day at which participants worked on the memory tasks in experiments 1 to 3 are documented in Table 4.1 as well. In the following, we give some reasons why time of day is an important variable that should not be

---

[5]The recency effect is usually no longer observed when a distractor task for about 30 seconds is added between the end of a list and a free-recall test (see Parkin, 1996).

TABLE 4.1
Overview of Experimental Variables Across Experiments 1 to 3

	N	Tasks	Stimulus Presentation	Goals	Additional Incentives	Time of Day
Exp. 1	44	WM	Cards	18 of 24	—	8–9 A.M. / 10–11 A.M. 1–2 P.M. / 3–4 P.M.
Exp. 2	42	STM	Computer ISI = 1 sec.	90 of 108	5 DM	8 A.M. / 10 A.M. 1 P.M. / 3 P.M.
		WM	Computer	27 of 36	5 DM	
Exp. 3	100	STM	Computer ISI = 0.5 sec.	90 of 108	5 DM	9 A.M. / 12 A.M. 3 P.M. / 6 P.M. / 9 P.M.
		WM	Computer	27 of 36	5 DM	

Note. WM = working-memory task; STM = short-term-memory task; ISI = interstimulus interval.

neglected if researchers attempt to explain inter- and intraindividual variance in short-term retention of information.

Memory Performance and Time of Day

Although diurnal variations in performance are fairly substantial (Birbaumer & Schmidt, 1991), the impact of different phases of circadian rhythms (around 24 hours) on human performance is a commonly neglected issue in cognitive and motivational psychology. Empirical evidence for the impact of time of day on performance in various tasks mainly stems from biological psychologists (Birbaumer & Schmidt, 1991) and researchers interested in the design of working-time systems (e.g., shift work) or in research on the effects of environmental stressors on performance (e.g., sleep loss; see Folkard & Monk, 1985; Hockey, 1984; Revelle, 1989). According to this work, for many tasks the time-of-day effect on performance shows a marked *parallelism* to diurnal variations in body temperature: performance is low in the morning, it increases over most of the day and reaches a maximum in the evening around 8 P.M. However, we should add that there is no causal relationship between performance and body temperature. Most researchers assume that changes in strategies and arousal (that are parallel to changes in temperature) are responsible for these effects. The most striking exception to this parallelism is observed for *short-term-memory* performance. In several studies an almost reversed trend was found. Short-term-memory performance (e.g., immediate memory, digit span) is high in the early morning and shows a general decrease over the day. In addition, it was found that the higher the working-memory load of a task, the earlier in the day a performance maximum is reached (Birbaumer & Schmidt, 1991; Folkard & Monk, 1983, 1985). Based on the assumption that higher arousal will decrease immediate memory performance, these observations were usually reconciled with the one-dimensional arousal theory that underlied theorizing in this field for a long time. However, in view of recent results (Birbaumer & Schmidt, 1991), multidimensional arousal theories seem to be more appropriate for explaining the joint effects of various task demands and time of day on human performance.

To control for possible differences in memory performance that are due to time of day, we noted the time when participants worked on the tasks in the first two experiments. Hence, assignment of participants to time of day was not completely randomized in experiments 1 and 2. All participants made their appointments together with the experimenter based on general time schedules that were available for both experiments. We will handle this factor as a fixed, almost randomized factor in the statistical analysis because these appointments were partially based on random influences (e.g., previous appointments made by the experimenter, available days, and times of day). In contrast, time of day was a deliberately planned and random experimental factor for experiment 3. Appointments with participants were made according to a randomized sequence in such a way that they started solving the memory tasks at five different times of day (see Table 4.1).

RESULTS

The design of experiment 1 is a 2 (specific, difficult goals vs. "do your best" = DYB) × 4 (time of day) × 3 (memory load of three, four, or five words) factorial design, with repeated observations on the last factor. Between 8 and 9 A.M., seven participants worked under goal-setting instructions and five under DYB instructions; between 10 and 11 A.M. the corresponding values were seven/five; between 1 and 2 P.M. five/five, and between 3 and 4 P.M. three/seven participants. Scores for the dependent variables of experiment 1 are presented in Table 4.2. Based on this data, it can be concluded that the assigned goal was difficult: only 4 of 22 participants reached the goal under goal-setting instructions, and 3 participants from the DYB group were able to remember at least 18 words out of 24.

A three-way analysis of variance (ANOVA) for the number of recalled words showed three significant effects. First, we found a main effect for the goal setting factor, ($F(1, 36) = 6.1$; $p \leq .02$; Eta$^2 = .14$), that supported our hypothesis. Goal setting increases memory performance in the working-memory task. In addition, there was a significant main effect for memory load, $F(2, 72) = 3.8$; $p \leq .03$; Eta$^2 = .10$. Participants recalled less words from sets with four and five sentences compared to sets with three sentences, $F(1, 36) = 6.4$; $p \leq .02$; Eta$^2 = .15$. However, there was no significant difference between sets with four and five

TABLE 4.2

Means and Standard Deviations for Performance of the Working Memory Task in Experiment 1

	DYB		Goal	
	M	SD	M	SD
Recalled Words	13.7	3.6	15.6	2.1
Recalled Words by Memory Load				
Three Sentences	5.1	1.1	5.3	0.8
Four Sentences	4.6	1.9	5.4	1.3
Five Sentences	4.0	1.6	5.0	1.2
Recalled Words by Time of Day				
8/9 A.M.	15.8	4.5	13.6	1.1
10/11 A.M.	10.2	3.5	18.0	1.4
1/2 P.M.	15.0	2.0	15.6	1.5
3/4 P.M.	13.7	2.3	15.0	0.3
Reading Times by Memory Load				
Three Sentences	45.3	4.7	44.6	4.0
Four Sentences	60.1	6.8	59.7	7.5
Five Sentences	80.7	9.8	78.7	7.9
Recall Times (sec.)	9.8	5.0	11.4	4.3
Recall Times by Memory Load				
Three Sentences	13.2	9.4	10.5	4.2
Four Sentences	27.3	17.8	25.2	13.2
Five Sentences	23.5	12.7	34.8	15.2

Note. DYB = "do your best" condition; Goal = goal-setting condition; $n = 22$ for each group.

sentences. Finally, a significant two-way interaction between goal setting and time of day was observed, $F(3, 36) = 8.8$; $p \leq .001$; Eta$^2 = .42$. This interaction is due to the fact that goal setting had a small but not significant negative impact on memory performance early in the morning (8–9 A.M.), whereas working-memory performance around midday (10–11 A.M.) was substantially higher in the goal setting condition than in the DYB condition.[6] In the afternoon (1–4 P.M.), both groups did not differ from each other with respect to their memory performance. If we consider performance in the DYB condition as a valid description of diurnal

---

[6]This interaction was also significant for words recalled on a correct position. In all experiments we used Helmert contrasts to handle the memory load and the time-of-day factor. The reported two-way interaction is based on the first parameter (8–9 A.M. vs. the rest of the day, Eta$^2 = .23$) and the second parameter (10–11 A.M. vs. 1–4 P.M.; Eta$^2 = .28$). If one considers only those groups working in the morning (8–11 A.M.), this interaction is again significant, $F(1, 20) = 19.1$; $p \leq .001$; Eta$^2 = .49$. For all other dependent variables there were no interactions with time of day.

variations that are usually observed in this kind of task (see previous discussion), these results seem to indicate that goal setting can overcome the impairment of short-term memory around midday that is based on circadian rhythms.

With respect to reading times and recall times, no significant differences between both groups emerged,[7] but the two-way interaction between goal setting and memory load was significant for recall times, $F(2, 72) = 12.9$; $p \leq .001$; $Eta^2 = .26$, indicating that goal setting leads to longer recall times in sets with five sentences. Longer recall times in these sets, however, can not explain the main effect of goal setting on memory performance that is primarily based on performance around midday (neither the three-way interaction including time of day nor any parameter of this interaction was significant for the variables reading time and recalled words). Hence, subjects in DYB and goal-setting conditions worked on the task in a similar way. There are no differences with respect to the use of time-consuming strategies during reading (e.g., hidden rehearsal) that might have been employed in order to attain the difficult performance goal. Moreover, even though recall times are not perfectly identical across the two goal-setting conditions, recall strategies within both conditions were similar since a further examination with respect to the sequence of recalled words (words recalled on the right position or on wrong positions) and the number of errors (falsely recalled words) showed no difference between groups.

The *second experiment* was conducted to replicate these findings and to overcome some shortcomings that were linked with our first study (e.g., uncommon procedures for time measurement, a rather small number of sets). A further goal of experiment 2 was to extend our analysis with the examination of a second memory task (a short-term-memory task). The design of the second experiment is again a 2 (specific, difficult goals vs. DYB) × 4 (time of day) × 3 (memory load of three, four, or five words) factorial design with repeated observations on the last factor. Between 8 and 8:15 A.M. five participants worked under goal-setting instructions for the working-memory task and five under DYB instructions; between 10 and 10:15 A.M. the corresponding values were eight/four participants, between 1 and 1:15 P.M. six/six, and between 3 and 3:15 P.M. four/four (for the short-term-memory task these numbers are exactly reversed). Let us first consider the results for the working-memory task (see Table 4.3).

Our attempt to measure reading times and recall times in the working-memory task more accurately (by presenting the sentences on the computer screen) was quite successful. On the other hand, we had to learn that our participants had no problem deceiving the experimenter under these experimental conditions (self-paced stimulus presentation). Several participants made short pauses before they pressed the button on the keyboard, and some participants moved their hands very

---

[7]The ANOVA's showed two significant main effects for the factor memory load [$F(2, 72) = 663.9$; $p \leq .001$; $Eta^2 = .94$ for reading times and $F(2, 72) = 61.2$; $p \leq .001$; $Eta^2 = .63$ for recall times)]

TABLE 4.3
Means and Standard Deviations for Performance of the Working Memory Task in
Experiment 2

	DYB		Goal	
	M	SD	M	SD
Reading Times (sec.)	248	41.4	300	60.0
Reading Times by Memory Load				
Three Sentences	60.1	10.8	70.3	11.9
Four Sentences	85.9	13.2	105.2	20.9
Five Sentences	102.1	18.4	125.4	29.2
Recall Time (sec.)	207	53.6	250	73.1
Recalled Words	26.8	2.4	27.6	4.7
Recalled Words by Memory Load				
Three Sentences	8.3	1.0	8.4	0.8
Four Sentences	9.5	1.7	9.0	1.8
Five Sentences	9.0	1.7	10.3	2.7
First Words	6.5	1.6	7.1	1.7
First Words by Memory Load				
First Words—3	2.7	0.6	2.7	0.5
First Words—4	2.3	0.8	2.3	0.8
First Words—5	1.6	0.8	2.2	0.9
Last Words	8.8	0.4	8.9	0.2

Note. DYB = "do your best" condition ($n = 19$); Goal = goal-setting condition ($n = 23$).

slowly to call for the presentation of the next sentence on the screen. As a consequence, participants with difficult performance goals had much longer reading times than participants in DYB groups, $F(1, 34) = 7.2; p \leq .02; \text{Eta}^2 = .18$. Especially for sets with four and five sentences, reading times were longer under goal-setting conditions (the two-way interaction between goal setting and memory load is significant, with $F(2, 68) = 4.2; p \leq .02; \text{Eta}^2 = .11$, and the corresponding contrast was significant, with $F(1, 34) = 5, 6; p \leq .03; \text{Eta}^2 = .14$. The fact that goal setting was successful in motivating our subjects to attain the assigned performance goals can also be recognized with respect to their high persistence in trying to recall the words they should remember, $F(1, 34) = 3.4; p \leq .07; \text{Eta}^2 = .09$. However, for the number of correctly recalled words the main effect of goal setting was not significant in this experiment. Nevertheless, we found a significant two-way interaction between goal setting and memory load, $F(2, 68) = 4.2; p \leq .02; \text{Eta}^2 = .11$. Improvements of memory performance due to goal setting were only observed for subtasks with a very high memory load (for sets with five sentences, the contrast comparing sets with four to five sentences was significant, with $F(1, 34) = 5.7$; $p \leq 0.03$; Eta$^2 = .14$. A more detailed analysis with respect to the most difficult words to remember in this task (the last word of the *first* sentence read in a set of sentences, first words in Table 4.3) gives us some idea why memory performance was superior for this subtask. Participants in goal setting conditions recalled these (first) words more often than participants in the DYB group (the two-way interaction between goal setting and memory load for this variable is significant, with $F(2, 68) = 3.4$; $p \leq .04$; Eta$^2 = .16$, and the corresponding contrast comparing performance for sets with 4 and 5 sentences is marginally significant, with $F(1, 34) = 3, 5$; $p \leq .07$; Eta$^2 = .10$. Finally, we found no differences with respect to the number of errors (falsely recalled words), and, more important, we were not successful in replicating the interaction between goal setting and time of day in this experiment (no interactions were significant[8]). One possible explanation for this failure might be that the extensive use of a (hidden) rehearsal strategy did mask the effects of endogenous rhythms on immediate memory performance (subjects had longer reading times, and a small primacy effect emerged for subtasks with memory load 5). In our view, this speculation is supported by the data we found for the short-term-memory task (see Table 4.4).

For this memory task, no systematic differences with respect to recall times were found.[9] Furthermore, memory performance of participants working under goal setting and "do your best" instructions was not different (see Table 4.4). However, identical presentation times (controlled by the computer for the short-term-memory task) and identical recall times might have been a necessary precondition for detecting the impact of circadian rhythms on short-term retention of information. The interaction between time of day and the two goal setting conditions for the number of correctly recalled words in the short-term memory task, $F(3, 34) = 3.3$; $p \leq .03$; Eta$^2 = .23$,[10] is almost identical to the interaction we found for the working memory task in experiment one (see Table 4.2). The second contrast of this two-way interaction, comparing memory performance at 10 A.M. to that in the afternoon, is significant, $F(1, 34) = 8.6$; $p \leq .01$; Eta$^2 = .19$. If we consider only those groups that solved the task at 8 A.M. and at 10 A.M., this interaction is significant too: $F(1, 18) = 5.9$; $p \leq .02$; Eta$^2 = .25$. Thus, especially shortly before or around midday, goal setting can help to overcome the impairment of short-term retention of information due to circadian rhythms. If this argument is

---

[8]We should add that for reading times, recall times, recalled words, and first words the main effect of memory load was significant (all $p \leq .001$).

[9]In this experiment, the main effect for the factor memory load was again significant for recalled words, recall times, and number of last words (all $p \leq .01$).

[10]A second, almost identical significant interaction was found for the number of words that were recalled on the right position. However, for all other variables (e.g., recall times, recalled words on wrong positions) there were no significant interactions with time of day.

TABLE 4.4
Means and Standard Deviations for Performance of the Short-Term-Memory Task
in Experiment 2

	DYB		Goal	
	M	SD	M	SD
Recall Time (sec.)	352	94.2	335	110.3
Recalled Words	89.0	11.2	92.1	7.2
Recalled Words by Memory Load				
Five Words	27.4	2.9	27.6	2.2
Six Words	29.7	3.9	31.6	2.5
Seven Words	31.8	5.3	32.9	3.5
Recalled Words by Time of Day				
8 A.M.	93.0	7.3	90.6	8.5
10 A.M.	79.6	9.9	95.2	4.4
1 P.M.	97.8	9.3	92.8	5.6
3 P.M.	89.7	7.6	89.7	10.8
First Words	17.5	0.8	17.5	0.7
Last Words	12.3	3.2	13.1	2.6

Note. DYB = "do your best" condition ($n = 23$); Goal = goal-setting condition ($n = 19$).

correct, both tasks should be comparable to some degree.[11] Therefore, we should also find a pronounced performance facilitating effect of goal setting for subtasks with a higher working-memory load (lists with six and seven words). The data indicate that this is the case, although differences between groups are only marginally significant (the term for the corresponding two-way interaction between memory load [5 vs. 6/7] and goal setting is $F(1, 34) = 2.9$; $p \leq .10$.

A possible reason for this missing difference in performance could be that the goal assigned to our participants in this task (recall 90 out of 108 words) was too easy. In the goal-setting group, 14 of 19 participants reached this goal, and in the DYB group, 13 of 23 participants recalled at least 90 words. That is why we decided to increase goal difficulty in the third experiment (by shortening the interstimulus interval during presentation of the words on the screen). Furthermore, the purpose of experiment 3 was to (a) examine more participants in order to have

---

[11]In contrast to the working memory task, it was not difficult to remember the first words presented in the short-term-memory task (see Table 4.4). These differences between both tasks are due to a varied use of rehearsal strategies. Whereas subjects in the short-term-memory task used a rehearsal strategy extensively (and in part even loudly), the use of this strategy is almost not possible for solving the working-memory task because subjects had to read out the sentences.

TABLE 4.5
Means and Standard Deviations for Performance of the Working Memory Task in
Experiment 3

	DYB		Goal	
	M	SD	M	SD
Reading Time (sec.)	297	64.8	305	65.2
Recall Time (sec.)	268	88.3	278	83.0
Recalled Words	25.2	4.9	26.2	4.6
Three Sentences	7.8	1.2	8.1	1.0
Four Sentences	8.0	2.0	8.8	2.0
Five Sentences	9.3	2.5	9.3	2.5
First Words	6.2	1.9	6.8	2.0
First Words—3	2.6	0.7	2.6	0.7
First Words—4	1.8	0.8	2.2	0.9
First Words—5	1.9	1.0	2.0	0.9
Last Words	8.9	0.3	8.9	0.2

Note. DYB = "do your best" condition; Goal = goal-setting condition; $n = 50$ for each group.

sufficient data for analyzing other times of day, and (b)"optimize" the behavior of our subjects while solving the working-memory task by instructing participants more clearly that it was *not* allowed to hesitate or to make pauses during reading the sentences. Let us consider again data for the working-memory task first (see Table 4.5).

As expected, there were no longer any remarkable differences regarding reading times and recall times between groups so that the preconditions for a more accurate replication of our findings from the first analysis of the working memory task should be given. Based on the data of all 100 participants that were tested in this experiment (from 9 A.M. to 9 P.M.), a main effect of goal setting on working-memory performance was not significant. Only one parameter of the two-way interaction between goal setting and memory load was marginally significant, $F(1, 90) = 3.3$; $p \leq .07$; Eta$^2 = .05$, indicating that participants striving for a difficult goal recalled more words correctly for memory load 4 than for memory load 5 (compared to performance of the DYB group). In addition, the results show that participants in goal setting conditions had a slightly superior performance for the last words of the *first* sentence (first words in Table 4.5) for this subtask. However, they recalled these first words not more often than participants in DYB groups (neither the main effect of goal setting is significant, $F [1, 90] = 2.3$; $p \leq .14$, nor the contrast comparing performance for memory loads 4 and 5; $p \leq .17$).

TABLE 4.6
Interactions Between Time of Day, Goal Setting, and Memory Load for
Performance in the Working-Memory-Task in Experiment 3

	DYB		Goal	
	M	SD	M	SD
Recalled Words				
9 A.M.	25.9	3.4	24.6	3.6
12 A.M.	26.7	4.7	29.1	4.5
3 P.M.	23.5	2.5	25.1	5.7
6 P.M.	22.4	6.7	24.6	4.3
9 P.M.	27.6	4.9	27.7	3.3
Recalled Words by Memory Load and Time of Day				
9 A.M. / 3 Sentences	7.8	0.8	7.6	1.2
9 A.M. / 4 Sentences	8.0	1.4	8.6	1.6
9 A.M. / 5 Sentences	10.1	2.0	8.4	1.9
12 A.M. / 3 Sentences	8.5	0.8	8.4	0.7
12 A.M. / 4 Sentences	8.5	2.5	9.5	2.2
12 A.M. / 5 Sentences	9.7	1.8	11.2	2.2

Note. DYB = "do your best" condition; Goal = goal-setting condition; $n = 10$ for each subgroup.

Taking into consideration that we added new groups in this experiment that solved the task at 6 P.M. and 9 P.M., we did not expect a main effect for goal setting on memory performance (see Table 4.6 for performance values by time of day).

However, we expected to find again a two-way interaction between goal setting and time of day in the morning (between 8 A.M. and noon). Moreover, this effect should be especially pronounced for subtasks with a high memory load. And indeed, this three-way interaction (Goal Setting × Time of Day × Memory Load) was significant, $F(2, 72) = 4.7$; $p \leq .01$; $Eta^2 = .12$; see Table 4.5. As we observed before, goal setting had a small (nonsignificant) negative impact on memory performance early in the morning (9 A.M.), whereas working-memory performance around midday (12 A.M.) was substantially higher in the goal setting condition than in the "do your best" condition.[12] In addition, this overall interaction is mainly based on performance variations in subtasks with a high working-memory load. The two contrasts of this three-way interaction ($F[1, 36] = 2.8$; $p \leq .10$; $Eta^2 = .07$ for comparing sets 3 vs. 4/5 and $F[1, 36] = 7.0$; $p \leq .01$; $Eta^2 = .16$ for comparing sets 4 vs. 5) demonstrate that goal setting improved memory performance

[12]If we consider those words that were recalled on a correct position, this interaction is significant, too. With respect to all other dependent variables, there were no significant interactions with time of day.

especially for sets with five sentences. Furthermore, in the critical conditions (noon, memory load of 4 or 5) there were again no significant differences between groups with respect to reading times and recall times. Participants in the DYB condition needed 298 seconds to read all sentences, and those in the goal setting condition needed 306 seconds (the corresponding values for recall times are 248 seconds and 256 seconds at 12 A.M.; for subsets with four and five sentences there were again no substantial differences). Therefore, we can conclude once again that goal setting reduces the impairment of short-term memory that is based on circadian rhythms especially around midday for conditions with high memory load. In addition, these changes in working memory performance are probably not based on differences in the use of time-consuming strategies.[13]

The results we found for the short-term memory task in experiment three are shown in (Table 4.7). Our manipulation of the interstimulus interval for this task was successful because participants recalled fewer words, but there was no indication of a goal setting effect on memory performance in the short-term-memory task (see Table 4.7), although subjects in the goal setting condition used even some more time for recalling the words, $F(1, 90) = 3.0$; $p \leq .09$; $\text{Eta}^2 = .04$. Finally, we found no significant two-way interaction between the goal-setting factor and the time of day factor. Nevertheless, participants in the goal-setting condition who worked on the task around midday showed again the highest performance compared to all other groups (see Table 4.7). When we consider the various parameters of the three-way interaction (Goal Setting × Time of Day × Memory Load), only one parameter approaches significance $(F[1, 90] = 3.1$; $p \leq .08$; $\text{Eta}^2 = .04$; the comparison of list length 6 vs. 7 for participants working around midday vs. those who solved the task later in the day, see Table 4.7). Around midday, participants in the goal-setting condition showed higher performance in lists with seven words than in lists with six words, whereas in the "do your best" condition memory performance for both lists is almost identical. For the 60 participants who were tested later in the day there were no substantial differences in memory performance due to goal setting. Hence, similar to the results for the working-memory task, assigning difficult goals around midday improved memory performance only for longer lists of the short-term-memory task. The reason for this finding might be that the use of a rehearsal strategy is no longer helpful to keep all information activated in memory and, as a consequence, working memory load increases for these lists substantially. Although there is no doubt that both memory tasks require different processes (the correlation between performance in both tasks for experiment 3 is $r = .34$; $p \leq .01$), this finding indicates that goal setting can improve memory performance especially under those conditions in which a continuous rehearsal of

---

[13] There were again significant main effects for memory load in this task. The number of recalled words, reading time, and recall time increased, and the number of recalled words presented first decreased with higher nmemory load (all $p \leq .01$). Moreover, there was also a main effect of time of day, $F(4, 90) = 3.7$; $p \leq .01$; $\text{Eta}^2 = .14$), for the number of recalled words (especially at noon and at 9 P.M. memory performance was high).

TABLE 4.7
Means and Standard Deviations of Performance for the Short-Term-Memory Task
in Experiment 3

	DYB		Goal	
	M	SD	M	SD
Recall Time (sec.)	370	88.5	416	101.8
Recalled Words	85.9	8.0	84.4	9.7
Recalled Words by Time of Day				
9 A.M.	86.2	8.2	82.8	9.5
12 A.M.	86.2	5.4	87.2	6.8
3 P.M.	86.6	9.2	82.0	7.4
6 P.M.	84.6	8.3	83.6	12.2
9 P.M.	85.5	9.7	85.6	9.5
Recalled Words by Memory Load				
Five Words	27.1	2.1	26.7	2.2
Six Words	29.7	3.1	28.4	4.1
Seven Words	29.1	4.3	29.2	4.8
Recalled Words by Time of Day and Memory Load				
12 A.M. / 6 Words	29.6	2.6	28.1	4.2
12 A.M. / 7 Words	29.7	3.7	32.2	3.6
3–9 P.M. / 6 Words	29.8	3.4	28.6	4.1
3–9 P.M. / 7 Words	28.9	4.6	28.5	4.9
First Words	17.4	1.1	17.3	0.9
Last Words	12.4	2.8	12.9	2.8

Note. DYB = "do your best" condition; Goal = goal-setting condition (n = 50); for 12 A.M., n = 10, and for 3–9 P.M., n = 30.

the stimulus material is no longer possible or effective (sets with five sentences or lists with seven words).

DISCUSSION

In five out of five experimental tests we found a significant impact of goal setting on performance in short-term-memory tasks. This impact showed up either in form of a two-way interaction between goal setting and time of day or as a three-way interaction between goal setting, time of day, and memory load (see Table 4.8). In none of the five tests there was evidence for a reversed effect. Moreover, the only test in which no interaction between goal setting and time of day could be observed was flawed because participants deceived the experimenter by working

TABLE 4.8
Significant Improvements (Eta^2) in Short-Term Retention Due to Goal Setting
Across Experiments 1 to 3

Tasks	Goals	Goals × TOD	Goals × Memory Load	Goals × TOD × Memory Load
Exp. 1 WM	.14	.49 8 A.M. vs. 11 A.M.		
Exp. 2 STM		.25 8 A.M. vs. 10 A.M.		
WM			.14 4 vs. 5 Words	
Exp. 3 STM				.04 12 A.M. vs. 3–9 P.M. for 6 vs. 7 Words
WM				.16 9 A.M. vs. 12 A.M. for 4 vs. 5 Words

Note. TOD = time of day; WM = working-memory task; STM = short-term-memory task.

very slowly.[14] The consistent replication of this interaction-effect is encouraging because motivational forces induced in these experiments were slightly different (see Table 4.1). Monetary rewards for goal attainment were added in experiments 2 and 3. This in turn suggests that the element of goal setting is sufficient to induce these interactions.[15]

In view of the existing studies regarding the effects of goal setting on various tasks (Locke & Latham, 1990), all this might have been expected. It would appear, then, that we just added some more experimental evidence to show the effectiveness of goal setting on very simple tasks. May be we could also draw the conclusion that difficult and specific goals work not so well on traditional short-term-memory tests. However, let us reconsider our findings and their theoretical implications in more detail. We found consistently that goal setting improved short-term retention of verbal information (a) especially during midday, (b) for subtasks with high memory load, and (c) when the use of a simple rehearsal strategy is almost impossible. Can this be explained by current cognitive or motivational theories of human performance? We do not believe this.

---

[14]Nevertheless, we count this test as a successful one because goal setting improved memory performance for subtasks with high memory load (five sentences). We should add that this effect is partially based on an increased primacy effect, indicating the violation of instructions for this task.

[15]It will remain to be seen if incentives alone would yield similar results.

Cognitive performance theories assume that performance in short-term memory tasks is mainly a function of the use of more or less effective encoding strategies (e.g., level of processing, chunking, rehearsal, imagery) and recall strategies (Baddeley, 1996; Engelkamp & Cohen, 1991; Parkin, 1996; Raajmakers & Shiffrin, 1992; Roediger et al., 1994). Thus, one might assume that the effects of goal setting on short-term retention of information we found are totally mediated by the availability and use of these strategies. In our view, this is probably not the case. Of course, we can not prove perfectly that participants in goal-setting conditions used the same (mental) encoding and recall strategies as subjects in "do your best" conditions. However, (a) participants were assigned randomly to experimental conditions, (b) instructions in both experimental conditions were not specific with respect to the type of encoding or recall strategies that should be used, (c) the use of some strategies (e.g., rehearsal) was almost impossible for the working-memory task, and (d) our behavioral measures (e.g., sequence of recalled words) and our time measures (reading times and recall times) would have detected differences with respect to the use of some of these strategies. In addition, in a recent experimental test with a slightly varied German version of the working memory task it was observed that (e) compared to control groups with DYB instructions even explicit instructions to use specific strategies (e.g., reading the last words very concentrated, constructing semantic relations between last words) did not improve memory performance in a substantial way (Hacker, Veres, & Wollenberger, 1994). Finally, the most convincing argument against this assumption is that (f) goal-setting effects were found under conditions when the simple use of a rehearsal strategy was almost impossible (sets with five sentences and lists with seven words) and that (h) the effects under discussion were dependent on time of day. If we assume that the use of different strategies is responsible for the impact of goal setting on memory performance, the interactions between time of day and goal setting would indicate that the use of performance-enhancing strategies in goal-setting conditions was promoted only around midday. Why should this be the case? In view of all findings, our explanation for this pattern of results is that improvements in short-term memory performance due to goal setting are probably based on a temporary increased level of cognitive arousal (working-memory capacity) that facilitates the reactivation of previously activated information in memory[16] (similar observations were made by Goschke & Kuhl, 1993; Gollwitzer, 1996 and Kluger & DeNisi, 1996[17]). In addition, the possibility to make use of this arousal mechanism is dependent on the phase of circadian

---

[16]Higher working-memory capacity may rely on a better supply of excitatory processes (e.g., more concepts can be held active in working memory at the same time) or on a better supply of inhibitory processes that help to reduce interferences due to task-irrelevant information (see Baddeley, 1996, p. 25 for recent discussions regarding this issue).

[17]The assumption that motivational variables can improve performance in memory tasks is also corroborated by the results of the meta-analysis of Kluger and DeNisi (1996). Among other things, they found that feedback interventions improved performance especially well on memory tasks.

rhythms, and for reasons that we do not know, this might happen especially around midday. However, as mentioned before, there is no motivational theory that can explain our data either. Most theories of work motivation, especially expectancy–value theories, analyze and explain human behavior usually on a static and molar level, not considering the various mechanisms and processes (e.g., rehearsal) that are involved in the translation of goals into action. Moreover, they include no assumptions about (a) changes in behavior over time (see also Hanisch et al., this volume) and (b) the impact of many task demands that are important for understanding inter- and intraindividual variance in performance outcomes (e.g., memory load). Hence, the scope of these models is mainly limited to predicting predecisional phenomena (e.g., goal choice). Due to these limitations, recent motivational theories have focussed more on the processes that are linked to the phase of goal striving, e.g., goal-setting theory, feedback intervention theory (Kluger & DeNisi, 1996; see also Erez & Earley, 1993; Gollwitzer, 1996), and dynamic resource-allocation models of goal-directed behavior (Kanfer & Ackerman, 1989). By integrating knowledge from cognitive psychology and other psychological disciplines, for example, with respect to the development of strategies, self-regulation activities, and processes linked to skill-acquisition, these approaches are much more successful in explaining outcomes of task performance. Nevertheless, even these theories are still oversimplistic with respect to the various micro-level processes that are involved in task solution. Therefore, at least in our view, there is a very important lesson to be learned from the findings presented here. Motivational psychologists who are interested in explaining human performance should start to analyze micro-level processes involved in task solution. This goal can and should be attained by integrating motivational theories with cognitive theories of human performance (Kluger & DeNisi, 1996; Kuhl, 1994; Simon, 1994). Such an integration will allow one to identify those mechanisms that underly changes in human performance that are induced by various motivational states (Wegge, 1998; Wegge, 2001). Finally, in keeping with the work of many other researchers (e.g., Boekaerts, Pintrich, Zeidner, 2000; Eysenck, 1992; Gollwtzer & Bargh, 1996; Kanfer & Ackermann, 1989; Kluger & DeNisi, 1996; Hockey, 1984; Humphreys & Revelle, 1984; Pekrun & Frese, 1992; Revelle, 1989; Sanders, 1983; Schiefele, 1996; Wood, 2000), we propose that an adequate theory of human performance has to integrate assumptions about energetical issues (e.g., arousal, activation, emotions) and their dynamic variations (e.g., diurnal) variations over time, too.

AUTHOR NOTES

Research reported here was supported by a grant from the German Research Foundation (DFG) and a grant from the Ministry of Science and Research (MWF-NRW). We wish to thank Dov Eden, Avraham N. Kluger, Abraham Korman, and Ed Locke for valuable comments on an earlier version of this chapter. Correspondence concerning this chapter should be addressed to Jürgen Wegge, Universität Dortmund, FB 14 Organisationspsychologie, Emil-Figge-Strasse 50, 44227 Dortmund, Germany (e-mail: *wegge@fb14.uni-dortmund.de*).

REFERENCES

Audia, G., Kristof-Brown, A., Brown, K. G., & Locke, E. A. (1996). Relationship of goals and microlevel work processes to performance on a multipath manual task. *Journal of Applied Psychology, 81*, 483–497.

Baddeley, A. D. (1986). *Working memory.* Oxford, England: Oxford University Press.

Baddeley, A. D. (1996). Exploring the central executive. *Quarterly Journal of Experimental Psychology, 49*, 5–28.

Bettman, J. R., Johnson, E. J., & Payne, J. W. (1990). A componential analysis of cognitive effort in choice. *Organizational Behavior and Human Decision Processes, 45*, 111–139.

Birbaumer, N., & Schmidt, R. F. (1991). *Biologische Psychologie.* Berlin: Springer.

Boekaerts, M., Pintrich, P. R., & Zeidner, M. (2000). *Handbook of self-regulation.* San Diego: Academic Press.

Daneman, M., & Carpenter, P. A. (1980). Individual differences in working memory and reading. *Journal of Verbal Learning and Behavior, 19*, 450–466.

Daneman, M., & Carpenter, P. A. (1983). Individual differences in integrating information between and within sentences. *Journal of Experimental Psychology: Learning, Memory and Cognition, 9*, 561–584.

Düker, H. (1949). Über ein Verfahren zur Untersuchung der psychischen Leistungsfähigkeit (A test to examine psychic concentration and performance). *Psychologische Forschung, 23*, 10–24.

Engelkamp, J., & Cohen, R. L. (1991). Current issues in memory of action events. *Psychological Research, 53*, 175–182.

Erez, M., & Earley, P. C. (1993). *Culture, self-identity, and work.* New York: Oxford University Press.

Eysenck, M. W. (1992). *Attention and arousal: Cognition and performance.* Berlin: Springer.

Folkard, S., & Monk, T. H. (1983). Chronopsychology: Circadian rhythms and human performance. In A. Gale & A. Edwards (Eds.), *Attention and Performance* (Vol. 2, pp. 57–78). London: Academic Press.

Folkard, S., & Monk, T. H. (1985). Circadian performance rhythms. In S. Folkard & T. H. Monk (Eds.), *Hours of work: Temporal factors in work scheduling* (pp. 37–52). New York: Wiley.

Ford, M. E. (1992). *Motivating humans: Goals, emotions, and personal agency beliefs.* London: Sage.

Gollwitzer, P. M. (1996). The volitional benefits of planning. In P. M. Gollwitzer & J. A. Bargh (Eds.), *The psychology of action. Linking cognition and motivation to behavior* (pp. 287–312). New York: Guilford Press.

Gollwitzer, P. M., & Bargh, J. A. (1996). *The psychology of action. Linking cognition and motivation to behavior.* New York: The Guilford Press.

Goschke, T., & Kuhl, J. (1993). Representation of intentions: Persisting activation in memory. *Journal of Experimental Psychology: Learning, Memory and Cognition, 19*, 1–16.

Hacker, W., Sieler, R., & Pietzcker, F. (2000). Dekompositionsuntersuchungen zu Kernfunktionen des Arbeitsgedächtnisses [Decomposition studies on the core functions of working memory]. *Zeitschrift für Experimentelle Psychologie, 47*, 195–218.

Hacker, W., Veres, T., & Wollenberger, E. (1994). Verarbeitungskapazität für Text: Ergebnisse der Entwicklung eines deutschsprachigen Prüfverfahrens des Arbeitsgedächtnisses. *Zeitschrift für Psychologie, 202*, 295–320.

Heckhausen, H., & Gollwitzer, P. M. (1987). Thought contents and cognitive functioning in motivational versus volitional states of mind. *Motivation and Emotion, 11,* 101–120.

Hockey, G. R. J. (1984). Varieties of attentional state: The effects of environment. In R. Parasuraman & D. R. Davies (Eds.), *Varieties of attention* (pp. 449–483). London: Academic Press.

Hockey, G. R. J., Coles, M. G. H., & Gaillard, A. W. K. (1984). Energetical issues in research on human information processing. In G. R. J. Hockey, A. W. K. Gaillard, & M. G. H. Coles (Eds.), *Energetics and human information processing* (pp. 3–21). Dordrecht: Martinus Nijhoff Publishers.

Humphreys, M. S., & Revelle, W. (1984). Personality, motivation, and performance: A theory of the relationship between individual differences and information processing. *Psychological Review, 91,* 153–184.

Kanfer, R. (1992). Work motivation: New directions in theory and research. In C. L. Cooper & I. T. Robertson (Eds.), *International Review of Industrial and Organizational Psychology* (Vol. 7, pp. 1–53). London: Wiley.

Kanfer, R., & Ackerman, P. L. (1989). Motivation and cognitive abilities: An integrative/aptitude-treatment interaction approach to skill acquisition. *Journal of Applied Psychology (Monograph), 74,* 657–690.

Kluger, A. N., & DeNisi, A. (1996). The effects of feedback interventions on performance: A historical review, a meta-analysis and a preliminary feedback intervention theory. *Psychological Bulletin, 119,* 254–284.

Kuhl, J. (1994). Motivation and Volition. In G. d'Ydewalle, P. Eeelen, & P. Bertelson (Eds.), *International perspectives on psychological science* (Vol. 2, pp. 311–340). Hillsdale, NJ: Erlbaum.

Locke, E. A., & Latham, G. P. (1990). *A theory of goal setting and task performance.* Englewood Cliffs, NJ: Prentice-Hall.

Parkin, A. J. (1996). *Gedächtnis. Ein einführendes Lehrbuch* (Memory, Phenomena, Experiment, and Theory). Weinheim: Beltz.

Payne, J. W., Bettman, J. R., & Johnson, E. J. (1993). *The adaptive decision maker.* Cambridge, UK: Cambridge Press.

Pekrun, R., & Frese, M. (1992). Emotions in work and achievement. In C. L. Cooper & I. T. Robertson (Eds.), *International Review of Industrial and Organizational Psychology* (Vol. 7, pp. 153–200). New York: Wiley.

Raajmakers, J. G. W., & Shiffrin, R. M. (1992). Models for recall and recognition. *Annual Review of Psychology, 42,* 205–234.

Revelle, W. (1989). Personality, motivation, and cognitive performance. In R. Kanfer, P. L. Ackerman, & R. Cudeck (Eds.), *Abilities, motivation, and methodology: The Minnesota symposium on learning and individual differences* (pp. 297–341). Hillsdale, NJ: Erlbaum.

Roediger, H. L., Guynn, M. J., & Jones, T. C. (1994). Implicit memory: A tutorial review. In G. d'Ydewalle, P. Eeelen, & P. Bertelson (Eds.), *International perspectives on psychological science* (Vol. 2, pp. 67–94). Hillsdale, NJ: Erlbaum.

Sanders, A. F. (1983). Towards a model of stress and human performance. *Acta Psychologica, 53,* 61–97.

Sanders, A. F. (1990). Issues and trends in the debate on discrete vs. continuous processing of information. *Acta Psychologica, 74,* 123–167.

Schiefele, U. (1996). Topic interest, text representation and quality of experience. *Contemporary Educational Psychology, 21,* 3–18.

Schmidt, K.-H. & Kleinbeck, U. (1990). Effects of goals and feedback on performance — Mediating mechanisms and structures of information processing. In P. J. D. Drenth, J. A. Sergeant, & R. J. Takens (Eds.), *European Perspectives in Psychology. Work and Organizational Psychology* (Vol. 3, pp. 55–66). Chichester, England: Wiley.

Schütte, M., & Jordan, C. (1996). Dependence between performance, strain and strategies for an activity involving informational load. *Ergonomics, 39,* 903–923.

Shacter, D. L. (1989). Memory. In M. I. Posner (Ed.), *Foundations of cognitive science* (pp. 683–725). Cambridge, MA: MIT Press.

Simon, H. A. (1994). The bottleneck of attention: Connecting thought with motivation. In W. D. Spaulding (Ed.), *Nebraska Symposium on Motivation* (Vol. 41, pp. 1–21). Lincoln: University of Nebraska Press.

Waters, G. S., & Caplan, D. (1996). The measurement of verbal working memory capacity and its relation to reading comprehension. *The Quarterly Journal of Experimental Psychology, 49*, 51–79.

Wegge, J. (1998). Lernmotivation, Informationsverarbeitung und Leistung (Academic motivation, information processing, and performance). Münster: Waxmann.

Wegge, J. (2001). Motivation, information processing and performance: Effects of goal setting on basic cognitive processes. In A. Efklides, J. Kuhl & R. Sorrentino (Eds.), *Trends and prospects in motivational research* (pp. 271–298). Dordrecht: Kluwer.

Wood, R. E. (2000). Special issue on Work motivation: Theory, research and practice. *Applied Psychology: An International Review, Vol. 49*.

Wood, R. E. & Locke, E. A. (1990). Goal setting and strategy effects on complex tasks. *Research in Organizational Bevhavior, 12*, 73–109.

5

Means Efficacy: External Sources of General and Specific Subjective Efficacy

Dov Eden
Faculty of Management, Tel Aviv University

I felt pretty confident with Buzz.

—Mary Ann, a New Yorker who, accompanied by her bulldog Buzz, chased a would-be robber 10 blocks in Uptown Manhattan until the police finally caught up with them and arrested the suspect, interviewed on NBC's *Today* show, August 1, 1995.

Self-efficacy is only half of the efficacy story. The aim of this chapter is to advance efficacy theory by conceptualizing previously undefined dimensions and sources of efficacy beliefs. This is an elaboration of propositions first introduced in the Pygmalion-at-Work model (Eden, 1988, 1990). It partially builds on some ideas developed by Gist and Mitchell (1992). The overall result is to broaden our understanding of efficacy beliefs to encompass sources of work motivation previously ignored by self-efficacy theory.

SUBJECTIVE INTERNAL AND EXTERNAL EFFICACY

Subjective efficacy is defined as one's overall assessment of all available resources that may be applied toward successfully performing a job. Some of these resources

73

are internal to the individual and are encompassed within the concept of self-efficacy. These sources include such talents, knowledge, endurance, willpower, or other traits that the individual deems useful for performance. However, the internal sources of self-efficacy are only part of the subjective efficacy picture.

Subjective external efficacy is defined as the individual's belief in the utility of the means available for performing the job. The individual attaches instrumental value to myriad means that may facilitate—or hinder—performance. The aggregate subjective utility of these external resources is dubbed *means efficacy*. Some means are helpful in promoting efficiency and effectiveness and are viewed as assets. Other means are inadequate, unreliable, and irksome to the user. Such means are impediments to excellence, are viewed as liabilities rather than assets, and have a demotivating effect on workers because they reduce their overall sense of efficacy and expectations for success. It is hypothesized that means efficacy is as motivating as self-efficacy; just as a high level of self-efficacy imbues one with expectations for success and thereby augments motivation to exert effort (Bandura, 1986), so a high level of belief in the efficacy of the means available impels one to use those means more energetically. Furthermore, the motivating effects of a high level of internal efficacy ("I am an accomplished sharpshooter") can be neutralized by low external efficacy ("The weapon is miscalibrated"). Similarly, a marvelous tool will have little impact on motivation for the individual who has low self-efficacy for using it ("I'm sure it's a great laptop but I'll never be able to learn how to use it"). Maximal motivation results when workers believe themselves to be highly skilled at what they do and believe that they have the best means for doing it, that is, when *total subjective efficacy* is high.

So far, scholars have considered only internal efficacy (i.e., self-efficacy) in their theories of work motivation. The present chapter is dedicated to illuminating the other, external half of the subjective efficacy construct. Adding external efficacy expands the efficacy concept and leads to greater understanding of motivated effort. It also opens the way for practical applications not implied by previous self-efficacy conceptualizations.

There has been some previous recognition of the importance of the individual's appraisal of the utility of the means available when estimating capability to perform a task. However, when considered at all, external efficacy has been given insufficient weight. For example, Gist and Mitchell's model (1992, Figs. 1 and 2) includes an analysis of situational resources and constraints as external cues that determine one's assessment of self-efficacy. Gist and Mitchell's external–internal dimension classifies the various determinants of self-efficacy as to whether the organization or the individual, respectively, controls each determinant. As a consequence, none of Gist and Mitchell's three intervention strategies for changing (i.e., increasing) self-efficacy involves changing assessments of the utility of the available means. In contrast, the internal–external dimension in the present approach includes different sources of total subjective efficacy and defines the external sources as determinants of means efficacy, not of self-efficacy. In determining work motivation, the present model gives consideration to workers' estimates both of the efficacy of their internal resources and of the efficacy of the available means. Thus, the present conceptualization lends the external determinants their due weight as independent variables that can be influenced in practical attempts to increase overall subjective efficacy, and hence motivation, effort, and performance.

Both internal and external efficacy may be higher or lower than would be corroborated by objective appraisal. The kinds of efficacy dealt with in this article are all subjective, and the adjective *subjective* will be dropped. Unless stated otherwise, the term *efficacy* used below refers to subjective efficacy.

EFFICACY AND EFFORT

For management, the most important implication of efficacy beliefs is their effect on motivated effort (Bandura, 1986; Eden, 1988, 1993; Locke & Latham, 1990). For this reason, it is more useful for total efficacy, regardless of its source, to be high than for it to be accurate. High performance expectations often become self-fulfilling. The self-fulfilling prophecy (SFP) is the reason for the emphasis on high expectations in the Pygmalion approach to management (Eden, 1990). Explicating the role of self-efficacy in motivation, Maddux (1995) made essentially the same point: "Motivation toward difficult goals is enhanced by overestimates of personal capabilities . . . which then become self-fulfilling prophecies when people set their sights high, persevere, and then surpass their usual level of accomplishment" (p. 13). Thus, various approaches converge in emphasizing the role of high self-efficacy in motivating intensification of effort.

GENERAL AND SPECIFIC EFFICACY

Researchers have followed Bandura (1986) in focusing on specific self-efficacy (SSE), largely ignoring general self-efficacy (GSE). SSE is a situation-specific cognition that is highly focused on a particular task. Studying it requires devising an ad hoc measure for each task; such measures are rarely used twice. In contrast, personality psychologists conceive of self-efficacy as a generalized trait comprised of one's belief in one's overall competence to effect requisite performances across a wide variety of achievement situations. Sherer et al. (1982) reasoned that expectations formed in one situation generalize and influence mastery expectations in new situations. They developed and validated the *General Self-efficacy Scale*. The GSE Scale has served many populations and situations. Recently, Chen, Gully, and Eden (2001) developed and validated a new general self-efficacy (NGSE) scale recommended for use in organizational research. The present treatise identifies and describes the sources of means efficacy, separating them into general and specific in parallel to GSE and SSE.

MEANS EFFICACY

Well, well, well, well, now. I met with Stalin this morning. He said he had some more
questions to present and I told him to fire away, and he did, too, and it was dynamite.
But now I have some dynamite, too. This gives me a completely new feeling of
confidence.

—Harry S Truman in Potsdam, upon being informed of the first successful atomic
detonation in New Mexico on July 16, 1945, in Peter Wyden's *Day One: Before
Hiroshima and After.*

President Truman's statement is a marvelous expression of means efficacy. Learning that he now held the power of *"the bomb"* in his hands drastically bolstered
his sense of being able to stand up successfully to Stalin's bullying threats. It in-
vigorated his efforts to pursue American interests in the face of militant Soviet
expansionism.

The concept of means efficacy was first introduced to refer to one's subjective
assessment of the adequacy of the tools available for performing a job (Eden, 1993).
Regarding the tools available as modern, efficient, well-maintained, and appropriate for the job increases one's confidence in being able to accomplish what needs
to be done. Disbelief in the efficacy of the tools is frustrating and demoralizing,
as inadequate means can threaten to neutralize even abundant internal resources.
Some means are permanently available, "fixed assets" that can be utilized over
and over. These comprise the sources of general external efficacy and appear on
the left side of Table 5.1. Some means are only temporarily available or are appropriate only for particular tasks. These are classified as sources of specific external
efficacy and appear in the right side of Table 5.1. The sources of external efficacy
are not encompassed within previous self-efficacy theory and have therefore been
largely ignored in work motivation theory.

TABLE 5.1
Sources of General and Specific Means Efficacy

General Sources	Specific Sources
Organization	Internal Services
Technology	Tools
e.g., Hardware	e.g., Software
Managerial Leadership	Supervisory Leadership
Team in General	Team on Specific Tasks
Permanent Work Group	Ad Hoc Task Force

Organization and Internal Services

The first entry for general means efficacy in Table 5.1 is "Organization." This is paralleled in the specific external cell by "Internal services." The modern organization is the consummate tool for accomplishing work. The very word *organization* is derived from the Greek *organon*, meaning tool or instrument. Current social constructionist conceptualizations notwithstanding, organizations are first and foremost rational tools contrived by a few to direct the productive efforts of the many. Some organizations are designed so well that they inspire confidence in their members. An efficient bureaucracy that solves problems in a timely fashion can facilitate feelings of efficacy among those it serves. This feeling of having an effective organization behind them motivates those employees. Conversely, some organizations are designed so poorly that they dissipate any willingness on the part of their members to exert effort.

Sometimes it is a specific function within the organization that is perceived as especially effective or ineffective ("The home office processes the forms right away; that keeps customers satisfied and helps me get repeat business" vs. "It takes them forever to process a sale; how can I ever build up a satisfied clientele?"). This would be an example of an internal service as a source of specific means (in)efficacy. It is hypothesized that, when members believe in their organization as a whole, or in a specific important part of it, as an effective apparatus that facilitates work, their overall efficacy increases. Conversely, when employees believe that "The only law around here is Murphy's Law," they see the organization more as a hindrance than an aid, and their sense of efficacy is thereby reduced.

Technology and Tools

Knowing that the technology behind the capital goods with which one does a job is the best available arouses a sense of efficacy. One example is an information-processing system. Belief in its quality is supremely important in instilling a sense of efficacy in the user. A military example is the soldier's belief in the efficacy of the weapon he has been issued. Factor analyzing the Combat Readiness Morale Questionnaire among combat soldiers in the Israel Defense Forces (IDF), Gal (1986) found that items assessing soldiers' confidence in their senior commanders and confidence in their weapons loaded on the first factor. In a replication in the U.S. Army, Gal and Manning (1987) revealed that confidence in weapons again loaded on the first factor. Moreover, confidence in weapons was correlated with both personal morale and company morale even more strongly in the U.S. Army than in the IDF. It is likely that confidence in commanders and weapons is a universal source of morale among combat soldiers. Both the commander and the weapon are sources of external efficacy, as both are prime means that determine the likelihood that the soldiers will accomplish their mission and return home safely.

Enthusiasm wanes among workers who do not believe that the technical means at their disposal are up to par. Having to use equipment considered to be outmoded can be devastating for work motivation, especially when believing that competitors have better means. Thus, for motivational purposes, it is important to equip workers with the best technical means the organization can afford, and to make sure they *know* they have the best.

The next row on both sides of Table 5.1 instantiates the distinction between general and specific sources of means efficacy. Computer *hardware* usually represents a heavy capital investment. Having a high-power computer is an indispensable means for doing many jobs. Furthermore, having state-of-the-art *software* may be crucial for a specific job. Both must be appropriate in order for subjective efficacy to be high; perceiving either as inadequate erodes confidence ("The computer is great but the program is out of date" or "This is the best software there is but it won't run right on the old computer we have").

Mary Ann, the courageous New Yorker quoted in the prologue to this chapter, expressed feelings of efficaciousness because of Buzz, her bulldog, who was accompanying her on her jog and subsequently on her chase after the bad guy. Viewing Buzz as an instrument used by Mary Ann, she was expressing means efficacy when she said she "felt pretty confident with Buzz." This exemplifies specific means efficacy because Buzz can inspire such confidence only in quite limited circumstances, such as warding off an intruder. Having Buzz alongside would not increase Mary Ann's sense of efficaciousness in balancing her checkbook or in conducting viewer surveys in her advertising firm. Similarly, efficient, user-friendly software designed to aid keeping track of household finances would be a source of means efficacy for balancing her checkbook, but not for anything else. Thus, listing a particular source of external efficacy under the general or specific column depends on a judgment as to how general or specific the usefulness of the means is. The same is true of all the entries in the table.

Managerial and Supervisory Leadership

Leadership is arguably the most important means organizations make available to their members. All organizations provide their employees with leadership—or at least provide managers who are supposed to lead. When employees believe in their leaders, they are more willing to make the sacrifices and to exert the effort necessary to succeed. When they do not believe in the leader's aptitude or dedication, they hold back on their own commitment and effort. Thus, belief in the leader's ability to lead them to success is a major source of followers' confidence in achieving that success. In this sense, the leader is a crucial means that, by being perceived as effective or ineffective, ignites or squelches followers' enthusiasm. The finding cited above, that belief in the immediate commander's leadership is the prime determinant of morale among combat soldiers, illustrates the importance of leadership as a source of means efficacy.

Table 5.1 distinguishes between the general leadership provided by upper-level managers and the more specific leadership provided by immediate supervisors. These are different, and not necessarily consistent, sources of means efficacy. Top management might be superb and the immediate boss might be awful, or vice versa. Soldiers need to know that they can rely on the top brass to devise the best strategy and on their immediate field commanders to lead them in implementing the best tactics. For civilian personnel, it is important to believe in top management's capacity to create effective corporate strategies and derive profitable business policies, as well as in the ability of lower echelon supervisors to guide everyday activities along the proper course. Strategy without capacity for implementation, or excellent immediate supervision in a policy void, arouses feelings of helplessness among workers, who need adequate input from both these levels of management in order to succeed in doing their jobs.

Inasmuch as leadership is not crucial for every aspect of job success, it should be viewed as a means of varying importance. As Kerr and Jermier (1978) have pointed out, there are characteristics of jobs that take on certain leadership functions, rendering the leader's action superfluous and leaving the leader free to do other things. A testable hypothesis is that leadership is less a source of external efficacy when substitutes for leadership are built in to the job setting. According to Kerr and Jermier, substitutes may include employee characteristics such as a strong professional orientation and abundant job knowledge derived from rich experience and training; task characteristics such as intrinsically satisfying work or structured, routine, and unambiguous tasks; and organizational characteristics such as a cohesive work group and formalization that is manifested in explicit plans, goals, and areas of responsibility. When such substitutes are lacking, leadership takes on much greater importance as a means of getting the job done, and hence, as a source of external efficacy.

Like the organization and any other means, leadership can become a liability when it hinders, rather than promotes, performance. We can hypothesize that experiencing poor leadership being exercised on the part of one's supervisor diminishes efficacy ("With a dodo like him in charge, what chance do we stand of meeting our goal?"). In like manner, any means can be perceived as a source that augments efficacy or acts as a barrier to performance and vitiates efficacy and motivation.

Peers as a Source of Collective Efficacy

The last two rows of Table 5.1 display two different ways of thinking about an individual member's colleagues collectively, as a work group or team. For an individual with a job to do, the other workers in the organization can be viewed as a means for getting work done. Therefore, collective efficacy is a special case of means efficacy. Collective efficacy is the individual's belief in the capacity of his or her team, department, division, or other relevant organizational unit to execute the courses of action required to perform its mission effectively. Whereas self-efficacy is a self-referent percept, the referent of collective efficacy is the competence of one's organizational unit. This definition is focused on the individual, defining collective efficacy in terms of the individual's belief in his or her group's capability, not members' collective sense of their capability. The latter is encompassed in Shea and Guzzo's (1987; see also Guzzo, Yost, Campbell, & Shea, 1993) concept of group potency.

Zaccaro, Blair, Peterson, and Zazanis (1995) carried over the specificity from Bandura's highly particularized definition of self-efficacy and likewise confined their concept of collective efficacy to the group's "perceived competence in a specific or single performance domain" (p. 313). They went on to cite organizational scholars who have argued that groups and organizations develop

> beliefs [that] are invariably more general than the efficacious beliefs prescribed by Bandura. Indeed, organizational researchers have identified other psychological concepts that reflect perceptions of collective competence, share many of the properties of collective efficacy, but operate at a much more general level. . . . These constructs refer to members' perceptions that their group can successfully resolve *any* task or demand it may confront. Such beliefs may influence group risk taking and group persistence in novel situations significantly more than specifically targeted competence beliefs. (p. 314, italics in original)

Notwithstanding this insight into the validity of a generalized conceptualization, Zaccaro et al. deferred to Bandura's microanalytic approach and retained specificity as part of their definition of collective efficacy.

Contrary to this unnecessarily restrictive specificity, Table 5.1 distinguishes between the team as a source of general means efficacy and the team when performing specific tasks as a source of specific means efficacy. It can be highly empowering to belong to a team whose members have great overall capacity for meeting challenges, adapting to changing conditions, enduring stress without losing cohesiveness, providing support to a member in need, and integrating new members efficiently. All this would make them a source of high general collective efficacy. If, however, the same team is inept at meeting the deadline for submitting its weekly quality report, then the team would be a source of low collective efficacy for performing this particular task. Conversely, a team might be perceived as incompetent in almost every kind of performance except, say, winning the monthly attendance award: they have a knack for getting everybody there every day on time no matter what, but once there, they do a dreadful job. Thus, as self-efficacy, collective efficacy can be conceived as both general and specific.

Table 5.1 also distinguishes between the work group to which one is permanently appointed and *ad hoc* task forces to which one may be temporarily assigned. Some workers report to the same place and crew day after day; others have *ad hoc* assignments in which their peers may change every few days or so (Bennis &

Slater, 1968; Fine, 1971). The permanent or temporary nature of the assignments makes the peers a source of general or specific efficacy, respectively. Some workers have both permanent and temporary assignments. One's permanent team may not engender much collective efficacy, whereas an *ad hoc* task force to which one has been temporarily assigned may be comprised of stars. In such a case, the worker will have much greater enthusiasm for working on the task force than on his or her permanent team. For all these reasons, peers are entered as a source of both general and specific external efficacy in Table 5.1.

The relative importance of collective efficacy compared to other sources of efficacy hinges on the degree of synergistic teamwork required for job performance. The growing trend toward self-managed teams (e.g., Wellins, Byham, & Wilson, 1991) will decrease the importance of leadership as a source of efficacy and increase the importance of collective efficacy. Similarly, the trend toward self-managed individuals (Sims & Manz, 1993) will decrease the importance of both leaders and colleagues as sources of means efficacy and increase the importance of self-efficacy. It is a testable proposition that, for an individual who works quite independently, such as a lone equipment installer, solo salesperson, self-employed mechanic, or independent professional (e.g., lawyer, architect, physician, or accountant), collective efficacy and leadership efficacy count for little, and self-efficacy counts for quite a bit more, in determining one's total subjective efficacy and overall assessment of the likelihood of success.

Summary of General and Specific Sources of Means Efficacy

Viewing the entries in Table 5.1 columnwise, we may predict that the more the individual (a) believes in the overall prowess of the organization in which is he or she a working member, (b) estimates highly the superiority of the technology made available for getting a job done, (c) holds top management in high regard, and (d) considers his or her teammates to be competent at what they do, the greater will be his or her overall general means efficacy. Likewise, the more the individual (a) values the quality of the organization's sundry internal services for facilitating his or her particular job performance, (b) appreciates the specific tools available, (c) respects the expertise of his or her immediate supervisor, and (d) esteems his or her teammates as highly skilled at performing their jobs, the greater will be his or her overall specific means efficacy. Combining both columns, the greater the sum of one's overall general means efficacy plus one's overall specific means efficacy, the greater the total means efficacy. Beyond bolstering employees' self-efficacy, management's task in motivating employees is to act in ways that maximize all these sources of means efficacy.

This completes the description of the external sources of general and specific subjective efficacy. Further thought could surely expand the entries in Table 5.1. Undoubtedly, some of the entries could be debated, as could some of the definitions and arguments made above. Nevertheless, expansion of the Banduran self-efficacy conceptualization to increase its appropriateness for management theory and research is overdue. Hopefully, emphasis on previously ignored general self-efficacy and means efficacy will spur intensification of efficacy research, help explain more variance in motivation and effort than has been possible to date, and lead to new applications.

RECIPROCAL RELATIONSHIP BETWEEN SELF-EFFICACY AND MEANS EFFICACY

Internal and external efficacy can compensate for each other. High means efficacy can give confidence of success to an individual lacking in self-efficacy for the task at hand, provided that person believes in the usefulness of the available tool. For example, a poor marksman may expect great success at hitting the target with a weapon that has an ultra-accurate targeting system; the efficacy of the means compensates for the dearth of the relevant internal resource. Conversely, a highly skilled marksman may be confident in his or her ability to correct for deficiencies in a targeting mechanism, a case of high SSE compensating for low specific means efficacy.

Furthermore, tasks differ in the extent to which they are tool-dependent. Some tasks, such as auto repair, nursing, and air traffic control, require constant use of tools, whereas other tasks, such as proofreading, playing chess, and most kinds of retail sales, require little or none. Similarly, a resourceful individual who believes in his or her capacity to improvise and make the best of whatever is available to succeed in getting a job done will not be so demoralized by having only second-best equipment. A testable hypothesis is that self-efficacy and means efficacy interact, such that if either one or both are high, motivation is high; only when both are low do performance expectations and motivation plummet.

A good example of extreme incongruity between self-efficacy and collective efficacy is the plight of the college athlete who is number one draft choice this season (high self-efficacy) but must now play for the professional team that finished the season in last place (low collective efficacy). His justified disbelief in his teammates' abilities will cause him to expect little success despite his own proven talents ("I can get the ball to their numbers every time, but none of them can catch it. Some career I'm gonna have!"). The reverse incongruity is experienced by the mediocre athlete who is the nth-round pick of last season's Super Bowl champions ("What a break! With a team like this, I can't help but have a great career."). The extreme interdependence that is characteristic of team sports magnifies the weight of perceived peer competence in determining the individual's overall subjective efficacy.

This sporting example also illustrates the team-as-means notion. One's teammates are an indispensable means of achieving personal success in any highly interdependent endeavor. Thus, collective efficacy is one kind of means efficacy.

PRELIMINARY RESEARCH
AND APPLICATION

Much research on training and self-efficacy has shown that SSE can augment training outcomes, and that training can augment SSE. Little research has been done on training designed to boost GSE. Exceptions are Caplan, Vinokur, Price, and van Ryn (1989), Eden and Aviram (1993), and Smith (1989). Beyond general and specific self-efficacy, can we enhanced means efficacy? Can training be used to augment means efficacy?

Preliminary answers to these questions come from two recent field experiments conducted to test some of the above propositions. Eden and Granat-Flomin (2000) randomly assigned branches of a governmental social service organization to experimental and control conditions. To test the hypothesis that raising means efficacy enhances performance, employees in the experimental branches were told that they were about to get a new computer system proven to be the best of its kind; control personnel got the same computer system with no means-efficacy treatment. Means efficacy increased in both conditions, but significantly more in the experimental condition. Self-efficacy, which was not targeted by the treatment, remained unchanged. The experimental branches improved service-time performance more than the controls, confirming the means-efficacy hypothesis. Next, Eden and Sulimani (2001) randomly assigned 14 anti-aircraft gunnery instructors to experimental and control conditions. The six experimental instructors received a one-day Pygmalion workshop with special emphasis on boosting self-efficacy and means efficacy before beginning instruction in a new round of a course; eight control instructors got an interpersonal-communication workshop. The trainees of the experimental instructors reported higher self-efficacy, means efficacy, and motivation, and obtained higher scores on written tests and on performance tests than did the trainees of the control instructors. Thus, these preliminary findings show that means efficacy can be measured, raised, and utilized to bring about enhanced performance, as hypothesized.

CONCLUSION

The practical upshot of the concept of total subjective efficacy is that managers can look both at workers and at their tools for sources of workers' sense of efficacy that they can—and should—augment through their leadership. It is not enough for managers to cultivate subordinates' self-efficacy, and it certainly is not enough to be concerned mainly about their efficacy beliefs regarding microperformances like those investigated in most self-efficacy research. Limiting efficacy augmentation to such narrow domains needlessly fetters leadership and squanders the motivational potential that could be actualized by considering both internal and external sources of efficacy. To achieve maximal motivation, it is incumbent upon the manager to lead employees to believe in their own competence, general and specific, as well as to be confident in the efficaciousness of the general and specific means available to them. This calls for leadership that makes people aware of every possible source of strength, and helps prevent or overcome the kind of self-doubt that demotivates effort and stymies progress toward success. This is the essence of Pygmalion Leadership Style (Eden, 1988, 1990, 1992).

REFERENCES

Bandura, A. (1986). *Social foundations of thought and action: A social-cognitive view.* Englewood Cliffs, NJ: Prentice-Hall.

Bennis, W. G., & Slater, P. E. (1968). *The temporary society.* New York: Harper & Row.

Caplan, R. D., Vinokur, A. D., Price, R. H., & van Ryn, M. (1989). Job seeking, reemployment, and mental health: A randomized field experiment in coping with job loss. *Journal of Applied Psychology, 74,* 759–769.

Eden, D. (1988). Pygmalion, goal setting, and expectancy: Compatible ways to raise productivity. *Academy of Management Review, 13,* 639–652.

Eden, D. (1990). *Pygmalion in management: Productivity as a self-fulfilling prophecy.* Lexington, MA: Lexington Books.

Eden, D. (1992). Leadership and expectations: Pygmalion effects and other self-fulfilling prophecies in organizations. *Leadership Quarterly, 3,* 271–305.

Eden, D. (1993, April, May). *Organizationwide self-fulfilling prophecy: Boosting member self-efficacy to enhance effectiveness.* Paper presented at the Eighth Annual Meeting of the Society for Industrial and Organizational Psychology, San Francisco.

Eden, D., & Aviram, A. (1993). Self-efficacy training to speed reemployment: Helping people to help themselves. *Journal of Applied Psychology, 78,* 352–360.

Fine, B. D. (1971). Comparison of work groups with stable and unstable membership. *Journal of Applied Psychology, 55,* 170–174.

Gal, R. (1986). Unit morale: From a theoretical puzzle to an empirical illustration—An Israeli example. *Journal of Applied Social Psychology, 16,* 549–564.

Gal, R., & Manning, F. J. (1987). Morale and its components: A cross-national comparison. *Journal of Applied Social Psychology, 17,* 369–391.

Gist, M. E., & Mitchell, T. R. (1992). Self-efficacy: A theoretical analysis of its determinants and malleability. *Academy of Management Review, 17,* 182–211.

Guzzo, R. A., Yost, P. R., Campbell, R. J., & Shea, G. P. (1993). Potency in groups: Articulating a construct. *British Journal of Social Psychology, 32,* 87–106.

Kerr, S., & Jermier, J. M. (1978). Substitutes for leadership: Their meaning and measurement. *Organizational Behavior and Human Decision Processes, 36,* 375–403.

Locke, E. A., & Latham, G. P. (1990). *A theory of goal setting and task performance.* Englewood Cliffs, NJ: Prentice-Hall.

Maddux, J. E. (1995). Self-efficacy theory: An introduction. In J. E. Maddux (Ed.), *Self-efficacy, adaptation, and adjustment: Theory, research, and application* (pp. 3–33). New York: Plenum.

Shea, G. P., & Guzzo, R. A. (1987). Groups as human resources. In K. Rowland & G. Ferris (Eds.), *Research in personnel and human resources management* (Vol. 5, pp. 323–356). Greenwich, CT: JAI Press.

Sims, H. P., & Manz, C. C. (1994). *Business without bosses: How self-managing teams are building high-performing companies.* New York: Wiley.

Smith, R. E. (1989). Effects of coping skills training on generalized self-efficacy and locus of control. *Journal of Personality and Social Psychology, 56,* 228–233.

Wellins, R. S., Byham, W. C., & Wilson, J. M. (1991). *Empowered teams: Creating self-directed work groups that improve quality, productivity, and participation.* San Francisco: Jossey-Bass.

Zaccaro, S. J., Blair, V., Peterson, C, & Zazanis, M. (1995). Collective efficacy. In J. E. Maddux (Ed.), *Self-efficacy, adaptation, and adjustment: Theory, research, and application* (pp. 305–328). New York: Plenum Press.

6

Increasing Reemployment Through Training in Verbal Self-guidance

Zeeva Millman
A&M Human Resources Consultants
Toronto, Canada

Gary Latham
University of Toronto
Joseph L. Rotman School of Management
Toronto, Canada

Goal-setting theory (Locke & Latham, 1990) states that given goal commitment, setting specific hard goals leads to higher levels of performance than is the case when no goals are set or when the goal is vague, such as to do one's best. Seeking reemployment, particularly during an economic recession, constitutes a hard goal, one for which numerous failures are likely to precede success. A lay article indicated that during a two-month period 45,000 job seekers in Canada gave-up looking for work (McCarthy, 1992). Frustration and discouragement over failure to get a job were cited as reasons. A second article stated that the current 8.5% rate of unemployment in the industrial world would be approximately 40% higher if discouraged workers who had given up looking for a job were included (Crane, 1994).

A theory that explains why some people persist in the face of adversity to attain a difficult goal while others give up is social cognitive theory (Bandura, 1977a, 1986). This theory states that people learn ways of managing situations not only through enactive mastery, but also through vicarious experience, verbal persuasion, and physiological responses. People who either experience frequent failure or observe similar others fail in their efforts may conclude that they too will fail. Self-talk that is negative may lower both perceived self-efficacy and outcome expectancies. When this is done repeatedly it may eventually result in learned helplessness.

An assumption underlying the present study is that many individuals who experience failure repeatedly develop a profoundly low sense of personal efficacy. Their self-talk is highly negative, hence their outcome expectations are very low. Persuasion is a key factor affecting self-efficacy and outcome expectancies (Bandura, 1986). Persuasion is a function of conversations with significant others, especially oneself. Self-talk refers to the individual's self-referent dialogue that serves to organize relevant information, devise plans and strategies of action that guide and motivate, and consequently serve as a basis for self-instructed performance.

Because self-talk occurs on a continuous basis (Meichenbaum, 1971, 1977), it plays a central role in self-regulation (Dush, Hirt, & Schroeder, 1989). Through negative self-talk and the individual's ability for symbolic visualization and forethought, a single failure may be experienced repeatedly (Bandura, 1986). Thus training designed to change negative self-talk into positive self-guidance fosters self-regulatory motivation and adaptive behavior. The first hypothesis tested in this study was that training in functional self-talk regarding a job search leads to reemployment. The second and third hypotheses focused on the process, namely, the cognitive changes through which functional self-talk exerts a positive effect on job search behavior.

Social cognitive theory (Bandura, 1986) states that failure experiences can undermine self-efficacy and lower outcome expectancies. The unemployed managers in this study had not only experienced a highly aversive outcome, namely loss of their jobs, but also failure in their attempts to find new jobs. Through media reports, they were repeatedly reminded that countless others had been unsuccessful in gaining reemployment. The second hypothesis stated that training in functional self-talk would increase perceived self-efficacy. The third hypothesis stated that training in functional self-talk would raise outcome expectancies that renewed job search efforts would lead to suitable employment. These hypotheses were based on the fact that persuasion, in this case self-guidance, is an effective technique for increasing efficacy beliefs and outcome expectations (Bandura, 1977a).

METHOD

Sample

Thirty-five unemployed managers from two outplacement firms in Toronto attended an information session where the purpose and the format of the training program were discussed. The participants had been identified by the outplacement firms as having given up searching for a job. Prior to this study, all outplacement clients had received job search training from these two firms. Specifically, they had received training in resume writing, interviewing, and networking. In addition, they participated in a session on possible career moves within one's occupation, and external to it. Both outplacement firms dealt with the same type of clients, namely, males from large corporations between the ages of 30 and 60.

The unemployed managers from one outplacement firm were told that because the intervention constituted a research program, not all of them would be able to participate immediately in the training program. These managers were randomly assigned to the training ($n = 20$) and control ($n = 8$) groups. As a condition for participating in the study, the second outplacement firm insisted that its 11 unemployed managers be assigned to the training group. Thus this was a quasi experimental field study.

Of the 35 managers from the outplacement firms who attended the orienting information session, three declined to participate, one was expecting a job offer, and two declined to participate without providing an explanation. Eleven from one outplacement firm were assigned to the experimental group. Twenty-one from the second outplacement firm were randomly assigned to the two conditions. Of the 21, 11 were assigned to the experimental group and 10 were assigned to the control group. Finally, 20 in the experimental group and 8 in the control group completed both the pre- and posttest assessments.

The mean length of unemployment was 13 months. Of the participants, 22 were male and 6 were female. They ranged in age from 25 to 64 years. Nine had completed high school, 16 were university graduates, and 3 had completed technical training. Seven of the displaced managers had held senior management positions, 10 were from middle management and the remaining 11 had held supervisory or staff positions. The managers represented a number of different industries, including financial services (e.g., banks, insurance companies), automobile, oil, food manufacturing, and real estate development. A preintervention questionnaire assessed the frequency with which the participants engaged in job search behaviors such as mailing resumes, networking, and calling people in companies. The results indicated that these managers were engaging in little or no serious job search activity. Nine of them reported that they no longer mailed any resumes, 13 mailed resumes occasionally, six mailed numerous resumes but never followed through by contacting anyone in those organizations. These reports were corroborated by their outplacement counselors.

Procedure

Managers in the training group participated in seven 2-hour sessions over a period of $2\frac{1}{2}$ consecutive weeks. Control group participants continued their job search as before. The training was conducted with two groups of 10 people each and was based on the self-talk training described by Meichenbaum (1971, 1977).

In the first session, the rationale for the training was explained. The managers' reported their thoughts and feelings about their unemployed status. Their self-statements were recorded by both the trainer and the managers themselves. Similarities and differences among the managers' self-statements were noted. The negative self-statements expressed by the group members were recorded for discussion in the next session.

To increase awareness of the effect of self-statements on behavior, the trainer asked the managers to discuss how their self-statements affected their job search activities. The strategy for altering their dysfunctional self-talk was then presented. The managers were given logs and asked to record their negative self-statements and any job search activities they pursued until the next session.

In the second session, the participants reevaluated the job search self-statements they had recorded. Through group discussion, the managers began to realize that their self-talk with regard to their job search expectancies consisted of generalizations rather than attributions to specific factors. Specifically, the managers began to realize that self-talk statements such as "there are no jobs" were based on a lack of job search activity on their part. Thus, monitoring their job search behaviors and self-talk provided them feedback regarding their job search efforts, and enabled them to realize that they had not searched sufficiently to conclude that there were, in fact, no jobs for them.

In the second session, examples of positive and negative self-talk regarding a job search were generated and discussed. Negative self-talk included statements such as "I feel age is against me," "I'm too senior, too costly," and "Headhunters know they are on to a loser." Based on the trainees' awareness of their dysfunctional self-talk, the trainees were asked to generate and record an alternate set of positive, functional self-statements. Positive self-talk included statements such as "People know about me and my skills—I have a positive reputation," "I have valuable skills and can make a positive contribution to an organization."

In both the third and fourth sessions, summaries of their self-statements generated during and between the previous meetings were reviewed. Using these self-statements, the trainer modeled job search behavior cognitively aloud while performing a job search task such as looking through employment advertisements. Consistent with Meichenbaum (1971), the cognitive modeling began with negative self-statements, moved to a neutral position, and ended with positive self-guidance. For example, the trainer opened the career section of the newspaper and looked through the advertisements. She verbalized the negative views about the lack of jobs that the managers expressed (i.e., "Why am I looking? There are never any jobs for me"), then verbalized transition statements (i.e., "Wait a minute, let me look at my job search behaviors; I haven't sent out any resumes in the past few weeks; I haven't received any rejections"), and then moved on to positive self-guidance (i.e., "I do have valuable skills and there are lots of companies in this city that can use my skills; besides I only need one offer"). Each task was first modeled by the trainer and then the trainees performed the task, talking to themselves aloud at first, and then covertly. The managers were then instructed to perform the same job search activity and talk to themselves aloud at first, then covertly. Several different job search activities were used, including examining the career classifieds, cold calling, and dealing with rejection letters.

In the fifth session, the trainer again modeled the self-talk technique for cold calls and networking. Each manager then used the self-talk technique for one of these two job search activities. Spontaneous positive self-talk with regard to the job search activity was also encouraged.

In the sixth session, relapse prevention techniques were discussed and rehearsed. Each manager identified possible obstacles to conducting an effective job search, as well as obstacles to using the self-talk technique. The managers were asked to generate a list of ways in which they could cope with these obstacles. Finally, the unemployed managers, together with the trainer, developed specific coping strategies that would enable them to deal with obstacles that arise, and consequently, combat learned helplessness.

In the seventh session, the self-statement modification and relapse prevention procedures were reviewed. Job search situations such as asking friends and acquaintances about potential jobs were identified, and the self-guidance technique was applied. Finally, the participants in both the training and control groups completed a questionnaire on self-efficacy, outcome expectancies, and job search behaviors.

Measures

Reemployment was measured by asking the participants whether they had found employment during the six months following the self-guidance training program. The measures of cognitive self-regulatory factors were administered before and after the study. Consistent with Bandura (Bandura & Jourden, 1991), self-efficacy strength regarding the job search was measured using a two-item scale (i.e., "I am able to overcome any obstacle standing in the way of finding a job"; "I am able to handle an interview effectively"), ranging from no confidence (1) to complete confidence (10) about securing a job.

Outcome expectancies were measured using four open-ended items adapted from Napier and Latham (1986) designed to identify the outcomes managers anticipated would result from their efforts. Examples of the items include, "To what extent do you believe that job search behaviors will enable you to find reemployment?" and "To what extent are you affected (feel good or bad) by your job search behaviors?" The participants recorded their expected outcomes on a scale ranging from not at all (1) to completely (5).

Because the questionnaire data were based on self-reports that could be biased, peers and outplacement counselors completed an eight-item questionnaire measuring changes in the unemployed managers' behavior. Behaviors such as manner of speaking, dress, and participation in outplacement counseling meetings were assessed using a behavioral observation scale (Latham & Wexley, 1994).

RESULTS

Reaction Measures

The assessment of employee reactions to a training program is an important part of its evaluation (Kirkpatrick, 1976). Members of the organization are more likely to support programs that are perceived to be useful to them, and trainee motivation is enhanced when the training program is received favorably (Wexley & Latham, 1991). Upon completion of the training program, participants in the experimental group rated their reactions on a seven-item questionnaire using a 5-point Likert-type scale (e.g., "Was the training program content useful? Do you believe that the technique will help you in the job search?"). The alpha coefficient was .98. The managers' reactions to the training program were highly favorable, $\mu = 4.12$, $SD = .44$.

Behavioral, Self-efficacy, and Outcome Expectancy Measures

Forty-five percent, $n = 9$, of the managers in the training group obtained re-employment within 6 months and 50%, $n = 10$, obtained reemployment within 9 months of the training. Only 12% ($n = 1$) of the managers in the control group did so. Of the remaining managers in the experimental group, one decided to return to school and another to retire, five did not find employment and four could not be located. A Fisher's exact test revealed that the difference in reemployment rates was significant ($p < .03$). Thus the hypothesis that training in self-talk fosters success in reemployment was supported. Three members of experimental group and one member of the control group found employment in their former industry, two managers in the experimental group were reemployed in a related industry, and the remaining four managers changed industries. All the managers stated that all or nearly all of their job skills were being used in their new positions. Three managers reported that their salary was 10% higher than it had been in their previous jobs, five managers reported that their current salaries were the same as they had been in their previous position, and two people accepted jobs that paid 10% less. The coefficient alpha for changes in the unemployed managers' behavior was .82. A marginally significant difference was found between the training and the control group, with the training group exhibiting better job search behaviors, $F(1, 26) = 3.27$, $p < .08$, than the control group.

The remaining two hypotheses focused on why training in functional self-talk is an effective means of helping people find reemployment. Specifically, it was hypothesized that training in functional self-talk increases beliefs of personal efficacy and positive outcome expectancies that suitable employment can be found.

T tests of the premeasures revealed no significant differences in efficacy beliefs and outcome expectancies between the training and the control groups.

Nevertheless, because of lack of complete randomization of participants to conditions, analysis of covariance (ANCOVA) was used with the pretest scores serving as covariates. Because the questionnaire was computed by the managers pre- and posttraining, a repeated measures ANOVA was conducted and showed support at the same level of significance. The alpha coefficient for self-efficacy was .55 at both times 1 and 2. The pretest means for the training and the control groups were 5.85 (SD = 1.41), and 6.75 (SD = .92), and the posttest scores were 7.43 (SD = 1.03), and 6.38 (SD = 1.73), respectively. ANCOVA revealed that this difference was significant, $F(1, 25) = 11.56$, $p < .01$. Thus the second hypothesis was supported.

The alpha coefficient for outcome expectancies was .56 and .52 at times 1 and 2, respectively. The pretest means for the experimental and control groups were 3.53 (SD = .80), and 3.97 (SD = .57), and the posttest means were 3.67 (SD = .94), 3.58 (SD = .66), respectively. ANCOVA revealed that the difference between the experimental and control groups was not significant. Thus the third hypothesis was rejected.

Qualitative Data

Qualitative support for the quantitative findings was obtained from interviews with counselors and peers. One manager in the training group received an offer for a job as vice president of a personnel agency while he was participating in the training course. His initial self-talk, shared with the group, consisted of doubts as to whether he could work effectively with the person who would be his boss. During the course of the training, he decided to accept the job offer. This decision reflected his recognition that the boss would be in the organization for only another year and a half. If there were difficulties in dealing with this supervisor, the difficulties would be temporary. Finally, he acknowledged that his contact with this individual had been insufficient to determine the suitability of the fit.

Another participant, who had been searching for a job for 8 months, was described as depressed by his peers because of his persistent negative self-talk. He expressed fears of failing, and he constantly questioned whether changing careers was the right thing to do for a person over 55 years of age. He had spent 25 years in the computer department of one company. During the course of the training session, his peers and counselor confirmed that the manager's doubts were fewer and farther between, and that he was successful in pursuing a lifetime dream, namely, finding employment as a real estate salesperson.

A third participant was described by his peers and counselor prior to attending the training program as quiet and reserved during lunchtime meetings conducted by the outplacement agency. Both his peers and counselor stated that during the course of the training program, he became an active participant in the meetings.

A fourth participant who had been unemployed for about a year and a half was described by his counselor as a highly negative person. For the entire year and a half during which he had been coming to the outplacement office, he always dressed in casual attire, such as jeans, that was inappropriate for an office setting. During the training program he came to the office in a suit and tie. His counselor remarked that this was the first time in a year and a half that he had dressed in a businesslike manner. She also commented that he attended several networking meetings for the first time. Finally, his counselor reported that this unemployed manager publicly stated that he would cease his negative ways. She remarked that he stopped her several times to remind her that he did not want to focus on negative things and that he was going to adopt a more positive outlook. He shared his self-talk with the training group concerning his negative attitude toward his wife and son, stating that he was now trying to adopt a more positive attitude toward them and was feeling better about himself as a result of the change in his behavior. He obtained employment 9 months after the training.

A fifth participant had ceased to search for employment for eight months prior to the training program. She did not examine the career advertisements nor engage in any networking. Nor was she making any cold calls or speaking to friends, acquaintances or company representatives about potential employment. She had a doctorate in the area of food science. When she was encouraged to participate in the training program she stated that she did not have the time to do so, as she was receiving out of town guests in a few weeks. When contacted a second time a week before the start of the training program, she said that she would try to come to the first meeting but would not commit to any further meetings. She not only came to the first meeting, but participated in the entire program. During the program she reported that it had been very painful for her to search for employment and continually receive rejections. She stated that she did not believe that there were any jobs that met her criteria and, consequently, that she had ceased all job search activities. During the course of the training program she started to check the newspaper career advertisements and send out resumes. Within a period of two months she received an offer for part-time employment in her area of expertise, as a part-time instructor at a local university. While this was not what she ideally wanted as a job, she realized that the work was relevant and that it enabled her to use her skills.

Finally, a sixth participant who had expressed much negativity and uncertainty about his future made the decision to return to school. He stated that he was able to make the decision to do so only after he had participated in this program.

Discussion

The present study sheds light on the determinants and processes of reemployment. Social cognitive theory (Bandura, 1977a,b, 1986) places a premium on self-regulation in which individuals serve as the principal agents of their own change. Persuasion is one of four factors that help to enable people to develop self-regulative capabilities regarding commitment to an extremely difficult goal. The present study showed that training in verbal self-guidance is an effective method of self-persuasion. Managers who had the benefit of the training exhibited stronger self-efficacy than did those in the control group and hence were more successful in attaining their goal to be reemployed. The findings suggest that self-persuasion influences self-efficacy with respect to finding reemployment. Instructions once instilled serve as powerful internally generated guides and motivators (Locke & Latham, 1990).

Although verbal self-guidance enhanced beliefs of personal efficacy, it did not raise outcome expectancies. This may be due to the fact that the items measuring outcome expectancies focused too heavily on the employment situation than on beliefs about the possible outcomes of specific job search activities. A comprehensive measure would assess the expected positive and negative outcomes of various aspects of job search behaviors.

The study shows that social cognitive theory provides a useful framework for explaining why some people who lose their job remain committed to their goal of finding reemployment while others abandon their goal. The findings suggest that people who find employment are those who have high self-efficacy created by positive self-guidance. They tell themselves that success is the result of their own efforts.

The qualitative data confirm that highly self-efficacious people who take responsibility for their successes present themselves in a positive manner during the job search process. They convey the attitude that they can succeed in their efforts and hence they attain difficult goals. Low self-efficacious people present themselves less positively and lack strong conviction regarding their ability to attain a difficult goal. Thus this study suggests that people act in accordance with the beliefs they express to themselves.

This study also has important practical implications. First, it provides external validity of training in positive, functional self-talk for senior- and middle-level managers from a variety of industries to overcome their rejection of a difficult goal.

Second, the study showed the effectiveness of training in positive, functional self-talk on a problem that had not previously been studied using this technique, namely, job search. Job search, when conducted by outplacement firms, is very costly to the sponsoring companies; hence, it is in the interest of the paying company to find ways of shortening the search time for reemployment.

Third, the study provided an effective method for teaching self-regulation skills. The managers themselves were taught the skills for dealing with repeated rejections in job searches, and its resulting effect on negative self-talk and low self-efficacy regarding goal attainment. By providing managers with skills in positive, functional self-guidance, the managers learned ways to exercise control over their job search. Thus, companies who intend to lay off employees should consider providing these people with training in self-guidance as a way of enhancing employees self-efficacy in the job search process.

Fourth, the study provided a straightforward, cost-effective way of training displaced managers in self-talk that enables them to find a job. The training took only 6 hours a week for $2\frac{1}{2}$ weeks. It was conducted by a doctoral student, namely the first author, who had little experience in training.

The above findings provide empirical support for what practitioners such as Tice (1989), have argued, namely, the importance of affirming to oneself that one can attain one's goals, if difficult goals are, in fact, to be attained.

A major limitation of a quasi experimental design is the lack of randomization of participants to conditions. ANCOVA was used to control for pretest differences. However, it cannot control the infinity of potential confounders not entered as covariates, an infinity that should be controlled for through randomization of participants in a future field study.

A second potential limitation is the Pygmalion effect, namely, the positive impact on managers' performance that results from a leader's expectations for them. In a study involving unemployed vocational workers, Eden and Aviram (1993) found that persuasion, in the form of feedback, from significant others, was effective in increasing general self-efficacy, job search activity, and hence reemployment.

The Pygmalion effect as a rival hypothesis for the present findings was rejected because the trainer emphasized the following disclaimer to the managers: she did not have a doctoral degree; this program constituted research rather than training per se, consequently no fee was charged; there was no evidence to date that the training would be effective; she had no prior experience working with unemployed people; and she had no prior experience working in outplacement firms. Finally, the trainer stated that she had no prior experience as a trainer in industry and that she was not an employee of the outplacement firm. The present study is an example of what Eden and Kinnar (1990) labeled the *Galatea effect*, whereby a person's own positive performance expectations increase self-efficacy and hence lead to high performance. Future research should examine a treatment package that includes instilling the Pygmalion effect as an integral part of the present training program.

This study focused on the quantity of job search behaviors. The qualitative data suggest that it was not the number of resumes sent, networking meetings attended, or number of people contacted, that changed significantly as a result of training. Rather, it was the way in which these behaviors were demonstrated to counselors within the outplacement firm, to headhunters, and most probably to interviewers that enabled managers to regain employment. Further research should measure the ways in which managers engage in job search activities to obtain reemployment as a result of changing their verbal self-guidance.

Finally, subsequent research requires a sufficient sample size to permit tests of self-efficacy and outcome expectancies as mediators. Ideally, a large sample would facilitate a follow-up study to determine how long the participants continue to use the skills they acquire from the training, and to see if they apply these skills to other areas of their lives.

ACKNOWLEDGEMENTS

The authors wish to thank Albert Bandura, Dov Eden, and E. A. Locke for their critical comments on a preliminary draft of this manuscript. The manuscript is based on the first author's doctoral dissertation completed at the University of Toronto under the guidance of the second author. The authors wish to thank Hugh Arnold and Martin Evans, who served on the dissertation committee. This research was supported in part by a Social Sciences and Humanities Research Council grant to the second author.

REFERENCES

Bandura, A. (1977a). *Social learning theory*. Englewood Cliffs, NJ: Prentice-Hall.

Bandura, A. (1977b). Self efficacy: Toward a unifying theory of behavior change. *Psychological Review, 84*, 191–215.

Bandura A. (1986). *Social foundations of thought and action*. Englewood Cliffs, NJ: Prentice-Hall.

Bandura, A., & Jourden, F. J. (1991). Self-regulatory mechanisms governing the impact of social comparison on complex decision making. *Journal of Personality and Social Psychology, 60*, 941–951.

Crane, D. (1994, July 20). Best jobs require education, skills, OECD report says. *The Toronto Star*, p. A3.

Dush, D. M., Hirt, M. L., & Schroeder, H. E. (1989). Self-statement modification in the treatment of child behavior disorders: A meta-analysis. *Psychological Bulletin, 106*, 97–106.

Eden, D., & Aviram, A. (1993). Self-efficacy training to speed reemployment: Helping people to help themselves. *Journal of Applied Psychology, 78*, 352–360.

Eden, D., & Kinnar, J. (1990). Modeling Gelatea: Boosting self-efficacy to increase volunteering. *Journal of Applied Psychology, 76*, 770–780.

Kirkpatrick, D. L. (1976). Evaluation of training. In R. L. Craig (Ed.), *Training and Development Handbook: A guide to human resource development*. New York: McGraw-Hill.

Latham, G. P., & Wexley, K. N. (1994). *Increasing productivity through performance appraisal*. Reading, MA: Addison-Wesley.

Locke, E. A., & Latham, G. P. (1990). *A theory of goal setting and task performance*. Englewood Cliffs, NJ: Prentice-Hall.

McCarthy, S. (1992, January 11). Bitter job-seekers giving up. *The Toronto Star*.

Meichenbaum, D. (1971). Examination of model characteristics in reducing avoidance behavior. *Journal of Personality and Social Psychology, 3*, 298–307.

Meichenbaum, D. (1977). *Cognitive behavior modification: An integrative approach*. New York: Plenum Press.

Napier, N. K., & Latham, G. P. (1986). Outcome expectancies of people who conduct performance appraisals. *Personnel Psychology, 39*, 827–837.

Tice, L. (1989). *A better world, a better you*. Englewood Cliffs, NJ: Prentice-Hall.

Wexley, K., & Latham, G. P. (1991). *Developing and training human resources in organizations*. New York: HarperCollins.

7

Personal Initiative (PI): The Theoretical Concept and Empirical Findings

Michael Frese
University of Giessen, Germany

In this chapter I want to discuss the concept of personal initiative (PI). I shall first argue that it is practically and theoretically useful. Then I shall discuss the concept and a theoretical framework. Further I present what we know about PI and what we still need to know.

PI is an important concept both for practical and theoretical reasons. Practically, PI has been used, for example, in assessment centers. PI will become more important in the future because future workplaces will require a high degree of self-reliance (Frese, 1997). Companies are interested in PI because it increases organizational effectiveness.

Theoretically, PI is related to a number of new performance concepts that are indirectly related to organizational effectiveness: intrapreneurship (Hisrich, 1990), organizational citizenship behavior (Organ, 1988), organizational spontaneity (George & Brief, 1992; Katz, 1964), generic work behavior (Hunt, Hansen, & Paajanen, 1994), and contextual performance (Borman & Motowidlo, 1993).

THE CONCEPT OF PERSONAL INITIATIVE

We think of PI to be a behavior syndrome resulting in an individual's taking a self-starting, active, and persistent approach to work. Additional aspects of the concept are that this behavior is consistent with the organization's mission, goal directed, and action oriented (cf. Frese, Fay, Hilburger, Leng, & Tag, 1997; Frese, Kring, Soose, & Zempel, 1996). An updated review of the concept of personal initiative is available in Frese and Fay (2002).

A syndrome is a set of co-occurring behaviors that together signify initiative. In our view this behavior syndrome can best be explained within an action theoretical approach (Frese & Sabini, 1985; Frese & Zapf, 1994; Hacker, 1985). Actions are goal oriented and guided by the goal. At work, the goals are heavily influenced by the tasks required of the individual job incumbent. However, there is a translation process from the outside task into goals—the redefinition process (Hackman, 1970). For example, a secretary may redefine her task to imply that she should also make sure that her boss is updated on problems in the work group, although this is not mentioned in the official task description. This redefinition process allows to define *extrarole goals* and goals that require a self-starting approach, and thus PI (Staw & Boettger, 1990).

Self-starting implies that the goals are not given by somebody else but that the person him- or herself develops those goals. At work, tasks are usually presented within a given occupational role (Katz, 1964). Thus, extrarole behaviors can be counted as self-started behaviors. For this reason, we used to operationalize PI by extra-role behavior (cf. Frese, et al., 1997). This has led to the conceptual problem that in some jobs the role ascriptions are so broad that practically any behavior is within-role behavior, for example, in the case of entrepreneurs or top managers who have to do everything to make the company survive and grow. When roles expectations do not really specify the expected behavior in some detail, then the issue of extrarole behavior becomes meaningless. However, self-starting behavior is still possible in such cases, although it may refer to the development of subgoals. Although all entrepreneurs have the general goal of producing efficiently, excellent entrepreneurs use the strategy more frequently to enhance PI in their employees (Goebel, 1998). In this case, it is the formation of the subgoal—enhancing PI—that is self-starting.

An active approach implies that a person is proactive. This means that they should attempt to get feedback and develop signals that signify future problems and to develop plans to actively prevent these problems from occurring.

Implementation of long-term goals often leads to new problems, barriers, and setbacks. Since new suggestions for work improvement, new procedures to do things, and other attempts have not been tried before, one will experience difficulties. For example, the supervisor may not like the new idea, or a new work procedure cannot be performed correctly in the beginning. If one does not overcome these difficulties or gives up quickly in face of barriers, there is no initiative.

Initiative, therefore, implies that one will deal with these obstacles actively and persistently.

Personal Initiative, Entrepreneurship and Organizational Citizenship

PI is related to but not identical with other constructs, such as entrepreneurship and intrapreneurship (Hisrich, 1990) and organizational citizenship behavior (OCB; Munene, 1995; Organ, 1990). PI and entrepreneurship both imply the use of productive, creative, and active strategies and to overcome problems in case they occur. However, the commercial component is not included in the concept of initiative.

Both OCB and PI go beyond direct role requirements, and both are seen to contribute indirectly to organizational effectiveness (Organ, 1988). However, there are also differences. Empirically, OCB is mainly made up of two factors: altruism and compliance. Compliance has a more passive connotation, e.g., conscientiousness in attendance ("does not take extra breaks"), adherence to rules, and other behaviors. In contrast, the concept of PI often implies a certain rebellious element towards the supervisor. OCB takes the framework of the supervisor as the starting point—how helpful the worker is from the supervisor's perspective. However, supervisors often fail to support PI and even punish active approaches. We think that the time perspective is different. A worker with high PI contributes to long-range positive outcomes for the organization, but in the short term he or she may well be a nuisance factor to the boss because he or she is constantly pushing new ideas (cf. some graphic descriptions on this issue appear in Peters & Waterman, 1982). In contrast, OCB is more oriented toward a short-term positive social orientation at the workplace; some even argue that OCB and ingratiation behaviors are similar (Eastman, 1994). Additionally, as George and Brief (1992) have pointed out, OCB includes role-prescribed behaviors whereas PI does not.

Personal Initiative and Organizational Effectiveness

PI should be related to organizational effectiveness (Motowidlo & Scotter, 1994). There are two avenues why this should be so. First, on the level of the organization and the team, there are no perfect production or service systems, and, therefore, there is some need for PI to uphold and to improve production or service (Katz, 1964; Organ, 1988). For example, if a machine breaks down and the worker is able to fix it or tell the repairperson what to do (although all of this is not part of his or her job description), organizational effectiveness is enhanced.

Second, there should be a higher degree of task performance of employees with higher initiative. Hacker (1992; cf. also Frese & Zapf, 1994) and Klemp and McClelland (1986) have shown that excellent employees are characterized by a longer time perspective in their work, a better developed mental model of it, and a more proactive approach to work. The long-term orientation and the proactive approach is shared by our concept of PI and the behavior and strategies of superworkers.

A MODEL OF PERSONAL INITIATIVE

Figure 7.1 displays a model of PI. Similar to other motivational theories (e.g., Ford, 1992), we assume that behavior is a function of Motivation × Skills × Responsive Environment, given some (biological or biographical) prerequisites (the latter is not included in our model). Thus, there is a differentiation between skills, a responsive environment (environmental supports), and motivation (personality and orientations). The motivational constructs are differentiated into distal and proximal (Kanfer, 1992) or generalized and specific constructs (Rotter, 1975)—the distal/generalized constructs being personality factors and the proximal/specific constructs being orientations.

The model roughly assumes that environmental supports, skills, and personality factors contribute to orientations that in turn lead to PI. Thus, orientations are mediators in this model. There are three entry points for the change of initiative: first, the environmental supports may be increased; second, the skills can be enhanced;

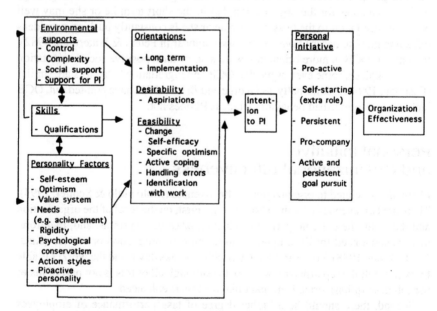

FIG. 7.1. A model of the functioning of personal initiative (PI).

and third, the orientations can be changed. Personality factors are assumed to be more constant.

Orientations

Orientations are behavior tendencies of moderate situational specificity. Thus, all the orientations in the figure refer to work. PI should be influenced by aspiration for control, that is, a desire to "be on top of things" (De Charms, 1968; Deci & Ryan, 1985; Frese, Garst, & Fay, 2001).

Self-efficacy (Bandura, 1986, 1977) is related to PI because one should have the expectation that one is able to do things adequately in order to show initiative (Speier & Frese, 1997). Self-efficacy implies that one achieves the positive outcomes through one's own actions. This is in contrast to optimism, which implies that positive outcomes may come about without having to do something for it. Thus, there may be optimism because one perceives oneself as the "mover" of things (and, thus, shows initiative) or one may be optimistic because things will work out by themselves. S. Taylor (1989) has argued that optimism has an energizing function leading to a higher degree of active approaches to life. If she is right, there should be a correlation between (specific) optimism and initiative.

Change orientation is necessary because PI usually changes the work situation in one way or the other. If one is afraid of such changes, there should be little initiative.

Active coping strategies (Folkman & Lazarus, 1980) imply that one actively deals with problems that are perceived to be aversive. Often, a person will show PI because something is bothering her or him at work.

Another issue refers to error handling. PI often implies that *new* activities have to be attempted and, therefore, some degree of uncertainty of outcomes exists. Thus, the more a person shows initiative, the more there are chances of making errors. We assume, therefore, that confidence of error handling, risking errors, and a low anxiety of errors should be related to PI (Rybowiak, Garst, Frese, & Batinic, 1999).

Finally, identification with work should be related to PI because work then is valued more strongly (as in optimism, this should be a low relationship because a person might think that work is very important without showing initiative).

Personality Factors

Both orientations and personality factors are action tendencies. We think that the personality factors are different from orientations on four dimensions:

- action tendency
- generality: cross-situational consistency
- endurance: consistency over time
- modifiability

Within action theory, we conceptualize personality constructs to consist of three aspects: propensities to act; a generalized, and automatic use of a tendency to act (Baron, 1981; Frese, Stewart, & Hannover, 1987). Propensity to act means that a certain action pattern comes to mind first and is put into effect as long as there are no situational constraints (or affordances) to do otherwise. Orientations should be more highly related to actions because they are more specific to the area of behavior (work, in our case); (cf. Fishbein & Aijzen, 1975, for a similar argument on the match between attitude and behavior).

A personality trait to be generalized implies that a certain action pattern is shown in different situations. Of course, there is a dimension from specificity to generality (Rotter, 1975). Personality factors are more general than orientations.

Automaticity means that the use of a metacognitive approach has been over-learned and is habitual. This does not mean that one automatically uses a certain behavior pattern. Rather, it means, for example, that a rule of thumb (heuristic) to develop long-range goals is developed quickly vis-à-vis a new task without having to make a conscious decision that one wants to develop a long-range goal. The person may still choose not to act according to a long-range goal; it is just the first idea that comes to mind. Personality factors are probably more strongly automatized than orientations.

Modifiability, that is, the degree to which change occurs because of experiences and training, should be higher for orientations than for personality variables. Modifiability should be related to both automaticity and generality. If an action tendency is automatically invoked and quite general, it is less likely to be to be changed even if somebody is trained not to use this action, because every training is specific. While I may change my approach toward a specific object, I do not necessarily have to change my general action tendencies. The more it is automatic, the more it will be resistant to change because it is overlearned (similar to habits that are difficult to break even if one actually wants to get rid of them).

The higher modifiability of orientation is one reason why orientations are entry points for change. Thus, if one wants to change initiative, we assume that it is useful to change responsibility and control aspirations, self-efficacy, and change orientation (which empirically are most closely associated with initiative) (Frese et al., in press).

Important personality factors for PI are self-esteem, general optimism, need for achievement, flexibility (the reverse of psychological conservatism), proactive personality (Crant, 1995), and action styles (like goal orientation and action orientation). All of these personality traits are factors activating people and should, therefore, contribute to initiative.

It is important to note that a certain construct may appear both as a personality factor and an orientation. For example, a generalized form of self-efficacy (orientation) is self-esteem (personality). Specific forms of hope (with regard to work and unemployment) are orientations, whereas general optimism is a personality factor. Need for achievement is a general trait, whereas control and responsibility aspirations for work is an orientation.

The more specific orientations should be influenced by personality factors as described in Fig. 7.1. Thus, a highly generalized concept (e.g., self-esteem) should have an influence on the more specific orientation (e.g., self-efficacy).

Skills and Environmental Supports

There are three environmental conditions that help the development of PI: control at work, complexity of work, and the support for PI given by the company and the immediate supervisor. All three are supposed to activate people and to make it possible for them to overcome barriers, once they occur. A similar argument can be made for skills. Control at work, complexity, and social support have been shown to be important parameters of occupational socialization (Frese, 1982; Semmer & Schallberger, 1996). Qualifications are obviously important to understand the workplace better and to produce ideas for changing the workplace (which is one prerequisite of initiative).

Environmental supports and skills should be related to PI via the mediators orientations. Two examples: Control and complexity at work should have an influence on self-efficacy (Speier & Frese, 1997) and control aspirations. One important source for developing self-efficacy is enactive mastery. "In the work context, enactive mastery can be experienced when one is able to make decisions, to work on challenging tasks, and to make use of one's competencies"—variables that are related to control and complexity (Speier & Frese, 1997, p. 175). Similarly, control aspirations are hypothesized to be lowered or increased by whether or not one actually has control at work (Frese, 1984). Reasons for this are similar: If workers do not have access to control their environment and their own behaviors at the workplace, their aspirations for control are reduced because of helplessness (Frese et al., 2001).

EVIDENCE FOR THE MODEL

With three steps we have attempted to test the overall model in a longitudinal study in eastern Germany (details on sample and measures in Frese, Kring, Soose, & Sempel, 1996; Frese, Fay, Hilburger, Leng, & Tag, 1997). First, a multiple correlation of all predictors, that is, environmental supports, skills, personality factors, and orientations with PI was .63 for the questionnaire measure of PI and .57 with the interview-based behavioral measure. Since the latter does not have common method variance with the questionnaire-based predictors, this is a good correlation. Figure 7.2 presents the results when the three best predictors (measured at the third measurement point of our study) were related to whether or not people showed a high degree of PI (operationalization of high initiative: M plus 1 SD at measurement wave 4). Only 4% of those with low control at work, low qualifications, and low aspirations for control and responsibility showed a high degree of initiative, whereas 29% of those with high scores on the predictors showed a high degree of initiative.

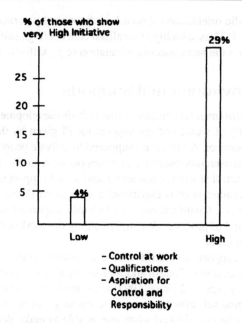

FIG. 7.2.   Prediction of initiative (t4) by 3 important predictors (t3).

Second, in a longitudinal analysis, change of interview-based PI was predicted with a significant increment. A hierarchical regression analysis showed that all predictors (environment, skills, personality lagged, orientations concurrent) produced an increment of 11% over and above earlier PI in the prediction of later initiative.

Finally, using the same approach as in the second step, a multiple partial correlation procedure substantiated the mediator function of the orientations (James & Brett, 1984). The three predictor areas of environmental support, skills, and personality without orientations predicted change in PI with an increment of R2 delta of .06 ($p < .01$). When orientations were partialled out in addition to the effect of earlier initiative, this led to a nonsignificant R2 delta of .02.

This speaks for the viability of the model. Obviously, this can only be a first test of the full model. Further LISREL analyses that look at the processes in much more detail are currently undertaken (Frese et al., 2001).

FUTURE RESEARCH ISSUES

There are at least four future research issues. First, the effect of each of the orientations has to be looked at in much more detail. An example of how this should be done is our article on self-efficacy (Speier & Frese, 1997).

Second, there should be reverse causations, in line with Kohn's and Schooler's (1978) concept of reciprocal relationship between job conditions and personal effects. We hypothesize that PI has have an influence on skills and on control and complexity of work (Frese et al., 2001). Since high PI also implies the motivation to get additional vocational education, skills should be enhanced with initiative. People with high PI will attempt to get jobs with higher control and complexity of work.

Third, one would suppose that there are interaction effects of orientations with environmental supports, skills, and personality factors. One example may suffice: Self-efficacy may have a compensatory relationship with control at work and complexity. Having little control at work may be an important predictor for people with high PI because they will show high PI in any case (because of their subjective expectations of effectiveness). In contrast to people with low self-efficacy, the degree of control at work should be a more important determiner of PI because they will depend much more on job characteristics to instigate PI (cf. Speier & Frese, 1997, for the evidence).

Fourth, we ought to look into the process of the development of PI in much more detail. For example, we should know in much more detail what is the actual trigger of PI: Is it the feeling that one needs to do something because nobody else will? Is it the feeling of being fed up with an inefficient procedure at work, the positive concept that one can do much better, and other factors? Both Kuhl's (1992) as well as Gollwitzer's (1993) work are examples of such process analyses in a related area.

Since PI is of high importance in most jobs and will be of higher importance in the future, it is tantamount to understand which organizational and individual conditions increase or undercut personal initiative.

ACKNOWLEDGEMENTS

The project AHUS (Aktives Handeln in einer Umbruchsituation—Active Actions in a Radical Change Situation) was supported by the Deutsche Forschungsgemeinschaft (DFG, No. Fr. 638/6); principal investigator: Frese). Other members of the project have been: Doris Fay, Harry Garst, Sabine Hilligloh, Christa Speier, Thomas Wagner, and Jeannette Zempel. Thanks are due to Doris Fay, Avi Kluger, and Kwok Leung, who have commented on prior versions of this article.

REFERENCES

Bandura, A. (1977). *Self-efficacy: The exercise of control.* New York: Freeman.
Bandura, A. (1986). *Social foundations of thought and action.* Englewood Cliffs, NJ: Prentice-Hall.
Baron, J. (1981). Reflective thinking as a goal in education. *Intelligence, 5,* 291–309.

Borman, W. C., & Motowidlo, S. J. (1993). Expanding the criterion domain to include elements of contextual performance. In N. Schmitt & W. C. Borman (Eds.), *Personnel selection in organizations* (pp. 71–98). San Francisco: Jossey-Bass.

Crant, J. M. (1995). The proactive personality scale and objective job performance among real estate agents. *Journal of Applied Psychology, 80,* 532–537.

De Charms, R. (1968). *Personal causation.* New York: Academic Press.

Deci, E. L., & Ryan, R. M. (1985). *Intrinsic motivation and self-determination in human behavior.* New York: Plenum.

Eastman, K. K. (1994). In the eyes of the beholder: An attributional approach to ingratiation and organizational citizenship behavior. *Academy of Management Journal, 37,* 1397–1391.

Fay, D., & Frese, M. (2001). The concept of personal initiative (PI): An overview of validity studies. *Human Performance, 14,* 97–124.

Fishbein, M., & Ajzen, I. (1975). *Belief, attitude, intention and behavior: An introduction to theory and research.* Reading, MA: Addison-Wesley.

Folkman, S., & Lazarus, R. S. (1980). An analysis of coping in a middle-aged community sample. *Journal of Health and Social Behavior, 21,* 219–239.

Ford, M. E. (1992). *Motivating humans.* Newbury Park, CA: Sage.

Frese, M. (1982). Occupational socialization and psychological development: An underemphasized research perspective in industrial psychology. *Journal of Occupational Psychology, 55,* 209–224.

Frese, M. (1984). *Do workers want control at work or dont't they: Some results on denial and adjustment* (IfHA - Berichte). Berlin: Institut für Humanwissenschaft in Arbeit und Ausbildung der Technischen Universität Berlin.

Frese, M. (1997). Dynamic self-reliance: An important concept for work. In C. L. Cooper & S. E. Jackson (Eds.), *Creating tomorrow's organizations* (pp. 399–416). Chichester, England: Wiley.

Frese, M., & Fay, D. (2002). Personal Initiative (PI): An active performance concept for work in the 21st century. In B. M. Staw & R. I. Sutton (Eds.), Research in organizational behavior. Greenwich, CT: AI Press.

Frese, M., Fay, D., Hilburger, T., Leng, K., & Tag, A. (1997). The concept of personal initiative: Operationlization, reliability and validity in two German samples. *Journal of Occupational and Organizational Psychology, 70,* 139–161.

Frese, M., Garman, G., Garmeister, K., Halemba, K., Hortig, A., Pulwitt, T., & Schildbach, S. (in press). Training zur Erhöhung der Eigeninitiative bei Arbeitslosen: Bericht über einen Pilotversuch [Training to increase personal initiative in unemployed: a pilot study). *Zeitschrift für Arbeits- und Organisationspsychology.*

Frese, M., Garst, H., & Fay, D. (2001). Control and Complexity in Work and the Development of Personal Initiative (PI): A Four-Wave Longitudinal Structural Equation Model of Occupational Socialization . *Univ of Giessen: submitted for publication.*

Frese, M., Kring, W., Soose, A. & Zempel, J. (1996). PI at work: differences between East and West Germany. *Academy of Management Journal, 39,* 37–63.

Frese, M., & Sabini, J. (Eds.). (1985). *Goal-directed behavior: The concept of action in psychology.* Hillsdale, NJ: Erlbaum.

Frese, M., Stewart, J., & Hannover, B. (1987). Goal orientation and planfulness: Action styles as a personality concepts. *Journal of Personality and Social Psychology, 52,* 1182–1194.

Frese, M., & Zapf, D. (1994). Action as the core of work psychology: A German approach. In H. C. Triandis, M. D. Dunnette, & J. M. hough (Eds.), *Handbook of industrial and organizational psychology* (Vol 4., 2nd ed., pp. 271–340). Palo Alto, CA: Consulting Psychology Press.

George, J. M., & Brief, A. P. (1992). Feeling good–doing good: A conceptual analysis of the mood at work-organizational spontaneity relationship. *Psychological Bulletin, 112,* 310–329.

Goebel, S. (1998). Persoenlichkeit, Handlungsstrategien und Erfolg [Personality, action strategies, and success]. In M. Frese (Ed.), *Erfolgreiche Unternehmensgruender [Successful start-ups]* (pp. 99–122). Goettingen, Germany: Verlag fuer Angewandte Psychologie.

Goebel, S. (in press). Persoenlichkeit, Handlungsstrategien und Erfolg. In M. Frese (Ed.), *Erfolgreiche Unternehmensgruender: Psychologische Analysen und praktische Anleitungen fuer Unternehmer in Ost- und Westdeutschland.* Goettingen: Verlag Angewandte Psychologie.

Gollwitzer, P. M. (1993). Goal achievement: The role of intentions. In W. Stroebe & M. Hewstone (Eds.). *European review of social psychology* (Vol. 4, pp. 141–185). London: Wiley.

Hacker, W. (1985). Activity: A fruitful concept in industrial psychology. In M. Frese & J. Sabini (Eds.), *Goal directed behavior: The concept of action in psychology* (pp. 262–284). Hillsdale, NJ, London: Erlbaum.

Hacker, W. (1992). *Expertenkönnen.* (Expert Knowledge). Göttingen Verlag für Angewandte Psychologie.

Hackman, J. R. (1970). Tasks and task performance in research on stress. In J. E. McGrath (Ed.) *Social and psychological factors in stress* (pp. 202–237). New York: Holt, Rinehart & Winston.

Hisrich, R. D. (1990). Entrepreneurship/intrapreneurship. *American Psychologist, 45,* 209–222.

Hunt, S. T., Hansen, T. L., & Paajanen, G. E. (1994). *Generic work behaviors: The components of non-job specific performance.* Paper presented in a symposium on "The Construct of Job Performance" at SIOP, Nashville, Tennessee.

James, L. R., & Brett, J. M. (1984). Mediators, moderators, and tests for mediation. *Journal of Applied Psychology, 69,* 307–321.

Katz, D. (1964). The motivational basis of organizational behavior. *Behavioral Science, 9,* 131–146.

Kanfer, R. (1992). Work motivation: New directions in theory and research. In C. L. Cooper & I. T. Robertson (Eds.), *International review of industrial and organizational psychology, 1992* (Vol. 7, pp. 1–54). Chichester, England: Wiley.

Klemp, G. O., & McClelland, D. C. (1986). What characterizes intelligent functioning among senior managers. In R. J. Sternberg & R. K. Wagner (Eds.), *Practical intelligence. Nature and origins of competence in the everyday world* (pp. 51–83). Cambridge, NY: Cambridge University Press.

Kohn, M. L., & Schooler, C. (1978). The reciprocal effects of the substantive complexity of work and intellectual flexibility: A longitudinal assessment. *American Journal of Sociology, 84,* 24–52.

Kuhl, J. (1992). A theory of self-regulation: Action versus state orientation, self-discrimination, and some applications. *Applied Psychology: An International Review, 41,* 97–129.

Motowidlo, S. J., & Scotter, J. R. V. (1994). Evidence that task performance should be distinguished from contextual performance. *Journal of Applied Psychology, 79,* 475–480.

Munene, J. C. (1995). Not-on-seat: An investigation of some correlates of organizational citizenship behavior in Nigeria. *Applied Psychology. An International Review, 44,* 111–122.

Organ, D. (1988). *Organizational citizenship behavior: The good soldier syndrome.* Lexington, MA: Lexington Books.

Organ, D. (1990). The motivational basis of organizational citizenship behavior. In B. M. Staw & L. L. Cummings (Eds.), *Research in organizational behavior* (vol. 12, pp. 43–72). Greenwich, CT.: JAI Press.

Peters, T. J., & Waterman, R. H. (1982). *In search of excellence.* New York: Warner.

Rotter, J. B. (1975). Some problems and misconceptions related to the construct of internal versus external control of reinforcement. *Journal of Consulting and Clinical Psychology, 43,* 56–67.

Rybowiak, V., Garst, H., Frese, M., & Batinic, B. (1999). Error Orientation Questionnaire (EOQ): Reliability, validity and different language equivalence. *Journal of Organizational Behavior, 20,* 527–547.

Semmer, N., & Schallberger, U. (1996). Selection, socialization, and mutual adaptation: Resolving discrepancies between people and work. *Applied Psychology: An International Review, 45,* 263–288.

Speier, C., & Frese, M. (1997). Generalized self-efficacy as a mediator and moderator between control and complexity at work and Personal Initiative: A longitudinal field study in East Germany. *Human Performance, 10,* 171–192.

Staw, B. M., & Boettger, R. D. (1990). Task revision: A neglected form of work performance. *Academy of Management Journal, 33,* 534–559.

Smith, C. A., Organ, D. W., & Near, J. P. (1983). Organizational citizenship behavior: Its nature and antecedents. *Journal of Applied Psychology, 68,* 653–663.

Taylor, S. E. (1989). *Positive illusions. Creative self-deception and the healthy mind.* New York: Basic Books.

8

Feedback-Expectation Discrepancy, Arousal and Locus of Cognition

Avraham N. Kluger
The Hebrew University of Jerusalem, Israel

Feedback interventions (FIs), that is, providing people with some information regarding their task performance, yield highly variable effects on performance (Balcazar, Hopkins, & Suarez, 1985; Ilgen, Fisher, & Taylor, 1979; Kluger & DeNisi, 1996; Latham & Locke, 1991; Salmoni, Schmidt, & Walter, 1984). Indeed, a meta-analysis suggested that FIs reduce performance in over one third of the cases (Kluger & DeNisi, 1996), a fact that is contrary to the common belief that FIs most often improve performance. Furthermore, Kluger and DeNisi (1996) found no evidence that the effects of FIs are moderated by FI sign. That is, negative FIs (information about failure) and positive FIs (information about success) do not differ on average in their performance effects (Kluger & DeNisi, 1996). The goal of this chapter is to investigate the possible causes for this counterintuitive finding. Specifically, the aim of this chapter is to investigate the effects of FI sign on affect and cognition. Understanding the effects of FI sign on affect and cognition is a first step towards understanding the role of FI sign in moderating the effects of FIs on performance.

The central argument of this chapter is that FI sign triggers a reaction from two parallel mechanisms that support adaptation. One mechanism operates with a symmetrical rule and the other with an asymmetrical rule. The symmetrical rule is manifested in a theoretical approach that emphasizes the sensitivity of people to discrepancies between standards and feedback (e.g., control theory).

111

The asymmetrical rule is manifested in a theoretical approach that emphasizes the sensitivity to the valence of the discrepancy (e.g., Taylor, 1991). Both the symmetric and the asymmetric rules are found in many self-regulation theories. However, self-regulation theories tend to emphasize only one of the rules, but then allow the other rule as an exception, as an escape clause, or as an unresolved issue. What follows are a few examples of the tendency to treat one of the rules as central and the other as a nuisance factor that needs an additional consideration.

Feedback Intervention Theory (FIT; Kluger & DeNisi, 1996) and control theory (e.g., Carver & Scheier, 1981) claims that behavior is regulated through the control of discrepancies, or errors. This regulation requires an evaluation of feedback against internal standards. The evaluation of feedback-standard (or feedback-goal) discrepancies is considered a fundamental source for motivational processes even among competing cognitive theories, such as self-efficacy theory (Bandura, 1986; see Phillips, Hollenbeck, & Ilgen, 1996). The theoretical disagreement among cognitive theories regards only the motivations that are triggered by the perception of discrepancies, but not to the fundamental sensitivity to feedback-standard discrepancy. However, most cognitive treatments of the process of discrepancy evaluation are indifferent to the valence of the discrepancy. That is, it is claimed that both a positive discrepancy and a negative discrepancy yield a self-regulatory action that is a mere function of the absolute magnitude of the discrepancy. Similarly, behaviorism (Thorndike, 1927) has symmetrical predictions. That is, both rewards and punishment can equally produce learning. All of the above are predictions that feedback-standard discrepancy produces symmetric effects.

In contrast, other theorists have argued that the reaction to positive and negative events is vastly different (cf. Taylor, 1991). That is, the direction of the feedback-standard discrepancy has major consequences. In other words, reinforcement and punishment have different and asymmetric effects on behavior (Taylor, 1991). Indeed, modern brain research point to different types of changes in the brain that occur as a function of the valence of emotions (Damasio, 1995).

Yet, the theories that emphasize symmetry recognize asymmetry, and vice versa. For example, classical control theory suggests that negative and positive discrepancy may activate different effectors (e.g., the same room temperature thermostat may activate the heating or the air-conditioning system as a function of the valence of the discrepancy). Also, Thorndike found that the word *wrong* yielded lower performance consistency than the word *right* (leading both him and Skinner to concentrate on rewards rather than punishment; see Adams, 1978). Similarly, the theories that emphasizes asymmetry recognize symmetry. For example, Taylor (1991) reviewed evidence for situations in which the reaction to positive surprise is similar to reactions to negative surprise.

I will argue that both theoretical approaches may be correct. People may possess parallel systems that in concert support survival; one operates with symmetric rules and the other with asymmetric rules. These systems may contain both affective and cognitive subsystems. Specifically, the valence of feedback may have asymmetric effects on pleasantness (the first dimension of affect; Russell,

1980) and breadth of cognition. In contrast, the magnitude of the discrepancy may have symmetric effects on arousal (the second dimension of affect; Russell, 1980) and on concentration of thoughts on the feedback-relevant task.

These two mechanisms may be related to two different types of cognitive appraisals (Lazarus, 1991); that is, feedback sign (the discrepancy between the feedback and the standard) is evaluated both for its harm–benefit potential and for the need to take new action (Kluger, Lewinsohn, & Aiello, 1994). The harm–benefit appraisal is a monotone function of the feedback signs. The need for action appraisal is a function of the magnitude of the deviation of the feedback from the standards (i.e., a curvilinear U-shaped function of the feedback sign centered on the standard).

The harm/benefit (punishment/reward) appraisal is reflected in the primary dimension of mood (i.e., pleasantness), and may affect the type of cognitive processes. That is, with a perception of benefit people can afford to regulate either the task at hand or other tasks that are not related to the current discrepancy. On the other hand, a perception of potential harm should mobilize resources to protect the system (Taylor, 1991).

The need for action appraisal is reflected in the secondary dimension of mood— arousal. The need for action should also manifest itself in elevated cognitive activity. The elevated cognitive activity may be aimed either at a preparation for an overt action or at a preparation for a cognitive action. Cognitive actions may include restructuring the cognitive system itself (e.g., reappraisal of the world or the self); that is, with a perception of large discrepancy there should be both an elevation in arousal and in cognitive activity with respect to the task. Furthermore, elevation in cognitive activity that is task related may be at the expense of the regulation of other tasks, and thus there should be a reduction in cognitive activity that is not task related.

There is no doubt that FI sign creates strong affective reactions (Kluger, Lewinsohn, & Aiello, 1994). For example, midterm grades alone may explain up to 50% of the variance in pleasantness (Kluger et al., 1994). However, the evidence regarding the effects of FI sign on arousal is still scarce, and it seems that there is no research on the effects of feedback-standard discrepancies on cognitive activity. In summary, it is hypothesized that: (a) FI sign (feedback-standard discrepancy) has a positive correlation with pleasantness and with nontask thoughts; (b) the absolute magnitude of the discrepancy has a positive correlation with arousal and task thoughts, and a negative correlation with nontask thoughts.

METHOD

Participants

University students in fifteen undergraduate classes were asked to volunteer to answer a survey during a class in which a midterm exam was returned. Over 90% of students, totaling 478, agreed to participate. However, missing data reduced the

TABLE 8.1
Means, Standard Deviations (*SD*), Intercorrelations and Sample Sizes
for Each Correlation

Variables	Mean	SD	1	2	3	4	5	6
1. Grade	0	0.98						
2. Expected	0	0.98	.33* 437					
3. Pleasantness	0	1.00	.41* 372	.03 399				
4. Arousal	0	1.00	.27* 372	.02 399	.00 478			
5. Task Thoughts (TT)	3.43	1.89	−.02 235	−.06 241	−.14* 212	.43* 212		
6. Nontask Thoughts (NTT)	2.24	2.12	.20* 231	−.06 237	−.02 210	.44* 210	.38* 240	
7. NTT Relative to TT	−0.40	0.86	.14* 230	−.00 236	.07 209	−.02 209	−.45* 239	.55* 239

Note. *$p < .05$.

sample size. Each hypothesis was tested separately, and thus pairwise deletion was used. The sample size for each analysis appears in the Tables 8.1 and 8.2.

Measures

Grades and Expected Grades

All grades and expected grades were standardized within each class because several grade formats were used by different instructors.

Feedback-standard Discrepancy (Grade-expectation Discrepancy)

The surface-response method (Edwards & Parry, 1993) was used to overcome psychometric problems inherent in difference scores. **Locus of attention** was measured with a 34-item thoughts frequency questionnaire. The questions asked the respondents to mark how frequently they thought about each item in the past few minutes on a 0 to 10 scale. Examples of items are: "what the grade says about me," "how difficult was the exam," "the course material," and "something that happened in the past." A factor analysis yielded five clear factors (self-related thoughts, course-related thoughts, grade-related thoughts, course-details thoughts, and nontask thoughts). However, the effects of grade-expectation discrepancy on

TABLE 8.2
Simultaneous Regression Models Results: Standardized Beta Coefficients
and T-tests

Predictor	Nontask Thoughts (NTT) N = 228		Pleasantness N = 435		Task Thoughts (TT) N = 228		Arousal N = 435		NTT Relative to TT N = 228	
	β	t	β	t	β	t	β	t	β	t
1. Grade (G)	.30	3.92**	.48	9.83**	−.01	−0.15	−.01	−0.15	.22	2.83**
2. Expect (E)	−.21	−2.65**	−.11	−2.23*	.03	0.36	.03	0.36	−.10	−1.31
3. G²	.12	1.46	.10	1.68	.11	1.32	.22	2.02*	.10	1.20
4. E²	.02	0.20	−.10	−1.89	.31	3.83**	.28	2.89**	−.24	−2.87*
5. E*G	−.13	−1.49	.05	0.90	−.40	−4.61**	−.42	−3.19**	.19	2.16**

Note. *p < .05; **p < .01.

the scales constructed on the basis of the factor analysis were similar for the first four scales, which, not surprisingly, were highly intercorrelated. Also, the first dimension of a multiple-dimension scaling showed that the items that loaded on the first four factors were different from the items loading on the fifth factor that measured nontask thoughts (e.g., something that happened in the past). Therefore, two scales were constructed: **task thoughts** (twenty five items; alpha = .92), and **nontask thoughts** (nine items; alpha = .82).

Arousal and Pleasantness

Mood items from mood questionnaires by Mano (1992) and Kluger et al. (1994) were translated from English into Hebrew and were augmented with arousal-related mood adjectives. This resulted in a 42-item mood questionnaire. Dimension scores were factor scores created by a principal component analysis (PCA). The PCA was performed on all the 42 mood items without rotation and with a forced two-factor solution. As was found in numerous studies (e.g., Kluger et al., 1994), the first unrotated factor of the principal component analysis reflected pleasantness, whereas the second factor reflected arousal.

Procedure

The procedure is similar to that used by Kluger et al. (1994) in study 2. Instructors asked their respective classes to take a survey during class time. In the beginning of the session in which the midterm was returned, the author or a research assistant distributed a short questionnaire (on a small paper strip). This questionnaire asked,

"What is the grade you expect to receive on the midterm?" Students were instructed to keep this slip. Then the instructor returned the graded exams, and the researchers immediately gave all students the main questionnaire. The main questionnaire had several versions, described later. Students were asked to indicate the grade they had just received on the top of the main questionnaire, to answer the main questionnaire, and then to attach the expected-grade questionnaire to the main questionnaire. This procedure protected their anonymity, yet allowed the data to be matched.

The main questionnaire contained two pages measuring moods and loci of attention, respectively. The order of these pages was randomized such that approximately half of the participants responded to the mood section first. The loci of attention section were measured only in eight of the classes ($N = 241$). The other half worked on a sentence-completion task that was a part of research beyond the scope of this chapter (including additional control classes that received no grades).

RESULTS

Table 8.1 shows the correlations among all the variables. Table 8.2 shows hierarchical regressions designed to test the effects of discrepancies (Edwards & Parry, 1993). These regressions show both asymmetric and symmetric effects, as predicted. The asymmetric effects are found for pleasantness and nontask thoughts. That is, the higher the grade (the more positive is the gap from an unmeasured standard), the more positive is the mood and the more likely are thoughts regarding nontask issues (for a discussion of multiple standards see Kluger et al., 1994). Moreover, once the grade is controlled for, the expectation effects reflect the asymmetric effects of grade-expectation discrepancies. That is, for a given grade, the lower the expectation (the more positive is the grade-expectation discrepancy) the more positive is the mood and the more likely are nontask thoughts. Taken in combination, these results are consistent with an asymmetric response model.

Table 8.2 also show clear symmetric effects for arousal and for task thoughts with no evidence for asymmetric effects (nonsignificant linear effects in the regression models). The symmetric effects are largely evidenced in the negative and significant beta of the "Expectation × Grade" product. Specifically, students receiving a grade discrepant from their expectation have a negative product (positive Z score on expectation and negative Z score on grades, or vice versa). For these students, the level of arousal is predicted to be high (the negative beta is multiplied by their negative product). To visualize these effects, see Figs. 8.1 and 8.2. These results show that as the expectation-grade discrepancy grows, irrespective of the valence of the discrepancy, arousal goes up, as well as task-related thoughts. It was also expected that nontask thoughts would show symmetric effects that are the inverse of the effects on task thoughts. This was not found. However, the nontask

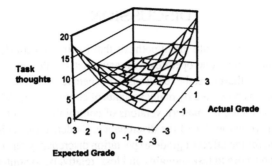

FIG. 8.1. The effect of feedback-expectation discrepancy on task–thoughts frequency.

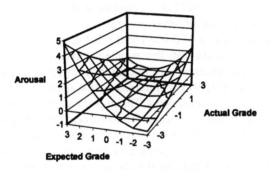

FIG. 8.2. The effect of feedback-expectation discrepancy on arousal.

thoughts correlated with arousal as high as did task thoughts. These correlations indicated that discrepancies are linked both to arousal and amount of cognitive activity, irrespective of content. To control for amount of cognitive activity, a new score for nontask thoughts was calculated. To calculate this score, the five scales created on the basis of the factor analysis were used (see "Method"). Across the five scales, I calculated the within-person mean and standard deviation. Then, the within-person standardized score of the nontask thoughts was calculated. This measure indicates the amount of nontask thoughts relative to all types of thoughts. This new measure was not correlated with arousal (Table 8.1), but it did show the predicted symmetric effect of discrepancy in the direction inverse to the one found both for task thoughts and arousal. Thus, it seems that whereas arousal is correlated with the *amount* in cognitive activity, arousal is not correlated with the relative *distribution* of cognition. The relative distribution of cognition, in turn, seems to be affected by the magnitude of feedback-standard discrepancy. Taken in combination, these results are consistent with a symmetric response model.

DISCUSSION

The results are congruent with the hypothesis that FI simultaneously triggers two types of reactions, where one operates with asymmetric rules and the other with symmetric rules. Furthermore, the reactions to FI seem to be regulated by monitoring discrepancies, as predicted by many variants of control theory. The symmetric rules are those predicted by modern versions of control theory. In these versions, people are sensitive to the size of the discrepancy. Evidence for such FI effects is most compelling for the effect of grade-expectation discrepancy on arousal and the locus of attention (more to task thoughts and less, relatively, to nontask thoughts). The effect on arousal that was measured here in Hebrew replicates previous findings in English (Kluger et al., 1994), whereas the effects on locus of attention are new findings. All of these effects show strong effect sizes that are induced by discrepancies in accordance with FIT and control theory that argue that discrepancies serve as one important basis for behavior regulation.

The asymmetric rule is well documented (Taylor, 1991) and is predicted by common sense. This rule suggests that people are very sensitive to the valence of the discrepancy. Such effects were found for the effect of FI on pleasantness (conceptually replicating Ilgen, 1971) and also for the amount of nontask thoughts. These results, per se, are not interesting. The important finding is that asymmetric effects coexist with symmetric effects. The asymmetric effects may be stronger in magnitude and more noticeable both for the lay person and for the researcher looking at the data. However, the symmetric effects (arousal, task thoughts) may have an important role in modulating the asymmetric effect. Also, the symmetric effects entail that for some affective and cognitive variables FI sign does not have linear effects. Taken as a whole, the results suggest that FI sign influences behavior through at least two paths, where one is insensitive to valence. These findings may be the clue for the lack of simple FI sign effects on FI effectiveness.

The present study suggests that the motivational effects of FI generalize across cultures (some of the present results replicated U.S. findings in Israel). Yet, we still lack a complete picture of the motivational (and learning) processes induced by FIs (Kluger & DeNisi, 1996).

This state of affair has implications both for research and practice. Researchers interested in the processes that mediate feedback sign effects on performance, should consider the effects reported here in combination with recent developments in self-regulation theory (e.g., Higgins, 1997). Specifically, arousal may be determined both by the magnitude of feedback discrepancy from a standard (found here) and by the salient goal of the recipient (prevention goal or promotion goal). Arousal may be at its peak either for positive feedback when a promotion goal is salient or for negative feedback when a prevention goal is salient (see Kluger & DeNisi, 1998; Van-Dijk & Kluger, 2000). Merging the current findings with Higgins's work is a major theoretical challenge for feedback researchers.

Given the little than we understand about FI effects on behavior, practitioners interested in increasing work motivation should use FIs very carefully. That is, practitioners should introduce effectiveness measures to the intervention, rather than assume that FI improves motivation and hence performance. Alternatively, practitioners interested in increasing work motivation should seriously consider alternative and safer interventions (such as goal setting.)

REFERENCES

Adams, J. A. (1978). Theoretical issues for knowledge of results. In G. E. Stelmach (Ed.), *Information processing in motor control and learning*. New York: Academic Press.

Balcazar, F., Hopkins, B. L., & Suarez, Y. (1985). A critical, objective review of performance feedback. *Journal of Organizational Behavior Management, 7*, 65–89.

Bandura, A. (1986). *Social foundations of thought and action: A social cognitive theory*. Englewood Cliffs, NJ: Prentice-Hall.

Carver, C. S., & Scheier M. F. (1981). *Attention and self-regulation: A control theory to human behavior*. New York: Springer-Verlag.

Damasio, A. R. (1995). *Descartes' error : Emotion, reason, and the human brain*. New York: Avon Books.

Edwards, J. R., & Parry, M. E. (1993). On the use of polynomial regression equations as an alternative to difference scores in organizational research, *Academy of Management Journal, 36*, 1577–1613.

Higgins, E. T. (1997). Beyond pleasure and pain. *American Psychologist, 52*, 1280–1300.

Ilgen, D. R. (1971). Satisfaction with performance as a function of the initial level of expected performance and the deviation from expectations. *Organizational Behavior and Human Performance, 6*, 345–361.

Ilgen, D. R., Fisher, C. D., & Taylor M. S. (1979). Consequences of individual feedback on behavior in organization. *Journal of Applied Psychology, 64*, 349–361.

Kluger, A. N., & DeNisi, A. (1996). The effects of feedback interventions on performance: Historical review, a meta-analysis and a preliminary feedback intervention theory. *Psychological Bulletin, 119*, 254–284.

Kluger, A. N., & DeNisi, A. (1998). Feedback interventions: Toward the understanding of a double-edged sword. *Current Directions in Psychological Science, 7*, 67–72.

Kluger, A. N., Lewinsohn, S., & Aiello, J. (1994). The influence of feedback on mood: Linear effects on pleasantness and curvilinear effects on arousal. *Organizational Behavior and Human Decision Processes, 60*, 276–299.

Latham, G. P., & Locke, E. A. (1991). Self-regulation through goal setting. *Organizational Behavior and Human Decision Processes, 50*, 212–247.

Lazarus, R. S. (1991). Progress on a cognitive-motivational-relational theory of emotion, *American Psychologist, 46*, 819–834.

Locke, E. A., & Latham, G. P. (1990). *A theory of goal setting and task performance*. Englewood Cliffs, NJ: Prentice-Hall.

Mano, H. (1992). Judgments under distress: Assessing the role of unpleasantness and arousal in judgment formation. *Organizational Behavior and Human Decision Processes, 52*, 216–245.

Phillips, J. M., Hollenbeck, J. R., & Ilgen, D. R. (1996). Prevalence and prediction of positive discrepancy creation: Examining a discrepancy between two self-regulation theories, *Journal of Applied Psychology, 81*, 498–511.

Russell, J. A. (1980). A circumplex model of affect. *Journal of Personality and Social Psychology, 36*, 1152–1168.

Salmoni, A. W., Schmidt, R. A., & Walter, C. B. (1984). Knowledge of results and motor learning: A review and critical reappraisal. *Psychological Bulletin, 95*, 355–386.

Taylor, S. E. (1991). Asymmetrical effects of positive and negative events: The mobilization-minimization hypothesis. *Psychological Bulletin, 110*, 67–85.

Thorndike, E. L. (1927). The law of effect. *American Journal of Psychology, 39*, 212–222.

Van-Dijk D., & Kluger, A. N. (April, 2000). *Positive (Negative) Feedback: Encouragement or Discouragement?* A paper presented at the 15th annual convention of the Society for Industrial and Organizational Psychology, New Orleans, LA.

9

Self-enhancement and Self-protection: Toward a Theory of Work Motivation

Abraham K. Korman
Baruch College, City University of New York

Among the most significant characteristics of the work setting of the 1990s has been the explosive growth of anxiety at all levels of the occupational spectrum. While this emotion has not been unknown in work organizations prior to this time and has in fact been the subject of considerable interest among some behavioral scientists (Kets de Vries & Miller, 1986), events of the last decade have made anxiety and its related emotions of increasing relevance. Spurred by the loss of millions of jobs due to corporate downsizing and the strong indications that such practices will continue despite their questionable financial outcomes, decreases in employer support of health and pension benefits, the difficulties of recounciling work and family demands among both men and women, the growth of temporary/part-time jobs, and the consequent decline of job security in general, the world of work has become characterized by levels of anxiety barely envisioned a decade ago.

We believe that these changes, dramatic in their impact but in reality reflecting events that have been developing over a period of years, suggest the need for a paradigm of work motivation that reflects these newer patterns as well as those that have dominated our perspectives during the past half century. In brief, this paradigm would include both the positive intrinsic and extrinsic goal-oriented perspectives that have been dominant in work motivation theory (e.g., as utilized by such theories as expectancy-value, self-actualiztion, and goal seeking) as well as the increasingly pervasive anxieties of the world of work.

The theory we develop in this chapter stems from this perspective. In the following we propose that motivation in the work setting consists of two independent processes that we conceptualize as the desire for self-enhancement and the desire for self-protection. Furthermore, it is our view that the likelihood of occurrence of either of these forms of behavior will be a function of the relative strength at the time of the dispositional and situational factors that generate these patterns.

In addition, as part of our presentation, we include a review of relevant research literature concerning our proposals as well a discussion of findings from our own research program.

A THEORY OF WORK MOTIVATION

We have indicated that the theory we present here derives from the need to account for the increasing anxiety in work settings in recent years as well as the desirability of continuing to recognize the relevance, at least under some conditions, of the motivation to attain positive goals. Thus, the paradigm we propose includes constructs emphasizing both the desire for positive outcomes obtainable from the work experience and also the need to reduce the anxiety that is also likely to be found in these contexts (c.f. Atkinson, 1974).

With this as a point of departure, we propose that work-related motivation reflects two independent processes, which we call self-enhancement and self-protection. The former is defined as the motivation to attain outcomes that signify personal growth on the part of the individual and/or the approval of others for attaining socially desirable goals. Among these outcomes may be vocational/career/personal goals that match and fulfill one's needs and desires, the obaining of information that is useful for self-growth, higher levels of work performance and effectiveness, and the achievement of goals that legimately enhance one in the eyes of the self and others. It may also be noted that these types of outcomes are typically utilized as dependent variables in research studies testing such frameworks as expectancy-value theory, goal-setting, and the self-actualization proposals of Maslow and Alderfer.

It is our view that self-enhancement motivation is most likely to occur among those individuals and in those situations in which individuals see the work environment as encouraging certain views concerning work opportunities. Three such views are involved. One is when the work setting is seen as providing the opportunity and the encouragement to attain positive goals. A second instance is when individuals see themselves as deserving of and competent to attain goals that reflect such positive self-feelings. Such encouragement can come from the work environment in two ways. One is by reinforcing already existing positive self-evaluation or self-esteem. Second, it can, by appropriate situational work design, encourage increasing levels of such self-feelings on the part of the individual. A third important view of the work setting that can also generate self-enhancement motivation is when the person is encouraged to believe that the positive goals that are available and that she/he believe they deserve are, in fact, capable of attainment by their own efforts and not by the permission of others. Here, also, these views can occur by either the work setting reinforcing an existing belief that one can achieve positive goals by one's own efforts, or by the development of a situational work environment that stimulates the growth of such beliefs in the individual.

In contrast to self-enhancement, we define self-protection motivation as the defense of the sense of oneself from threatening environmental or personal forces that, if unleashed, would result in the destruction of one's sense of personal identity. Individuals view the work setting in these cases as potentially threatening punishment for actual or believed imperfections and as encouraging them to focus attention on the need to protect the self from these actual or potential threatening forces. Among the behaviors reflecting these processes may be engaging in social and information manipulation for self-protection regardless of the implications for performance effectiveness, preferring coworkers who agree with the self regardless of the topic, issue at hand, or potential work outcomes, making decisions that only confirm what one has already decided (particularly publicly), and denying reponsibility for any action resulting in negative outcomes (c.f. Ashforth & Lee, 1990). A theoretical discussion that has provided both a useful integration of these types of behaviors and a number of illustrations is Greenwald's (1980) analysis of the similarity of ego-defensive processes at the individual level to the use of information-suppression and distortion techniques by both totalitarian leaders and theoreticians more involved in protecting their own work than in obtaining meaningful or accurate research data. It is the similarity between these processes, as seen by Greenwald, that led him to propose three types of cognitive biases that illustrate the obtaining and use of information for self-protection. Among these biases are "egocentricity," where only the self is seen to serve as the focus of knowledge; "benefectance," where the self is considered as responsible for desired but not for undesired outcomes; and "cognitive conservatism," when meaningful information exists that indicates that change is both desirable and necessary but which is still resisted. It is through the use of these biases that the ego, totalitarian organizations, and theoreticians engage in information control that protect the self from information inconsistent with one's position, values, and previous actions. Furthermore, Greenwald suggests, these processes are more likely to occur the more the individual is ego involved in a stated position (and thus more likely to be anxious and defensive).

As with self-enhancement, self-protective motivation occurs as a function of both dispositional and situational factors. Thus, it is most likely to occur among those individuals for whom the work setting is a source of anxiety and potentially debilitating outcomes. One such type of anxiety of particular relevance is the fear that one will be found "failing" in some way, in that the demand for

excellent (perfect?) outcomes will not be met and the person will be blamed for
such imperfection.

Anxiety may also develop as a result of work-setting characteristics. Thus, individuals might see the work environment as a setting that promises punishment
of a serious nature if performance schedules are not met or if hierarchical leadership dictates are not acceded to appropriately. Such settings may also increase
anxiety, because hierarchical control may encourage individuals to see themselves
as incompetent to attain goals on their own. Similarly, the organization can increase anxiety in the individual by engaging in confusing and contradictory leadership patterns and/or by providing guidelines to actions that are ambiguous and
meaningless.

It is our view that self-enhancement and self-protection are motivational processes that are independent of one another and that each can occur in varying
degrees depending on the configuration of dispositional and situational factors
that may be influential at that particular time. As we outline in Fig. 9.1, we
also suggest that both dispositional and situational variables may be influential in

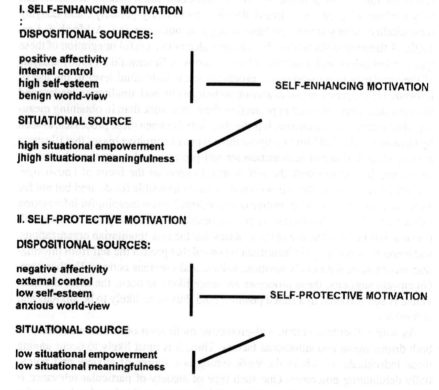

FIG. 9.1. Work motivation theories and their sources.

impacting on the degree to which either motivational process may occur in a specific setting. Thus, we may find in any given context some individuals virtually exclusively dominated by the need for self-protection, some by the need for self-enhancement, and some reflecting both motivational processes to an intermediate degree. In the following we identify and clarify the nature of these dispositional and situational factors.

Dispositional Variables and Motivational Processes

There are a number of dispositional variables that may influence the degree to which motivational processes reflect self-enhancement or self-protection. In the former instance, we propose that self-enhancement motivation is more likely to occur as a function of the degree to which individual dispositions are marked by three characteristics. One disposition is a sense of optimism about the world, for example, one's feelings of "positive affectivity"; the second is the belief that one is deserving of goals signifying the attainment of self-enhancement on the part of the individual, that is, one's degree of self-esteem; and the third is the degree to which one is capable of engaging in those behaviors that will lead to self-enhancing outcomes, that is, one's sense of "internal control."

Considering the first of these, *positive affectivity* can be defined as indicating an overall sense of positive well-being resulting from the tendency to see people, both others, the self, and the world in a positive light and to experience positive emotional states because desirable, self-enhancing goals are viewed as possible of attainment. Given this definition, it would be expected that effective performance in task settings would be positively related to positive affectivity (or generalized optimism), and there is considerable evidence to support this prediction in the research literature. Sheier, Weintraub, and Carver (1986) have shown that dispositional optimism (which they define as a generalized expectancy for positive outcomes) is associated with better adaptation under stress and problem-focused coping, whereas dispositional pessimism is related to denial, distancing, and disengagement from goals. Similarly, Seligman, and Schulman (1986) have shown dispositional optimism to be associated with success as a life insurance agent, and Staw and Barsade (1993) have found those with a more positive world view to be more accurate in their decision making and to be more capable interpersonally. Also relevant here is a series of studies by Isen and her coworkers in which she found that people made to feel happy by experimental manipulation performed better than a control group on complex tasks and also processed information more effectively and/or creatively (Isen & Daubman, 1984; Isen, Daubman, & Nowicki, 1987; Isen, Johnson, Mertz, & Robinson, 1985; Isen & Means, 1983). In sum, these studies indicate that those who see the world as positive are more likely to perform effectively in work settings and to attain outcomes that are self-enhancing.

Also relevant here are the results of our own research concerning the implications of positive and negative emotional states (Korman, 1996). Working with a group of 74 male managers enrolled in an executive development program, we found that those marked by negative affectivity (i.e., self-described as tense and jittery) did not see themselves as using those behaviors and attitudes more likely to make them effective as managers. Among these characteristics that they did *not* see themselves as likely to develop or utilize were an achievement orientation, interpersonal skills, verbal ability, an ability to cope with stress, an ability to take advantage of opportunities, and a knowledge of the relevant industry in which they are working. On the other hand, these are precisely the skills that those high in positive affectivity (i.e., self-described as calm, relaxed, and at ease) saw themselves as more likely to develop and use; that is, they were more likely to adopt and utilize the skills that would help them attain effectiveness and success.

A second dispositional factor we propose to be associated with the attainment of goals supporting feelings of self-enhancement is *self-esteem*, which we define as the degree of belief that one is a capable, competent individual and deserving of outcomes that are positive in both a personal and social sense.

The literature supporting the positive implications of high self-esteem is substantive. Korman (1977), citing his own work and that of others, found considerable support for this proposition in both his work and the work of others, and additional research since that time continues to be supportive. For example, high-self-esteem individuals are more successful in job search behavior than those with low self-esteem (Ellis & Taylor, 1983), and they are also more likely to take steps to try to resolve job-related problems (Pierce, Gardner, Dunham, & Cummings, 1993). Similarly, in a general review of the literature, Wagner and Hollenbeck (1992, p. 101) concluded that high-self-esteem individuals are more driven to meet their self-set goals (that tend to be high and resistant to change) than those with low self-esteem and to expect to succeed regardless of the context.

A third construct we believe influencing self-enhancing motivation is the degree to which the individual views her- or himself as capable of internal control as opposed to being subject to external control. Defined as the extent to which an individual believes that her or his own actions can influence the attainment of outcomes, individuals who are high in this characteristic believe they can attain desirable goals by their own actions, whereas individuals low on this factor believe their own actions cannot help the attainment of outcomes, desirable though they may be. Given this definition, we would expect this dispositional variable to be related to self-enhancing motivation, an expectation that both Spector (1982) and Miner (1988) have supported in separate research reviews. Among the studies they cite in this context are some showing that those with an internal sense of control are more likely to attain self-enhancing goals because they seek out and attempt to attain rewards indicating high performance, are better at collecting and processing complex information, and perform better even when general mental ability is held constant.

There are also dispositional variables associated with self-protective motivation. Of particular relevance in the work setting is fear of failure, defined as the desire to avoid failure when one can be blamed for it. Thus, it is not the failure itself that is the problem for those high on this disposition but the fact that one must assume responsibility for such an outcome.

Research on fear of failure has found it to be consistently related to self-protective motivation. Birney, Burdick, and Teevan (1969) have reported that those with high fear of failure are likely to (a) avoid situations where they will be evaluated precisely, (b) prefer comparing themselves against those greatly deviant from themselves, (c) prefer vague and imprecise measures of performance, (d) reject responsibility, and (f) blame others when failing to meet a performance standard. Also supportive of the view that fear of failure is associated with self-protective motivation is a more recent review by Lowman (1993), which concluded that fear of failure is related to withdrawing prematurely from a goal or career, failure avoidance, protecting the self by ascribing negative attributions to others, and exhibiting greater concern with favorable-impression management rather than focusing on problem-solving efforts that might result in task accomplishment.

Situational Variables and Motivational Processes

A major assumption underlying our view of motivational processes is that they are dynamic in nature as well as a function of dispositional trait characteristics. That is, we view the motivation toward self-enhancement and/or self-protection to be a function of situational job characteristics as well as the dispositional variables we have noted above.

More specifically, we propose that a major key to understanding relationships between the work setting and the two motivational processes is the degree to which the job characteristics encourage feelings of positive affectivity, self-esteem and internal control on the one hand and feelings of fear of failure on the other.

Theoretically, such influence processes can occur from a number of sources. For example, organizations that are undergoing downsizing and encourage strict hierarchical practices in decision-making are likely to generate high levels of anxiety in individuals about failing in a performance demand, the former because of the uncertainty involved about the prospect of job loss and the latter because of the fear of negative evaluation. In both instances the individual is powerless to impact the situations involved, and the result is a high level of anxiety concerning the implications of job failure. On the other hand, organizations that encourage autonomy and a sense of empowerment in decision making and emphasize job enrichment and participative practices in general are more likely to generate feelings of positive affectivity, self-esteem, and internal control, with a resulting motivational impetus towards self-enhancement.

Situations encouraging feelings of empowerment are not the only settings that may generate a more optimistic, internal-control view of the world. Also potentially influential is when job characteristics encourage the belief that job demands and goals are meaningful and not ambiguous or conflicting. In these instances, we would expect that individuals working in such settings will develop, because they know what to know and what to expect, a more optimistic view of the world, and engage in behavior reflecting the desire for self-enhancement. On the other hand, self-protection will be more likely to occur the more the situational job variables are ambiguous and conflicting, because these patterns are more likely to generate anxiety in those working in such settings.

We have completed three preliminary investigations designed to test these proposed relationships, and all provide considerable support for these hypothesized relationships (Korman, 1996). In the first of these studies, we compared the responses of 65 managers and professionals who were asked to indicate how they would behave if they were in organizations marked either by high centralization (e.g., low empowerment) and high ambiguity as opposed to one characterized by low centralization and consistency in decision making. The results were as expected. Those responding to the former organizational description were far more self-protective in their expected behaviors than those responding to the latter.

Following this, we then conducted an interview survey of 67 managers and professionals from a number of business organizations in a large northeastern city. In this interview we first asked the respondents to describe the degree to which the leadership-management characteristics of their organization were empowering and meaningful and, a week later, to describe the behavior of their fellow employees along self-enhancing and self-protective dimensions. The results provided considerable but not complete support for our hypothesized framework. More than half of the proposed relationships were significant as proposed, whereas none were significant in the opposite direction.

In addition to these studies, we have also tested hypotheses relating to this theory utilizing 39 MBA students at a northeastern university who were employed full-time and who were enrolled in a course in organizational behavior at the graduate level. In this case, we found, as we expected, fear of failure and fear of success to be positively correlated with self-protective motivation, and to be negatively correlated with self-enhancing motivation.

CONCLUSIONS

Theories can be of value for a number of reasons. Most important, theories are of value if they have the capability of accounting in a coherent manner for known research findings and if they are potentially fruitful in generating new research of a meaningful nature. Within this context, the theory we are proposing here may be of value for several reasons. One is that we are suggesting a model of motivation in the work setting that is a rather complex one. It suggests an individual whose motivational processes may vary in different contexts as a result of situational influences and who may also reflect varying dispositional characteritics, not all of which are consistent with one another. Thus, it is not out of the case that individuals may have a strong fear of failure and may also have at least a moderate sense of internal control. Similarly, other such combinations may also be possible, particularly in conjunction with situational influences.

In another direction, the theory we have outlined here may also suggest potential directions for responding to some of the problems of current theories in the areas of work motivation and leadership. Consider the frameworks that have come to be known as expectancy-value, goal setting, and self-actualization, each of which can be characterized by several patterns. One is that they are popular and frequently cited as the more important theories of work motivation. Second, each is built around and assumes a desire for positive (e.g.,"self-enhancing") outcomes, as a metatheoretical key for understanding work motivation. Third, and of importance for us here, is that expectancy-value, self-actualization, and goal-setting theories have long been recognized to have limitations in their empirical validity (c.f. Korman, 1977; Kopelman, 1977; Miller & Grush, 1988; Wahba & Bridwell, 1976). Given the empirical and conceptual limitations of these theories, it may be suggested that the undertaking of research studies evaluating the theory we have proposed here may provide guidelines as to the dispositional and situational conditions under which, for example, expectancy-value predictions (or goal setting or self-actualization) will prove to be of value and when an anxiety-reduction model is more appropriate. In support of this expectation, we may note that there already is some research indicating that expectancy value theory works best for those high on internal control and not for those high on external control (Miner, 1988, p. 83). However, more work is clearly needed concerning these possibilities and the general usefulness of the framework we have presented here.

REFERENCES

Ashforth, B., & Lee, R. (1990). Defensive behavior in organizations: A preliminary model. *Human Relations, 43*(7), 621–648.

Atkinson, J. W. (1974). *An introduction to motivation.* Princeton, NJ: D. Van Nostrand and Co.

Birney, R. C., Burdick, H. J., & Teevan, R. C. (1969). *Fear of failure.* Princeton, NJ: Van-Nostrand-Reinhold.

Ellis, R. A., & Taylor, M. S. (1983). Role of self-esteem in the job search process. *Journal of Applied Psychology, 68,* 632–640.

Greenwald, A. G. (1980). The totalitarian ego: Fabrication and revisions of psychological history. *American Psychologist, 35*(7), 603–618.

Isen, A. M., & Daubman, K. A. (1984). The influence of affect on categorization. *Journal of Personality and Social Psychology, 47,* 1206–1217.

Isen, A. M., Daubman, K. A., & Nowicki, G. A. (1987). Positive affect facilitates creative problem-solving. *Journal of Personality and Social Psychology, 52,* 1122–1131.

Isen, A. M., Johnson, M. M., Mertz, E., & Robinson, G. F. (1985). The effect of positive affect on the unusualness of word associations. *Journal of Personality and Social Psychology, 48*, 1413–1426.

Isen, A. M., & Means, B. (1983). The effect of positive affect on decision-making strategy. *Social Cognition, 2*, 18–31.

Kets de Vries, M. F. R., & Miller, D. (1986). *The neurotic organization.* San Francisco: Jossey-Bass.

Kopelman, R. (1977). Across-individuals, within-individuals and return on effort version of expectancy-theory. *Decision Sciences, 8*, 651–662.

Korman, A. (1977). *Organizational behavior.* Englewood Cliffs, NJ: Prentice-Hall.

Korman, A. (1996). *Self-enhancement and self-protection: Towards an expanded theory of motivation in the work setting.* Paper presented at the International Conference on Individual, Group and Cultural Factors in Motivation, Israel.

Lowman, R. L. (1993). *Counseling and psychotherapy of work dysfunctions* (pp. 43–44). Washington, DC: American Psychological Association.

Miller, L. E., & Grush, J. E. (1988). Improving prediction in expectancy-theory research: Efforts of personality, expectations and norms. *Academy of Management Journal, 31*(1), 107–123.

Miner, J. B. (1988). *Organizational behavior: Performance and productivity* (p. 83). New York: Random House.

Pierce, J. G., Gardner, D. G., Dunham, R. B., & Cummings, L. (1993). Moderation by organization-based self-esteem of role condition-employee response relationships. *Academy of Management Journal, 36*, 271–288.

Scheier, M. F., Weintraub, J. K., & Carver, C. S. (1986). Coping with stress: Divergent strategies of optimists and pessimists. *Journal of Personality and Social Psychology, 48*, 1162–1172.

Seligman, M. E. P., & Schulman, P. (1986). Explanatory style as a predictor of productivity and quitting among life insurance agents. *Journal of Personality and Social Psychology, 50*, 832–838.

Spector, P. E. (1982). Behavior in organizations as a function of employee locus of control. *Psychological Bulletin, 91*, 482–497.

Staw, B. M., & Barsade, S. G. (1993). Affect and managerial performance: A test of the sadder-but-wiser vs. happier-and-smarter hypotheses. *Administrative Science Quarterly, 38*, 304–331.

Wagner, J. A., III, & Hollenbeck, J. A. (1992). *Management of organizational behavior,* Englewood Cliffs, NJ: Prentice-Hall.

Wahba, M., & Bridwell, L. S. (1976). Maslow reconsidered: A review of the research on the need-hierarchy theory. *Organizational Behavior and Human Performance, 15*, 212–240.

10

VIE Functions, Self-set Goals, and Performance: An Experiment

Wendelien Van Eerde
University of Amsterdam, The Netherlands

Henk Thierry
University of Tilburg, The Netherlands

The Valence Instrumentality Expectancy (VIE) model (Vroom, 1964) has been one of the most influential theories in work motivation. However, the reviews that appeared over the years (Mitchell, 1974, 1982; Pritchard & Campbell, 1976; Schwab, Olian-Gottlieb, & Heneman, 1979; Wanous, Keon, & Latack, 1983) raised several questions concerning its validity. In a meta-analysis (Van Eerde & Thierry, 1996) we gave an overview of effect sizes of nonexperimental research. The results of the meta-analysis show different average correlations across the criterion measure categories, whereas the average correlations referring to models, such as the Expectancy-valence (EV) or VIE model, did not differ from those referring to the single constructs valence, instrumentality, and expectancy, or across different operationalizations. Within-subjects correlations were not found to be clearly superior to between-subjects correlations, although this may have been partly due to the fact that relatively few within-subjects correlations were available. We concluded that the issue of which criterion variable is to be predicted is more important than which form and operationalization of expectancy theory is used.

The relation between the VIE variables and assigned goals has been the subject of several empirical studies, in which the dependent variables were goal commitment (Henry & Strickland, 1994; Hollenbeck and Brief, 1987; Klein & Wright, 1994; Locke, Latham, & Erez, 1988; Tubbs, 1993; Wofford, Goodwin, & Premack, 1992) and goal level (Campbell, 1982; Mento, Locke, & Klein, 1992; Riedel, Nebeker, & Cooper, 1988; Wofford et al., 1992). However, the relation between the VIE variables and self-set goals has not been studied extensively. A self-set goal may be viewed as a measure of intended performance. Tubbs, Boehne, and Dahl (1993) assessed the perception of the difficulty of assigned goals on within-subject functions of valence, expectancy, force, and subsequent self-set goals.

The current study is a follow-up on our meta-analysis of nonexperimental data in an experimental design. Experiments on the VIE model are relatively rare. Examples of between-subjects experiments are those conducted by Graen (1969), Peters (1977), and Pritchard and DeLeo (1973). Others have used within-subjects experimental designs, which are also known as decision modeling or policy capturing studies, for example, Arnold (1981), Tubbs and Dahl (1991), and Zedeck (1977). Here, we will discuss some of the manipulations of valence, instrumentality, and expectancy that have been used.

MANIPULATION OF VALENCE

Valence, or the anticipated satisfaction associated with an outcome, can be manipulated by varying the attractiveness of the outcome. In practice, valence has usually been manipulated by varying the size of a monetary reward. Experiments using incentives for performance illustrate this type of manipulation, and these usually yield strong effects.

MANIPULATION OF INSTRUMENTALITY

Instrumentality, or the perceived relation between an outcome and a second level outcome, can be manipulated by relating performance and reward in different ways, such as contingent versus noncontingent rewards upon performance (e.g., Jorgenson, Dunnette, & Pritchard, 1973), or by offering a high or low probability of winning a reward in a lottery (e.g., Folger & Doherty, 1993). Theoretically, the avoidance of a negative outcome would have the same effect, but this condition of instrumentality has been used only rarely (e.g., Wright, Kelley, & Bramwell, 1988).

The manipulation of instrumentality has often been confounded with that of valence, that is, the relation between performance and a reward have been manipulated together with the value of the reward. This is unfortunate, because it does not allow for a separate analysis of the main effects of each construct.

MANIPULATION OF EXPECTANCY

Expectancy, or the subjective probability that an action will lead to an outcome, can be influenced in several ways so as to establish a norm or point of comparison. This can be manipulated by emphasizing that task performance is to a greater or lesser extent dependent on effort (e.g., Henry & Strickland, 1994), by giving hard or easy tasks (e.g., Cellar, Posig, Johnson, & Janega, 1993), by assigning difficult or easy goals (e.g., Tubbs et al., 1993), or by giving a high or low task load (e.g., Wright & Gregorich, 1991).

In this study, we combined the between-subjects manipulations of the VIE variables with Tubbs et al.'s (1993) approach, who used within-subjects functions of expectancy and valence. These functions consist of potential performance levels on the x-axis, and the rating of expectancy, and respectively, valence of performance on the y-axis. The expectancy function decreased as a function of increasing potential performance levels, and the valence of performance function increased. Tubbs et al. (1993) showed that these functions shifted to the right when the assigned goal was perceived as more difficult. Force, computed as the product of expectancy and valence, shifted accordingly as an inverted U function, of which the top signifies the maximum force. This maximum force—according to Vroom (1964)—should predict performance, in combination with a persons' ability.

We hypothesized that those who perceive valence, instrumentality, or expectancy as high will set higher goals and have a higher performance level than those who perceive these variables as low. Based upon the results of our meta-analysis, we did not predict any interaction effects. Further, we expected that the level of the within-subjects functions of valence, instrumentality, expectancy, and direct ratings of force would reflect the manipulations of between-subjects manipulations. Also, we explored gender differences. Although gender differences in self-confidence in future performance are not always consistent, some studies showed that women have lower performance expectations in achievement settings (e.g., McCarthy, 1986; Sleeper & Nigro, 1987).

METHOD

Subjects and Design

Subjects were 80 students of the Dutch Royal Military Academy (69 men and 11 women) who cooperated for one hour in their time off in between classes. Subjects were randomly assigned to conditions in a 2 (expectancy high/low) × 2 (instrumentality high/low) × 2 (valence high/low) between-subjects design. The rating of the VIE variables and force was obtained for 18 levels of performance in order to permit the computation of within-subjects correlations.

Performance Task and Procedure

The task consisted of solving 40 problems in which the number of kilometers from one train station to another had to be given. The subjects first looked at a map or in an index in order to find the table with the right route. At the first page of each table, the number of kilometers from the beginning of the route to each of the train stations along that route are indicated at the entrance of the rows. This meant that the subjects must subtract the kilometers between the stations asked in order to get the right answer. Some problems were slightly more complicated because they included one stopover. Although some subjects were familiar with looking up the times and connections of routes,—the actual use of the train schedule—looking up the number of kilometers is an unknown task, because the schedule is normally not used for this purpose.

The subjects participated individually in the experiment with one of the five experimenters, all female psychology students.[1] The experimenter explained the task, and solved two problems together with the subject to familiarize him or her with the task and encouraged to ask questions if he or she did not understand the task fully. Subsequently, the experimenter presented four trial problems of different difficulty levels. She recorded the time needed to complete a problem correctly and provided feedback on the time taken for the four problems. Thereafter, she introduced the experimental condition (explained in detail below) and requested the subjects to rate the VIE variables and the variable force, as well as to set a goal. After the ratings the subjects continued to work on the task for 25 minutes, and subsequently some background questions were obtained, such as the perceived knowledge of Dutch topography relevant for the map reading, experience with the use of the train schedule, and attributions for their self-set goals and performance. If the subject had met the criterion for winning the reward according to the instrumentality condition, he or she threw a die. Depending on the outcome of the throw, the subject was promised the reward or not. All subjects finished the procedure within one hour, and those who won the reward were told that it would be given after all subjects had participated. In reality, all subjects were given the highest reward in the week following the experiment.

Between-Subjects Independent Variables

Valence

In order to affect the anticipated satisfaction with the outcome of their performance, the subjects were told they could win a monetory reward. In the low-valence condition, subjects could win five guilders, an equivalent of about $2.50, which

---

[1] We would like to thank Chantal Couvreur, Esther Geven, Marja Stuifbergen, Renske Valk, and Larissa Wladimiroff for their help in the data collection.

would only allow them for example to buy a pack of cigarettes, and in the high-valence condition they could win 25 guilders. The subjects were asked how they planned to spend this money in case they would win it, as to increase the salience of the manipulation.

Instrumentality

The objective of the instrumentality manipulation was to affect the perceived relation between performance and the outcome of the performance. Subjects in the low-instrumentality condition were told that they were allowed to throw a die once for each set of eight problems finished correctly, and that throwing a six meant winning the reward. Subjects in the high instrumentality condition were told that they were allowed to throw the die three times for every set of eight problems finished correctly, and that throwing a six meant winning the reward.

Expectancy

The goal of this manipulation was to influence beliefs about the probability that a certain performance level could be obtained. The subjects in the low-expectancy condition were told that the average number of problems finished was 25 in 25 minutes, that is, a low probability of reaching it. The subjects in the high-expectancy condition were told that the average number of problems finished was ten, a high probability. Both of these conditions are plausible, because the subjects could relate this information to the trial problems, some of which were very easy and some were more time-consuming.

Within-Subjects Independent Variables

The following measures were obtained: (a) valence of performance, measured as the anticipated satisfaction associated with reaching 18 performance levels, ranging from 8 to 34 problems solved; (b) instrumentality, measured as the relation of performance and winning the reward for four levels of performance (8, 16, 24, and 32 problems); expectancy, measured as the subjective probability of successfully reaching the 18 performance levels; (d) force, measured directly as the rated motivation to reach the 18 performance levels. The scale used for all measures was a continuous 10-cm line, with anchors 0 and 100 on which the subjects could place a tick.

Dependent Variables

Two dependent variables were obtained: (a) a self-set goal, the number of problems the subjects indicated they planned to finish within the time given, and (b) performance, the number of problems finished correctly. This meant that if subjects did not find the correct answer, they repeated the problem until it was solved correctly.

RESULTS

Manipulation Checks

Expectancy

The manipulation check showed that we succeeded in creating two levels of expectancy. Those in the high-expectancy conditions perceived the average number of problems finished as a low performance, and in the low-expectancy condition as high performance, $M_{high} = 28.17$ vs. $M_{low} = 72.85$; range 0–100 on a continuous scale of 10 cm, $F(1, 78) = 9.29$, $p < .001$.

Instrumentality

The check measuring whether subjects believed that it was advantageous to finish many problems in order to win the reward did not differ for the subjects in the two instrumentality conditions. However, the wording of this single check may not have been appropriate, because the within-subjects instrumentality ratings, on which the subjects indicated the relation between performance and winning the reward for four levels of performance, did differ significantly between the two conditions. We interpreted this as a sufficient indication that the manipulation was indeed successful.

Valence

The reward was perceived as significantly less attractive by the subjects in the low-valence condition than by those in the high-valence condition ($M_{low} = 49.33$ vs. $M_{high} = 64.40$; $F = 2.15$, $p < .05$).

Between-Subjects Results

An overview of the between-subjects correlations is given in Table 10.1. As may be expected, the duration of solving the trial problems is highly related to the subsequent performance, and to a lesser extent, to the self-set goal. The indicators of ability, such as the experience with the train schedule and the self-rated knowledge of topography, are related to performance to a somewhat lesser extent. In particular, the duration of answering the trial problems is not related to the experience with the train schedule.

The effects of the experimental manipulations on the dependent variables are presented in Table 10.2. Analysis of variance, using experience with a train schedule

TABLE 10.1
Between-Subjects Correlations

	1	2	3	4
1. Performance	—			
2. Self-set Goal	.41**	—		
3. Duration Trial Problems	−.63**	−.37**	—	
4. Experience with Train Schedule	.33**	−.09	−.16	—
5. Knowledge of Topography	.33**	.01	−.20	.21

Note. N ranges between 76 and 79; ** $p < .01$.

TABLE 10.2
Analysis of Variance for VIE Variables on Self-set Goal and Performance (Using
Experience with Train Schedule and Knowledge of Topography as a Covariate)

		F	
Source	DF	Self-set Goal	Performance
Covariates	2	.39	8.43***
Experience with Train Schedule	1	.77	7.34**
Knowledge of Topography	1	.08	5.94*
Main Effects	3	2.91*	.35
Valence	1	.11	.50
Instrumentality	1	.91	.14
Expectancy	1	7.50**	.51

Note. * $p < .05$; ** $p < .01$; *** $p < .001$.

and knowledge of topography as a covariate, revealed that there are no main effects
of expectancy, instrumentality, or valence on performance, and no main effects of
instrumentality or valence on personal goal. There is a main effect of expectancy
on self-set goal contrary to our prediction: Subjects in the low expectancy condition set higher goals, $m = 21.61$, than those in the high condition, $m = 17.90$ or,
in other words, the higher the norm, the higher the goals set.

Within-Subjects Results

The manipulation of valence, instrumentality, and expectancy between subjects affected the level of ratings in the within-subjects functions. In addition, the shape of the VIE functions varied among subjects, and as these functions seemed to have four distinct shapes, we coded them. The decision as to which function a subject belonged to was based on the correlation between the VIE ratings and the performance levels. A high, > .50 positive or negative correlation was coded as an increasing or decreasing function, and a low correlation meant that a nonlinear regression was performed. If the variance explained by the nonlinear regression was higher, it was classified as an inverted U. No other shape of function was discovered. When no variance was explained, it was coded as a constant function. These four functions of force are each relevant to a particular theory of motivation (cf. Landy, 1994, p. 408; Thierry, 1998) and are shown in Fig. 10.1. We interpreted the increasing function as indicative of the goal setting theory of motivation, in which people are more motivated to perform more when the task is seen as challenging. The decreasing function appears to indicate that motivation is based on expectancy only: Motivation decreases as performance level increases, a realistic but pessimistic view. The inverted U function was interpreted as indicative of an optimal motivation level at the level of performance of which the probability of success and failure are judged equally, as, for example, in the theoretical notion of need for achievement. The interpretation of the constant function is that the subjects are indifferent towards the performance levels, and yet are highly or

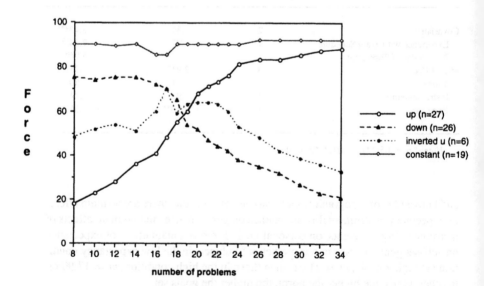

FIG. 10.1.   Mean force scores per function type.

TABLE 10.3
Classification of Subjects According to Type of VIE Function

	Valence	Instrumentality	Expectancy	Force
Increasing	65	72	—	27
Decreasing	—	1	72	26
Inverted U	3	—	7	6
Constant	10	6	—	19

moderately motivated. The codings were independent of between-subjects conditions of valence, instrumentality and expectancy. It can be seen in Table 10.3 that the classifications of the functions for the VIE variables are mainly as expected, whereas the force variable does not show a single dominant pattern.

An analysis of variance showed no differences in the dependent variables between the four coded groups. Subsequently, we repeated this procedure after removing the constant function, as these subjects may have been indifferent and may not have participated fully. An effect was found for force on the self-set goal: those who were coded as having a linear increasing function of goals set higher goals than those who had linear decreasing or inverted U functions of force, $F(56, 2) = 3.94, p < .05$. This would seem to support our tentative interpretation of the codings.

Gender Differences

The distribution of gender was found to be independent of the VIE conditions, $\chi^2(7) = 8.93, p > .20$ (see Wickens, 1989, for a discussion of the appropriateness of the use of the χ^2-test for small numbers), and men and women did not differ in their performance ($M = 18.83, SD = 5.80$) or task appreciation ($M = 43.97, SD = 29.37$). Although the number of women in the sample is small ($n = 11$), the results show interesting differences between men and women. Women set lower goals ($M_{women} = 17$ and $M_{men} = 20, t = 2.61, p < .05$), and performed more problems than for which they set their goal, whereas men performed less than their self-set goals (goal performance discrepancy: $M_{women} = -2.55$ vs. $M_{men} = 1.35, t = 2.02, p < .05$). Also, the average within-subjects VIE functions differed between men and women. Women were more easily satisfied with low performance levels, estimated the probability to win the reward significantly lower for the higher performance levels, and had lower expectancies for higher performance levels.

DISCUSSION

The manipulation of valence, instrumentality, and expectancy between-subjects affected the within-subjects VIE-functions. However, the manipulation did not affect performance, and self-set goals were only influenced by the expectancy manipulation, in that people set higher goals when average performance was introduced as high. This finding reflects the results of Tubbs et al. (1993) and Meyer and Gellatly (1988). In addition, four types of within-subjects functions for force were discovered.

Actual performance was not affected by the manipulation of the VIE variables. There may be at least two explanations for this result: first, the type of performance task may be one in which exerted effort is actually not seen, but this is not very likely. Perhaps controlling for previous experience as a measure of ability is not good enough and a better indicator of ability might have caused the effect of the VIE variables to appear; second, the manipulations to the group of subjects may not have been relevant for them. There are a few indications in favor of this argument, such as the constant within-subjects functions of some of the subjects and the failure of the instrumentality manipulation check: The participants were requested to indicate to what extent it was advantageous to finish more problems, but this may have been too strong in wording. Although the subjects indicated they perceived differences between the reward conditions, the fact that they could win a reward may not have been important to them. The expectancy manipulations appeared to have been more relevant: some subjects inquired how their friends had performed.

A related issue that limits our findings is that the manipulations were presented in the beginning of the experiment, so we can only say something about how the subjects started to work on the task and nothing about the process during the performance. Attitudes and other cognitive states may have changed throughout the task as a function of the subjects' own or the experimenters' behavior, or the passage of time.

Another limitation of this study is that the within-subjects force functions were coded based on post hoc judgments. We think that the functions reflect real differences, because those who had increasing force functions set higher goals for themselves, and the gender differences confirmed earlier findings. A replication study should be conducted in which the functions are predicted from individual difference variables. Another possibility is that the perception of the experimental situation may have been differentially influenced by variables such as boredom susceptibility, or the degree to which the subjects felt obliged to cooperate.

Although we found these differences between people in a laboratory setting, we expect them to be stronger in a situation where there is more room for different interpretations. That is, when a task or situation is unfamiliar and strong norms about performance are absent, the individual differences will be even more outspoken.

If the results relating to force can be replicated with a priori predictions about which subjects may respond according to the type of function, this would imply that different motivation theories may be appropriate for different groups of people. In an organizational setting, shared and individual work values, as well as individual differences may be relevant factors with important practical implications. The following study was conducted to explore variables that may have affected the functions for the subjects in the experiment.

FOLLOW-UP STUDY: INDIVIDUAL DIFFERENCES AND VIE FUNCTIONS

A follow up study was conducted 14 months after the experiment. A questionnaire was constructed to explore whether individual difference variables were related to the three dependent variables self-set goal, performance, and force function in the experiment. Also, measures that would provide information on the external validity of the dependent variables were collected: selection test data and grades.

First, reactions to the experimental situation may have influenced the responses in the experiment. Dominance was expected to influence the attitudes towards the experimenter, possibly leading to the effect in which the experiment may not have been taken seriously. We expected that those who had indifferent (constant) force functions, would score higher on dominance.

Second, those who have a positive view of themselves and life in general, and who see a task as an opportunity to learn, may have been more motivated in the experiment. The following variables were selected as potential explanatory variables: self-efficacy (Bandura, 1977), self-esteem (Rosenberg, 1965), optimism (vs. pessimism, Scheier & Carver, 1985), and learning orientation (vs. performance orientation, Button, Mathieu, & Zajac, 1995). These variables were expected to be related positively to the self-set goal and performance. And we expected that these variables would be higher on average for those who responded in an increasing force function, in comparison to the others who responded according to the decreasing, inverted U or constant function.

Finally, an attempt was made to establish external validity for the variables force functions, self-set goals, and performance. In the questionnaire, we requested permission to include archival data from tests obtained in the selection into the Dutch Royal Military Academy. The tests chosen for this study were achievement motivation, fear of failure (Hermans, 1968) and locus of control (Andriessen, 1972). We expected achievement motivation, and internal locus of control to be related to the self-set goal and performance in the experiment. It was expected that those who had increasing force functions would have higher scores on achievement motivation, lower scores on fear of failure, and would have an internal locus of control.

In addition, we collected the students' grades from the year in which the experiment took place. We expected the grades to be positively related to the self-set goal and performance in the experiment, and we expected the grades to be higher for those who had responded in the increasing force function, in comparison to those who had responded according to the other functions.

METHOD

Variables

A questionnaire was sent to the 79 participants of the experiment. The questionnaire contained the following scales (Cronbach's alpha's are given in Table 3): Dominance, 17 items from the Dutch Personality Test with three response categories: correct (2), ? (1), and incorrect (0) (Luteijn, Starren & Van Dijk, 1985). All other response scales ranged from 1 to 7. Self-esteem (Rosenberg, 1965), a 10-items scale; Performance and Learning Orientation (16 items) (Button, Mathieu, & Zajac, 1995); Self-efficacy regarding the experimental task was measured by two items: (a) I am good at looking up information in tables; (b) I am good at mental arithmetic; Optimism (4 items) and Pessimism (4 items) (LOT, Scheier & Carver, 1985).

In the questionnaire, the participants were requested permission to include the scores of the selection tests at the entry of the Military Academy. These had been gathered 2 to 6 years prior to the experiment. From these tests, three variables were collected: Achievement Motivation (range: 23 to 41), Fear of Failure (ranging from 0 to 8) (Hermans, 1968); and Locus of Control (Andriessen, 1972) (ranging from 0 to 9). This latter scale consists of two subscales: internal and external. The scores of the internal scale were reverse scored and summated, resulting in the degree to which a person has an external locus of control. Coefficient alpha's were not available for these test scores.

A third source of information was the school archive: grades of the past year were obtained for all participants in the experiment and averaged. The range of grades found was 5.20 to 8.13, whereas, in theory, they can range from 1 to 10.

To analyze the relation between the scales and the force functions, analyses of variance were performed, and if these revealed a difference between the conditions, univariate tests were performed between the functions.

RESULTS

Ten subjects could not be traced because they had moved, and 34 of the remaining subjects (49%) returned the questionnaire, 26 of which could actually be matched to the experimental data. A check for differential attrition was performed on the dependent variables of the experiment. The t-tests between those who did and did not send back the questionnaire revealed that no differential attrition had taken

TABLE 10.4

Descriptive Statistics, Coefficients Alpha, and Intercorrelations of the Follow-Up Questionnaire, Archival Data, and Dependent Variables from the Experiment

	n	m	SD	α	1	2	3	4	5	6	7	8	9	10	11	12	13
1. Dominance	31	2.38	.30	.68	—												
2. Optimism	33	5.42	.81	.69	.18	—											
3. Pessimism	33	2.51	1.00	.76	-.10	-.67**	—										
4. Performance Orientation	33	4.23	1.05	.85	-.13	-.57**	.42*	—									
5. Learning Orientation	33	5.80	.62	.80	.25	.69**	-.66**	-.40*	—								
6. Self-esteem	32	5.30	.45	.64	.26	.71**	-.56**	-.25	.62**	—							
7. Self-efficacy	33	5.03	1.41	.69	.19	.10	-.08	.00	.13	.07	—						
8. Grades	79	6.85	.59	—	-.39	-.04	-.09	.07	-.19	.18	-.32	—					
9. Achievement Motivation	15	3.53	4.87	—	.32	.40	-.43	.17	.33	.59*	.34	.15	—				
10. Fear of Failure	15	2.60	2.29	—	-.43	-.26	.13	.17	-.37	-.35	.12	-.07	-.23	—			
11. External Locus of Control	15	3.53	3.09	—	-.40	-.44	.32	.25	-.38	.23	-.39	.35	-.12	.18	—		
12. Self-set Goal	79	19.73	5.75	—	.25	.11	.29	.23	-.02	.09	.41*	-.35	.28	-.52*	.18	—	
13. Performance	79	18.86	5.30	—	-.08	-.10	.24	.04	-.19	-.28	.44**	-.35	.19	.07	.02	.41**	—
14. Gender	79	1.14	1.20	—	-.62***	.05	-.05	.30	-.13	-.25	-.14	.09	.09	.47	.41	-.20	.05

Note. Gender is coded as follows: Male = 1, Female = 2; * $p < .05$; ** $p < .01$; *** $p < .001$.

place that was related to the self-set goal: $t(74) = -.02$, $n.s.$, or performance $t(76) = -.38$, $n.s.$ An analysis of variance showed no differences between the force functions: ($F(3, 77) = 1.45$, $n.s.$).

Only 15 persons gave permission to obtain their information from the selection archive. Those who gave permission had set lower goals in the experiment ($m = 16.20$, $SD = 4.59$) than those who did not give permission ($m = 20.58$, $SD = 5.70$) ($t(74) = 2.77$, $p < .01$). Also, there was a difference on the force functions: those who gave permission to include the selection data were underrepresented in the group of subjects who had responded in an increasing force function as compared to the decreasing function ($F = 2.76$, $p < .05$, $m_{increasing} = .04$, $SD = .19$, $m_{decreasing} = .35$, $SD = .49$).

The intercorrelations between the scales and grades are given in Table 10.4. Of the variables in the questionnaire, only self-efficacy was related to the self-set goal ($r = .41$, $p < .05$) and performance ($r = .44$, $p < .05$) in the experiment. Table 10.5 shows the results of the analyses of variance. A significant difference in variation of self-efficacy according to the four force functions was found. However, there was no univariate effect, so that the expectation that those who had an increasing force function would have a higher self-efficacy for the experimental task cannot be confirmed.

Even for this small number of self-selected subjects who gave permission to view the data from the selection archive, fear of failure was significantly and negatively related to self-set goal in the experiment ($r = -.52$, $p < .05$). The other test results were not related to the dependent variables in the experiment.

The grades were unrelated to any of the variables in the experiment or the questionnaire.

TABLE 10.5
Analyses of Variance by Force Functions

	F
Dominance	2.11
Optimism	.27
Pessimism	.79
Performance Orientation	.06
Learning Orientation	1.62
Self-esteem	.48
Self-efficacy	3.17*

Note. $n = 26$, $df = 3$; * $p < .05$.

DISCUSSION

Although the response rate for the questionnaire was low, self-efficacy in the questionnaire was related to the self-set goal and performance in the experiment. Self-efficacy was found to be distributed unevenly over the force functions, but no univariate effect was found, and the significance is probably due to the large standard deviation in the inverted U function. The fact that performance and self-efficacy were related may or may not be an indication of real ability differences. The other variables in the questionnaire were not related to the dependent variables in the experiment.

The subjects who gave permission to include their selection test data were different from those that did not: they had set lower goals and had responded more often according to a decreasing force function. But even for this small group, fear of failure from the selection test was related to the self-set goal in the experiment.

The grades were not related to the dependent variables in the experiment, probably because of the lack of variance.

The low response rate makes this a purely exploratory study and these results are far from conclusive. Keeping this limitation in mind, some support for the external validity was obtained of the variables used in the experiment. The findings point to self-efficacy as the most important factor in predicting self-set goals and performance. Fear of failure may also influence self-set goals, but was not related to performance. In order to fully establish the validity of the within-subject functions, future research should ideally include an objective measure of ability, self-efficacy and fear of failure, and VIE functions, self-set goals, and performance.

REFERENCES

Andriessen, J. H. T. H. (1972). Interne of externe beheersing. [Internal or external control]. *Nederlands Tijdschrift voor de Psychologie, 27*, 173–198.

Arnold, H. J. (1981). A test of the validity of the multiplicative hypothesis of expectancy-valence theories of work motivation. *Academy of Management Journal, 24*, 128–141.

Bandura, A. (1977). Self-efficacy: Toward a unifying theory of behavioral change. *Psychological Review, 84*, 191–215.

Button, S. B., Mathieu, J. E., & Zajac, D. M. (1996). Goal orientation in organizational research: A conceptual and empirical foundation. *Organizational Behavior and Human Decision Processes, 67*, 26–48.

Campbell, D. J. (1982). Determinants of choice of goal difficulty level: A review of situational and personality influences. *Journal of Occupational Psychology, 55*, 79–95.

Cellar, D. F., Posig, M., Johnson, D., & Janega, D. (1993). Effects of social cues, task complexity, and sex on intrinsic motivation and task perceptions: A test of the task-instrumentality hypothesis. *Basic and Applied Social Psychology, 14*, 87–102.

Erez, M., & Zidon, I. (1984). Effect of goal acceptance on the relationship of goal difficulty to performance. *Journal of Applied Psychology, 69*, 69–78.

Folger, R., & Doherty, E. M. (1993). Perspectives on value creation: Variations on the energization model. *Basic and Applied Social Psychology, 14*, 421–436.

Graen, G. (1969). Instrumentality theory of work motivation. Some experimental results and suggested modifications. *Journal of Applied Psychology, 53*, 1–25.

Henry, R. A., & Strickland, O. J. (1994). Performance self-predictions: The impact of expectancy strength and incentives. *Journal of Applied Social Psychology, 24*, 1056–1069.

Hermans, H. (1968). *PMT*. Swets & Zeitlinger, Lisse.

Hollenbeck, J. R., & Brief, A. P. (1987). The effects of individual differences and goal origin on goal setting and performance. *Organizational Behavior and Human Decision Processes, 40*, 392–414.

Jorgenson, D. O., Dunnette, M. D., & Pritchard, R. D. (1973). Effects of the manipulation of a performance-reward contingency on behavior in a simulated work setting. *Journal of Applied Psychology, 57*, 271–280.

Klein, H. J., & Wright, P. M. (1994). Antecedents of goal commitment: An empirical examination of personal and situational factors. *Journal of Applied Social Psychology, 24*, 95–114.

Landy, F. J. (1994). *The psychology of work behavior* (5th ed.) Pacific Grove, CA: Brooks/Cole Publishing Co.

Locke, E. A., Latham, G. P., & Erez, M. (1988). The determinants of goal commitment. *Academy of Management Review, 13*, 23–39.

McCarthy, P. A. (1986). Effects of feedback on the self-confidence of men and women. *Academy of Management Journal, 29*, 840–847.

Mento, A. J., Locke, E. A, & Klein, H. J. (1992). Relationship of goal level to valence and instrumentality. *Journal of Applied Psychology, 77*, 395–405.

Meyer, J. P., & Gellatly, I. R. (1988). Perceived performance norm as a mediator in the effect of assigned goal on personal goal and task performance. *Journal of Applied Psychology, 73*, 410–420.

Mitchell, T. R. (1974). Expectancy models of job satisfaction, occupational preference and effort: A theoretical, methodological, and empirical appraisal. *Psychological Bulletin, 81*, 1053–1077.

Peters, L. H. (1977). Cognitive models of motivation, expectancy theory and effort: An analysis and empirical test. *Organizational Behavior and Human Performance, 20*, 129–148.

Pritchard, R. D., & Campbell, J. P. (1976). Motivation theory in industrial and organizational psychology. In M. D. Dunnette (Ed.), *Handbook of industrial and organizational psychology*. New York: John Wiley & Sons.

Pritchard, R. D., & DeLeo, P. J. (1973). Experimental test of the valence-instrumentality relationship in job performance. *Journal of Applied Psychology, 57*, 264–270.

Riedel, J. A., Nebeker, D. M., & Cooper, B. L. (1988). The influence of monetary incentives on goal choice, goal commitment and task performance. *Organizational Behavior and Human Decision Processes, 42*, 155–180.

Rosenberg, M. (1965). *Society and the adolescents' self-image*. Princeton NJ: Princeton Press.

Scheier, M. F., & Carver, C. S. (1985). Optimism, coping, and health: Assessment and implications of generalized outcome expectancies. *Health Psychology, 4*, 219–247.

Schwab, D. P., Olian-Gottlieb, J. D., & Heneman, H. G., III. (1979). Between-subjects expectancy theory research: A statistical review of studies predicting effort and performance. *Psychological Bulletin, 86*, 139–147.

Sleeper, L. A., & Nigro, G. N. (1987). It's not who you are but who you're with: Self-confidence in achievement settings. *Sex Roles, 16*, 57–69.

Thierry, H. (1998). Motivation and satisfaction. In P. J. D. Drenth, H. Thierry, & C. J. de Wolff (Eds.), *Handbook of work and organisational psychology* (Rev. ed.) Howe, England: Psychology Press.

Tubbs, M. E. (1993). Commitment as a moderator of the goal-performance relation: A case for clearer construct definition. *Journal of Applied Psychology, 78*, 86–97.

Tubbs, M. E., Boehne, D. M, & Dahl, J. G. (1993). Expectancy, valence, and motivational force functions in goal-setting research: An empirical test. *Journal of Applied Psychology, 78*, 361–373.

Tubbs, M. E., & Dahl, J. G. (1991). A within-persons examination of the effects of goal assignment on choice of personal goal. *Psychological Reports, 69*, 263–270.

Van Eerde, W., & Thierry, H. (1996). Vroom's expectancy models and work-related criteria: A meta-analysis. *Journal of Applied Psychology, 81*, 575–586.

Vroom, V. H. (1964). *Work and Motivation.* New York: Wiley.

Wanous, J .P., Keon, T. L., & Latack, J. C. (1983). Expectancy theory and occupational/organizational choices: A review and test. *Organizational Behavior and Human Performance, 32*, 66–86.

Wofford, J. C., & Goodwin, V. L. & Premack, S. (1992). Meta-analysis of the antecedents of personal goal level and of the antecedents and consequences of goal commitment. *Journal of Management, 18*, 595–615.

Wright, R. A., & Gregorich, S. E. (1991). Difficulty and instrumentality of imminent behavior as determinants of goal attractiveness. *European Journal of Social Psychology, 21*, 75–88.

Wright, R. A., Kelley, C. L., & Bramwell, A. (1988). Difficulty and effectiveness of avoidance behavior as determinants of evaluations of a potential aversive outcome. *Personality and Social Psychology Bulletin, 14*, 630–640.

Zedeck, S. (1977). An information processing model and approach to the study of motivation. *Organizational Behavior and Human Performance, 18*, 47–77

11

The Reflection Theory on Compensation

Henk Thierry
University of Tilburg, The Netherlands

Many work organizations are facing incisive changes, due to, for example, the increasing globalization of markets, the diversification of customer needs and expectations, technological innovations, the rising level of education of managers and employees, and, not the least, the emergence of different philosophies (or ideologies) of management. Consequently, "flexible" organization responses are required, including the redesign of organization structure (e.g., the introduction of business units), investments in new equipment (which leads to the obsolescence of some types of job and the creation of other ones), gaining access to unexplored markets (e.g., with customer-specified products and services), and different selection, training and education, and attrition strategies (in order to match managerial and employees' qualifications to current and future job requirements). Often, adaptive organizational responses also necessitate different leadership styles (e.g., more transformational behavior), a more supportive organizational culture, a better integrated human resource management (Pfeffer, 1994), a productivity level that exceeds the results gained by excellent competitors, and different instruments to motivate managers and employees.

Organizations differ greatly in how they tailor such adaptational policies and the actions to manage these. Basic to this chapter is the issue of *which role is*

149

usually assigned or attributed to financial compensation.[1] In many organizations, compensation is not considered to be a core strategic area (unless, of course, cost reductions are to be achieved through decreasing the pay level or reshuffling the pay structure). However, there are organizations using compensation in order to facilitate, or even to effect, organizational change (Lawler, 1980, 1990). Also, Gomez-Mejia and Balkin (1992) report in several studies that organizations in a more bureaucratic environment tend to use a compensation strategy that differs from the strategy identified in a more organic environment. Yet, many work organizations do not seriously consider using their total compensation package purposefully in the context of adaptive change. This may impede organizational change processes, but at least as important is the question why compensation is frequently so underutilized.

Remarkably, administrators and managers often have rather "extreme" beliefs about the impact of compensation upon work behaviors of employees and organizational performance. Some argue that pay is a more important reward category for eliciting effective performance behavior than any other outcome. Many more others hold, on the contrary, that pay is rather ineffective in this respect; although supportive research evidence is lacking, often (popularized versions of) Maslow's (1954) and Herzberg's, Mausner's, and Snyderman's (1959) ideas are referred to here. But many behavioral scientists also tend to underrate the impact of pay upon work behaviors. Current scientific jargon has it that pay is considered to be an extrinsic reward; intrinsic rewards (e.g., the experience to have meaningful work) are often believed to be more influential in eliciting effective and satisfactory work behaviors. It is our opinion that the intrinsic–extrinsic distinction is frequently misunderstood, and moreover tends to *blur* a better understanding of the role of financial compensation in affecting work behavior (e.g., Deci & Ryan, 1985; Thierry, 1990; Vinke, 1997).

Perhaps the conceptual confusion about the significance and effectiveness of pay is also due to the lack of a unifying, generally accepted theory on compensation. Moreover, psychological theories addressing pay have mostly not been explicitly designed with a focus on pay. Rather, psychological concepts and models regarding compensation stem from more general theories that address phenomena like motivation, learning, and social comparison. Most of these concern, for example, the notion of how pay may become important or meaningful to an individual organization member (Thierry, in press). But almost all theories fail to clarify which *kind of meaning* pay may have for that member; this neglect may explain why the intrinsic–extrinsic distinction could "move in" to help fill this gap.

It is here that our reflection theory on pay may shed some light. First, the theory's core characteristics will be described. Then, four meanings of pay will be highlighted, in the context of which several other (psychological and economic)

---

[1]In this text compensation is always understood in monetary terms. Concepts like pay, income, wage, salary, and remuneration are used liberally as akin to compensation.

theories on pay will be touched on. After a brief overview of the current status of the reflection theory, some suggestions for future research will be outlined.

REFLECTION THEORY

Background

The reflection theory on pay (Miedema, 1994; Shaw, 1996; Shaw & Jenkins, 1995; Thierry, 1992a, 1992b; Van den Heuvel & Thierry, 1995) was developed on the basis of some notions about meanings of pay, and addresses how pay through its meanings may affect an individual's behavior at work. As point of departure, we consider the development and maintenance of *self-identity* as an essential characteristic of the individual human being. The self-identity is a usually rather forceful principle for organizing a person's experiences, cognitions, emotions, interests, values, and preferences, with the purpose of establishing or maintaining his or her inner self. Through self-identity, the person is capable of integrating and unifying his or her past experiences with current events, preparing him or her to meet future challenges; Shamir, House, and Arthur (1993) coin this capability as "self-consistency." We assume, moreover, that the person is motivated to maintain his or her self-identity, and, if needed, to strengthen it. This implies that the individual person is scanning incoming information, among other things, from the perspective to which extent occurring changes in the "external" environment and in the self would necessitate behavioral action in order to maintain self-identity. Consequently, the person's behavior is to some degree initiated through the goal to restore, maintain, or enhance self-identity. Following Shamir et al. (1993), self-identity consists not only of individual, idiosyncratic components, but also of social, group- and societal-related, components. Both categories of components constitute the self-identity of the person, that is, his or her "construction" of who he or she is, as well as the meaning given to that construction (by others and the self). Shamir (1997) suggests interestingly that self-concepts (like self-identity) are more important in "weak" situations (Mischel, 1977) than in strong ones.

We assume that somebody who is regularly occupied with work (e.g., within an employment relationship), is particularly alert on scanning *work-related* information. Signals that changes in work are occurring may lead to a person's actions to effect internal and external changes in order to reaffirm his or her self-identity. An individual may "read" such signals to a large extent in performance results (of others and him- or herself), in power differentials, in leadership behaviors, in organizational rules and administrative procedures, in informal social relationships, and so forth. In interpreting such signals, the person will also compare him- or herself to referent others in order to confirm self-identity (Austin, 1977).

In a regular work situation, the pay an individual receives encompasses a variety of meanings that we consider to be vital to that person's self-identity. Of course, it is not exclusively compensation that conveys relevant information to the person.[2] Yet it is a very vital subject matter, which is expressing itself in terms of level (i.e., pay amount), structure (i.e., the design of the different pay forms and systems), differentials (i.e., differences in pay, both between people and over time), and administrative procedures (e.g., the extent of participation and degree of secrecy). Nonetheless, pay has no informational value and meaning in itself; pay gets significance, since it *refers* to other domains that are important to the individual person at work. That is why we call our theory a *reflection* theory of pay: pay "reflects" information about what is happening in other fields, the meaning of which connects to the person's self-identity. Pay does this through its amount, composition, differentials, and administrative procedures. Consider, for example, the case in which an employee's pay is almost exclusively determined by job value and tenure ("maturity"): this usually conveys the information to the employee that the level of his or her performance is not a very distinctive issue. Perhaps the employee's performance is closely monitored and taken for granted; possibly, a climate of trust has it that the employee takes responsibility for achieving good performance; it might also be that management considers performance measurement not to be feasible. Compare that to the business unit in which the application of performance-based pay signals to employees that the level of (group?) performance is vital to the unit's effectiveness. Particular targets are set that are supposed to challenge employees and managers to do their best. The performance bonus should add to that challenge as well as provide a reward for the result achieved.

Meanings of pay are also affected by the extent to which total pay is aligned to a company's strategic business policy. Lack of alignment would occur when strategic policy would, for example, stress the importance of innovative plans and actions (including suggesting new ideas, experimenting with new products, learning from failures, etc.), whereas pay policy would further stability in operations, experience, staying within the boundaries of one's job description, and so forth. This issue also addresses the degree in which main human resource practices (like selection, training, and performance appraisal) are tuned to the compensation domain, and vice versa.

Later, we return to the point how meanings of pay can be influenced by superiors and others. We now turn to the meanings pay may have. Four categories of meaning will be discussed: motivational properties, relative position, control, and spending.

Four Categories of Meaning
Motivational Properties

Pay is meaningful, according to the first category, to the extent that a person considers pay to be instrumental to effect his or her motives and personal goals.

---

[2]One other domain would be performance evaluation.

One example would be that an employee expects to gain more security in life by means of (a part of) his or her salary, for example, through buying an insurance policy. Another would be that a person expects to have influence upon other human beings, for example, through the status of the goods and services that he or she purchases. Also, the pay a manager or employee gets for the job level they occupy or for the quality of a particular job performance may be expected to provide an opportunity for getting recognition. These and other examples are based on expected means (pay) — > goal (motive) relationships. Such relationships may be modified through changes in the strength of relevant motives (e.g., when the need for exerting influence or control increases), and in the means other than pay to satisfy a need (such as when a new performance appraisal form hardly contributes to receiving signals of recognition). Also, changes in pay level or pay structure may lead to different actual or expected means — > goal relationships.

Theoretically, this meaning is rooted in the *instrumentality theory on pay*, as Lawler has proposed (cf. Lawler, 1971; Thierry, 1998), which is derived from the valence–instrumentality–expectancy theory on motivation (Van Eerde & Thierry, 1996; Vroom, 1964). Instrumentality theory holds that the importance of pay to an individual employee is determined by: (a) the extent to which he or she expects pay to be a vehicle to satisfy a motive and (b) the attractiveness or importance of that motive. Thus, as pay is seen as a signal of individual achievement and the experience of achievement is important to a person, pay is meaningful as a motivational property. However, as pay is considered to be indifferent in getting somebody's love, while the experience of love is pursued, pay is not meaningful *in that particular respect*. Another theoretical root of means — > goal relationships is embedded in the concept of *(partial) reinforcement*. Following Skinner's operant conditioning concepts (e.g., Skinner, 1969), such as in the Organizational Behavior Modification model (Luthans & Kreitner, 1985; Luthans & Stajkovic, 1999; Stajkovic & Luthans, 1997), it would not be necessary to assume the occurrence of "conscious" cognitions for making pay important to an individual. Particular behaviors are strengthened by effects that follow these behaviors. Consequently, pay may acquire secondary reinforcement properties, as it is tied directly and frequently to preceding performance actions or outcomes (initially jointly with primary reinforcers). Pay is meaningful, since it elicits and rewards preceding performance behaviors. But what will happen when a reward (like pay) is not given immediately subsequent to performance but after a while, and, moreover, in varied frequency rates? This "partial reinforcement" phenomenon has been shown in animal research to cause stronger and more persistent behaviors to occur than a "continuous" reinforcement schedule. Yet, evidence on partially reinforced human behavior, concerning, for example, planting of seedlings, catching small beavers, being absent from work, and sales performance, is ambiguous (Mawhinney, 1986; Thierry, 1998; Yukl & Latham, 1985; Latham, & Huber, 1992). Compared to instrumentality theory, the same dynamic concept is at stake in (partial) reinforcement models, that is behavior — > reward relationships, though not in a similar causal sequence.

According to instrumentality theory, the extent to which pay carries the meaning of motivational properties is determined by cognitions of the individual. Obviously, these cognitions are influenced—as we will see later—by various variables, some of which reside in a meso-level (e.g., kind of pay system; pattern of organizational culture) and a macro-level of analysis (like the industrial relations tradition within an economic sector). Still, it is the interpretation of the pay —> motive relationship given by the individual person, which is decisive for the motivational meaning pay has for that person.

Interestingly, the *neo-classical labor market theory*, which is of economic descent, also takes a means —> end perspective (which is *not* shaped by individual cognitions, however). The theory holds that the (effective) wage rate of a particular occupation is determined by the point on the curve where labor supply (employees looking for employment) and labor demand (vacant job positions) meet. To the extent that labor supply is abundant, wages are low; the more demand surpasses supply, wages are higher (cf. Cartter, 1959; Gomez-Mejia & Balkin, 1992). In other words, market forces determine the size of wages. The individual organization has no control whatsoever on wage levels; managers should merely observe the market rate and adjust the pay level. Another economic theory, the *neo-institutional model*, takes it that organizations tend to adopt systems, practices, and procedures that are applied by other organizations within their field (Balkin & Bannister, 1993; Dimaggio & Powell, 1984; Ross, 1957). Gerhart and Milkovich (1992) coin this conforming behavior as organizational "mimicry." Consequently, management should not only observe market rates, it should also make the company's wages conform to *relevant* others.

The latter two theories emphasize that the motivational meaning of pay (and other pay meanings as well) is not merely affected by individual cognitions and motives, but also to some extent by institutional factors.

Relative Position

Compensation is always embedded in a, more or less formalized, employment contract (e.g., Gerhart & Milkovich, 1992). In the individual contract, whether or not within the boundary conditions of a collective labor contract,[3] the employer and the employee lay down the contributions and the rewards they want to exchange. It is this *regulatory* character of work which qualifies pay's second-meaning category: relative position. In exchange for getting, in one way or another, a command (an assigned task) and for meeting particular performance requirements, the employee receives an agreed upon compensation (and other labor conditions). One of the ways in which regulation of work—the main purpose of which is the reduction of uncertainty about the other party's behavior—occurs is through setting goals, either

---

[3]Collective labor contracts are negotiated by employers' federations and unions, and are still prevailing in most countries in continental Europe.

self-set by the employee or assigned by somebody else. Short- and long-term goals specify the results that ought to be reached. The nature of the goal expresses also the degree to which more or less predictable behaviors of others—colleagues, superiors, suppliers, clients, and others—affect the work behavior of the individual worker.

This is a first aspect of relative position: Pay may allow the individual employee or manager to learn whether the set task was carried out well or whether ongoing task performance is on the right track. Thus, pay is an important component of goal-oriented task performance: It provides a signal that corrective actions are needed or that, if the same task is assigned again, a similar performance behavior cycle would be adequate. Pay has a strict feedback meaning: *it compares task performance with a standard or goal* (see also Greller & Parsons, 1995). The person does not only receive a financial reward for his or her work contribution, but also other rewards (like continued education, career opportunities, etc.). These rewards stem partly from the labor contract mentioned earlier; partly they are influenced by the particular task at hand, characteristics of mutual social relationships, and bio/demographical variables (like the career stage). There are no absolute standards to assess the fairness of these rewards: so the person compares his or her position to that of others in order to learn whether justice has been done. Here we meet the second aspect of relative position: pay reflects to the person *the evaluation (s)he got relative to significant social others*. Thus, pay's relative position meaning informs the employee or manager about his or her status within a group. This aspect relates to Lind's and Tyler's group-value model (Lind & Tyler, 1988; Tyler & Lind, 1992), which holds that people are concerned about their status within a group because a high status validates, for example, their self-identity. Hagedoorn (1998) shows that this concern is one explanatory factor for both distributive and procedural justice perceptions. Moreover, pay's relative position meaning informs the person also about the level of appreciation the organization has for him or her (usually voiced by the immediate superior), and, in a wider sense, about social evaluation yardsticks (e.g., DeCarufel, 1986).

This second meaning addresses two feedback characteristics: pay reflects the position of the person's task performance relative to a goal or standard, and it mirrors the position of his or her rewards received relative to the rewards significant others got. Various theories bear upon relative position (in addition to the group-value model and justice perceptions mentioned earlier). One perspective is that of *reward–contributions*, for example, as outlined by Barnard (1938) and March and Simon (1958) in terms of decisions taken by employees on their performance level. Belcher and Atchison (1976) note in their contract model that most expectations each party has about its own and the other party's contributions and rewards remain implicit. Current psychological contract research emphasizes the behaviors of one party concerned (mostly the employee), in particular when that party perceives the terms of the established contract to be violated (Robinson & Rousseau, 1994; Rousseau, 1989). Theories on *social comparison and equity* (e.g., Adams, 1965;

Hermkens, 1995; Homans, 1961) address, for example, the choice of the referent in "social" contribution—reward comparisons as well as the effects of perceived dissonance. A referent may be constituted by the person himself or herself (in the past or in the future, or regarding his or her own wants and preferences), another human being (whether or not interacting socially with the focal person), a group (Runciman, 1966), company policy, and institutional structures (cf. Berger, Zelditch, Anderson, & Cohen, 1972). The choice of who or what "significant social others" are—which concept is basic to the second aspect of relative position—is determined by the individual employee or manager.

Goal-setting theory (Locke & Latham, 1990a, 1990b) pertains to the first aspect of relative position: this theory specifies the conditions under which high and specific goals result in high performance. Evidence about the "additional" effect of pay on performance is mixed. Mowen, Middlemist and Luther (1981) showed that people with difficult goals had the highest performance with a piece rate system, whereas those with moderate goals did best with a bonus system that paid for goal success. Shikdar and Das (1995) found that when goals were set participatively, a large financial incentive resulted in higher performance. Bartol & Locke (2000) conclude that the effect of goal setting on pay may be phrased in terms of expectancy: if an individual believes that performing well leads to getting extra pay, pay for performance will motivate to perform higher.

In economics, a rather popular theory is tournament theory (e.g., Lazear & Rosen, 1981; Rosen, 1986). It conceives of relative position rather differently, as the company is seen as equaling an arena. On its playground competitive actors engage in games, which create winners and losers. The higher the performance, the better the pay, where differences in pay between two successive jobs should be so large that incumbents will perceive these and be motivated to exert at least as much effort as in their previous job. Pay differentials increase, moreover, as one moves up the ladder. Tournament theory helps in understanding that pay's relative position meaning is probably affected by company-internal asymmetrical power relations (as was earlier coined by us in terms of the "regulatory" nature of work).

The latter perspective is also taken by the well-known agency theory (cf. Eisenhardt, 1988; Holmstrom, 1979; Jensen, 1983; Nalbantian, 1987; Van Silfhout, 1995), which addresses the exchange process between two parties: principal and agent. Agency theory assumes that each party pursues his or her own interests and strives for maximum utility. What happens then if both parties' interests diverge? How should the principal (e.g., a manager) try to prevent that an agent (an employee) is taking it easy, looking for short-term gains, perhaps stealing company property, and so forth? That risk is easy to take if the principal is in a position to monitor the behaviors of the agent. But suppose that the costs for doing so are prohibitive, or that the agent is working on a geographically distant spot, or is perhaps a better expert than the principal. Then the principal will try to transfer the risk he or she runs through engaging the agent in an performance-outcome contract, which involves strong pay incentives, stock options, and the like. In return, the agent will bargain for a more stable pay level, or for more pay, and so forth.

Relative position as one of pay's meanings embodies two characteristics of regulation of work through an employment contract: achieved task performance relative to a goal or standard, and received rewards relative to significant social others. In particular, tournament theory and agency theory stress the asymmetrical power relationships within which these comparison processes occur. This characteristic qualifies the third meaning of pay.

Control

Since it is often the manager (whether or not in cooperation with others) who assigns tasks and sets goals, or helps in defining the boundary conditions within which employees set their own goals, another aspect of work regulation bears on the manager—employee relationship. Obviously, many others impact this relationship: Colleagues affect through their expectations, attitudes, and behaviors how tasks are performed (cf. Fishbein & Ajzen, 1975). An employee is moreover usually dependent on supporting activities from other units, the quality of equipment, opinions (and complaints) of customers, fluctuations on the stock market, and other conditions. This emphasizes the *network* of people and material means the employee is dependent upon. Dependence may be phrased in terms of relative power position; however, to avoid a confusion of terms, we will speak of *control*.

Thus, the control meaning of pay reflects to the person to which extent he or she regulates his or her own behavior and alters the behaviors of others toward what that person wants and, conversely, the extent to which the person's behavior is directed towards what others prefer. Pay, in other words, mirrors a manager's and employee's *rate of dependence*. Three aspects are distinguished:

Hierarchy. Somebody's job level specifies the organizational position of that person in general terms, such as authority level, responsibility for others, liability, and others. This implies the positioning of a manager or employee relative to incumbents having more, less, or an equal amount of power. Usually, pay levels and pay differentials correlate highly with this distribution. Jointly, they mirror the social position and remuneration of the job. Kipnis and Schmidt (1988) have shown that upward influence of a manager affects his or her salary level.

Role set. This embodies the organization members, groups, and units the person is dependent on to perform his or her work adequately. Role set is obviously also determined by hierarchical position. Thus, this set refers to the superior, staff members, supporting units, and subordinates whose expectations, attitudes, information, beliefs, values, and norms are of importance to the person. The person is also influenced by company-external actors, like customers, banks, and government agencies. In return, other organization members and external clients may be dependent on the person's views, values, and performance.

Autonomy and self-regulation. The individual's performance behavior is also affected by the nature and quality of the critical performance factors in his or her work (e.g., Pritchard, 1995). A first issue is whether those performance factors are indeed crucial to the job. A second concern is the extent to which the individual is able to regulate his or her performance and whether his or her performance quality affects these factors. A third point is the degree in which cooperation with others is vital to success in the job, such as when group tasks or project groups are at stake.

Of course, these three aspects are interrelated. Jointly, they explain that a person's compensation reflects the exertion of control *by and upon* that person. A manager or employee "reads" this meaning, similar to the other meanings, in the level of pay, in (the causes of) pay variation, in the (choices made in composing the) pay package, in the presence or absence of particular bonuses, and so forth.

Some of the theories touched upon in previous sections bear upon the control meaning of pay, such as instrumentality theory, tournament theory, and agency theory. As with relative position, control also relates to distributive and procedural justice. According to Thibaut's and Walker's *control model* (Hagedoorn, 1998; Thibaut & Walker, 1975), fairness perceptions do have an instrumental character. An individual strives for controlling his outcomes, either through determining these very outcomes or through the processes that result in these outcomes. So the more control that individual has over processes and outcomes, the fairer these are considered to be, whereas unfair outcomes may threaten a person's self-identity (cf. Brockner & Wiesenfeld, 1996).

Cognitive evaluation theory (e.g., Deci & Ryan, 1985; Vinke, 1997) holds that intrinsic motivation is high when a person perceives him or herself to be in a situation in which he or she constitutes the locus of control (and experiences to be competent as well). Yet, if an external source would control the outcomes that accrue to the person, the locus of control will shift from the person to the external source, causing intrinsic motivation to decrease. Performance-related pay would be an example of an external source, according to Deci and Ryan, and would consequently lead to less intrinsic motivation (see Thierry, 1990, and Vinke, 1997, for a critical review). Reflection theory suggests, however, that the more an employee reads the *degree of his or her dependence* in his or her pay, the more that employee's performance and satisfaction will be affected.

The *resource dependence model* (Balkin & Bannister, 1993; Pfeffer & Davis-Blake, 1987; Pfeffer & Salancik, 1978) stresses that the amount of control, of individuals or coalitions, is determined by the resources these "actors" are capable to provide or withhold. Whoever controls access to information, expertise, equipment, support and other resources—which are usually badly needed by a company—is gaining power and may effectively negotiate a comfortable pay level, an adequate pay structure, and so forth.

Both "relative position" and "control" are rooted in regulatory work processes. Yet each meaning highlights different—although interrelated—regulatory characteristics. Thus, we expect each meaning to be sufficiently independent. However, in some situations the two might partly overlap in practice.

Spending

The fourth category is perhaps slightly related to the first one. As "motivational properties" focus on pay as a source of *opportunities* to effect important motives and goals, spending addresses goods and services actually purchased through pay. But it is not the purchase itself that is at stake. Rather, spending reflects the extent to which motives and goals have been realized. In particular, it is the *utility* of spending, as well as the easiness or the hardship with which spending occurred.

Some theories mentioned in an earlier section apply to spending. Its mean −> goal relationship is outlined in *instrumentality theory*. By *comparing* the utility achieved with that of others, this meaning also relates to distributive and procedural justice perceptions. *Resource dependence theory* highlights sources of unequal spending opportunities. The *neo-classical labor market theory* and the *neo-institutional model* also bear upon such sources, mainly external to the organization.

MODEL

Core

Reflection theory holds that any pay system affects a person's behavior at work through the meanings which pay (through its level, structure, differentials, and procedures) reflects to that person. Figure 11.1 illustrates this.

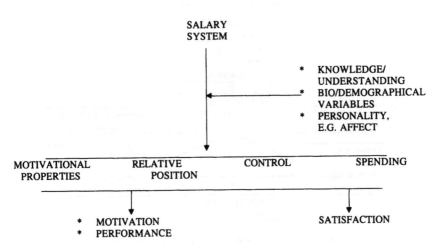

FIG. 11.1. Meanings of pay and work behavior.

The model outlined in Fig. 11.1 shows that a pay or salary system that is at least partly understood by an employee (or manager), affects that employee's performance and (pay) satisfaction more to the extent that this employee reads more meanings into his or her pay. In other words, as compensation is more "reflective" of events and changes in domains that connect to a person's self-identity, the person's performance and satisfaction level will be more influenced. Conversely, a pay system or form that is not very meaningful to a person will hardly impact that person's work behavior. There are no indications that the four meaning categories would differ in importance among each other. Yet, bio- and demographical variables, and personality characteristics (like negative affect), may have a moderating effect on meanings read in pay.

Multilevel

In discussing the four meaning categories (section 2), it was stressed repeatedly that some variables may impact a person's cognitions of these meanings and may also independently affect them. Fig. 11.2 contains a fuller model, including variables on various levels of analysis.

Reading Fig. 11.2 from the bottom line upwards, the "Applying Salary System" (box 1) equals "Salary System" in Fig. 11.1. Pay meanings are influenced by task characteristics (box 2), also since such characteristics may constitute the basis,

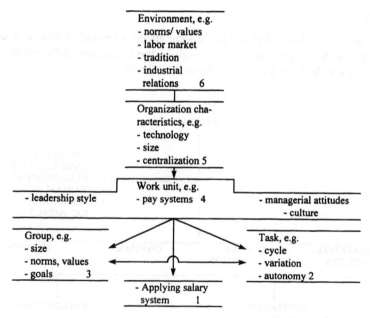

FIG. 11.2. Determinants of pay meanings.

through a regular process of task appraisal, for providing financial rewards. Group features impact pay meanings, such as the degree of mutual support in work and the nature of informal norms about an "adequate" performance level. The work unit (box 4) an employee belongs to encompasses not only the variety of applied pay and salary systems (perhaps differentiated according to category of personnel), but also leadership style (e.g., extent of feedback provided) and managerial attitudes and culture (such as more innovation or more rule oriented). All variables in boxes 2 to 4 are supposed to determine pay meanings directly. The aspects included in boxes 5 and 6—about organization characteristics, respectively environmental features—probably have an indirect effect.

In other words: There are some opportunities for choice. Managers may shape, to some extent, the total pay package for their employees.[4] They may try to strengthen the particular meanings (and, accordingly, the particular components of self-identity) to which means − > goal relationships apply, focussing, for example, on (individual) pay for performance plans. Also, the enhancement of self-efficacy may be furthered, for example, through skill-based pay. Moreover, managers may try to reinforce justice perceptions, perhaps through increasing the fixed part of the monthly pay. Alternatively, pay's control meaning may be addressed, for instance, by offering cafeteria plan options. On the contrary, managers may deemphasize some pay meanings (in particular, relative position and control) by outlining to their employees the determining impact of institutional (extra-organizational) factors upon which they cannot exert any control, and so forth.

REFLECTION THEORY IN PERSPECTIVE

Current Status

Most research on the reflection theory is occurring in the Netherlands. Miedema's study (1994) made a sizable contribution, by operationalizing the four meanings in four scales. More than 3,500 employees from organizations in industry and construction, commercial services, and the governmental and noncommercial sector participated in her research. Confirmatory factor analyses by means of LISREL showed that the predicted four-factor structure of pay meanings is supported. Shaw (1996) administered these scales to 182 MBA students at two regional universities in the southern United States. It was found that a three-factor solution provided for the best fit (relative position and control converged into one feedback factor).

Miedema (1994) also showed that, among some other determinants, both relative position and spending contributed to explaining pay satisfaction of employees. Shaw's data indicated that all four pay meanings explain considerably more variance in pay satisfaction than any other determinant. More recent research (which

---

[4]As the CEO may do for members of the management team, and so forth.

will not be detailed here) reveals that pay meanings usually explain a sizable part of pay satisfaction variance. However, while relative position always contributes, the contribution of the three other meanings varies; this may be due to differences in the nature of applied pay systems at stake. Since it is hard to assemble individual performance data, there is until now only one study in which pay meanings were related to both performance and satisfaction. The results suggest that performance level is not directly affected by pay meaning scores, but in an indirect way: pay meaning relates to pay satisfaction, which in turn correlates with performance. Further research should provide more evidence concerning both individual and group performance levels.

Some Research Issues

In a study by Langedijk (1998) pay meaning scores were related to choice behavior in a cafeteria pay plan (according to which employees may select alternative work conditions). Pay meanings appeared to be less predictive than expected. It has caused us to enlarge the current item pool with items that probably cover more pay systems and forms.[5] Obviously, more comparative research is welcome.

Our main research concerns bear upon themes that are related to the models shown in Figs. 11.1 and 11.2. First, the degree of *commitment* might moderate the effect of pay meanings on both performance and satisfaction. As commitment would be low, it is possible that even high scores on pay meanings do not have much impact upon both performance and satisfaction. But as commitment is higher, rather low pay meaning scores might be effective. Distinguishing between "instrumental" commitment on the one hand and both "affective" and "normative" commitment on the other, a higher level of instrumental commitment might relate mainly to a higher performance level, whereas higher affective and normative commitment might cause primarily more pay satisfaction. In other words: Commitment might be a condition for pay meanings to be effective.

Another condition might reside in the degree of *trust* between managers and employees, in the extent to which employees *participate* in designing, introducing, or administering a pay system, and, more in general, in the level of *organizational citizenship*. Pay meanings are thus supposed to be effective, contingent on particular "high-involvement" characteristics. This assumption is confronted with reflection theory's hypothesis that the extent of involvement is already embedded in how much a person reads meaning into his or her pay.

Following the model outlined in Fig. 11.1, the variable of knowledge/understanding was measured in several studies. It seems to be an obvious assumption: in order to impact somebody's work behavior, a pay system should be understood to some extent by that person. Data repeatedly show that this is *hardly* the case: Scores on perceived knowledge do not affect pay meanings, whereas factual knowledge

---

[5]Both item pools are available from the author.

has a minor impact. We speculate that the degree of understanding a person has of a particular pay system does not affect the impact that system has on the person's behavior, unless that person perceives that the pay system's outcome deviates from what he or she expected. Then additional information is needed to acquire more understanding. This line of "speculated" reasoning would be in agreement with a reinforcement, or control theory, perspective. This third concern surely calls for more research.

Finally, it is interesting to combine research on reflection theory with that on justice perceptions. In particular, relative position and control seem to reflect both distributive and procedural justice components. This suggests a rewarding common domain for future research.

ACKNOWLEDGEMENTS

The author has profited much from critical comments and suggestions made by Gerard Evers, Miranda Langedijk, Paul van der Maesen, Anat Rafaeli, Reiny van Silfhout, and Bob Wood.

REFERENCES

Adams, J. C. (1965). Inequity in social exchange. In L. Berkowitz (Ed.), *Advances in experimental social psychology* (Vol. 2). New York: Academic Press.

Austin, W. (1977). Equity theory and social comparison processes. In J. M. Suls, R. L. Miller (Eds.), *Social comparison processes*. Washington, D.C.: xxx

Balkin, D. B., & Bannister, B. D. (1993). Explaining pay forms for strategic employee groups in organizations: A resource dependence perspective. *Journal of Occupational and Organizational Psychology, 66*, 139–151.

Barnard, C. I. (1938). *The functions of the executive*. Cambridge, MA: Harvard University Press.

Bartol, K. M., & Locke, E. A. (2000). Incentives and Motivation. In: S. L. Rynes & B. Gerhart (Eds.). *Compensation in Organizations*. San Francisco: Jossey Bass.

Beatty, R. P., & Zajac, E. J. (1994). Managerial incentives, monitoring and risk bearing: A study of executive compensation, ownership and board structure in initial public offerings. *Administrative Science Quarterly, 39*, 313–335.

Belcher, D. W., & Atchison, T. A. (1976). Compensation for work. In R. Dubin (Ed.), *Handbook of work, organization and society*. Chicago: Rand McNally.

Berger, J., Zelditch, M. B., Anderson, B., & Cohen, B. P. (1972). Structural aspects of distributive justice: A status value formulation. In J. Berger, M. Zelditch, & B. Anderson (Eds.), *Sociological theories in progress* (Vol. 2). Boston: Houghton-Mifflin.

Brockner, J., & Wiesenfeld, B. M. (1996). An integrative framework for explaining reactions to decisions: Interactive effects of outcomes and procedures. *Psychological Bulletin, 120*, 189–208.

Cartter, A. M. (1959). *Theory of wages and employment*. Homewood, IL: Irwin.

DeCarufel, A. (1986). Pay secrecy, social comparison, and relative deprivation in organizations. In J. G. Olson, C. B. Herman, & M. P. Zauna (Eds.), *Relative deprivation and social comparison: The ontario symposium*. Hillsdale, NJ: Erlbaum.

Deci, E. L., & Ryan, R. M. (1985). *Intrinsic motivation and self-determination in human behavior.* New York: Plenum Press.

Dimaggio, P., Powell, W. (1984). The iron cage revisited: Institutional isomorphism, and collective rationality in organizational fields. *American Sociological Review, 48,* 147–160.

Eisenhardt, K. M. (1988). Agency and institutional theory explanations: The case of retail sales compensation. *Academy of Management Journal, 31,* 488–511.

Eerde, W. Van, & Thierry, H. (1996). Vroom's expectancy models and work-related criteria. *Journal of Applied Psychology, 81,* 575–586.

Fishbein, M., & Ajzen, I. (1975). *Belief, attitude, intention and behavior. An introduction to theory and research.* Reading, MA: Addison-Wesley.

Gerhart, B., & Milkovich, G. T. (1992). Employee compensation: Research and practice. In M. D. Dunnette, L. W. Hough (Eds.), *Handbook in industrial and organizational psychology* (2nd ed., Vol. 4). Palo Alto, CA: Consulting Psychologists Press.

Gomez-Mejia, L. R., & Balkin, D. B. (1992). *Compensation, organizational strategy, and firm performance.* Cincinnati, OH: South-Western Publishing Company.

Greller, M. M., & Parsons, C. K. (1995). Contingent pay systems and job performance feedback. *Group and Organization Management, 20,* 90–108.

Hagedoorn, M. (1998). *Employees' reactions to dissatisfying situations: Multi-method research with justice-based predictors.* Unpublished doctoral dissertation, University of Groningen.

Hermkens, P. (1995). Sociale vergelijking en rechtvaardigheid van beloning (Social comparison and justice of pay). *Gedrag en Organisatie, 8,* 359–371.

Herzberg, F., Mausner, B., & Snyderman, B. B. (1959). *The motivation to work.* New York: Wiley.

Heuvel, H. van den, Thierry, H. (1995). Over de reflectietheorie: Betekenissen van beloning (On the reflection theory: Meanings of pay). *Gedrag en Organisatie, 8,* 372–386.

Holmstrom, B. (1979). Moral hazard and observability. *Bell Journal of Economics, 10,* 74–91.

Homans, G. C. (1961). *Social behavior: Its elementary forms.* New York: Harper, Brace & World.

Jensen, M. C. (1983). Organization theory and methodology. *Accounting Review, 58,* 319–339.

Kipnis, D. & Schmidt, S. W. (1988). Upward influence styles: Relationships with performance evaluations, salary and stress. *Administrative Science Quarterly, 33,* 528–542.

Langedijk, M. C. (1998). *Flexibel belonen: de keuze voor arbeidsvoorwaarden op maat* (Flexible compensation: the choice for tailor made working conditions). Assen (The Netherlands): Van Gorcum.

Latham, G. P., & Huber, V. L. (1992). Schedules of reinforcement: Lessons from the past and issues for the future. *Journal of Organizational Behavior Management, 12,* 125–149.

Lind, E. A., & Tyler, T. R. (1988). *The social psychology of procedural justice.* New York: Plenum.

Lawler, E. E. (1971). *Pay and organizational effectiveness.* New York: McGraw-Hill.

Lawler, E. E. (1980). *Pay and organization development.* Reading, MA: Addison-Wesley.

Lawler, E. E. (1990). *Strategic pay.* San Francisco: Jossey-Bass.

Lazear, E., & Rosen, S. (1981). Rank order tournaments as an optimum labor contract. *Journal of Political Economy, 89,* 841–864.

Locke, E. A., & Latham, G. P. (1990a). Work motivation: The high performance cycle. In U. Kleinbeck, H. H. Quast, H. Thierry, & H. Häcker (Eds.), *Work motivation.* Hillsdale, NJ: Erlbaum.

Locke, E. A., & Latham, G. P. (1990b). *A theory of goal setting and task performance.* Englewood Cliffs, NJ: Prentice-Hall.

Luthans, F., & Kreitner, R. (1985). *Organizational behavior modification and beyond.* Glenview, IL: Scott, Foresman & Company.

Luthans, F., & Stajkovic, A. D. (1999). Reinforce for Performance: The Need to go Beyond Pay and Even Rewards. *Academy of Management Executive, 13,* 49–57.

March, J. G., & Simon, H. B. (1958). *Organizations.* New York: Wiley.

Maslow, A. H. (1954). *Motivation and personality.* New York: Harper & Row.

Mawhinney, T. C. (1986). Reinforcement schedule stretching effects. In E. A. Locke (Ed.), *Generalizing from laboratory to field settings.* Lexington, MA: Heath & Company.

Miedema, H. (1994). *De achterkant van het salaris* (The reverse side of salary). Assen (The Netherlands): Van Gorcum.

Mischel, W. (1977). The interaction of person and situation. In D. Magnuson & N. Endler (Eds.), *Personality at the crossroads*. Hillsdale, NJ: Lawrence Erlbaum.

Mowen, J. C., Middlemist, R. D., & Luther, D. (1981). Joint Effects of Assigned Goal Level and Incentive Structure on Task Performance: A Laboratory Study. *Journal of Applied Psychology, 66,* 598–603.

Nalbantian, H. R. (1987). Incentive compensation in perspective. In H. G. Nalbantian (Ed.), *Incentives, co-operation, and risk sharing. Economic and psychological perspectives in employment contracts.* Ottowa: Rowan & Littlefield.

Pfeffer, J. (1994). *Competitive advantage through people.* Boston: Harvard Business School Press.

Pfeffer, J., & Davis-Blake, A. (1987). Understanding organizational wage structures: A resource dependence approach. *Academy of Management Journal, 30,* 437–455.

Pfeffer, J., & Salancik G. R. (1978). *The external control of organizations: A resource dependence perspective.* New York: Harper & Row.

Pritchard, R. D. (1995). *Measuring and improving organizational productivity: a practical guide.* New York: Praeger.

Robinson, S., & Rousseau, D. M. (1994). Violating the psychological contract: Not the exception but the norm. *Journal of Organizational Behavior, 15,* 245–259.

Rosen, S. (1986). Prizes and incentives in elimination tournaments. *American Economic Review, 76,* 701–715.

Ross, A. M. (1957). The external wage structure. In G. W. Taylor, & F. C. Pierson (Eds.), *New concepts in wage determination.* New York: McGraw-Hill.

Rousseau, D. M. (1989). Psychological and implied contracts in organizations. *Employee Responsibilities and Rights Journal, 8,* 121–139.

Runciman, W. (1966). *Relative deprivation and social justice.* London: Routledge & Kegan Paul.

Shamir, B., House, R. J., & Arthur, M. B. (1993). The motivational effects of charismatic leadership: A self-concept based theory. *Organization Science, 4,* 577–594.

Shamir, B. (1997, March). *Leadership in boundaryless organizations: Disposable or indispensable?* Paper presented at the WORC Symposium on Transformational Leadership, Tilburg, The Netherlands.

Shaw, J. D. (1996). *A confirmatory factor analysis of pay meaning dimensions on an English-speaking sample.* Paper presented at the 1996 Southwest Academy of Management Conference.

Shaw, J. D., & Jenkins, G. D. (1995). *The role of pay meaning knowledge of the pay system, pay for performance perceptions and actual salary in determining group pay satisfaction.* Paper presented at the 1995 Annual meeting of the Southern Management Association.

Shikdar, A. A., & Das, B. (1995). A field study of worker productivity improvements. *Applied Ergonomics, 26,* 21–27.

Silfhout, R. K. van (1995). De effectiviteit van prestatiebeloning (The effectiveness of pay for performance). *Gedrag en Organisatie, 6,* 399–418.

Skinner, B. F. (1969). *Contingencies of reinforcement.* Englewood Cliffs, NJ: Prentice-Hall.

Stajkovic, A. D. & Luthans, F. (1997). A meta-analysis of the effects of Organizational Behavior Modification on task performance. *The Academy of Management Journal, 40,* 1122–1149.

Thibaut, J., & Walker, L. (1975). *Procedural justice: A psychological analysis.* Hillsdale, NJ: Lawrence Erlbaum.

Thierry, H. (1990). Intrinsic motivation reconsidered. In U. Kleinbeck, H. H. Quast, H. Thierry, & H. Häcker (Eds.), *Work motivation.* Hillsdale, NJ: Lawrence Erlbaum.

Thierry, H. (1992a). Pay and Payment systems. In J. Hartley & G. Stephenson (Eds.), *Employment relations: The psychology of influence and control at work.* Oxford, England: Blackwell.

Thierry, H. (1992b). Payment: Which meanings are rewarding? *American Behavioral Scientist, 35,* 694–707.

Thierry, H. (1998). Compensating work. In P. J. D. Drenth, H. Thierry, & C. J. De. Wolff (Eds.), *Handbook of work and organizational psychology* (Rev. ed., Vol. 4). Hove (England): Psychology Press.

Thierry, H. (in press). Enhancing Performance Through Pay and Reward Systems. In: S. Sonnentag (Ed.), *Psychological Management of Individual Performance*. Chichester: John Wiley.

Tyler, T. R., & Lind, E. A. (1992). A relational model of authority in groups. In M. Zanna (Ed.), *Advances in experimental social psychology*. San Diego: Academic Press.

Vinke, R. H. W. (1997). *Motivatie en belonen: De mythe van intrinsieke motivatie* (Motivation and compensation: The myth of intrinsic motivation). Deventer, The Netherlands: Kluwer.

Vroom, V. H. (1964). *Work and motivation*. New York: Wiley.

Yukl, G. A., Latham, G. P. (1985). Consequences of reinforcement and incentive magnitudes for employee performance: Problems encountered in an industrial setting. *Journal of Applied Psychology, 29*, 221–231.

II

The Group Level

INTRODUCTION—*UWE KLEINBECK*

Part 2 focuses on work motivation at the team level. Responsibility for work is shifting from individuals to work teams, and our knowledge of work motivation in teams is not keeping pace with this shift. Facing this situation of a changing world of work, **Chapter 11, by Daniel R. Ilgen and Lori Sheppard**, proposes a comprehensive model of *motivation in work teams*. The model assumes that motivation in teams presents a dilemma requiring trade-off between team-level and individual-level needs, goals and payoff. Team members must receive rewards that can be associated with individual level performance, but if these associations are too tightly established, team functioning often breaks down. Performance measurement, feedback, goals, job design, and incentive systems are the primary sources of influence on motivation in teams, and within each of these domains exist means of addressing a number of the complexities of individual motivation in teams. Recognizing the nature of the constructs and establishing contingencies between behaviors and outcomes as illustrated in their model should aid in addressing motivation in teams.

Uwe Kleinbeck, Jürgen Wegge, and Klaus-Helmut Schmidt, in their chapter, *"Work Motivation and Performance in Groups,"* propose a theoretical model that examines the relationship between group motivation and group effectiveness. The model describes four determinants of work motivation and group effectiveness: (a) the motivating potential of the group tasks; (b) the dispositional motives of group members, with the group composition of members with different motive profiles crucial for understanding effective team performance, (c) task and socially related factors in the *process* through which motivational states and group goals are translated into action and achievement, and (d) contextual variables, such as compensation systems. The chapter further discusses the causal links between all the variables in the model.

Jen A. Algera, in the chapter *"Performance Management for Self-managing Teams and Organizational Control Systems,"* presents a method for enhancing team motivation. In particular, he focuses on the design and implementation of the Productivity Measurement and Enhancement System (ProMES). The development of valid performance indicators is essential in this system. ProMES has been implemented mainly for work teams on the shopfloor level. However, the success of this type of intervention in practice is heavily dependent on the organizational context. The consistency of performance indicators throughout the whole organization turns out to be a necessary condition for successful implementation of ProMES. For this reason, his chapter proposes how performance indicators from a psychological viewpoint, such as ProMES, can be combined with performance indicators on the organizational level, including financial and logistic indicators. Algera's paper is mainly focused on the design of valid performance indicators.

George Graen examines the effect of leadership in project teams. The title of his chapter captures his approach: *"Approaches to Leadership: Toward a Complete Contingency Model of Face-to-Face Leadership."* The novel idea advocated is that contingencies can be applied to team settings. Specifically, contingencies may change during the life cycle of a team project, and they may be best understood at the dyadic level. In this context, Graen distinguishes between three types of leadership: leader based, relationship based, and follower based. He then identifies three contingencies that should be examined: problem ownership—or the domain of work, resources, and legitimacy. Graen proposes that when the leader possesses all three factors, the leader-based approach yields superior results. The follower-based approach is most effective when the follower possesses these three factors, and the relationship-based approach is the preferred one when both the leader and the followers share the three factors.

12

Motivation in Work Teams

Daniel R. Ilgen and Lori Sheppard
Michigan State University

Primary responsibility for work in organizations is shifting from individuals to teams (Hackman, 1987; Ilgen, 1994; Ilgen, Major, Hollenbeck, & Sego, 1995). To some, this shift goes beyond normal change to a revolutionary restructuring of the way work is accomplished. *Fortune* magazine ran a cover story entitled "The End of the Job," in which it was suggested that the whole concept of a job is outdated (Bridges, 1994). Few go as far as Bridges. However, regardless of how radical one views the expanded use of teams in organizations, there is little doubt that tasks and jobs formally assigned to individuals are today often accomplished by teams. Now, more than ever, organizational effectiveness depends on the performance of persons who work in teams.

Distributing work to teams shifts the unit of responsibility for work from individuals to teams and introduces a number of fundamental processes that exist only at the team level. Coordination, cooperation, cohesiveness, and conflict are just a few of the phenomena that play a crucial role in effective team performance but have no comparable analog at the level of individual performance. Yet, individuals, not teams, are the ones promoted, transferred, trained, and rewarded in organizations.

Most research and writing on team performance is descriptive, focusing on interaction processes within teams by exploring various inputs to these processes

169

and outcomes resulting from them (Hackman, 1987)[1]; that is, team interaction processes are the mediators between inputs brought to and impacting on these processes and key team outputs. In contrast to the descriptive approach, Hackman offered a normative model of work-team effectiveness. Work-team processes remained a central concern, but, rather than simply describe what teams do, he addressed what teams *should* do to be effective. The focus was on conditions in teams' environments that were potentially able to be manipulated. Normative models provide means for diagnosing the strengths and weaknesses of teams as performing units in such a way as to lead to recommendations for designing and influencing teams to perform effectively.

Our purpose is similar. It is both normative and descriptive as we focus on the motivation of individuals who are members of teams in organizations.

INDIVIDUALS' MOTIVATION IN TEAMS

Motivation is an internal state of the individual that influences the direction, intensity, and persistence of behavior (Kanfer, 1990). This internal state exists at some level regardless of the setting. Consistent with many others (e.g., Atkinson & Birch, 1978; Kanfer, 1990; Kanfer & Ackerman, 1989; Naylor, Pritchard, & Ilgen, 1980; Vroom, 1964), we view motivation as manifested in choices, choices to invest time and effort in various activities. These activities have direction and intensity and, when the individual's activity is measured over time, persistence. At any moment, the individual may or may not be aware of the choices made about investing time and effort. However, although through the establishment of habits or routines (Weiss & Ilgen, 1985) the individual may not be aware of choices that are made, it is assumed that these choices, at some earlier point in time, were consciously considered by the person and were influenced by some subjective evaluation of the consequences of choosing various alternative courses of action (Naylor et al. 1980; Vroom, 1964).

In the remainder of this chapter, we present a model of motivation in team settings. The model is based on the assumption that, in general, team members allocate personal resources of time and effort to behaviors that facilitate or inhibit team effectiveness. Their allocation of time and effort is based on their beliefs and expectations about their capability to perform the behaviors and their beliefs about the links of these behaviors to outcomes they value. The motivational theories of

---

[1] In this paper, we shall use teams to refer to collectives of two or more persons who interact with one another, are interdependent, and have a set of shared goals. Often such units have been called groups in the small groups literature. Although a distinction can be made between teams and groups (e.g., Guzzo & Salas, 1995), we shall not make a distinction because we feel it is often quite arbitrary. Rather, we shall use single label, teams, for units that possess the characteristics just mentioned regardless of whether authors whose work we cite called them teams or small groups.

Atkinson and Birch (1978), Kanfer (1990) and Naylor et al. (1980) represent the foundation on which our position rests. Although, since our concern is with teams, we shall not go into nearly the level of detail offered by these other positions for individual behavior.

The teams of interest are imbedded in organizations and have some identifiable task(s) to perform. The relationship between team members and the organization is assumed to be an exchange relationship that operates within the normal bounds of an employment contract, both implicit and explicit. That is to say, work team members are far from indifferent about their association with their organization and their team, but their association rarely is based entirely on the intrinsic value of the team task or other team members, as may be the case for amateur sports teams or families.

A MODEL OF MOTIVATION IN TEAMS

Figure 12.1 presents our model of individuals' performance in teams. Before discussing it in detail, two boundary conditions should be raised. First, since the focus of the model is on the motivation of *individual* team members, antecedents of team performance effectiveness are limited to those outcomes that are the result of team member behaviors. Team environmental characteristics such as the quality

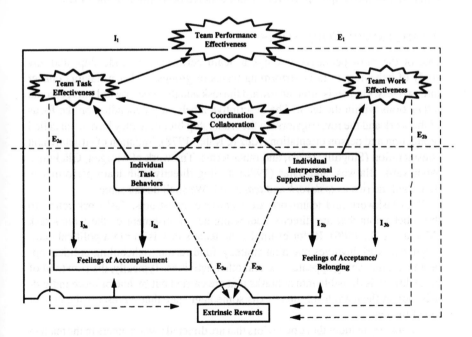

FIG. 12.1. A model of individuals' motivation in teams.

of technology or the availability of other resources to the team are beyond the scope of the model, although it is recognized that such factors often have strong influences on team performance.

The second issue is that of the level of analysis. Teams by their very nature are multilevel units. Some constructs (e.g., coordination) operate at the team level and have no analog at the individual level. Others, such as performance, exist at both the individual and the team level. While not downplaying the importance of multi-level issues, in the brief amount of space we have here we have chosen to address motivation in teams only at the individual level. Team-level issues are worked through the boundary between the individuals that make up the team and the team itself as we address the impact of team variables on individuals. To emphasize the differences in levels, in Fig. 12.1, team-level constructs are represented by stars and individual-level ones by boxes. A permeable boundary is drawn between the two. This boundary also represents an aggregation discontinuity. Constructs above the boundary represent aggregates of the team members in which aggregates are not necessarily averages but depend on the nature of the construct. Those constructs below the boundary are within individual ones. Arrows from below the boundary to above it are individuals' contributions to the team-level phenomena, and feedback loops from above represent team-level conditions that get fed back to individual team members through the latter's perceptions of the team-level phenomena. The remainder of the chapter provides a more detailed description of the model.

Team-Level Constructs

One of the most pervasive findings in team performance, leadership, and any study of behaviors in task-performing teams or groups, is that behaviors cluster into two sets. One set is directed toward the task and the other toward interpersonal interactions within the team. The descriptive labels vary depending on the focus of the work and the investigators. In the leadership literature they have been called production and person orientation (Katz & Kahn, 1978), initiation of structure and consideration (Stogdill, 1974), and other terms. The work of Morgan, Glickman, Woodward, Blaiwes, and Salas (1986) dealing directly with team performance described the two as *taskwork* and *teamwork*. We shall do the same.

Both taskwork and teamwork are team-level constructs. Taskwork refers to those behaviors that are directly addressing accomplishment of the team's task (Morgan et al., 1986). If, for example, the team's task is to run a political campaign, taskwork involves planning strategy, fund raising, scheduling political appearances, managing appearances, and other activities. Typically, the sum total of the taskwork is divisible into subtasks that are carried out by one or more individuals, but, at the team level, there exits some aggregate that represents the task or job of the team.

Teamwork includes those behaviors that are directed toward others in the team in contrast to the task itself. McIntyre and Salas (1995) proposed several dimensions of teamwork, four of which are particularly salient in all kinds of team-task settings:

performance monitoring, feedback, closed-loop communication, and backing-up behaviors. Performance monitoring is the extent to which team members keep track of the work of their fellow team members. Effective teams in a navy simulation task were those that developed norms for members to check on one another with the intention of helping each other accomplish the team task (Morgan et al., 1986). Feedback takes the monitoring one step further, providing team members with information about their own behavior and that of others. Effective team members both accept feedback about themselves and give feedback to others about their behavior. Closed-loop communication among team members is where the members are committed to making sure that the receiver of communications receives the message intended by the sender. Behaviorally, McIntyre and Salas suggest that the receiver must give some indication that he or she received a communication, and the sender must double-check that the received message was the intended message. Thus, closed-loop communication is similar to what most mean by simply effective communication, where the criteria of effectiveness are specified.

The final dimension of teamwork described by McIntyre and Salas (1995) is that of backing up teammates. Observations of teams indicated that better performing teams were composed of team members who were more likely to step in and help team members who needed help, and both those helping and those receiving help were unlikely to feel that needing it was a sign of weakness.

Taskwork and teamwork encompass a large number of behaviors in teams, but, as described, none deal with the critical needs of interacting team members to combine their behaviors in an overall team effort and/or to discuss, plan, and develop ways for working together. Coordination, collaboration, strategic planning, cooperation, and other team-level processes do not cluster clearly with teamwork or taskwork. There are elements of each in many team processes. Therefore, in our model we have separated out those team-level behaviors that are interactions among two or more team members. The nature and amount of these behaviors required for team effectiveness is strongly influenced by the task. For example, some team tasks may require little or no coordination among team members if the members work primarily alone and pool their products. Other team tasks may require high levels of coordination across time. Planning, developing the initial strategies for coordination and cooperation, and adjusting these strategies over time are all elements of all three team-level constructs illustrated in Fig. 12.1.

Individual-Level Constructs

All models of team performance effectiveness recognize that team-level performance outcomes result from the collective inputs of team members.[2] With this recognition, the vast majority of research then focuses on the effects of group

---

[2]Obviously, technology, support systems, and other conditions in teams' environments also affect team performance. However, for our purposes here, we are limiting our attention to those factors influenced by those who comprise the team.

interaction processes that affect team performance. Traditional models of team effectiveness go so far as to consider all inputs to team performance mediated by team interaction processes (Hackman, 1987). Hackman modified the traditional model somewhat by suggesting that team inputs directly affected team performance as well as interaction processes, but the emphasis remained on the team-level interaction processes.

While not denying the importance of team interaction processes on team effectiveness, we suggest that the exclusive emphasis on these team-level processes directs attention away from consideration of team member contributions. Motivationally, it is necessary to understand those factors that influence each team member's willingness to contribute his or her time and effort in such a way that the team performs effectively.

At the individual level, behaviors can be clustered into two primary sets—those directed toward tasks and those directed toward others on the team. The task-directed behaviors will vary, depending on the nature of the team's task and the subtasks allocated to specific individuals. Although a number of taxonomies have been offered for team tasks (e.g., Hackman & Morris, 1975; McGrath, 1984; Steiner, 1972), no one taxonomy dominates. For our purposes, the specific nature of the behaviors is unimportant. It is only important to recognize that team tasks usually are subdivided in some fashion. At any given time, each team member works on some part of the team effort. These parts may be done in relative isolation, in collaboration with others, or members may coordinate effort on their subtasks by working on them in some order. Often coordination requirements are a prescribed part of an individual's job. In other cases, they evolve as the team member performs his or her job in the team setting. In either case, individual-level task behaviors may link to joint behaviors represented by coordination and collaboration within the team.

The second set of behaviors illustrated in Fig. 12.1 are those directed to others on the team, either individually or as a team. These behaviors represent the socioemotional and supportive behaviors that constitute teamwork as described earlier. They may also support the collaboration and coordination process in such a way as to be difficult to disentangle from the latter.

The final set of elements in the figure are the outcomes individuals may receive as a result of their presence in the team. Consistent with motivational theories that see behavior as a function of the actor's commitment of time and effort to a course of action (e.g., Atkinson & Birch, 1978, Kanfer, 1990; Naylor et al., 1980), the extent to which the outcomes to be described influence the two sets of behaviors just described is related to beliefs about the association between the behavior and receipt of the outcome. The associations are the team member's perception of the contingency between his or her behavior and the outcome.

The outcomes of the model are classified into three sets. Feelings of accomplishment are those outcomes associated with both the performance of the task of the member herself or himself and from the team performance. The job design literatures (e.g., Campion & McClelland, 1993; Griffin, 1983; Hackman & Oldham,

1976, 1980) clearly have shown the importance of this outcome and its link to the nature of the job at the individual level. Since team members also contribute to the team's performance, it is expected that members may also experience a feeling of accomplishment resulting from the team's performance. Such feelings are seen as intrinsic to the task in the sense that they can be thought of as given to the member by himself or herself (Naylor et al., 1980); agents or conditions outside the person cannot provide feelings of accomplishment, per se. They can only provide conditions likely to lead the person to be able to experience such feelings. The lines of the model labeled I_{3a} and I_{2a} illustrate the member's perceived contingency between task behaviors (team or individual) and feelings of accomplishment. Finally, by isolating the team-task portion of overall team performance from that of teamwork and other behaviors on the team, we are suggesting that feelings of accomplishment are affected by overall performance. The solid line, I_1, represents this contingency.

In a similar fashion, feelings of acceptance and belonging are critical socially referenced outcomes potentially available to team members as a result of their interpersonal behaviors and association with the team. They are part of what Hackman (1987) calls the "group synergy." Just as is the case with feelings of accomplishment, others outside the focal person cannot provide him or her with feelings of acceptance or belonging; others can only create conditions likely to influence the extent to which the person will experience such feelings. Thus, we would argue that, in a way analogous to that with the task-directed behavior, group synergy provides conditions intrinsic to performing the behavior for motivating members socio-emotionally, and these outcomes in team settings result from the team members' behavior toward each other. The contingencies between a member's own behavior and that of the outcomes is represented by the line I_{2b} in the figure, and those between the behaviors of others on the team with I_{3b}. Furthermore, overall team performance may impact feelings of acceptance and belonging (I_1). Staw (1975, 1976) and others (DeNisi & Pritchard, 1978) showed that team members' ratings of cooperation and support among team members were directly affected by team performance. In all cases, positive correlations were found between member ratings and the level of team performance reported to the members prior to their ratings when the performance reports were *independent of* actual team performance.

In contrast to feelings of accomplishment and of acceptance or belonging are those outcomes that are not inherent in the behavior itself but are associated with it. The common characteristic among these outcomes is that contingencies between behaviors and them are typically created or established in the actor's (team member's) environment, although the perceptions of the contingencies obviously exist within the person's belief system. Pay is a commonly considered outcome of this nature, but many other outcomes fit this type of association. Promotions, recognition, and status are some examples. In all cases, there is nothing inherent in the behavior itself that would lead to the outcome. Policies and practices, reward system characteristics, supervisory or coworker responses, and other conditions encountered by the team members establish conditions that are likely to lead to perceptions of contingencies between team and/or individual behaviors and the receipt of the outcome. The dotted lines in Fig. 12.1 represent contingencies to outcomes that are imposed by the situation, whereas solid lines are to outcomes that result from the behavior itself in interaction with the actor's reactions to that behavior.

The distinction between the two sets of outcomes is consistent with what has been considered intrinsic and extrinsic outcomes with respect to individuals' motivation. For White (1959) and Ryan (1970), two outcomes were intrinsic to performing the task, personal control over the way in which the task was done and feelings of accomplishment that resulted from doing the task. Both of these points of view strongly influenced motivational considerations of job design (Campion, 1988; Campion & McClelland, 1991, 1993). The Job Characteristics model of Hackman and Oldham (1976, 1980) most clearly captures the intrinsic emphasis on the design of jobs. Extrinsic outcomes, on the other hand, are simply the remaining outcomes not included in the intrinsic subset. Although incentive and reward systems incorporate a number of extrinsic outcomes, pay is the one that has received the most attention.

The intrinsic–extrinsic distinction has a number of possible contributions to make to understanding motivation in teams. First, just as tasks have outcomes that are intrinsically associated with the nature of the task itself, we argue that teams have similar contingencies regarding social behaviors. Thus, the potential of the team for providing such outcomes is controlled primarily by the nature of the team design and the people who populate the team. Second, the distinction between the two outcomes provides a way of looking at the dilemma of attaching rewards to team or individual performance. The distinction clarifies that the dilemma relates only to extrinsic outcomes; by their very nature, intrinsic outcomes are associated with the task itself and really cannot be arbitrarily attached to one or the other (teams or individuals). The association is determined as soon as the task is designed. At the same time, the nature of the association between extrinsic rewards and either individual or team performance may influence both the display and nature of the association among interpersonal behaviors, teamwork, and team process (coordination/collaboration). These possible effects have been ignored in the past. We believe that they deserve consideration.

Individual- versus Team-Level Rewards

The primary controversies in team motivation arise from two well-established facts. The first of these is that outcomes tend to function best as rewards or incentives to individual performance the stronger the contingency between the outcomes and the behaviors of the individual, assuming that the outcomes are valued by the individual (Lawler, 1981). From the time that Thorndike presented his Law of Effect to the present, data support this conclusion whether the association is expressed in the stimulus–response terms of reinforcement theory or cognitive theories in which beliefs represent the connections.

The second well-established fact is that, in teams, making explicit and strong contingencies between *individual* team members' task behaviors and extrinsic outcomes often has very detrimental effects on team members' willingness to work together. Strong incentives for individual performance frequently create competitive relationships among team members and decrease cooperation (Johnson, Geofrey, Johnson, & Nelson, 1981). As a result, the team performance and interpersonal outcomes, such as cohesion or supportiveness, often suffer.

The two conditions above are in contradiction. The first suggests that individual members of teams will be most highly motivated to perform particular behaviors when the contingencies between the individuals' behaviors and the outcomes are strong. The latter implies that creating strong individual contingencies to rewards will decrease the probability of cooperative behavior and thus lower team performance. Argote and McGrath (1993) described the conflict of these two conditions as a classic dilemma facing teams.

Two responses to the conflict between the two conditions are frequently suggested. Neither, in our opinion, is satisfactory. One is to attempt to reward only team performance. Demming (1986) argues that performance appraisals or other policies and practices that emphasize individual performance or accomplishments must be eliminated in teams. The basis for this position is making salient and rewarding individual performance interfere with the willingness of team members to work for the good of the team rather than their own self-interest. Others simply have ignored individual-level contingencies. Profit sharing, gain sharing, and other compensation systems based on the performance of the firm or some identifiable unit of it are attempts to focus employees on the performance of the larger unit and encourage them to coordinate, cooperate, and work together with others for the common good of the unit.

The second general response to the tension between individual gain and the collective's performance is to continue to associate rewards with individual behaviors but to attach these rewards to behaviors that are not directly associated with either the team's task performance or the individual's task behaviors, per se. In particular, rewards are associated with developing new skills that should have potential for contributing to team performance, but the rewards themselves come from the total number of potentially important skills the team member possesses. Such reward systems are labeled skill-based pay systems (Lawler, 1981) and are frequently advocated for settings where work is organized into teams.

Although both the above approaches are in response to counteracting forces between individual and collective needs, they do so in very simplistic ways. The former ignores legitimate issues at the individual level in an effort to accommodate team process issues. The latter directs individual attention to an auxiliary set of skill-building behaviors, presumably assuming that these skills, once learned, will facilitate team performance and that taking direct attention away from individual task performance will allow more effective team-level processes to emerge.

CONCLUSIONS

The motivation of individuals in teams creates dilemmas—dilemmas between levels and dilemmas between types of outcomes. Like any dilemma, there exists no solution that optimizes on all dimensions. To address dilemmas, one must first recognize they exist and then consider the potential impact of alternative courses of action for dealing with them. These actions will represent a set of trade-offs. The model of Fig. 12.1 implies that the design of the team task and pattern of interactions among persons on the task creates the motivational potential for the team by its intrinsic motivational potential. The creation of paths to extrinsic rewards are added to the task over and above the design of the task. Whether the ties to extrinsic outcomes enhance or inhibit overall team motivation can only be decided empirically, although already existing literature on team and individual performance offer guidance with respect to what may be expected. Performance measurement, feedback, goals, job design, and incentive systems are the primary sources of influence on motivation in teams, and within each of these domains exist means of addressing a number of the complexities of individual motivation in teams. Recognizing the nature of the constructs as outlined in the model and establishing contingencies between behaviors and outcomes as illustrated should aid in addressing motivation in teams.

REFERENCES

Argote, L., & McGrath, J. E. (1993). Group processes in organizations: Continuity and change. In C. L. Cooper & I. T. Robertson (Eds.), *International review of industrial and organizational psychology*. Chichester, England: Wiley.

Atkinson, J. W., & Birch, D. (1978). *An introduction to motivation* (Rev. ed.). New York: Van Nostrand.

Bridges, W. (1994, September 14). The end of the job. *Fortune*, 62–74.

Campion, M. A. (1988). Interdisciplinary approaches to job design: A constructive replication with extension. *Journal of Applied Psychology, 73,* 467–482.

Campion, M. A., & McClelland, C. L. (1991). Interdisciplinary examination of the costs and benefits of enlarged jobs: A job design quasi-experiment. *Journal of Applied Psychology, 76,* 186–198.

Campion, M. A., & McClelland, C. L. (1993). Follow-up and extension of the interdisciplinary costs and benefits of enlarged jobs. *Journal of Applied Psychology, 78,* 339–351.

Demming, W. E. (1986). *Out of the crisis.* Cambridge, MA: MIT Press.

DeNisi, A. S., & Pritchard, R. D. (1978). Implicit theories of performance as artifacts in survey research: A replication and extension. *Organizational Behavior and Human Performance, 21,* 358–366.

Griffin, R. W. (1983). Objective and social sources of information in task design: A field experiment. *Administrative Science Quarterly, 28,* 184–200.

Guzzo, R. A., & Salas, E. (1995). *Team effectiveness and decision making.* San Francisco: Jossey-Bass.

Hackman, J. R. (1987). The design of work teams. In J. Lorsch (Ed.), *Handbook of organizational behavior* (pp. 315–342). Englewood Cliffs, NJ: Prentice-Hall.

Hackman, J. R., & Morris, C. G. (1975). Group task, group interaction process, and group task performance effectiveness: A review and proposed integration. In L. Berkowitz (Ed.), *Advances in experimental social psychology* (Vol. 8, pp. 45–99). New York: Academic Press.

Hackman, J. R., & Oldham, G. R. (1976). Motivation through the design of work: Test of a theory. *Organizational Behavior and Human Performance, 16*, 250–279.

Hackman, J. R., & Oldham, G. R. (1980). *Work redesign.* Reading, MA: Addison-Wesley.

Ilgen, D. R. (1994). Jobs and roles: Accepting and coping with the changing structure of organizations. In M. G. Rumsey, C. B. Walker, & J. H. Harris (Eds.), *Personnel section and classification* (pp. 13–22). Hillsdale, NJ: Erlbaum.

Ilgen, D. R., Major, D. A., Hollenbeck, J. R., & Sego, D. (1995). Decision making in teams: Raising an individual decision model to the teal level. In R. A. Guzzo & E. Salas (Eds.), *Team decision making in organizations* (pp. 113–148). San Francisco: Jossey-Bass.

Johnson, D. A., Geofrey, M., Johnson, R., & Nelson, D. (1981). Effects of cooperative, competitive, and individualistic goal structures on achievement: A meta-analysis. *Psychological Bulletin, 81*, 47–62.

Kanfer, R. (1990). Motivation theory and industrial and organizational psychology. In M. D. Dunnette & L. M. Hough (Eds.), *Handbook of industrial and organizational psychology* (2nd ed., Vol. 1, pp. 75–170). Palo Alto, CA: Consulting Psychologist Press.

Kanfer, R., & Ackerman, P. L. (1989). Motivation and cognitive abilities: An integrative/aptitude-treatment interaction approach to skill acquisition. *Journal of Applied Psychology, 74*, 657–690.

Katz, D., & Kahn, R. L. (1978). *The social psychology of organizations* (2nd ed.). New York: Wiley.

Lawler, E. E. (1981). *Pay and organization development.* Reading, MA: Addison-Wesley.

McGrath, J. E. (1984). *Groups: Interaction and performance.* Englewood Cliffs, NJ: Prentice-Hall.

McIntyre, R. M., & Salas, E. (1995). Measuring and managing for team performance: Lessons from complex environments. In R. A. Guzzo & E. Salas (Eds.), *Team effectiveness and decision making in organizations* (pp. 9–45). San Francisco: Jossey-Bass.

Morgan, B. B., Jr., Glickman, A. S., Woodward, E. A., Blaiwes, A., & Salas, E. (1986). *Measurement of team behaviors in a navy environment* (NTSC Rep. No. 86-014). Orlando, FL: Navy Training Systems Center.

Naylor, J. C., Pritchard, R. D., & Ilgen, D. R. (1980). *A theory of behavior in organizations.* New York: Academic Press.

Ryan, T. A. (1970). *Intentional behavior: An approach to human motivation.* New York: Ronald Press.

Staw, B. M. (1975). Attribution of the "causes" of performance: A general alternative interpretation of cross-sectional research on organizations. *Organizational Behavior and Human Performance, 13*, 414–432.

Staw, B. M. (1976). Knee-deep in the big muddy: A study of escalating commitment to a chosen course of action. *Organizational Behavior and Human Performance, 16*, 27–44.

Steiner, I. D. (1972). *Group process and productivity.* New York: Academic Press.

Stogdill, R. M. (1974). *Handbook of leadership: A survey of the literature.* New York: Free Press.

Vroom, V. H. (1964). *Work and motivation.* New York: Wiley.

Weiss, H. M., & Ilgen, D. R. (1985). Routinized behavior in organizations. *Journal of Behavioral Economics, 14*, 57–67.

White, R. W. (1959). Motivation reconsidered: The concept of competence. *Psychological Review, 66*, 297–333.

13

Work Motivation and Performance in Groups

Uwe Kleinbeck, Jürgen Wegge, and Klaus-Helmut Schmidt

University of Dortmund
Dortmund, Germany

WORK MOTIVATION AND GROUP EFFECTIVENESS: A CONCEPTUAL MODEL

Managers responsible for the design of work organization in Germany are more and more making use of group work as a basic principle of work organization (Antoni, 1994). Stimulated by the Japanese competitors, managers in car production and the machine construction industry started in the beginning of this decade to introduce group work in combination with increased efforts to improve productivity. One of the reasons they had in mind for such a change in work organization, from individual to group organization, was to design conditions for a better work motivation of their organizational members. They perceived work motivation as an influential factor for increasing flexibility and productivity of work. Although most of the managers had no conceptual knowledge of the psychological background for their interventions, they persistently stuck to their belief in the advantages of group work. In many cases they were deeply convinced that group work would help them to overcome their difficulties to stand the challenges arising from worldwide competition.

No doubt, there are conditions under which group work as an organizational principle will have a good chance to increase work motivation and thereby performance; however, studies on social loafing, for example, have documented (Karau & Williams, 1993) that the conceptual network for understanding the relations between group performance and work motivation is not so simple (McGrath, 1984); there might also be conditions in group work leading to a decrease in motivation (Shepperd, 1993) and thereby performance, too (French, 1958). To design group work that stimulates a high work motivation and an effective performance, it therefore should be helpful to consider a theoretical model and some of the empirical results collected to evaluate its validity. Models useful to be considered in this context have been developed, for example, by French (1958), Hackman (1987) and Weldon and Weingart (1993).

Our own research was strongly influenced by these authors. We designed studies in the organizational psychology lab and in the field to get a better understanding of the complex network of those variables responsible for group effectiveness and to support the designers of organizations in their efforts to improve the conditions for high work motivation and high productivity. The conceptual framework we used to derive our hypotheses focusses on the relation between work motivation of group members and group effectiveness. It states that higher motivation of group members will result in higher productivity in groups. Productivity is defined as the extent to which a group uses its resources to reach its goals. The model describes four determinants of work motivation and group effectiveness:

1. The *motivating potentials* of group tasks; they are—from the motivational point of view—the basic factors of the task structure;
2. The *motives* of group members; they represent dispositional individual factors constituting the personality of the group members. The composition of groups with persons who have different motive profiles may be important for successful group work.
3. Some variables concerning the *process through which motivational states and group goals are translated into action and achievement*; these variables can be divided into two groups. In the first group are those variables which are *task related*; the most important example is (task) *feedback*. In the other group we find *social variables* defining the degree of cooperation and understanding between group members;
4. *Contextual variables*, for example, *compensation systems* (see Fig. 13.1);

THE MOTIVATING POTENTIAL OF GROUP WORK

For a large group of researchers (see, for example, Hackman, 1987) the most important determinants of the motivating potential of group work are *task contents*. Hence, the design of the task is one crucial factor for the strength of the

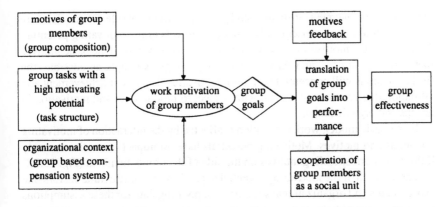

FIG. 13.1. Determinants of work motivation and group effectiveness.

motivating potential of the job. Using an old German concept, it is possible to summarize important components of the motivating potential of the task in a set of statements describing the course of an action. It was called by Hellpach (1922) the concept of the complete task. A complete task is composed of the following factors:

- Setting of personal goals that can be embedded in higher-ordered goal structures
- Preparations to take over responsibility of planning functions
- Choice of means for task accomplishment, including the necessary social interactions for adequate goal attainment
- Performance with process feedback to trigger necessary changes in action
- Action control with outcome feedback and with the opportunity to observe the fit between action outcomes and goal standards

The concept of the complete task describes the motivating potential from the perspective of an *achievement-oriented relation* between persons and tasks. In this respect, it is similar to the motivating potential of a job as it was described by Hackman and Oldham (1975). They defined it as composed of variables like task variety, job identity, imortance of the job, autonomy, and feedback. Other person–task relations also important for the effectiveness of groups in our organizations are described by concepts like *affiliation* and *power*. Group members have to work together as social partners in a group, and there will be incentives and requirements for using power to influence group members. Therefore, these issues of power and affiliation are also part of the motivating potential of work.

The above mentioned classification of components of the motivating potential of work (achievement, power, and affiliation) corresponds with the one that has been used for motives by McClelland (1987). In his theory of human motivation, the motives for achievement, affiliation, and power play a central role. Of course, there are other motives and consequently also other aspects of the motivating potential, for example, the motives of curiosity, aggression, anxiety and all the basic motives like sexuality, hunger, and thirst. For keeping things as simple as possible, the further sections will concentrate on those motivational issues of achievement and affiliation that are most important with respect to productivity and motivation in groups and organizations.

In our basic model, work motivation is affected by the interaction of motivating potentials and motives. Motivating potentials have an impact on motivation only if there are corresponding motives on the side of the group members (Fig. 13.2).

The strength of the motivating potential depends on some structural factors like task contents and organizational structures. Supporting data for these assumptions come from a set of field studies. They were done some years ago and are described by Kleinbeck (1987) and Schmidt and Rutenfranz (1989). The achievement motive (Atkinson, 1958; Heckhausen, 1989) and the achievement-related motivating potential were measured in three field studies; the results of these studies clearly demonstrated that the motivating potential of work (achievement oriented in content) influenced the attitudes (e.g., job satisfaction) ant the behaviors of persons with a high achievement motive more than those with a low one.

A convincing illustration for the validity of our approach comes from an older study reported by French (1958). She measured two motives (achievement and affiliation) and realized two experimental conditions to establish an achievement-related motivating potential on the one side and an affiliation-related one on the other. To present the situation as achievement related, she gave feedback during the task sessions directed to the individual abilities and efforts of group members (achievement-related feedback). The affiliation-related motivating potential was

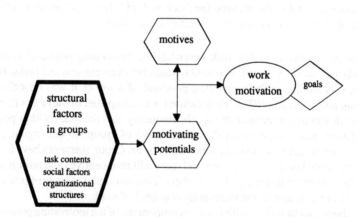

FIG. 13.2. Structural factors in groups as determinants of the motivating potential of work.

realized by giving feedback directed to the good cooperation between members of the group (affiliation-related feedback). Moreover, she instructed her subjects ($N = 256$) in two different ways. One group of participants in the experiment was asked to cooperate closely and find consensus with respect to task solution (group orientation); the other part had no such instruction (individual orientation).

Four subjects were allocated to one group. Each group member received five sentences, and their task was to put them together to form a complete story. Each group was composed of persons with a homogenous motive profile: Either the achievement motive was high and the affiliation motive was low or the affiliation motive was high and the achievement motive was low. Feedback was given during two short breaks during the experimental procedure.

The results show that the groups with a high achievement motive performed better when the feedback was given achievement related. Groups with a high motive for affiliation performed better when the feedback focused on the cooperation of their members (Fig. 13.3). The orientation given by the different instructions had no effect for groups in which the members had a high achievement motive. In groups with members having a high affiliation motive, the group orientation contributes to a high performance. There was no main effect of the three independent factors—the motive constellation, the instructional work orientation and the feedback—only the interactions between motives and feedback, $F = 60.83$; df 1/56; $p < 0.001$, and motives and orientation, $F = 6.29$; df 1/56; $p < 0.05$, proved to be significant.

Results like these indicate that motivating potentials and motives can explain different strengths of work motivation and perhaps group performance, but a positive relation between work motivation and performance does not turn out automatically. Whether high motivation really results in high effectiveness depends very much on the *process* through which motivation is translated into action.

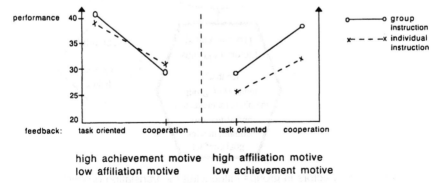

FIG. 13.3. Interaction between two motives and two motivating potentials (affiliation and achievement orientation).

FACTORS IN GROUPS INFLUENCING
THE TRANSLATION OF MOTIVATION
AND GOALS INTO ACTION

It is well-known by all of us that not every goal developed as a result of the interaction between motives and motivating potentials is realized in action. And even if persons start a goal-oriented action they sometimes are opposed to a lot of difficulties in pursuing these goals persistently. Therefore it becomes necessary for a psychology of work motivation in groups to take a closer look at the process by which goals are translated into action (Fig. 13.4).

As we know from the work of Locke and Latham (1990), goals influence behavior through various mechanisms (giving direction to behavior or controlling persistence) moderated by a set of variables such as task structure and goal commitment (these variables are called moderators). The most important factor for guaranteeing effectiveness in individuals and in group is feedback (Fig. 13.4). There are a lot of studies showing the importance of feedback (Algera, 1990; Locke & Latham, 1990). The influence of feedback in real-life groups in organizations was demonstrated in a set of studies using a systematic feedback report for groups to find out how powerful feedback can be to increase the group's productivity (Pritchard, 1995). One of these was carried out by our Dortmund group (Przygodda, Kleinbeck, Schmidt, & Beckmann, 1995).

The productivity measurement and enhancement system ProMES (in Germany called PPM, which means Participatory Productivity Management; Pritchard, Kleinbeck, & Schmidt, 1993) was implemented and used in an advanced

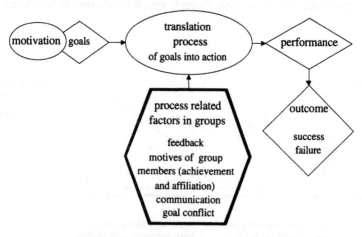

FIG. 13.4. Factors in groups influencing the translation process of goals into actions.

manufacturing system in a German factory producing electric safety devices. The central feature of PPM is the feedback report, which is developed on the basis of tasks and indicators showing how good the tasks of the group are accomplished. The indicators themselves and the indicator scores are further evaluated to find out to what extent they contribute to the productivity of the whole organization. The productivity values of each indicator score form the contingencies that are worked out by the group developing the PPM system participatively.

A salient feature of the production system in this organization was the complex technological equipment that made it difficult for working crews to know thoroughly how their behavioral input is transformed into the final output of the system. The project was designed to find out whether PPM provides the information necessary for operators to control advanced manufacturing systems more effectively and whether PPM will improve productivity.

The production section of the factory where PPM was implemented consisted of several interrelated manufacturing centers. Two of them formed the research setting of the present study. Both centers were characterized by a high degree of automation and allowed the flexible production of different product variants in varying lots. In comparison with conventional production units, advanced manufacturing systems like these are generally expected to offer better conditions for reacting rapidly to the increasing fluctuations and diversifications in market demands.

These technological facilities, however, are only to be realized with crews who thoroughly know how their behavioral input is transformed into the final output of such system. In practice, this knowledge is difficult to acquire because of the complexity and the multitude of intervening mechanical processes, which, in addition, are not all under the immediate control of the operators. Moreover, the commonly applied output measures for evaluating the system's functioning, such as the number of pieces produced or time per piece, neither provide clear information about what the crews can really influence nor how this influence can be actually used to contribute effectively to the productivity of the whole sociotechnical system. Modern production systems put increasingly higher demands on the abilities and skills of people necessary to cope with organizational complexity.

As a behavior-oriented measurement and feedback approach, PPM would represent an appropriate instrument for assisting the operators in overcoming these difficulties. PPM requires four steps of implementation:

1. Tasks of the working groups are described (products).
2. Indicators are identified to measure group performance.
3. Each indicator score is evaluated to find out the contribution of the group for the productivity of the whole organization.
4. A feedback report is developed.

In our study, PPM could provide the information needed for operators to control highly automated production systems more effectively (Przygodda, Kleinbeck, Schmidt, & Beckmann, 1995).

Before PPM had been introduced, members of the experimental groups did not dispose of any productivity indicators or of their own behavioral potentials to make use of the technical system. This lack of experience in managing an advanced manufacturing system could be successfully diminished by using PPM as a management system recording indicator data on a regular basis and feeding behavioral outcomes back systematically.

Taking all the results together, data seem to legitimate the assumption that PPM works under the conditions described above. It contributes to an increase of productivity in working groups. Further conclusions from these data with respect to psychological processes behind these PPM effects cannot be deduced. But some speculations might be helpful to get ideas about these processes, which could be examined in further experiments (Fig. 13.5).

The observed increase of productivity was related to the feedback phase of the study, pointing strongly to the fact that feedback might be a powerful variable to explain the results. Feeding back the information of the measurement system is not only expected to facilitate role clarification and to promote the building up of more effective work strategies, but also should enhance the motivation of the workers. At first, the feedback information may help the group members to see the results of their efforts. This should strengthen the connection between effort and productivity and thereby improve the effort–performance expectancies which, according to expectancy theory approaches, are considered strong determinants of work motivation (Campbell & Pritchard, 1976; Vroom, 1964). Furthermore,

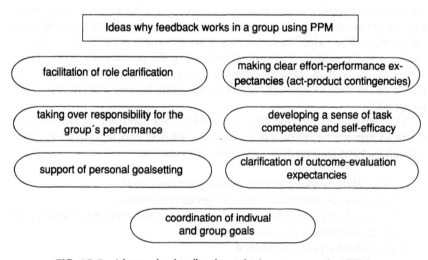

FIG. 13.5.   Ideas why feedback works in a group using PPM.

by separating out the effects of factors that group members cannot control, they are made accountable for their productivity. This may strengthen the workers' feelings of responsibility and at the same time prevent them from attributing low productivity rates to external conditions like technical processes, management strategies, and other causes. In addition, by experiencing the control they have over the production process, the workers develop a sense of task competence, or self-efficacy (Bandura, 1992; Whyte, 1959), which is another powerful determinant of high work motivation. Last, but not least, PPM helps to relate individual goals of group members to group goals, and even more to the goals of the departments groups are working in. According to recent results reported by Crowne and Rosse (1995), the coordination of personal and group goals is a necessary conditions for a group's high performance.

Moreover, the feedback information may stimulate the workers to set their own productivity goals. This process can be supported by formal training in goal-setting strategies that explains the effectiveness of goal setting and shows how goal setting is to be managed in a group of workers and supervisors. By this they learn to set specific and challenging but attainable goals that meet the unanimous approval of all involved in the goal setting process (Locke & Latham, 1990). On the basis of this training, a formal goal-setting program can be introduced to shape the group activities in line with the organizational goals.

EFFECTS OF MOTIVES OF GROUP MEMBERS ON THE DEVELOPMENT OF GOALS AND ON THEIR TRANSLATION INTO ACTION

In the field studies addressing the question how feedback influences the translation of goals into action, it was not possible to consider other important moderators. Nevertheless, according to our conceptual model, *motives* of group members should show a twofold influence on work motivation and group efffectiveness (see French, 1958, and Fig. 13.3). First, they interact with their corresponding motivating potentials to determine the strength of work motivation, and, second, they moderate the translation of motivational states into action. A laboratory study of Wegge and Kleinbeck (1996) addressed these issues. It was conducted in the Dortmund lab to examine the joint effects of group composition with respect to achievement and affilition motives of group members, and the influence of task complexity and task interdependence on performance in 27 three-person groups. Each group was asked to solve an anagram task, a motor coordination task, and a brainstorming task.

Consistent with motivation theory, our results documented that motives of group members affect those processes that are linked with self-setting of group goals.

Moreover, motives had an impact on overall group performance and performance changes due to group goal setting.

With respect to self-set group goals, it was observed that groups with a high affiliation motive set more difficult goals for the motor coordination task. Compared to the other group tasks studied, this task requires a higher degree of cooperation between group members (which means a high affiliative motivating potential). Therefore, the main effect for the affiliation motive might be based on more self-confidence with respect to acting in social situations and/or more experience with (real) group work for persons with a high affiliation motive. In addition, we observed that groups consisting of persons with high achievement motives who have also a high motive for affiliation agreed on more difficult goals in the brainstorming task than groups with mixed motives. Both effects indicate clearly that in the context of group performance the affiliation motive is at least as important as the achievement motive if the difficulty of self-set group goals has to be explained.

With respect to overall group performance (see Table 13.1), it was observed that groups with a low affiliation motive solved the anagrams faster than groups with high motive for affiliation. Moreover, groups composed of subjects with a high motive for achievement had a higher performance in the motor coordination task than those composed of low-motive achievers. In addition, especially groups with a high motive for achievement and affiliation performed this task better than groups

TABLE 13.1
Influences of Different Motives on Performance, Communication, and the
Translation of Goal Setting Into Performance for Three Different Tasks

	Performance	Communication	Effectiveness of Group Goal Setting
Anagrams	Low-affiliation-motive Groups Better Than High	High-affiliation-motive Groups Communicate More	
Motor Coordination	High-achievement-motive Groups Better Than Low High-achievement- and high-affiliation-motive Groups Better Than Mixed Motives	High-achievement-motive Groups Communicate More	High-achievement-, Low-affiliation-motive Groups Perform Better
Brainstorming			Low-achievement-, High-affiliation-motive Groups Perform Better

with a low motive score; these results clearly document *that effects of motives on group performance are task specific.* This notion is also valid for other aspects of group behavior. Whereas communication intensity between group members was especially high for groups with a high affiliation motive while solving the anagram task, group members talked more to each other during performance of the motor coordination task when they had a high motive for achievement. Intense communication between group members might facilitate group performance in task with high task interdependence (motor coordination) and hinder performance of group tasks that require problem solving (such as anagrams).

Therefore, it can be expected that the effects of motives on group performance mentioned above are mediated by communication processes. A test of this hypothesis revealed that both main effects were no longer significant when performance variance linked with communication intensity was removed. Thus, effects of motives on group performance are (partially) due to differences regarding communication processes in work groups.

Finally, the effectiveness of group goal setting was moderated by motives of group members (Table 13.1). In the brainstorming task, groups with a low achievement and a high affiliation motive increased performance more than groups composed of subjects high on both motives. Moreover, for the anagram task it was found that groups with a low achievement motive needed the same time to solve the anagrams in goal-setting trials than groups with a high achievement motive. This missing difference is important because in "do your best" trials, groups with a high achievement motive solved the anagrams faster than groups composed of persons with a low achievement motive. In addition, for the motor coordination task, groups with a high motive for achievement and a low motive for affiliation had higher performance improvements than groups with a high motive for achievement and affiliation.

What is the reason for this moderator effect of motives in the context of group goal setting? First, one might speculate that this pattern of results is due to those variations that were observed with respect to group goal commitment. For each of the three group tasks it was found that mixed-motive groups reported higher group goal commitment than homogenous motive groups. Moreover, performance differences between groups for the motor coordination task were no longer significant when group goal commitment was considered as a covariate. Hence, interactions between motives of group members and effects of group goal setting on performance improvements partially rely on differences regarding group goal commitment. Second, another explanation can be derived from the fact that two of the above mentioned interactions are built on the comparison of special groups: Groups with mixed motives are compared to groups with a high achievement and a high affiliation motive. Taking into consideration that groups with a high achievement and affiliation motive performed both tasks very well during "do your best" trials, it is possible that further performance improvements were very difficult to achieve for these groups. Hence, these interactions may have been caused by a ceiling effect. Although this possibility cannot be ruled out with the help of our data, we believe that the following propositon is the best explanation for the observed moderator effect. This third proposition holds that group goal setting works especially well for groups with mixed motives because (a) these groups are prone to show very low performance under "do your best" instructions, (b) that these performance decrements are due to processes of self-regulation based on goal conflicts with respect to individual standards of excellence, and (c) that the presence of specific and difficult group goals will reduce these goal conflicts and/or will promote a mode of self regulation in which individual performance standards are no longer considered.

The idea that goal conflicts might affect especially groups with mixed motives is based on the assumption that both motives are aroused in group work. Whereas group members with homogenous motives will feel a unique desire to perform very well in this situation or to leave this situation, in mixed motive groups members will experience a conflict between a standard of excellence (e.g., perform well, cooperate with other group members) and an opposite avoidance tentency (e.g., fear of failure, fear of social rejection). These conflicts may hinder smooth group performance because they induce conscious deliberations concerning conflicting goals (thoughts about fears and hopes). Assigning a specific group goal might help to reduce these conflicts in three ways: because (a) goal setting will promote higher self-efficacy; (b) group goals focus attention on the group level and stress standards of group performance, to that self-evaluative consequences linked with (individual) failure will become less important (e.g., responsibility for failures is distributed over group members); and (c) group goals implicate a strong pressure to contribute to the group product that helps to overcome fears concerning social rejection. These effects of group goal setting probably will also occur in groups composed of subjects with a high fear of failure and social rejection. However, we further suggest that these groups will show less performance improvement because (d) they will achieve better performance results under "do your best" instructions (e.g. superior performance compared to mixed-motive groups might be due to fewer conscious deliberations about goal conflicts; see the results of the brainstorming and anagram tasks); or (e) these processes have less impact on behavior when avoidance motivation is aroused intensively (see the results for the motor coordination task).

In summary, the findings with respect to achievement and affiliation motives of group members reveal that the composition of groups with respect to these motives is an important factor in the context of group work. Group composition will affect the difficulty of sef-set group goals, overall group performance (probably moderated by communication processes), and the effectiveness of group goal setting (probably moderated by variations in group goal commitment and/or differences with regard to self-efficacy, standards of self regulation, and the presence of conscious thoughts about goal conflicts).

CONTEXTUAL FACTORS IN GROUPS AND THEIR EFFECTS ON WORK MOTIVATION AND PERFORMANCE

In our comprehensive model of the determinants of work motivation and group effectiveness, there is a last group of variables, which are called the contextual factors of group work. The most prominent example of a contextual factor is group pay. Although commonsense provides some reasons to assume a positive effect of group performance based pay on group performance, empirical evidence for such effects is missing. Nevertheless, some thoughts will finally be presented about these issues, which could be the basis for further empirical work in the context of the comprehensive model presented at the beginning of this chapter (see Fig. 13.6).

Our hypothesis is that a group bonus based on the performance of the group will increase work motivation of the group's members and by that also performance. According to the model, and especially in combination with a management system like PPM, a plan for tying pay to group performance can be developed that could then be tested empirically. Such a plan should start with establishing the indicators used to measure group performance. This can easily be done by implementing PPM and then using the feedback reports. With PPM, contingencies will be established showing the amount of productivity for every indicator score describing the performance of the group with respect to a particular task. This transformation from indicator scores into productivity scores is important for the design of the pay

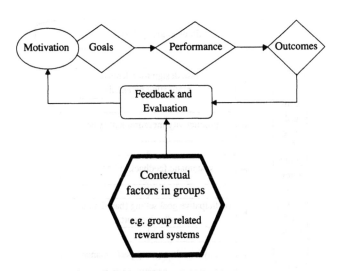

FIG. 13.6. Contextual factors as determinants of work motivation and group effectiveness.

system. It gives the opportunity to relate pay directly to group and organizational productivity. Using PPM brings other advantages. With PPM it is possible to derive indices for the group's effectiveness, which can be compared between groups. It thereby opens the opportunity to compare the performances of groups and relate the group bonus to the relative standing of groups in the organization.

STEPS IN GROUP DESIGN FROM THE PERSPECTIVE OF A MODEL OF WORK MOTIVATION

Based on our model of work motivation and group effectiveness, it is now possible to describe the steps to be done in a group design process (Fig. 13.7). For the first step, the designer has to consider the factors for a high motivating potential of the group task. In general, one can suggest to design a "complete task," as described in the first chapter. Such a "complete task" will interact positively with high achievement motives of group members. For persons with other motives (e.g., high affiliation), there should be other task components that stimulate the individual motives. Group work will in principle offer chances to design features of the group tasks creating high motivating potentials for both affiliation and power motives.

The second step on the way to effective group work should be the implementation of a measurement system at the level of group performance. PPM could be such a system; it has the advantage of combining the measurement system with

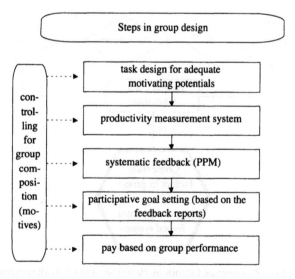

FIG. 13.7. Steps in the design process for effective group work.

systematic feedback, which already brings us to the third step in group design. On the basis of measurement and systematic feedback, the introduction of a system of (participative) goal setting will be appropriate. This goal setting could be participative when PPM has been used because the group members have dveloped the measurement system by themselves, and from the feedback reports they know exactly what their performance has been. After having done the first four steps, it will be easy to do the last one and develop a compensation system based on group performance.

Going through all the five steps guarantees that the components of the design process are compatible with each other. Other components of work organization should be restructured to adapt to the core design steps as they are described in Fig. 13.7 (e.g., leadership, training, staffing, and personnel development). This will prevent conflicts coming from heterogenous elements of organization that could be detrimental for the development of work motivation and the translation of high motivation into productive actions.

REFERENCES

Algera, J. A. (1990). The job characteristics model of work motivation revisited. In U. Kleinbeck H. H. Quast, H. Thierry & H. Häcker et al. (Eds.), *Work motivation*. Hillsdale NJ: Lawrence Erlbaurm.

Antoni, C. H. (1994; Ed.). *Gruppenarbeit: Konzepte, Erfahrungen, Perspektiven* (Group Work: Concepts, Experiences, Perspectives). Weinheim: Psychologie-Verlags-Union.

Atkinson, J. W. (1958). *Motives in fantasy, action and society*. Princeton, NJ: Van Nostrand.

Bandura, A. (1982). Self-efficacy mechanism in human agency. *American Psychologist, 37*, 122–147.

Campbell, J. P., & Pritchard, R. D. (1976). Motivation theory in industrial and organizational psychology. In M. Dunnette (Ed.), *Handbook of Industrial and Organizational Psychology*. Chicago: Rand McNally.

Crowne, D. F., & Rosse, J. G. (1995). Yours, mine, and ours: Facilitating group productivity through the integration of individual and group goals. *Organizational Behavior and Human Decision Processes, 64*, 138–150.

French, E. G. (1958). Effects of the interaction of motivation and feedback on task performance. In J. W. Atkinson (Ed.), *Motives in fantasy, action, and society* (pp. 400–408). Princeton, NJ: Van Nostrand.

Hackman, J. R. (1987). The design of work teams. In J. W. Lorsch (Ed.), *Handbook of Organizational Behavior* (pp. 315–342). Englewood Cliffs, NJ: Prentice-Hall.

Hackman, J. R, & Oldham, G. R. (1975). Development of the job diagnostic survey. *Journal of Applied Psychology, 60*, 159–170.

Heckhausen, H. (1989). *Motivation und Handeln* (Motivation and Action). (2. Aufl.). Berlin: Springer.

Hellpach, W. (1922). Sozialpsychologische Analyse des betriebstechnischen Tatbestandes "Gruppenfabrikation." (Social psychological analysis of "group production"). In R. Lang. & W. Hellpach, *Gruppenfabrikation* (5–186). Berlin: Springer.

Karau, S. J., & Williams, K. D. (1993). Social loafing: A meta-analytic review and theoretical integration. *Journal of Personality and Social Psychology, 65*, 681–706.

Kleinbeck, U. (1987). Gestaltung von Motivationsbedingungen der Arbeit (Design of motivational determinants of works). In U. Kleinbeck & J. Rutenfranz (Eds.), *Arbeitspsychologie (Enzyklopädie der Psychologie)*. Göttingen: Hogrefe.

Locke, E. A., & Latham, G. P. (1990). A theory of goal setting and task performance. Englewood Cliffs, NJ: Prentice-Hall.

McClelland, D. C. (1987). *Human motivation*. Cambridge, England: Cambridge University Press.

McGrath, J. E. (1984). *Groups: Interaction and performance*. Englewood Cliffs, NJ: Prentice-Hall.

Pritchard, R. D. (1995). *Productivity measurement and improvement—Organizational case studies*. Westport, London: Praeger.

Pritchard, R. D., Kleinbeck, U., & Schmidt, K. H. (1993). *Das Managementsystem PPM—Durch Mitarbeiterbeteiligung zu höherer Produktivität*. Munich: C. H. Beck.

Przygodda, M., Kleinbeck, U., Schmidt, K. H., & Beckmann, J. (1995). Productivity measurement and enhancement in advanced manufacturing systems. In R. D. Pritchard (Ed.), *Productivity Measurement and Improvement—Organizational Case Studies* (pp. 62–80). Westport, London: Praeger.

Schmidt, K. H., & Rutenfranz, J. (1989). Arbeitsstrukturierung in der Montage und Teilefertigung (AEG-Projekt) (Resolution of work in assembly lines and the production of parts). In S. Greif, H. Holling, & N. Nicholson (Eds.), *Arbeits- und Organisationspsychologie*. Munich: Psychologie Verlags Union.

Shepperd, J. A. (1993). Productivity loss in performance groups: A motivation analysis. *Psychological Bulletin, 113*, 67–81.

Vroom, V. H. (1964). *Work and motivation*. New York: Wiley.

Wegge, J., & Kleinbeck, U. (1993). Motivationale Faktoren betrieblicher Fehlzeiten: Zum Einfluβ leistungs und anschluβthematischer Variablen auf die Abwesenheit am Arbeitsplatz (Motivational factors of absenteeism in organizations: Influences of achievement and affiliation-oriented variables on absences). *Zeitschrift für Experimentelle und Angewandte Psychologie, 40*, 451–486.

Wegge, J., & Kleinbeck, U. (1996). Goal-setting and group performance: Impact of achievement and affiliation motives, participation in goal-setting. In T. Gjesme & R. Nygard (Eds.), *Advances in Motivation* (pp. 1–34). Oslo: Scandinavian University Press.

Weldon, E., & Weingart, L. R. (1993). Group goals and group performance. *British Journal of Social Psychology, 32*, 307–334.

Whyte, W. F. (1955). *Money and motivation: An analysis of incentives in industry*. New York: Harper.

14

Performance Management for Self-managing Teams and Organizational Control Systems

Jen A. Algera

*Eindhoven University of Technology
and Hoogovens Steel Works, The Netherlands*

In this chapter we discuss problems associated with applying motivational concepts in practice. In particular we will focus on the design and implementation of the Productivity Measurement and Enhancement System (ProMES) (Pritchard, 1990, 1995). The development of valid performance indicators is essential in this system. ProMES has been implemented mainly for work teams on the shopfloor level. However, the success of this type of intervention in practice is heavily dependent on the organizational context. The consistency of performance indicators throughout the whole organization turns out to be a condition for successful implementation of ProMES. Performance indicators on the strategic, tactical, and the operational level of the organization refer to different kinds of performance. For example, on the strategic and tactical level, financial and logistic performance indicators are used. We will go into the issue of how performance indicators from a psychological viewpoint, such as ProMES, can be combined with performance indicators from other viewpoints, e.g., financial and logistics. We first will indicate how the underlying motivational concepts of ProMES can be placed in a framework of motivation constructs.

In the discipline of psychology many motivation theories do exist. Kanfer (1992) gives an overview of examplar motivation theories embedded in a heuristic framework of motivation constructs. This heuristic framework differentiates between distal and proximal constructs. Proximal construct theories focus at the level of purposive action and concentrate on the processes and variables that affect the goal-behavior/performance relation. Distal theories of motivation focus on intermediate cognitive choice processes. These processes refer to an individual's intentions that prepare for action, rather than behavior or performance. Kanfer (1992) concludes in her overview that theories at the proximal end of the continuum get the most theoretical and empirical attention. As far as proximal theories is concerned, she points at the converging evidence for the joint importance of goals and self-regulation in work motivation. One of the traditional arguments against cybernetic control theories and mechanisms of self-regulation is that only negative discrepancy between goals and performance seems to motivate individuals. However, Bandura (1988) has suggested that feedback as well as "feedforward" is included in self-regulation processes. Feedforward mechanisms can foster persons to adjust goals upwards (discrepancy production). The underlying motivational concepts of ProMES (Pritchard, 1990) are at the proximal end of the continuum in Kanfer's (1992) framework.

Most theories on work motivation, as referred to by Kanfer (1992), are theories on the individual level. However, in the actual workplace, more and more individuals work in teams, and also organizations tend to change rather rapidly, especially in the face of global competition. It is not yet quite clear what this means for the validity of many work motivation theories. Another important issue is the actual translation from theories to the design of motivational interventions. In this chapter, the emphasis will be on the last issue, i.e., the design of motivational interventions in actual practice. We will go into experiences in implementing Pritchard's ProMES system, an intervention technique that is based on resource allocation perspectives (see Naylor, Pritchard, & Ilgen, 1980) and more generally on theoretical notions of feedback, goal setting, and rewards. In particular, we will focus on the design of valid performance indicators.

PRACTICAL APPLICATION: EXPERIENCES IN DEVELOPING ProMES IN ACTUAL WORK SETTINGS

Applying work motivation theories in actual practice is rather complex, because in actual work settings interventions take place in a specific organizational context with its own process dynamics. Besides that, many other organizational variables, such as reward systems, culture, leadership style, and organization structure will affect the results of the invervention. In many instances, research in actual work settings is less rigorous than laboratory studies and is often more qualitative than quantitative. Nevertheless, it can be very useful, especially for generating hypotheses.

An interesting example is the design and implementation of ProMES (Pritchard, 1990, 1995). ProMES (Productivity Measurement and Enhancement System) can be considered an intervention technique, based on Naylor's, Pritchard's and Ilgen's (1980) resource theory and goal-setting/feedback theory, which has been used to investigate the effects of group-based feedback and goal setting. After the original study in the U.S. Air Force, this system has been implemented in different countries and different types of organizations (see Pritchard, 1995). Most of the studies have been on the shop floor in manufacturing or in service on the group level. We will explore in some more detail what kind of conditions are relevant for the effects of ProMES. In general, the effect size is substantial. Pritchard (1995) reports a mean effect size of 2.3 across 26 organizational units (using the d-statistics approach; Hunter, Schmidt, & Jackson, 1982).

The basic characteristics of ProMES are to develop performance indicators for key result areas ("products") that can be controlled by the work group, using a bottom-up design methodology. Systematic feedback is periodically given to the work group. On the basis of this systematic feedback, and possibly goal setting, the work group is supposed to improve its performance. Performance improvement can be achieved, for example, by mobilizing on task effort, but also by developing new task strategies.

Taken together, this will mean that a work group needs to have discretion to decide on new task strategies, but also to have the feeling that resulting scores on the performance indicators reflect their efforts. It is not surprising that during the process of design a large part of the discussions within the ProMES design teams focus on the controllability of performance by the work group, as measured by the indicators. Stated negatively, work groups often say, "Management cannot blame us for performance outcomes we are not able to influence." This means that the organizational context in which ProMES is to be implemented is of utmost importance, not only in terms of conditions to start such a design process successfully (Pritchard, 1990), such as the willingness of both management and work groups to use such a performance measurement system, but also in terms of organizational structures that give discretion to work groups.

In the Netherlands, we have a number of cases (see e.g., Algera & van den Hurk, 1995; Janssen, van Berkel, & Stolk, 1995) in manufacturing settings where organization structures have changed, prior to the ProMES intervention or during the implementation process, in the direction of self-managing teams. The concept of self-managing teams fits very nicely with the implementation of ProMES in practice. These cases illustrate that motivational interventions, such as ProMES, can only be succesfull when the organizational context is taken into account. But even more important, it illustrates that ProMES is not an isolated intervention. In all cases in the Netherlands it was part of broader organizational change processes, such as changing organizational structures to self-managing work groups or introducing total quality management systems. As such, the distinction between ProMES implementation projects, and other organizational interventions becomes blurred in practice. Therefore, we will now delineate some contextual issues that are decisive for succesfull application of ProMES motivational interventions.

ORGANIZATIONAL CONTEXT: CONDITIONS FOR DESIGNING VALID PERFORMANCE INDICATORS

Over the last few years there has been a tremendous movement in organizations to delayer in combination with self-managing teams on the work floor in the Netherlands and other European countries. This trend is visible not only in manufacturing settings, but also in service organizations. The reason for this movement is that to stay competitive in global markets, organizations have to enhance performance on quality, delivery time, service, and flexibility. These outside pressures have led to adaptations of the internal organizational structures. Delayering organizations and introducing self-managing teams mean in terms of Mintzberg (1979) that the coordinating mechanism of direct supervision is replaced by the coordinating mechanism of standardization of outputs. This means that performance indicators that specify the required outputs become much more important. This is valid for all levels of the organization. These kinds of organizational changes, however, tend to differ in underlying philosophy. In the Netherlands, in many organizations changes are based on ideas from the sociotechnical systems approach. But also, lean production and business process redesign are labels used to indicate the basic philosophy underlying these organization restructuring processes. From a motivational point of view, the amount of discretion of work teams seems to be very important. .

The issue of performance indicators on different organizational levels is rather complex. Performance indicators are used in different disciplines, for example, management accounting and industrial engineering. Many different types of performance indicators are used in practice. Flapper, Fortuin, and Stoop (1994) give an overview of existing classifications as can be found in accounting, engineering, and production management literature, such as financial versus nonfinancial, global versus local, internal versus external, and so forth. They propose a new classification scheme that is based on three dimensions:

1. Decision type: strategic/tactical/operational.
2. Level of aggregation: overall/partial.
3. Measurement unit: monetary/physical/dimensionless. The first dimensions of their classification scheme, that is, performance indicators on the strategic, tactical, or operational level, is interesting for our discussion.

We will also discuss contextual issues based on experiences in implementing ProMES in a number of Dutch organizations. In designing and implementing

ProMES systems, some bottlenecks came out in many projects. One point relates to the consistency of performance indicators at different organizational levels.

Consistancy of Performance Indicators at Different Organizational Levels

In the bottom-up design methodology of ProMES, in the approval meetings between work groups and management, consistency between strategic, tactical, and operational performance indicators should be guarded. If management approves a specific performance indicator, it should also be good for the whole organization. This is especially valid in Step 3 of ProMES, where the contingencies are established. The establisment of contingencies is a unique feature of ProMES, as compared to other performance measurement systems. It is also where the basic theoretical notions from the resource theory of Naylor, Pritchard, and Ilgen (1980) come into play. A contingency specifies the relationship between the amount of the indicator and the overall effectiveness for the organization. The total set of contingencies for a work group should be used by the work group to decide on how to spend its time and energy to get a maximum total score.

In discussing the effect sizes of ProMES interventions, Pritchard (1995) argues that the motivational impact of ProMES covers many variables influencing the whole motivational process. Referring to the resources theory of Naylor, Pritchard, and Ilgen, Pritchard states that ProMES has impact on the contingencies between acts (behavior) and products (results of behavior), between products (results of behavior) and evaluations (performance) and between evaluations (performance) and outcomes (intrinsic and extrinsic rewards). We will confine our discussion to the second relation, between products (results of behavior) and evaluations (performance). This relation is, in fact, established in Step 3 of the ProMES intervention, as has been explained above.

In practice, in the approval meetings, management and the work groups discuss what is the right shape of this contingency. This procedure supposes that management is able to specify what a certain amount of the indicator means for the overall effectiveness of the organization. What management is asked for is to indicate what the value of scores on the indicator is for the organizations as a whole. This means in practice that management has to make its policy explicit.

This turns out to be a difficult task for management in many projects. In fact, management has to consider the value of performance indicator scores as well on a short-term as on a long-term basis. In addition, management has to weigh the value of quite different types of indicators and products. For example, quantitative indicators, as the amount of tons of steel production, have to be evaluated against safety. In some projects, management had some reservations concerning Step 3 (contingencies). We believe this is not primarily because of conceptual difficulties, but probably more because of the difficulty to make their evaluation explicit. This difficulty could be explained partly by the fact that management does not normally have objective and quantitative arguments for its evaluation. In fact, management has often only quite global ideas on how to evaluate the different indicators and products against each other. One reason could be that the priorities for management itself are not clear enough to quantify in terms of ProMES contingencies. Another reason could be that there is "vertical inconsistency." That is to say that management itself is evaluated by a set of performance indicators that is inconsistent with the performance indicators of the work groups. Stated otherwise, there is a (great) chance that performance indicators at different organizational levels are not consistent. This can be partly explained by the fact that strategic plans at the top level of the organization often are not translated into concrete performance indicators for the strategic and the tactical level. This can also be the case if one looks at the "operative" goals instead of the "official" strategy of the organization (Perrow, 1961). Another explanation could be that at higher organizational levels goal conflict is often quite normal. Probably one of the most important performance indicators for management itself are financial indicators. From the management accounting literature it is well-known that management accounting systems can have quite dysfunctional effects, because performance indicators at the strategic and tactical level are often not consistent with performance indicators at the operational level.

We will later describe some recent developments in the management accounting field. This is relevant because of the relations between strategic, tactical, and operational performance indicators.

Management Accounting Systems

For managers, financial performance indicators are often the most important, because they are primarily evaluated against these types of criteria. Traditional performance indicators in this field make use of analysis of differences, in particular between budget and reality. Analysis of differences is a technique used to explain global differences by splitting up in more detail, e.g., differences in financial yields are split up in price differences, volume differences, market share differences, etc. (see Bruggeman, Slagmulder, Waeytens, & Everaert, 1993).

Cost differences are split into variable and fixed cost differences, and within these two categories are even more differentiated, for example, differences in the use of available capacity. This technique of analysis of differences between budget and reality is made downwards in the hierarchy of the organization. The lower the level in the organization, the more detailed the analyses are. On the lowest level, differences are explained per "responsibility center," on the one hand to evaluate the functioning of the unit and on the other to learn lessons for the future.

These traditional performance indicators from the management accounting field, mainly based on cost information, are less useful for controlling companies

in new production environments and in fact work out negatively for the overall effectiveness of the organization.
Problems with this approach are:

1. Information is too late and too general; mostly provided on a monthly basis and summarizing across machines, so that positive and negative differences are no longer visible.
2. It generates dysfunctional behavior; for example, it creates overproduction by full use of capacity, whereas preventative maintenance and training of operators is punished by negative difference of capacity use.
3. It creates local optimalization instead of overall optimalization. Because each department or unit is evaluated separately, it does not give insight into the interdependencies between units in the total production process.
4. It does not stimulate continuous improvement. Historical standars are static and often imply an amount of slack and waste; only by benchmarking are standards made more dynamic.
5. It does not show all important improvements, because it only takes direct and indirect costs into account and not customer satisfaction or competitive advantage.
6. Interpretation of differences is dependent on strategy; for example, not using the budget fully for a R&D department must be evaluated quite differently depending on a low cost, milk strategy versus an invest strategy. If differences analysis is used, it should be done for each strategic business unit separately.

The same dysfunctional effects, as discussed above for financial differences analysis, can be seen in traditional productivity performance indicators at the tactical level, especially when single-factor productivity measures are used such as labor efficiency and capacity use per machine. These measures can be contradictory to modern philosophies such as just-in-time (JIT). In these new approaches, the interdependancies of machines are considered and capacity use is more dependent on the structure of the total production process and less controllable by production personnel of separate machines. In the JIT philosophy, machines are grouped into production cells. This also calls for organization structures based on (self-managing) teams. Bruggeman, Slagmulder, Waeytens, and Everaert (1993) argue that financial performance measures cannot give valid information on effectiveness and efficiency.

In organizations in new production environments more and more performance indicators at the operational and the tactical level are being used. These operational and tactical performance indicators can include:

1. Quality, measured in the process by statistical process control.
2. Delivery performance, measured by on time schedule.
3. Throughput time and process time, measured by delivery lead time.

4. Waste rate, for example, measured by non-added-value activities (e.g., transport).
5. Customer statisfaction, for example, measured by percentage repeat order by existing customers.
6. Flexibility, for example, measured by machine flexibility in terms of time needed to change to another manufacture.
7. Productivity, measured by delivered output.

Bruggeman et al. (1993) conclude that financial performance indicators are less useful when users of these indicators are closer to the production activities, when a company operates in a more dynamic competitive market, and when internal production processes become more integrated. Strategy has to be the integrating factor to combine financial and other performance indicators (see, e.g., Cross & Lynch, 1989).

In the traditional management accounting approach, costs are dominant and units have to report differences against the budget. Its prime orientation is in the past and not on the improvement of processes. In new approaches, such as JIT and total quality control, not costs but the improvement of processes are emphasized. The method of Activity-Based Costing, being a new approach in the management accounting field, can be useful because costs in this method are tied to activities and not to persons, jobs, or departments. Its focus is on improvement of activities leading to shorter throughput times, lower stock, and lower costs. We will give an example in the next paragraph.

Thus, a manager who is evaluated by traditional management accounting performance measures might have difficulty in translating performance indicators from management level to the shop floor. These developments from the field of management accounting illustrate the difficulties in designing performance indicators that are consistent across different organizational levels.

WHAT IS ORGANIZATIONAL EFFECTIVENESS?

The developments as sketched in the previous paragraphs make it clear that the basic question of what exactly is organizational effectiveness is strongly tied to organizational structure, logistic control systems, management accounting systems, and other components. Choices for organizational structure and control systems should be highly dependent on strategy. Going back to Step 3 of the ProMES intervention technique, it turns out that in the approval meetings management has to answers two questions. First, referring to the horizontal relations within the production process, what is the contribution of a self-managing team in relation to other teams in the total production process? Second, referring to vertical relations in the organization, how does the contribution of a self-managing team fit into organizational goals and performance indicators at higher levels such as delivery performance and flexibility?

Top-Down Definition of Performance Indicators

In practice, we found that management had some difficulty in deciding on the contingencies. One could argue that before starting a ProMES intervention, a top down establishment of performance indicators should first be done. Borg, Staufenbiel, and Pritchard (1995) present a method for identitifying strategic objectives in productivity management. In their approach they combine features of their method, called HISYS (Staufenbiel & Borg, 1992) and features of ProMES. The HISYS method contains four steps and is supported by a computer program that generates graphic displays for overhead projection, stores results, and computes statistics. In the case Borg et al. (1995) present, the management team worked as a design team in working out the system in four steps. Step 1 is stratifying the organizational objectives in terms of lower-level and higher-level objectives. Subordinate objectives are sorted into lower levels in terms of logical dependency or semantic overlap. In fact, this first step leads to sharpening objectives and avoiding vagueness of concepts. In Step 2, a qualitative hierarchy is built by connecting lower-level and higher-level objectives. Each objective on a given level is connected to at least one objective on the level below it. In Step 3, the hierarchy is quantified by using a pairwise comparison method. All objectives on a given level that contribute to a higher-level objective are expressed in a ratio that indicates the contribution to that objective. The observed ratios can be checked for logical inconsistencies and are fed back to the design team. Consistency was felt to be very important, because an inconsistent set of objectives would be difficult to communicate to subordinates.

In Step 4, the overall hierarchy of objectives is explored. This step can lead to redesigning the overall hierarchy, for example, because an objective with many paths leading upward leads to an accumulation of weights, giving a greater contribution to the overall objective than probably previously estimated. In the same way, the design team can conclude that some paths in the hierarchy are missing or should be deleted. In fact, this part of the HISYS method can be considered an interative design procedure, with many feedback loops supported by a computer program.

In the second part of HISYS, a four-step procedure is available to further define objectives in more concrete behavioral indicators that may help in practice. In steps 1 and 2, different behavioral facets and three behavioral anchors for each of the behavioral facets are defined. These three behavioral anchors define the minimum, maximum, and expected level of performance. In steps 3 and 4, the expected level is scaled and effectiveness scores are established, more or less similar to ProMES contingencies.

The methodology as used in HISYS provides a vehicle to organize and discuss complex sets of objectives in a systematic way. It is a top-down approach that can help when overall strategic objectives are not totally clear. As Borg et al. (1995) suggest, it could be used in addition to a bottom-up ProMES approach. The products, performance indicators, and contingenties suggested by self-managing teams designing ProMES could be evaluated by management against the outcomes of the HISYS approach. In this way a balance between top-down and bottom-up processes could be achieved.

An Empirical Illustration

An empirical illustration of generating a quantitative basis for discussions on the right shape of ProMES contingencies can be found in Kleingeld (1994). In his study, the ProMES methodology was applied to design a performance management system for maintenance technicians of a company leasing photocopiers. For product "quality" (to repair and maintain photocopiers as effectively as possible), two performance indicators were defined (Kleingeld, 1994):

1. Mean Copies Between Calls (MCBC): the average number of copies made between a technician's repair visits and the first malfunctions after those visits.
2. Percentage repeat calls: the percentage of repair visits made by a technician within five working days of the original repair. For the product "cost" (to repair and maintain photocopiers as efficiently as possible) two performance indicators were also defined (Kleingeld, 1994):
   (a) Parts cost per call: the average amount of money spent on replacement parts.
   (b) Labor time per call: the average amount of time used for repairing and maintaining photocopiers.

Initially, the relative importance of the indicators was established by subjective estimates of the ProMES design teams in two regions (the field service department was split up in 14 regions). In the approval meetings, management admitted that they were unable to evaluate the accuracy of the design groups' judgments. It was decided to verify the contingencies on a quantitative economic basis.

The Activity-Based Costing method (Cooper & Kaplan, 1988; Drury, 1989), mentioned before, was used to estimate the relative impact on cost reduction of comparable improvements on each of the indicators. For example, which cost reduction results from a 10% improvement on the indicator "parts cost per call" compared to a 10% improvement on "Mean Copies Between Calls"? This analysis was done for low-middle-and high-volume copiers and then generalized to the whole population of photocopiers.

TABLE 14.1
Results of Subjective Estimate by Design Teams and Activity-Based Costing

Indicator	Subjective Estimate of Design Teams	Cost Reduction Calculation (Activity-Based Costing)	Cost Reduction to Customer Satisfaction Subjective Estimate	Cost and Customer Satisfaction: Combined Assessment
Mean Copies Between Calls	100	100	Important	100
Percent Repeat Calls	86	30	Very Important	70
Parts Cost/Call	61	82	Unimportant	50
Labor Time/Call	67	96	Somewhat Important	85

In addition to this quantitative analyses, the relative strategic effects of improvements on the indicators were estimated in a discussion between management and the design teams. These strategic effects mainly included aspects of improved customer satisfaction and goodwill due to, for example, shorter reaction times and less frequent malfunctions.

The combination of cost-reduction-based and customer-satisfaction-based estimates of relative importance of indicators differed from the subjective estimates originally made by the design teams (see Table 14.1). Mean Copies Between Calls remained the most important indicator. The importance of labor time per call increased, whereas the importance of percentage of repeat calls and parts cost per call decreased slightly.

Interestingly, the importance of parts cost per call is the result of this indicators' impact on cost reduction. This indicator does not contribute to customer satisfaction, since a large majority of the customers had a maintenance contract, in which replacement of spare parts is free of charge. Conversely, the importance of percentage repeat calls is mainly determined by its influence on customer satisfaction, through the reduction of faulty or insufficient repairs, which compel a customer to again report a malfunction within a few days of the original repair.

This example from Kleingeld (1994) nicely illustrates that short-term financial perspectives as well as more long-term perspectives on customer satisfaction come into play to define the relationship between performance indicators and organizational effectiveness. It also illustrates that combining performance measurement approaches from different disciplines, for example, organizational psychology and management accounting, can be fruitful.

APPLICATION OF WORK
MOTIVATION THEORIES: CONTEXT
DEPENDENT DESIGNING

In this chapter we focus on the application of work motivation theories. Stated otherwise, we take a design-oriented perspective. In this perspective, it is inevitable to consider the situational context in which individuals or groups have to perform their work activities. A number of comments can be made.

First, the core question in ProMES interventions is: what exactly constitutes organizational effectiveness? The illustrations presented show that in the approval meetings, management often has difficulty to exactly indicate the right shape of the contingencies. It turns out to be difficult to translate the strategy of the organization into concrete contingencies. This is partly because financial and non-financial objectives on a short- and long-term basis are not easy to quantify. In any case, it urges management to make the strategy much more explicit. The bottom-up approach of ProMES in some cases needs to be accompanied by a top-down process of strategy formulation and translating strategy to lower organizational levels. The method presented by Borg et al. (1995) can help to structure such a process. However, this method is restricted because there are no direct relations with other organizational control systems, such as management accounting systems or logistic planning systems. Nevertheless, HISYS can help to clarify relationships between organizational goals at different organizational levels.

Second, in the illustrations we presented on ProMES interventions in Dutch organizations, most cases refer to work groups. The theoretical basis of ProMES can be found in resource theory (Pritchard, 1995; Naylor, Pritchard, & Ilgen, 1980). Basically, this theory is about motivation of individuals and not of groups. In Pritchard's studies, these theoretical notions are translated to the group level. However, work motivation of groups is more complicated than motivation of individuals. For example, Weldon and Weingart (1993) emphasize that in complex group tasks planning activities of group members are very important. In combining high group goals and complex tasks there is a risk that too less time is allocated to the development of effective and efficient task strategies, in particular with regard to internal coordination. The findings of Weldon and Weingart (1993) illustrate that the relation between goals and performance is much more complex for group tasks than for individual tasks. So, the allocation of time and energy is also dependent on group processes. One implication of resource theory, both on the individual and group level, is that the motivational effects of interventions will be stronger when there is more discretion in arriving at the required output. Therefore, effect sizes of ProMES interventions are expected to be greater in organizational structures that allow for autonomy and decision latitude for a work group, as is the case in self-managing teams.

Third, performance indicators and theories behind performance indicators come from different disciplines. In view of global markets, competition between organizations becomes much stronger. This leads to new approaches from production planning, management accounting, and organization theories. These new approaches have strong influence on the structuring of organizations, the adoption of logistic production planning models, and accounting systems, and thereby shape the context in which individuals and groups have to work.

Fourth, application of work motivation theories in practice always implies a design process wherein many pifalls can occur. Elsewhere (Algera, van Tuijl, & Janssen, 1995) we presented pitfalls in implementing ProMES in different phases of the design process in actual practice. As far as starting conditions is concerned, a check of congruence between principles underlying ProMES and the basic values of management, work groups, and supporting departments should be done. During system development, the time span for development, visible support of top management, and insufficient knowledge of work groups can be pitfalls. In the phase of actual implementation, the availability of computerized information systems and links with other control systems (e.g., reward systems) can hamper the process of arriving at an accepted performance management system. After implementation, in the phase of maintenance, the management attitude and skills in handling feedback data and also skills in problem-solving is essential to be sure the intervention has enduring success.

In the application of work motivation theories, the design of valid performance indicators for work teams turns out to be rather complex. But it is even more difficult to let the organization adopt the intervention permanently, because we then have to change, most likely, many organizational control systems.

REFERENCES

Algera, J. A., & van den Hurk, A. M. C. M. (1995). Testing the feasibility of ProMES before implementation: A case study in the Dutch steel industry. In R. D. Pritchard (Ed.), *Productivity measurement and improvement. Organizational case studies.* Westport, CT: Praeger.

Algera, J. A., van Tuijl, H. F. J. M., & Janssen, P. M. (1995, October). *Pitfalls in implementing participative management of work groups: Dutch experiences in the design process of ProMES.* Paper presented at Conference Participative Management of Work Groups. Dortmund.

Bandura, A. (1988). Self-regulation of motivation and action through goal systems. In V. Hamilton, G. H. Bower, & N. H. Frijda (Eds.), *Cognition, motivation and affect: A cognitive science view* (pp. 37–61). Dordrecht, Holland: Martinus Nijhoff.

Borg, I., Staufenbiel, T. & Pritchard, R. D. (1995). Identifying strategic objectives in productivity management: Combining features of HISYS and ProMES. In R. D. Pritchard (Ed.), *Productivity measurement and improvement. Organizational case studies,* Westport, CT: Praeger.

Bruggeman, W., Slagmulder, R. Waeytens, D., & Everaert, P. (1993). *Management accounting in de nieuwe produktieomgeving.* Antwerp: Maklu.

Cooper, R, & Kaplan, R. S. (1988). Measure costs right: Make the right decisions. *Harvard Business Review,* September/October, 96–103.

Cross, K., & Lynch, R. (1989). Accounting for competitive performance. *Journal of Cost Management, 3*, 20–28.

Drury, C. (1989). Activity Based Costing. *Management Accounting (CIMA), 67*, 60–66.

Flapper, S. D. P., Fortuin, L., & Stoop, P. P. M. (1996). Towards consistent performance management systems. *International Journal of Operations and Production Management, 16 (7)*, 27–37.

Hunter, J. E., Schmidt, F. L. & Jackson, G. B. (1982). *Meta-analyses: Cumulating research findings across studies*. Beverly Hills, CA: Sage Publications.

Janssen, P. M., van Berkel, A., & Stolk, J. (1995). ProMES as part of a new management strategy. In R. D. Pritchard (Ed.), *Productivity measurement and improvement. Organizational case studies*. Westport, CT: Praeger.

Kanfer, R. (1992). Work motivation: New directions in theory and research. In C. L. Cooper & I. T. Robertson. (Ed.), *International review of industrial and organizational psychology* (Vol. 7). Chichester, England: Wiley.

Kleingeld, P. A. M. (1994). *Performance management in a field service department*. Dordrecht, The Netherlands: ICG Printing.

Mintzberg, H. (1979). *The structuring of organizations*. Englewood Cliffs, NJ: Prentice-Hall.

Naylor, J. C., Pritchard, R. D. & Ilgen, D. R. (1980). *A theory of behavior in organizations*. New York: Academic Press.

Perrow, C. (1961). The analysis of goals in complex organizations. *American Sociological Review, 26*, 854–66.

Pritchard, R. D. (1990). *Measuring and improving organizational productivity: A practical guide*. New York: Praeger.

Pritchard, R. D. (1995). Lessons learned about ProMES. In R. D. Pritchard (Ed.), *Productivity measurement and improvement. Organizational case studies*. Westport, CT: Praeger.

Staufenbiel, T., & Borg, I. (1992). HISYS, a program for the scaling and measurement of hierarchical systems. In F. Faulbaum (Ed.), *Softstat '91* (161–166). Stuttgart: Fisher.

Weldon, E., & Weingart, L. R. (1993). Group goals and group performance. *British Journal of Social Psychology, 32*, 307–334.

15

Approaches to Leadership: Toward a Complete Contingency Model of Face-to-Face Leadership

George B. Graen
International Leadership Center
The University of Louisiana
Lafayette, Louisiana

Chun Hui
Department of International Management
The Chinese University of Hong Kong
Shatin, N. T., Hong Kong

This chapter is an attempt to build a *contingent–holistic model of leadership* based on our earlier three-approach model (Graen & Uhl-Bien, 1995; Graen & Wakabayashi, 1994). This means that we seek to answer the question: When to use which leadership approach? The novel idea advocated here is that contingencies can be applied to team settings. Specifically, contingencies may change during the life cycle of a team project, and they may be best understood at the dyad level. These ideas contribute to the literature by extending the view of leadership contingencies, which can be employed over multiple followers and situations. In this paper, we identify and discuss (1) a taxonomy of approaches to leadership, (2) contingency factors that theoretically might affect the relative organizational effectiveness of these approaches, (3) the application of this contingency approach to teams, (4) preliminary tests of the model, and (5) how this model can yield a holistic picture of leadership.

Research on face-to-face leadership has contributed much to our understanding of the various aspects of leadership-driven work motivation (Graen, 1969; Graen

211

& Uhl-Bien, 1995; Uhl-Bien, Graen & Scandura, 2000). Among other approaches, for example, the trait approach focuses on the personal aspect of the leader (e.g., Galton, 1869; Stogdill, 1984), the behavioral approach distinguishes the different behavioral styles of leadership (e.g., Fleishman, 1973; Yukl, 1989), whereas the relational approach highlights the importance of leader-member relationship to the effectiveness of a leader (e.g., Graen, 1976; Graen & Wakabayashi, 1994; Graen & Uhl-Bien, 1995). The analysis on the different aspects of leadership, the contributions of which notwithstanding, leaves two fundamental issues in leadership to be resolved. The first deals with contingency factors. Specifically, are there situations in which one approach would be more appropriate and effective than another? Answers to this issue fall generally into the form of contingency theories of leadership. For example, Fiedler's (1967) contingency model of leadership distinguished the situations in which task- or person-oriented behavioral styles are more appropriate. Hersey's and Blanchard's (1982) situational theory of leadership is another attempt to analyze leadership effectiveness in terms of contingency factors. Even though Hersey and Blanchard focused on a different set of contingency factors than Fiedler, they still employ task or person orientation as the content of the leadership practice. These contingency theories of leadership call into question the kinds of contingency factors to consider. However, what also warrants a deeper understanding is the kind of leadership approaches in these models.

The second issue that is fundamental to the understanding of leadership deals with the very demarcation of the various aspects of leadership. Whereas research on single aspects of leadership has enhanced conceptual clarity, it is doubtful whether any one aspect in isolation is sufficient for understanding leadership practices in complex situations. For example, a leader is typically confronted with the task of handling multiple followers under multiple situational constraints. In these complex situations, the analysis of whether a leader should be task or person oriented becomes not only tedious, but may fail to capture the richness of actual leadership practices. More importantly, most, if not all, leaders possess personal characteristics, behavioral and management styles, and relationships with followers varying in degree of quality. Thus, to fully appreciate leadership, attention must be given to how the various aspects of leadership can be put back together to yield a *holistic picture of leadership.*

LEADERSHIP VERSUS MANAGERSHIP

Before discussing the details of our model, the issue of what we think constitutes leadership should be addressed. We distinguished leadership from managership, (Graen & Wakabayashi, 1994; Graen & Uhl-Bien, 1995) and suggested that our model is more appropriate for understanding leadership than managership. In fact, the distinction between managers and leaders has not been an unfamiliar one in leadership literature. For example, Zalesnik (1977) argued that managers are different from leaders. Burke (1982) extended such a distinction to understanding empowerment. Burke argued that leaders and managers differ in terms of how they empower followers. In sum, we suggest that leadership deals with incremental influences a leader has on followers, with incremental meaning above and beyond formal authorities, rules, and regulations. Managership, on the other hand, deals with formal influences a leader has on followers, with formal meaning authorities, rules, and regulations legitimized by the organizational system. As such, we can also talk about leadership as influence on extra-role behavior, whereas, managership is influence on in-role behavior (Graen, 1989; Graen & Wakabayashi, 1994; Uhl-Bien & Graen, 1992). Leadership involves the use of interpersonal influence above and beyond that prescribed by the organizational role. In other words, leadership can motivate followers and leaders to perform extra-role behavior using interpersonal means instead of formal authority. On the other hand, managership involves the motivation of role-prescribed behavior using rules, rewards, and punishments to induce subordinates to perform.

The fundamental difference between leadership and managership described above can be concretized in terms of where, when, why, and how each approach functions, and the cost and benefit of each approach. Table 15.1 summarizes these differences between managership and leadership. For example, managers are more likely to exert their influence on jobs, whereas leaders use their influence on projects. When it's business as usual, influence from leaders is not needed. When innovation and change are required, however, leaders' social influence is more effective than managers' inducement of minimal role compliance in followers. When the objective is to create integrated teamwork, again leadership is more appropriate than managership. Managers manage by written rules and procedures, whereas leaders lead by transformational appeals and unwritten rules (Graen, 1989). The cost of leadership is in the investment in relationship, which is a time-consuming as well as a risky process. However, if outcomes such as innovation and change are desired, leadership—not managership—is required (Imai, 1991; Nemoto, 1994).

We believe that the distinction between managership and leadership is an important one because one has to know what kind of outcome is desired before one can decide on the means to the end. In this case, leadership and managership serve as the means to different ends. If one wants to continue business as usual, is willing to settle for minimal role compliance from followers, and accepts minimum acceptable performance, competent managership without leadership will be sufficient. On the other hand, if one wants committed innovation and change toward continuous effectiveness improvement, leadership is necessary. *Ours is a model of leadership.* In other words, we concern ourselves with how leaders can exert incremental influence effectively to induce extra-ordinary outcomes. This requires a careful explication of the influence process. The influence process for managers is much more straightforward. To the extent that a manager can implement rules and procedures and have effective control mechanisms, minimal role compliance

TABLE 15.1
Leadership Continuum

	Managership	*Leadership*
Where?	Jobs	Projects
When?	Business as usual	Innovation and change
Why?	Overdetermine minimal routine	Create integrated teamwork
How?	Efficient use of rules and resources	Transformation of self-interest into team interest via incremental influence
Cost?	Elaborate communication and control	Investment in relationships
Benefit?	Minimal role compliance	Continuous improvement
Process?	Role Giving	Role Making

TABLE 15.2
Combinations of Managership and Leadership

	Leadership	
	Lower	*Higher*
Managership		
Lower	(a) Unacceptable performance and unresponsive to needed change	(b) Rule violation but responsive to needed change
Higher	(c) Minimal role compliance and unresponsive to needed change	(d) Beyond role compliance and continuous efforts toward needed improvement

can be determined. Thus, it is our belief that the leadership process warrants careful consideration as a means of motivating extra-role behavior required for innovation and change in organizations.

The interaction of managership and leadership is illustrated in Table 15.2. As shown, cell (a) consists of lower (less-competent) managers with lower (less skillful) leadership, cell (d) includes higher (more-competent) managers with higher (more skillful) leadership. Cells (b) and (c) contain the two combinations, which are higher on one and lower on the other. Clearly, those in cell (a) are the targets for "rightsizing," and those in cell (d) are the future executives if they continue to grow in managerial competence and leadership skill. In the off diagonals, those in cell (c) are most effective in stable and simple processing situations (e.g., production of mature products or services of routine nature), and those in cell (b) are most effective in units that can be undermanaged but which require innovation and change of a dramatic kind (e.g., the more creative functions of research and development, design, advertising, marketing, sales, public relations, or turnaround executives. Comparisons of the people in these four cells contrasting middle managers with executives in lean and competitive companies generally should reveal that cells (b) and (d) contain disproportionately higher percentages of executives relative to the middle manager base if leadership is more valued at the executive level.

LEADERSHIP APPROACHES

Our taxonomy of leadership approaches is shown in Table 15.3 (Graen & Uhl-Bien, 1995; Graen & Wakabayashi, 1994). The primary approaches to leadership focus tightly on the leader, the follower, and their relationship. In the leader-based approach, the primary focus is on the leader. The critical issue of interest concerns the question: What is the proper mix of personal characteristics and leader behavior to promote desired outcomes? Based on this viewpoint, the focus is on leader behaviors and characteristics, such as leader traits, leader behaviors, personality variables, and leader attitudes, perceptions, power, influence, and other qualities. Adopting a follower-based perspective, on the other hand, generates approaches that focus primarily on follower issues. In this case, the critical question of interest becomes: What is the proper mix of follower characteristics and follower behavior to promote desired outcomes? Like the leader-based approach, this approach focuses on how traits, behaviors, attitudes, perceptions, expectations, and so forth affect the type and effectiveness of certain leadership styles and techniques, but this time with respect to followers. Finally, a relationship-based approach focuses on the dyadic relationship between the leaders and the followers and between followers within teams and networks. The critical question of interest in this case is: What is the proper mix of relational characteristics (e.g., trust, respect, mutual commitment) to promote desired outcomes? This approach focuses on how traits, behaviors, attitudes, expectations, and so forth of both leaders and followers affect the type and effectiveness of particular leadership styles and techniques.

As described in the leadership taxonomy, each of these approaches should then be considered in combination with the others. This generates a whole new set of issues of how the characteristics of leaders, followers, and relationships in combination interact with each other to influence leadership outcomes. Clearly, all three approaches to leadership can and often should (contingency specified) be used at the same time *by the same leader but with different followers*. Moreover, leaders can and often should (contingency specified) *move from one approach to*

TABLE 15.3
Approaches to Leadership

	Leader-Based	Relationship-Based	Follower-Based
What is leadership?	Behavior of the person in leader role that generates influence of leader over followers	Mutual trust, respect, and commitment that generates mutual influence between parties	Ability and motivation to manage one's own performance through a team
What behaviors constitute leadership?	Establishing and communicating vision; inspiring, instilling pride	Building strong relationships with followers; mutual learning and accommodation	Empowering, coaching, facilitating, giving up control
Advantages?	Leader as rallying point for organization; common understanding of mission and value; can initiate wholesale change	Accommodates differing needs of subordinates; can elicit superior work from different types of people	Makes the most of follower capabilities; frees up leaders for other responsibilities
Disadvantages?	Highly dependent on leader; problems if leader changes or is pursuing inappropriate vision	Effort-requiring; relies on high quality relationships between specific leaders and members	Highly dependent on follower initiative and ability
When appropriate?	Fundamental top-down improvements; charismatic leader in place; limited diversity among followers	Continuous dyadic improvements; adequate diversity among followers	Integrated team improvements; highly capable and team-committed followers

Note. James Dean collaborated with authors.

another over time as conditions change. One *caveat* is that the relationship-based approach requires more investment over time than the other two and hence requires more lead-time and effort.

Each of the three approaches has advantages and disadvantages and is more appropriate in specified situations. However, we need to specify in detail under what conditions each of these three complementary, not competing, approaches is warranted and under what conditions it should be changed. As shown in Table 15.4, two complementary roles must be played with cooperation and commitment for any of the three approaches to be effective: The active role and the reactive role. Although these roles have often been confused with the actors (leader and follower),

TABLE 15.4
Roles to Be Played

Mission	Active (Leader Role)	Reactive (Follower Role)
Vision	Create	Accept
Objectives	Develop	Implement
Procedures	Design	Trust and Follow
Processes	Enforce	Respect and Maintain
Evaluate and Correct	Assess and Adjust	Accept and Comply
Reward	Establish Criteria, Judge, and Mediate	Acknowledge Fairness
Team Enhancement	Initiate	Follow Through

the leader can play the reactive role and the follower can play the active role. In sum, both roles must be played effectively, but different actors play these roles under the three primary approaches. In the leader-based role, leaders must be convinced that they need to play the active role and followers the reactive role. In contrast, the follower-based approach requires that followers accept the need for the roles to be reversed somewhat: If all are reversed, self-leadership; if all but vision are reversed, self-directing; if all but vision and objectives are reversed, self-implementing. Finally, the relationship-based approach requires that followers accept the need to share and reciprocate the role elements (they can play either roles as the situation dictates).

APPLYING THE MODEL TO TEAMS

A leader is not a leader without followers. Typically, leadership involves multiple people. Thus, it appears that researchers should consider applying models of leadership to group or team settings. Unfortunately, this has not been done consistently. The model we propose may be meaningfully applied to group or team settings. We begin with the proposition that leadership within teams can have a work and a social component. The work component on which we are focusing (working relationship) is different from the task orientation identified in previous team research, (e.g., Beene & Sheats, 1948). Task orientation refers to the emphasis on getting the job done. We are focusing on the nature of dyadic relationships within a team. In terms of relationship building, we suggest that there can be a kind of relationship that is developed within the context of work, and with quality in the relationship, can be conducive to task performance. For example, the relationship between a leader and a follower can be highly effective in that both have trust and respect for the other's work and a sense of obligation towards the other's work-related problems. This kind of relationship can be exemplified, for example, when one is required to bail the other out in emergency work situations. This relationship is developed within the work context and takes on its meaning within the work context, but in itself is not restricted to a task orientation. This kind of relationship has been conceptualized and examined extensively in leadership research. Specifically, Graen and his colleagues argue that effective work relationships can be distinguished from ineffective work relationships (e.g., Graen, 1976; Graen & Uhl-Bien, 1995; Graen & Wakabayashi, 1994). An effective work relationship is referred to as having a high-quality leader–member exchange and an ineffective work relationship is referred to as having a low-quality leader–member exchange. Leader–member exchange (LMX) is the quality of the relationship that emerges between leaders and their direct reports over time, given the unique characteristics of each and within complex organizational contexts (Graen & Scandura, 1987; Klein & Kim, 1998; Scandura & Lankau, 1996).

Graen and his colleagues described a three stage role-making process between different dyads of a team that may be relevant to team building (Graen & Uhl-Bien, 1995; Graen & Wakabayashi, 1994; Maslyn & Uhl-Bien, 2001). According to this process model, working relationships can develop from the initial stage of strangers, to the middle stage of acquaintances, to the mature stage of partners. As relationships move from strangers to partners, the interactions between the parties move from "economic" to "trust-based" ones (Blau, 1964). Economic-based exchange in the initial stage of relationship building is contractual in nature, and is characterized by having careful definition of obligations for parties involved in the exchange, specific time spans and terms for exchange, and enforceable terms of exchange. Trust-based exchange in the mature stage of relationship building is characterized by implicit felt obligations between the parties involved, nonspecific time spans or terms for exchange, lack of absolute certainty for fulfillment of the exchange obligation by the other party, or the lack of absolute certainty for effective enforcement of such exchange obligations. Thus, the working relationship is transformed from a barter partner to that of a trusted teammate. It should be noted that trusted teammates are not necessarily close friends. LMX is a valid measure of the maturity of the work relationship between two workers (Gerstner & Day, 1997).

We suggest that within team contexts, effective work relationship between team members described by the LMX theory may be useful in helping us understand the dynamics of team building. First, since our objective is to understand relationship building within work teams and not social teams, it only seems natural to focus on effective work relationships. Second, more recent work has extended the LMX literature stream to the team level and results are promising (Uhl-Bien & Graen, 1992). Third, research has illustrated that LMX relationships are related to organizational effectiveness (for a review, see Graen & Uhl-Bien, 1995), leading to the proposition that LMX may also in some way contribute to team effectiveness.

TABLE 15.5
Three Approaches to Team Leadership

Focus	Approach	Collaboration
Downward	Leader-based	Singular
Upward	Relation-based	Shared
Horizontal	Follower-based	Partner

For example, through the use of mature leadership relationships, teams are able to develop, when needed, additional resources beyond those formally defined by the organization (Zalesny & Graen, 1986). Mature leadership relationships are also suggested to lead to an internalization of team interests—a transformation of self-interest to team interests (Burns, 1978; Graen & Uhl-Bien, 1993), which has been linked to better team development and output success (Locke & Latham, 1990). Therefore, a theoretical foundation exists that the development of a network of mature leadership-exchange relationships within teams should be positively associated with team effectiveness.

Team leadership can be deconstructed into (a) leader-based (leader's view of relationships with followers), (b) follower-based (followers view of relationships with each other), and (c) relation-based (follower's view of relationships with their leader). Is it conceivable that across teams with different levels of success, one type of team composition may be more important than another? This is of interest because teams may have top-down leaders (leader-based), bottom-up leaders (follower-based) or shared leadership (relation-based) as shown in Table 15.5. As shown, focus and collaboration can characterize the three approaches.

TESTING THE MODEL

Leadership researchers have long been interested in defining and enhancing leader effectiveness (cf. Bass, 1981; Eden, 1993; House 1977, 1988; House & Baetz, 1979; Stogdill, 1984; Yukl, 1989). For example, Yukl (1989) created a taxonomy of leader behavior after reviewing previous conceptualizations and categorizations of leader behavior. Yukl's taxonomy included giving-seeking information, making decisions, influencing people, and building relationships. Interestingly, a key operationalization of leader effectiveness in most previous research is follower, group, or organizational performance. Our conceptualization of leadership effectiveness includes previous operationalizations by considering both team outcomes and teamwork process.

To examine the dual nature of relationships in project team settings, we distinguished the working relationship from the friendship relationship. An effective work relationship as conceptualized by LMX represents only one of several types of relationships in teams. Relationships in teams can also be focused outside of work. These are commonly known as dyadic friendships. There exists a good deal of work in the social network literature extolling the need for "liking" relationships at the team level (e.g., Krackhardt & Stern, 1988; Nelson, 1989; White, 1961). Moreover, dyadic friendship networks can be related to team communications and conflict (Krackhardt & Kilduff, 1990; Labianca, Brass, & Gray, 1998). At the organizational level, however, as far back as the Hawthorne studies (Rothlisberger & Dickson, 1939), the importance of friendships, or liking relationships, in organizations have been investigated. Friendships in organizations are suggested to provide useful emotional support. For example, "Employees who find little satisfaction in a dull, repetitive job may refrain from quitting because they really like their coworkers" (Steers & Porter, 1991; p. 196). In such situations, coworkers provide comfort, support, and satisfaction on an otherwise meaningless job. In fact, there is work suggesting that affective liking, or friendship, particularly of one's leader (upward), may be critical to organizational success (Moore, 1996). Fraternization among workers (horizontal) is suggested to help morale and give people a reason for going to work. Finally, there is work which suggests that the metaphor of the organizational leader as a pseudo-military commander must be replaced by a metaphor based on friendship; the basic assumption is that friendship provides connection and interdependence, and that this changes the relationship between leader and follower from that of superior and subordinate to one of friend and friend. The goal is mutual actualization that affirms the best in human beings both as leaders and followers (Parraault, 1991). Finally, Boyd and Taylor (1998) proposed a promising developmental model of friendships in leader-follower exchanges based partly upon the developmental model of LMX (Graen & Uhl-Bien, 1995).

In our preliminary tests of the model, we investigated the separate contributions of leader-based, relationship-based, and follower-based approaches to team outcomes and teamwork processes. Furthermore, we distinguished an LMX from friendship in these relationships. Leadership approaches were measured on quality of work-focused trust, respect, and commitment of the other(s) (LMX) and outside work-focused interpersonal friendship. These two measures of a relationship were factorally orthogonal and analyzed as such in the following two studies. In each study, 40 teams of engineers worked on industrial design projects for six months. At the project deadline, teams presented their products for evaluation by company clients.

Results of the investigations are shown in Table 15.6. As shown, team performance (the company evaluated ratings of the engineering design project) was related to the three different leadership approaches. In the Leader-based approach, the evaluation of the trust, respect, and commitment (LMX), and friendship of the

TABLE 15.6
Mean Differences Between Higher and Lower Performing Teams on LMX and
Friendship by Leadership Approach

	Leader-Member Exchange		Friendship	
Approach	Study 1	Study 2	Study 1	Study 2
Leader-based	.47	.73	−.74	NS
Relation-based	.55	1.01	−.63	−.30
Follower-based	.56	1.17	−.79	NS

Note. LMX and friendship measured at time 3 and performance at time 4.

followers by the leader contributed to team performance based on LMX in both studies and based on friendship in only study 1. In the Relation-based approach, the evaluation of trust, respect, commitment (LMX), and friendship of leader by followers contributed to team performance based on LMX and friendship in both studies. Finally, in the follower-based approach, the evaluation of trust, respect, commitment (MMX), and friendship of peer by peer contributed to team performance based on MMX in both studies and based on friendship in Study 1 only. Although all three approaches contributed to team performance, the contributions of LMX and MMX were positive (higher LMX and MMX were related to more effective performance) but the contributions of friendship were negative (higher friendship was related to less-effective performance). Moreover, the contributions of the three different approaches were not the same. In terms of LMX and MMX, all three approaches contributed about the same in Study 1, but in Study 2, relation-based and follower-based contributed more than leader-based. Also in terms of friendship, all three approaches contributed about the same in Study 1, but only relation-based contributed in Study 2. Clearly, the three different approaches tap different aspects of the team's leadership context.

In this team situation, trust, respect, and commitment, the critical dimensions of the leader–member exchange model, contributed positively to team performance. In the first study, all three approaches contributed about the same, but in the second study the leader-based contributed less than the other two. Leader's evaluation was relatively less important. In contrast, friendship in Study 1 on all three approaches showed negative contributions, but in Study 2 only relation-based showed a negative contribution. In these studies, LMX and MMX appeared to facilitate team performance, and friendship appeared to interfere with it.

The manager of all project teams in the second study evaluated teamwork effectiveness. As expected, the sum of the three approaches on LMX and teamwork effectiveness produced a correlation of +.64, and that on friendship generated a correlation of −.27. In this team situation, LMX appears to facilitate and friendship appears to interfere with teamwork effectiveness; however, in other team situations friendship may be seen to facilitate it.

In the studies, teams of engineers were attempting to bring about innovations in their client organizations. Other studies of innovation also have produced supportive results (Graen & Uhl-Bien, 1995). Mayfield and Mayfield (1998) reported that improved LMX work relationships can enhance worker performance of over 20%, and worker satisfaction improvements of over 50%. Clearly, research on the relationship between leader–member exchange and innovation demonstrates the importance of all three leadership approaches to innovation (Basu, 1991; Tierney, 1992; Scott, 1993; Tierney, Farmer, & Graen, 1999). These field studies found that innovative behavior was a function of all three bases of leadership: charisma of the leader (leader based), interest of the follower in innovation (follower based), and the leader–member exchange between leader and follower (relational based). In the Tierney and Scott studies, innovative behavior was measured as the quality and quantity of research and development contributions reported by their organizations. In the Basu study, it was measured as the improvement suggestions contributed. In all three studies, the contribution of the leader-based approach was negative, and relation-based and follower-based approaches were positive.

CONCLUSION

Over the life of a complex project, the situational factors may change several times and require appropriate changes be made in leadership approaches. Moreover, because a relation-based approach takes a longer lead time to develop but allows the most flexibility in transitioning, it should be built first (Graen & Uhl-Bien, 1995). Teams with mature leadership relations can quickly and easily change from leader driven to follower driven to partner driven (Uhl-Bien, Graen, & Scandura, 2000). Although all three approaches require a quality of relationship between leader and follower above the stranger level, only the relation-based approach requires the partnership level (Graen & Wakabayashi, 1994). Therefore, we recommend that people concerned with issues of work motivation in organizations of the future pay particular attention to the question raised in this chapter: When to use which leadership approach? Leadership is a critical motivating process in work organizations and should not be considered handicapped by a single approach. As the U.S. military learned in Vietnam at a tremendous cost, (Hal Angle, personal communication, 1992) the leader-based approach cannot be the only one. Rather, follower-based and relational-based must be options. Let's not forget this costly lesson.

Let us highlight our key points:

1. Face-to-face leadership requires an understanding of how it differs from managership.

2. Holistic thinking is required: Leadership involves three different role-based approaches (not merely styles).
3. Contingency factors that involve key operating parameters should be considered.
4. Leadership outcomes should be carefully defined.
5. Complex tasks involving multiple contingencies necessitate the relation-based approach.

As leaders and their followers transform their organizations from the obsolete Ford/Sloan "Silo design" to the newer "Toyota overlapping team design" (Graen & Wakabayashi, 1994), leaders and followers will require the flexibility inherent in our complete contingency model of face-to-face leadership. Our preliminary tests of the model were encouraging. We agree that the contingency theorists were on the right track, but they needed to break out of their oversimplified, confounded, and resistant-to-change paradigm. We welcome them to try this new paradigm.

ACKNOWLEDGEMENTS

The authors would like to thank Joan Graen for her editing, and management support, Mary Uhl-Bien for reading a earlier version of this chapter, and two reviewers for their useful comments and suggestions.

REFERENCES

Bass, B. M. (1981). *Stogdill's handbook of leadership* (Rev. ed.). New York: Free Press.
Basu, R. (1991). *An empirical examination of leader–member exchange and transformational leadership as predictors of innovation behavior.* Unpublished doctoral dissertation, Purdue University.
Beene, K. D., & Sheats, P. (1948). Functional roles of group members. *Journal of Social Issues, 4,* 41–49.
Blau, P. M. (1964). *Exchange and power in social life.* New York: John Wiley & Sons.
Boyd, N. G., & Taylor, R. R., (1998). A developmental approach to the examination of friendship in leader-follower relationships. *Leadership Quarterly 9,* (1) 1–25.
Burke, W. W. (1982). *Organization development: Principles and practice.* Boston: Little, Brown.
Burns, J. M. (1978). *Leadership.* New York: Harper & Row.
Eden, D. (1993). Leadership and expectations: Pygmalion effects and self-fulfilling prophecies in organizations. *Leadership Quarterly, 56,* 215–239.
Fiedler, F. E. (1967). *A theory of leadership effectiveness,* New York: McGraw-Hill.
Fleishman, E. A. (1973). Twenty years of consideration and structure. In E. A. Fleishman & J. G. Hunt (Eds.), *Current development in the study of leadership* (pp. 1–37). Carbondale: Southern Illinois University Press.
Galton, F. (1869). *Hereditary genius: An inquiry into its laws and consequences.* London: Macmillan. (Paperback edition by Meridian Books, New York, 1962).
Gerstner, C. R., & Day, D. V. (1997). Meta-analytic review of leader-member exchange theory: correlates and construct ideas. *Journal of Applied Psychology, 82,* 827–844.

Graen, G. B. (1969). Instrumentality theory of work motivation: Some experimental results and suggested modifications. *Journal of Applied Psychology, 53,* Whole No. 2, Part 2.

Graen, G. B. (1976). Role-making processes within complex organizations. In M. D. Dunnette (Ed.), *Handbook of industrial and organizational psychology* (pp. 1201–1245). Chicago: Rand McNally.

Graen, G. (1989). *Unwritten rules for your career: 15 secrets for fast-track success.* New York: John Wiley & Sons.

Graen, G. B. (1996). At last a production system that works and allows everyone to be an insider. *Applied Psychology: An International Review. 45* (2), 12–17.

Graen, G. B., & Scandura, T. (1987). Toward a psychology of dyadic organizing. In B. Staw & L. L. Cumming (Eds.), *Research in organizational behavior* (Vol. 9, pp. 175–208). Greenwich, CT: JAI Press.

Graen, G. B., & Uhl-Bien, M. (1993). Team leadership–making theory: From mature dyads grow high-performance teams. In A. Kieser, G. Reber, & R. Wunderer (Eds.), *Handbook of Leadership* (2nd ed.). Stuttgart, Germany: Poeschl Verlag.

Graen, G. B., & Uhl-Bien, M. (1995). Development of leader-member exchange (LMX) theory of leadership over 25 years: Applying a multi-level–multi-domain perspective. *Leadership Quarterly, 6,* (2), 219–247.

Graen, G. B., & Wakabayashi, M. (1994). Cross-cultural leadership-making: Bridging American and Japanese diversity for team advantage. In H. C. Triandis, M. D. Dunnette, & L. M. Hough (Eds.), *Handbook of industrial and organizational psychology* (Vol. 4, pp. 415–446). New York: Consulting Psychologist Press.

Hersey, P., & Blanchard, K. H. (1982). *Management of organizational behavior: Utilizing human resources* (4th ed. pp. 150–161). Englewood Cliffs, NJ: Prentice-Hall.

House, R. J. (1977). A 1976 theory of charismatic leadership. In J. G. Hunt & L. L. Larson (Eds.), *Leadership: The cutting edge* (pp. 189–207). Carbondale: Southern Illinois University Press.

House, R. J. (1988). Leadership research: Some forgotten, ignored, or overlooked findings. In J. G, Hunt, B. R. Baliga, H. P. Dachler, & C. A. Schriesheim (Eds.), *Emerging leadership vistas.* Lexington, MA: Lexington.

House, R. J., & Baetz, M. L. (1979). Leadership: Some empirical generalizations and new research directions. In B. M. Staw (Ed.), *Research in Organizational Behavior* (Vol. 1, pp. 341–423). Greenwich, CT: JAI Press.

Imai, M. (1991). *Kaizen: The key to Japan's competitive success.* New York: McGraw-Hill.

Klein, H. J., & Kim, J. S. (1998). A field study of the influence of situational constraints, leader–member exchange and goal commitment on performance. *Academy of Management Journal, 41,* 88–95.

Krackhardt, D., & Kilduff, N. (1990). Friendship patterns and culture: The control of organizational diversity. *American Anthropology, 92,* 142–154.

Krackhardt, D., & Stern, R. N. (1988). Informal networks and organizational crisis: An experimental simulation. *Social Psychology Quarterly, 51,* 123–140.

Labianca, G., Brass, D. J., & Gray, B. (1998). Social networks and perceptions of intergroup conflict: The role of negative Relationships and third parties. *Academy of Management Journal, 41*(1), 55–67.

Locke, E. A., & Latham, G. P. (1990). *A theory of goal setting and task performance.* Englewood Cliffs, NJ: Prentice-Hall

Maslyn, J. M., & Uhl-Bien, M. (2001). Leader-member exchange and its dimensions: Effects of self and other effort on relationship quality. *Journal of Applied Psychology,* in press.

Mayfield, J., & Mayfield, M., (1998). Increasing worker outcomes by improving leader follower relations. *Journal of Leadership Studies, 5,* (1), 72–81.

Moore, J. (1996). Light side of the sun. *Executive Excellence, 13,* (6), 14–16.

Nelson, R. E. (1989). The strength of strong ties: Social networks and intergroup conflict in organizations. *Academy of Management Journal, 32,* 377–401.

Nemoto, M. (1994). The complete Toyota system: Toyota production system, Toyota quality control,

Toyota human resource management, and Toyota strategic management system. Presented at the Graduate School of International development, Nagoya University, Japan, December 6.

Parraault, G. (1991). Leadership as friendship. *Executive Excellence, 8* (6), 8–9.

Rothlisberger, F., & Dickson, W. J. (1939). *Management and the worker.* Cambridge, MA: Harvard University Press.

Scandura, T. A., & Lankau, M. J. (1996). Developing diverse leaders: A leader–member exchange approach. *The Leadership Quarterly, 7,* 243–263.

Scott, S. (1993). *The influence of climate perceptions on innovation behavior.* Unpublished doctoral dissertation, Department of Management, University of Cincinnati.

Steers, R. M., & Porter, L. W. (1991). Motivation in work behaviors (5th ed.). New York: McGraw-Hill.

Stogdill, R. M. (1984). *Handbook of leadership.* New York: Free Press.

Tierney, P. (1992). *The contribution of leadership, supportive environment, and individual attributes to creative performance: A quantitative field study.* Unpublished doctoral dissertation, Department of Management, University of Cincinnati.

Tierney, P., Farmer, S. M. & Graen, G. B. (1999). An examination of leadership and employee creativity: The relevance of traits and relationships. *Personnel Psychology, 52,* 591–620.

Uhl-Bien, M. & Graen, G. B. (1992). Self-management and team-making in cross-functional work teams: Discovering the keys to becoming an integrated team. *Journal of High Technology Management, 3,* 225–241.

Uhl-Bien, M., Graen, G., & Scandura, T. (2000). Implications of Leader-Member Exchange (LMX) for Strategic Human Resource Management Systems: Relationships as Social Capital for Competitive Advantage. In G. R. Ferris (Ed.), *Research in Personnel and Human Resources Management,* Vol.18 (pp. 137–185). Greenwich, CT: JAI Press.

White, H. C. (1961). Management conflict and sociometric structure. *American Journal of Sociology, 67,* 185–199.

Yukl, G. A. (1989). *Leadership in organizations* (2nd ed.). Prentice-Hall, NJ:

Zalesnik, A. (1977). Managers and leaders: Are they different? *Harvard Business Review, 55,* 67–78.

Zalesny, M. D., & Graen, G. B. (1986). *Exchange theory in leadership research.* In G. Reber (Ed.), *Encyclopedia of Leadership.* Linz, Germany Linz University Press.

III

The Organizational Level

INTRODUCTION—HENK THIERRY

When work motivation is considered from an organizational perspective, as is characteristic of the chapters adopted in this part of the book, our subject matter is further complicated. This adds a series of potentially conditioning and intervening variables that affect one or more phases of the motivation of employees and managers, or that are, in turn, affected by these. This part of the book stresses that motivation does not necessarily apply exclusively to the behavior of an individual organization member, as it may also be related to the behavior of members of a group, business unit, or organization at large. In other words, in this part the emphasis will shift from the micro-level up to the meso- and macro-level, and backward again.

Ben Schneider's, D. Brent Smith's, and Michelle Paul's chapter 15, on *P–E fit and the Attraction-Selection-Attrition model of organizational funtioning*, touches on the issue of levels of analysis. He signals various ambiguities regarding the definition of the still popular concept of "fit" and notes that there is a distinct bias in favor of the individual level of analysis criteria. Moreover, most fit theories posit that merely positive outcomes accrue from fit. Shneider holds that in addition to the effects of "person–related" variables and those of "environmentally related" attributes, the impact of their interaction should be assessed. In his well-known ASA theory, Schneider takes a person–related perspective to the concept of environment: An organization's environment is best conceptualized in terms of the characteristics of the people in it, in particular those of the founder. The founder's values, competencies, interests, and personality characteristics tend to determine the objectives, strategies, and internal processes of an organization. Thus, an organization will increasingly attract individuals whose attributes match the founder's. Interestingly, the more homogeneous an organization's population, the less probable it will be able to cope with change, to adapt to new challenges, and to innovate when needed.

In chapter 16, **Anat Rafaeli** examines *employee–organizational relationships in employment ads*. Her underlying assumption is that organizations differe in the psycho-social environment they offer employees. Yet little is known about how information concerning the organizational environment is obtained. Rafaeli studies employment ads as a source of implicit information about organizational employment arrangements. She proposes that ads can and should be viewed as potential representations of reality in an organization. Thus, the text and structure of employment ads reveals expectations that job applicants or newly hired employees hold regarding their employee–organizational relationships. One interesting implication may be that employment ads are public forums in which a collective sharing of information about alternative employment relationships in a given society takes place. In aggregate, the set of ads appearing in a given newspaper or a given society may offer information about employment in the society.

Chapter 17, **by Katherine Klein**, focuses on *creating a strong, positive climate for technology implementation*. Klein explores the antecedents that affect the successful implementation of computerized technologies. The chapter highlights the perhaps inevitable tensions between the three organizational groups involved in the adoption and implementation of major new computerized technologies: managers, computer technicians, and targeted technology users. These three groups differ in power, expertise, values, and roles, which results in a weak climate for technology implementation. Klein proposes more moderating factors that may facilitate or inhibit the creation of a strong climate for technology implementation. She proposes that the more employees engage in upward communication of problems and concerns, and the more managers are responsive to employee problems and concerns, the stronger an organization's climate for technology implementation.

The purpose of **Lyman Porter and Gregory A. Bigley's** chapter 18, on *motivation and transformational leadership*, is to demonstrate that the nature and scope of the linkage between employee motivation and transformational leadership can be more fully understood through an explicit consideration of organizational context factors. Conceptual models and empirical studies of transformational leadership have tended to focus narrowly on the leader–follower relationship. Consequently, motivational effects that are revealed when transformational leadership is viewed as a process embedded within an organization have been neglected. The authors examine three situations involving such leadership: (a) the possible effects on followers of multiple transformational leaders, (b) some likely unintended consequences of transformational leadership occurring in one part of an organization, and (c) the potential sustainability of high levels of transformational leadership. The concluding section of this paper highlights some implications for organizations and sets out several suggestions for future research.

Several studies indicate that employees spend a very considerable amount of their "work" time to behaviors not required because of their work roles, for example, coffee breaks, late starts early departures, and chatting. **Kathy A. Hanisch, Charles L. Hulin, and Steven T. Seitz** argue in chapter 19 on *temporal dynamics and emergent properties of organization withdrawal models*, that such behaviors have attitudinal antecedents and might be indicative of these employees' general job attitudes These withdrawal behaviors may function to diminish stress or to decrease disssatisfaction. The authors hold that the causal nature of antecedents, behavioral effects, and organizational consequences should include a concern for the development of those patterns over time. After discussing a few organizational withdrawal models, they present a new computational modeling program, WORKER. Simulation data with this model demonstrated that instead of single behaviors, composite withdrawal patterns should be identified. Such patterns bear on both micro- and meso-levels of analysis.

In chapter 20, **Meni Koslowsky** discusses *some new organizational perspectives on moderators and mediators in the stress-strain process—time urgency, management, and work control*. Koslowsky proposes that time urgency, often considered to be a personal disposition, can be imposed by the environment or the organization. In both cases, it acts as a moderator in a stress model. On the other hand, time management is considered a mediator. Its role in a stress model is to increase a person's control over the situation and to minimize or attenuate the negative effects of stressors. The article discusses the advantages of such a model, its theoretical and practical contributions, as well as some of its limitations.

In conclusion, the chapters in this part witness the diversity of work motivation approaches in the organizational context. One of their merits is the opulence of research ideas, which will hopefully result in more research, both fundamental and applied, in the new millennium. Another merit is a host of suggestions to reconceptualize parts of the cycle of motivated behavior and to add other potentially explanatory variables. But these chapters also reflect the viewpoint that the study of work motivation cannot be restricted anymore to one—the individual—level of analysis only. Multilevel theorizing and research is called for, it not combined with concepts brought forward by disciplines neighboring psychology. These changes make the study of work motivation probably more complex than it already is. Yet it makes it also more challenging, which is a concept still close at heart of being motivated.

16

P–E Fit and the Attraction-Selection-Attrition Model of Organizational Functioning: Introduction and Overview

Benjamin Schneider
University of Maryland, College Park, MD

D. Brent Smith
Rice University, Houston, TX

Michelle C. Paul
In Momentum, Inc., Palo Alto, CA

There is an institutionalized distinction in the organizational sciences segregating those who focus on individual or micro-level phenomena, such as motivation and job attitudes, and those who study organizational or macro-level phenomena, such as strategy, structure, and culture (Staw, 1991). These two perspectives comprise nearly parallel literatures, with one side studying people who work and the other side studying the organizations in which people work. Although some recent research recognizes the need to cross these levels of analysis and identify both individual and organizational contributions to effectiveness (Klein, Dansereau, & Hall, 1994), there has been a failure to integrate these tangential literatures.

Consequently, little progress has been made in the exploration of this "meso" level (House, Rousseau, & Thomas-Hunt, 1995). With few exceptions (e.g., the work of Chatman and her colleagues; Chatman, 1989, 1991; O'Reilly, Chatman, & Caldwell, 1991), research proceeds either at the micro-level, studying individual variables, or at the macro-level studying organizational attributes (Schneider, 1996).

Within the realm of meso-level research, the dominant theoretical framework has been "person–environment (P–E) fit." Historically, the roots of this approach can be traced to Murray's (1938) need-press theory. Murray proposed that when people's needs fit the nature of the environment (the "press"), the match yields positive individual adjustment outcomes. The P–E fit framework lies at the intersection of "situationist" and "personologist" perspectives on the origins of human behavior in general (e.g., Walsh, Craik, & Price, 1992), and of human behavior in organizations in particular (e.g., Kristof, 1996). The P–E fit framework argues that behavior and effectiveness are ultimately a joint function of characteristics of the environment (or organization) and characteristics of the individual.[1] In contrast, situationists see behavior as determined largely by the attributes of the environment within which people behave (e.g., organizational reward system, culture), and personologists see attributes of individuals behaving in organizations as the main cause of behavior (e.g., ability, personality).

However, even within the P–E fit framework, the person and the environment are conceptualized as distinct entities with little regard to, or research on, the manner in which the attributes of people affect (or define) the environment or for the role of the environment in understanding people. Such research would emphasize the reciprocal nature of person and environment, one having influence on the other in a cyclical or nonrecursive fashion. With the exception of the fruitful research program of Kohn and Schooler (1983), such research is rare.

In what follows, we first review some conceptualizations of person–environment fit and some emerging themes from that research. Then, we present an alternative view of P–E fit, the Attraction-Selection-Attrition (ASA) model (Schneider, 1987). The ASA model assumes an extreme, personological position (Schneider, 1989) on the nature of organizational behavior, a position that emphasizes the attributes of people as the defining characteristics of an organization and as the principle determinants of organizational behavior.

Finally, we present summaries of two recent studies carried out by Schneider and his colleagues (Schneider, Smith, Taylor, & Fleenor, 1998; Simco & Schneider, 1997) to test a central proposition of ASA theory—the hypothesis that, over time, organizations tend towards homogeneity of personality. In the first study (Simco & Schneider, 1997), people within an organization are shown to share similar life history experiences (biodata), whereas people in different organizations vary with respect to life history experiences. In the second study (Schneider et al.,

---

[1]In what follows, we use the term *environment* as if it were synonymous with both *situation* and *organization*.

1998), people within an organization are shown to share personality characteristics, whereas people in different organizations are shown to vary with respect to personality. Both studies suggest preliminary support for the hypothesis that the people within an organization tend towards homogeneity of personality.

MAIN CONCEPTS IN PERSON–ENVIRONMENT FIT THEORY

Generally, P–E fit theorists propose that not only do both person and environment function to influence behavior, but it is the *fit* between person and environment that is critical. These theorists operationalize fit as an index of the degree of similarity, overlap, or convergence between a particular set of person-related attributes and a set of environmentally related attributes. Admittedly, there exists ambiguity in how "fit" may be operationalized, and recent articles by Edwards (1991, 1994) have encouraged alternatives to the ubiquitous "difference scores." Generally, difference scores are used to contrast a profile of the attributes of individuals, with a profile of attributes of the environment and for each point in the respective profiles, that difference is calculated and squared. These squared differences are then summed (Cronbach & Gleser, 1953), with larger sums representing poorer fit. Edwards (1991, 1994) has recommended the use of a polynomial regression procedure rather than difference scores because this procedure simultaneously considers the main effects of the individual and the environmental variable *as well as their interaction* as potential correlates of a criterion of interest. Such a procedure, he appropriately argues, permits researchers to apportion variance to main effects and interactions, thus more fully understanding the importance of "fit." However, the calculation of fit is, itself, but one of many important methodological issue in conducting P–E fit research.

A second issue, one we consider to be of fundamental importance, concerns the criterion variable employed in most P–E fit theory and research. Most fit research employs one or more indices of individual affect (e.g., adjustment, satisfaction, commitment) as the criterion of interest. Perhaps this concentration on affect stems from the early conceptual work by Murray (1938), followed by adoption of a variant of the "need–press" model in Holland's (1985) theory of vocational choice or Dawis and Lofquist's (1984) Theory of Work Adjustment (TWA). Holland's theory proposes that individuals whose vocational interests fit the career environments they enter will experience greater satisfaction in those careers. The latter theory, TWA, makes a similar proposal, this time regarding the fit of individual desires (e.g., for autonomy, variety, considerate supervision) to organizational rewards (on these same dimensions), with the outcome being satisfaction and adjustment. Infrequently has research on P–E fit been concerned with individual performance or productivity (for an exception see O'Reilly, Chatman, & Caldwell, 1991). Furthermore, the relationship between P–E fit and indicators of organizational outcomes has yet to be addressed.

A central purpose of this paper is to summarize a recent framework that proposes a new perspective on P–E fit, including ways of conceptualizing possible relationships among P–E fit and organizational outcomes. Prior to describing that framework, however, it is important to review a sampling of more traditional P–E fit research efforts. This will provide the ground against which the figure of ASA will be presented.

A SAMPLING OF PERSON–ENVIRONMENT FIT THEORIES AND RESEARCH

There are two broad approaches to theory and research concerning the person–environment nexus. One approach views aspects of the environment (or the person) as moderating relationships between the person (or environment) and some individual-level criterion of interest. Hackman's and Oldham's (1980) theory of work motivation is one example of a person variable moderating the relationship between an environmental variable and some criterion. Hackman and Oldham propose that jobs with high motivating potential yield increased levels of motivation, especially for people with strong higher-order need strength; that is, the relationship between job attributes and motivation is enhanced for people with strong higher-order needs. Fiedler's (1967) leadership contingency theory is another prominent person–environment fit theory in which individual-level variables moderate environment-criterion relationships. Fiedler proposed that leaders will be effective to the degree that their own personality is appropriate for the "situational favorableness" they encounter. In his framework, more task-oriented personalities are hypothesized to function more effectively using certain styles when situational favorableness is high and others when situational favorableness is low; for more socioemotionally oriented leaders an opposite pattern emerges.

The other approach to P–E fit theory views fit as a predictor of outcomes such as an individual's vocational choice, adjustment, and long-term satisfaction. Research typical of this approach examines multiple dimensions of person and environment simultaneously, indexes the degree to which they fit, and uses that index as a predictor of various individual outcomes. Holland's (1985) theory of vocational choice is perhaps the most widely studied example of this approach. Holland proposed that people choose careers based on the perceived fit of their interests to different career environments. For Holland, the career environment is a function of the interests of the people in the career, making the environment a direct function of people. He describes an interactive relationship between people and environments such that "... the character of an environment reflects the nature of its members and the dominant features of an environment reflect the typical characteristics of its members" (Holland, 1985, p. 35).

Artistic careers, for example, are characterized by people who are complicated, disorderly, emotional, expressive, idealistic, imaginative, impractical, impulsive, and so forth (Holland, 1985, p. 21). Thus, the environments peopled by artistic types stimulate people to engage in artistic activities, foster artistic competencies and achievements, encourage people to see themselves as they are (complicated, disorderly, emotional, expressive), and reward people for the display of artistic values (p. 38). There is a mutually reinforcing reciprocity between the nature of the environment and the people who choose particular careers, and, thus, a particular career environment emerges. Three decades of research on Holland's theory reveals that people seek and choose careers such that their interests fit their career environment and, when they succeed, they are more satisfied and better adjusted to their career.

Holland's (1985) conceptualization of fit is but one of many contemporary P–E fit models. For example, the person–environment fit model that has received perhaps the most recent attention in organizational science is the one proposed by Chatman (1989, 1991) and her colleagues (O'Reilly, Chatman, & Caldwell, 1991). In this research, the values of individuals (assessed prior to the time they join an organization) are compared to the culture of the organization they join. Here, organizational culture is operationalized in terms of the values incumbents ascribe to the organization (these values are the same ones to which newcomers respond; however, in this case, incumbents are making attributions concerning organizational values not representing their own individual values). Research indicates that the stronger the fit between an individual's values and the organization's culture, the more satisfied, committed, and productive he or she is likely to be (O'Reilly et al., 1991).

EMERGENT THEMES
IN PERSON–ENVIRONMENT FIT
THEORY AND RESEARCH

The conceptualizations of person–environment fit theories reviewed here, although clearly not exhaustive (see Kristof, 1996), reveal some common themes. First, there is a clear bias for an individual level of analysis in criteria—primarily job satisfaction, adjustment, and commitment, with a few additional studies employing turnover and performance criteria (Schneider, 1996). To our knowledge there is no research on the relationship between fit and organizational outcomes.

Second, with the exception of Holland's theory, the environment is conceptualized in terms of nonperson attributes; these theories make the implicit assumption that the attributes of people are neither relevant nor important with regard to what the environment is or contains. Thus, for Hackman and Oldham, the job is something "out there," as is culture for Chatman and her colleagues (Schneider, Goldstein, & Smith, 1995). Last, all fit theories implicitly propose only positive consequences to arise from fit despite considerable evidence for the advantages of heterogeneity or diversity in solving at least some classes of problems (cf. Herriot & Pemberton, 1995).

The ASA model, to be presented next, suggests that the consequences of fit may not be all positive. In fact, good fit may result in diminished "effectiveness" for both individuals and organizations. However, these potential negative consequences of good fit emerge as one moves beyond the individual level of analysis to the group or organization level and this, as noted, would be inconsistent with the focus on individual outcomes dominating existing research on person–environment fit.

What does it mean to "move beyond the individual level of analysis"? Researchers with a psychological perspective study individual outcomes. Thus, regardless of whether the predictor or independent variable is conceptualized and measured at the group or organizational level of analysis, outcomes are assessed at the individual level of analysis. Consider the Hackman and Oldham (1980) research referenced earlier. In this work on job characteristics, the attributes of jobs are identified, and then those attributes are used to predict individual outcomes like job satisfaction and effort expended on the job. An alternative approach would still assess the attributes of jobs but then explore the degree to which people, in the aggregate, are more productive or more satisfied when they work at jobs that have higher motivating potential scores.

Or, consider the research that has been accomplished on the relationship between job satisfaction and performance. Schneider (1985) has proposed that this research, which has generally yielded at best a slightly positive relationship in the literature, has a "levels problem." Specifically, the hypothesis of a relationship between satisfaction and performance is, in actuality, an hypothesis at the group or organizational level of analysis that was tested by psychologists at the individual level of analysis. Thus, consultants going from organization to organization hypothesized that when morale was high productivity would be high; they made an organizational-level hypothesis. Psychologists then translated this hypothesis into an individual level phenomenon and, within single organizations, assessed the individual-level job satisfaction of workers and related these data to individual-level assessments of performance. In fact, research by Ostroff (1992) finds that satisfaction aggregated to the organizational (school) level of analysis is significantly correlated with school performance.

The point is that simply because one has an hypothesis does not mean the pattern of relationships derived from that hypothesis will be identical at different levels of analysis. More specifically, because positive outcomes accrue to individuals when they are in homogeneous work environments does not mean that those environments will necessarily accrue positive outcomes. Care must be taken to specify not only the hypothesized relationship between the variables but the level of analysis of both the predictor and the criterion for which the hypothesis is likely to hold. In ASA theory, the predictor of interest is individual-level personality data, and the criteria of interest are organizational structure, process, culture, and effectiveness. Explicit in ASA theory is the idea that individuals with similar personality, through the ASA cycle, tend to people a common organization, and consequences for the organization can be negative.

ASA THEORY

Schneider (1983, 1987, 1989; Schneider et al., 1996) outlined a theoretical framework of organizational behavior based on the mechanism of person–environment fit that integrates both micro (individually focused) and macro (organizationally focused) theories. This view proposes that the outcome of three interrelated dynamic processes, attraction, selection, and attrition (ASA), determines the kinds of people in an organization. Those people, in turn, define the nature of the organization as well as its structure, processes, and culture.

In contrast to the theories presented earlier, ASA (an individual-based framework, like Holland's [1985] theory) proposes that environments are most appropriately conceptualized in terms of the characteristics of the people in them. In addition, as a meso, cross-level, or person–environment model, ASA theory is focused not so much on individual-level outcomes but on organizational-level outcomes, with the criteria of interest including the resultant structure, culture, and effectiveness of organizations rather than individual affect and behavior. The ASA model explicitly acknowledges the potential negative consequences of good P–E fit. Obviously, certain positive consequences, such as harmony, positive affect, effective socialization, and adjustment, are assuredly associated with good fit. However, ASA theory suggests that good fit and homogeneity may lead to an organization's inability to adapt and change when the strategic environment demands change, there is a lack of innovation or an unchallenging acceptance of established norms, and, in general, "dry rot" (Argyris, 1964) or "group think" (Janis, 1972).

In fact, ASA theory proposes a number of testable theoretical propositions. What occurs when the range of personality attributes of a particular organization's members is narrowed as a direct function of them being attracted to, selected by, and remaining in that organization? In addition, Schneider proposed that research on socialization, job attitudes, and leadership might profit from exploration of potential effects of differences in personality on those three constructs. For example, he (1983) noted that socialization research was accomplished most frequently in "total institutions," settings characterized by rigid rules and requirements like police departments, forest rangers, and hospitals. Findings from such research, namely that there is a strong effect of the environment on socialization, could be attributed to the kinds of people who enter these occupations. Research conducted in different organizational settings, such as financial companies or advertising firms, might reveal more of an effect for the person than the organization on socialization (Gundry & Rousseau, 1994; Louis, 1990). Or, consider the issue of job attitudes and the recent finding that job satisfaction may be a function of more than the attributes of the setting; it may also be a function of the worker's personality (Judge, 1992).

Schneider (1987) originally offered seven propositions having numerous implications for the recruitment, selection, and socialization of newcomers as well as for organizational effectiveness interventions and management philosophy. However, these propositions are driven by two central research issues. The first concerns the criticality of the founder in ultimately determining the "character" of an organization; the second suggests that organizations are inclined to, over time, achieve relative homogeneity in their members' individual attributes. We will discuss each of these in turn.

The logic of the ASA framework begins with the personality of an organization's founder. Like Schein's (1992) writings on organizational culture, Schneider (1987) views the founder as the central determinant of organizational behavior. The founder's decisions and actions early in the life of the organization are said to be driven by and reflections of his or her personality. The founder's actions reduce the inherent ambiguity associated with the formative period in an organization's life. In addition, it is through the founder's actions that the organization articulates its goals and basic managerial philosophy (McGregor, 1960) and begins to evolve a particular strategy, structure, and culture. ASA theory essentially proposes that the personality of the founder is projected onto the organization through the goals established for the organization and the strategies, processes, and structures enacted to accomplish those goals. In other words, the blank canvas of the new organization is painted on by the founder; the colorful painting that results is a reflection of the founder's personality (Schneider et al., 1995). Therefore, ASA theory proposes that the so-called environmental attributes of organizations (practices, policies, structure) are enacted by the founder in pursuit of goals and are reflections of the founder's personality.

Based on the early decisions made by founders, organizations can grow and prosper, requiring increasingly large numbers of employees. ASA proposes that potential employees are initially attracted to the founder and the organization he or she has created. This is followed by hiring decisions that tend to reproduce the way the founder thinks and behaves. As Schein (1992) remarks:

> Founders not only choose the basic mission and the environmental context in which the new group will operate, but they choose the group members and bias the original responses that the group makes in its effort to succeed in its environment and to integrate itself. Organizations do not form accidentally or spontaneously. . . . Founders not only have a high level of self-confidence and determination, but they typically have strong assumptions about the nature of the world, the role that organizations play in that world, the nature of human nature and relationships, how truth is arrived at, and how to manage time and space. They will, therefore be quite comfortable in imposing those views on their partners and employees as the fledgling organization copes . . . (pp. 211–213).

These selection strategies and procedures driven by the founder are subsequently utilized by the organization in future recruitment and hiring. Organizations therefore have a basic proclivity to choose those individuals who match the collective characteristics of current members or who fit the basic competencies, interests, personality, and culture of the organization.

Argyris (1958) proposed that organizations indeed attract and select what he called "right types." For Argyris, right types are managers who conform in background and personality to the existing power elite in an organization. Incidentally, empirical evidence exists supporting this view. Jackson, Brett, Sessa, Cooper, Julin, and Peyronnin (1991) studied the homogeneity of top management teams over time and found that demographic-based similarity is likely in top management teams. Likewise, the central proposition of the ASA framework is that an outcome of the ASA cycle is relative homogeneity of the kinds of persons in an organization, especially homogeneity among the leaders of that organization. In other words, organizations are homogeneous with respect to the attributes of their members.

Most person–environment theories propose that the good fit between individuals and organizations yields desirable, beneficial outcomes. Schneider (1987) and his colleagues (Schneider et al., 1995; Schneider, Kristof, Goldstein, & Smith, 1997) do not ascribe to this commonly held belief. Good fit may yield primarily positive outcomes for individuals over the short term; individuals are more likely to be adjusted, satisfied, and committed to the organization. However, research indicates that over the long term, good fit can yield homogeneity in thinking, decision making, and action (Denison, 1990; Miller, 1990). Thus, ASA theory proposes that for organizational and longitudinal outcomes, good fit may be detrimental to organizational health. Good fit may produce a shared perspective on the part of an organization's principle decision makers that leads to strategic myopia, ultimately hindering their ability to both perceive, and consequently adapt to, environmental changes. By implication of the ASA cycle, the organization's strategy and its environment will become misaligned over time. In practice, ASA suggests that homogeneity may be useful in the early stages of an organization's life cycle to promote growth through harmony, collegiality, and focus on the organization's initial goals (Schneider et al., 1997), but, through time, a shift towards heterogeneity (at least, in the perspectives, backgrounds, and personalities of the principle decision-makers) will increase the likelihood of an accurate assessment of an organization's strategic environment.

Schneider (1987), Schneider et al. (1995), and Schneider et al. (1997) have reviewed the literature that is relevant to the ASA framework. At this point, these studies suggest support for the attraction (A) and attrition (A) portions of ASA; little evidence on the selection (S) phase of the model exists and there has been only one direct test of the degree to which homogeneity of personality exists in organizations. For example, research reveals that people are attracted to organizations with characteristics that match their own personalities (Tom, 1971) or that they think will be instrumental for them to attain highly valued outcomes (Vroom, 1966). There is also research that reveals that people are likely to leave organizations they do not fit (Jackson et al., 1991; O'Reilly et al., 1991) and that people choose organizations that fit their need structures, e.g., high-need-for-achievement people choose to work in organizations with individual incentive systems (Bretz, Ash, & Dreher, 1989; Turban & Keon, 1993).

There is also research suggesting that organizations consciously make selection and promotion decisions that serve to clone the personality attributes of the dominant coalition (Pinfield, 1995) and/or fit the personality of the founder of the organization (Schein, 1992). Pinfield (1995) not only notes the use of political, historical, and social issues in making selection and promotion decisions, he also documents how those making such decisions attempt to guarantee, after the fact, that their decisions were appropriate. Schein (1992) also presents several case studies demonstrating the inclination of founders to choose managers and executives similar to themselves as they strive to achieve early successes in their newly formed organizations. In sum, research provides some indirect support that certain kinds of actions on the part of individuals and organizations do in fact promote homogeneity in organizations.

To our knowledge, however, there is only one published study that directly tests the extent to which there is actually homogeneity of personality in organizations. Research of this kind is sparse probably for methodological reasons—it requires very large individual sample sizes from multiple organizations (Schneider et al., 1995). This published study was conducted in England by Jordan, Herriot, and Chalmers (1991), who sampled four organizations containing 344 managers. Jordan et al. (1991) demonstrated that the factors of the 16PF (a factor analytically derived personality measure authored by Cattell) significantly discriminated both among incumbents' occupations and organizations. In other words, they found that different personalities characterized various occupations as a function of the organization in which that occupation exists. Therefore, Jordan et al. (1991) provide evidence supporting the notion that personality is related to the occupations in which people work and that specific personality attributes related to a given occupation varies across organizations. So far as ASA theory is concerned, this suggests that the well-known relationship between personality and occupation is, once again, substantiated (e.g., Holland, 1985) but that organizational differences in personality within occupations is also true—as ASA theory would predict. Indeed, in Schneider's (1987) original paper he cites the hypothesis that accountants who work for the YMCA would likely share some attributes with accountants who work for a stock brokerage house but that, on other attributes, the two sets of accountants would differ. In the first study to be described below, this idea of personality similarity within occupations with differences across organizations is pursued in greater detail using biodata as the individual differences variable of interest. Then a large-scale study across 132 organizations is summarized directly assessing the extent to which there is homogeneity of personality in organizations.

THE BIODATA STUDY OF HOMOGENEITY

Simco and Schneider (1997) proposed that, since life history experiences contribute to personality and interests, such experiences should prove useful in segmenting people into careers and, further, into the organizations in which they carried out their careers (Schneider & Schneider, 1994). The two careers they studied were accountants and attorneys. The accountants ($N = 309$) worked in four different accounting firms, and the attorneys ($N = 378$) worked in two different law organizations (one in the private sector and one in the public sector). A series of stepwise multiple discriminant analyses, using biodata items as predictors, revealed the following:

1. Biodata is a significant discriminator of accountants from attorneys, not an unusual finding in the career literature (Holland, 1985). The squared canonical correlation for this discrimination was .60 ($p < .01$), based on 26 biodata items.
2. Biodata significantly discriminates between attorneys working in private sector versus public sector law organizations. The squared canonical correlation for this analysis was .55 ($p < .01$), based on 27 biodata items.
3. Biodata significantly discriminates among the four accounting firms in which the accountants worked. The squared canonical correlation for this analysis was .29, based on 15 items.

Some additional information about this study is important. First, differentiating accountants from attorneys was made difficult by choosing two adjacent careers from Holland's hexagonal model. In that model, adjacent careers are hypothesized to be more similar to each other than careers further away. In other words, first separating accountants from attorneys was hypothetically difficult, and then separating the members of each career further into their membership organization should have proven even more difficult. Second, the biodata items that differentiated attorneys from accountants were different from those items useful for distinguishing between members of the two law organizations on the one hand, and the members of the four accounting firms on the other hand.

The results of the Simco and Schneider (1997) study extend the work of Jordan et al. (1991) and provide another piece of evidence supporting the homogeneity of persons within organizations, this time based on life history experiences.

THE PERSONALITY STUDY
OF HOMOGENEITY

The central proposition of ASA theory is the prediction that organizations tend towards homogeneity of personality. As noted earlier, only one study, that of Jordan et al. (1991), has directly tested this idea, and some support for the proposition was found. In addition, the study using biodata just reviewed (Simco & Schneider, 1997) provides support for the general notion of homogeneity with regard to individual attributes.

In a second study (Schneider et al., 1998), supported by the Center for Creative Leadership (CCL) and the U.S. Army Research Institute for the Behavioral and

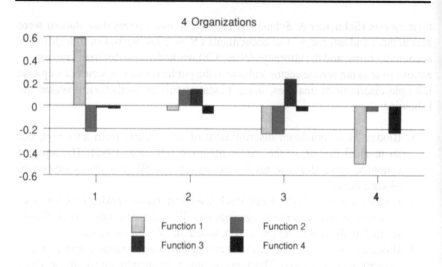

FIG. 16.1. Discriminant function scores.

Social Sciences (ARI), personality data for 12,379 individuals in 142 U.S. public and private businesses were analyzed. Personality was measured using the Myers-Briggs Type Indicator (MBTI), a measure administered to participants in various leadership and management development programs at the CCL. The sample of 142 organizations represents all those organizations for whom at least 25 participants completed the MBTI; thus, the minimum sample of respondents for any one of the 142 organizations was 25 managers.

The analysis of the data employed stepwise multiple discriminant analysis with the four MBTI continuous scale scores used to predict organizational membership. In fact, four discriminant functions were extracted with a squared multiple canonical correlation of .24 ($p < .001$).

Figure 16.1 reveals the personality profiles for four randomly chosen organizations based on the four discriminant functions extracted in the stepwise analysis. In the figure, the first bar for each organization represents that organization's score on the first discriminant function, the second bar the results for the second discriminant function, and so forth. This figure reveals the dramatic differences in profiles that characterize the modal personalities of different organizations.

In fact, the MBTI is most frequently used by consultants and vocational counselors in the form of profiles or types, not based on discriminant function weights but on dichotomies of each of the four continuous scales used in the discriminant analysis. In combination, this produces the 16 MBTI types that have become so familiar to managers and executives in the public and private sectors.

Treating the MBTI as categorical data, a nonparametric chi-square likelihood ratio test of the relationship between the 16 MBTI types and the 142 organizations produced a chi-square of 4308.64 ($p < .0001$), again suggesting a significant relationship between personality and organizational membership. For this analysis, each of the 12,379 individual managers was "typed" and placed in one of the 16 (types) by 142 (organizations) cells of the resultant matrix. The chi-square analysis tests for the degree to which these placements are different from the chance expectations of people in the cells of the matrix. The significant effect indicates that, as predicted by ASA, people are not randomly distributed in the matrix.

SUMMARY AND CONCLUSION

We have tried to summarize a considerable amount of information in this chapter. ASA theory in its original formulation (Schneider, 1987) contained seven propositions regarding attraction, selection, attrition, and homogeneity, as well as a proposition concerning the hypothesized long-term negative consequences of homogeneity for organizational effectiveness. In this chapter, the focus has been on P-E fit, especially as it emerges over time through the ASA cycle, and the consequences of that fit for homogeneity of personality and, in the case of Simco and Schneider (1997), life history experiences. We note here that there are also consequences of fit and homogeneity for organizational outcomes, although neither the research literature nor the present paper has much attended to this possibility (Schneider et al., 1997).

We, and Schneider in his earlier papers (e.g., Schneider 1983, 1987), have written as if homogeneity of personality in organizations is entirely caused by the ASA cycle. In the ASA model, little credence is given to the role of "the environment" in creating personalities. That is, "the environment" is frequently considered to affect an individual's personality through the process of organizational socialization (e.g., Louis, 1990). In the socialization literature, however, "the environment" to which people are socialized is separated conceptually from the socialization practices used. Schneider (1983) noted that much socialization research has been dominated by the study of what happens in total institutions (such as police forces, the military, and the priesthood), settings characterized by people who are oriented towards structure to begin with, and who create structured environments for newcomers because that structure fits both those who steer socialization and those who are socialized. Indeed, Schneider (1983) argued that socialization is smooth in most organizations precisely because those who are attracted to and selected by the organization come, in some sense, already partially "socialized."

It is very hard to break away from the situationist perspective in the interpretation of why organizations may be characterized by people with similar life history experiences and/or similar personalities. Even in the research literature on P-E fit, the "E" is conceptualized as if it were somehow separate from the "Ps" there. Thus, with the exception of Holland's theory of career environments, all other perspectives on and approaches to the measurement of environments places the environment "out there" and separate from the attributes of people in the environment. In the present effort, the focus has been on the organizational consequences of P–E fit, especially the consequences in terms of the personality of the members of the organization. In our view, it is the people present who make an environment (or organization) what it is.

However, we currently have no evidence concerning the implications of such homogeneity for the ways recruitment, selection, and socialization are actually practiced in organizations, or the strategies, structures, and cultures that evolve in organizations characterized by different modal personalities. We also lack evidence concerning potential implications of homogeneity for eventual organizational effectiveness. The present results, however, do contribute to the evidence beginning to accumulate concerning the potential role individual differences might play in understanding organizational phenomena. As noted in the introduction, there has been a tendency in the organizational sciences to ignore the attributes of individuals when conceptualizing and studying the behavior of organizations; people are interesting, the literature seems to say, but not when it comes time to understand important *organizational* phenomena. The conceptual and empirical literature in the organizational sciences implicitly presents the argument that it is okay to study individual differences in skills and personality as correlates of individual outcomes but to not muddy the organizational behavior and effectiveness waters with such individual phenomena.

Schneider (1996) has recently suggested that a failure of academics and practitioners to explore the linkages between individual differences and organizational phenomena could marginalize the contribution of such efforts to organizational interventions conducted by executives. Typically, executives are unconcerned with individual differences and are more concerned with broader issues of organizational behavior and effectiveness. Research that explores the links across levels of analysis might demonstrate the usefulness of increased attention to individual differences in skills, personality, values, and so forth, thereby furthering the kind of cross-level interest demonstrated by the present conference.

It is time for those of us interested in the study of people in the workplace, in all of their individual differences glory, to reclaim rights to the understanding of organizational behavior and organizational effectiveness. The kinds of data we have summarized in the present paper hopefully begins to reveal how such radical cross-level conceptualization may be possible (Schneider, 1996).

REFERENCES

Argyris, C. (1958). Some problems in conceptualizing organizational climate: A case study of a bank. *Administrative Science Quarterly, 2*, 501–520.
Argyris, C. (1964). *Integrating the individual and the organization.* New York: Wiley, 1964.
Bretz, R. D., Jr., Ash, R. A., & Dreher, G. F. (1989). Do people make the place? An examination of the attraction-selection-attrition hypothesis. *Personnel Psychology, 42*, 561–581.

Chatman, J. (1989). Improving interactional organizational research: A model of person–organization fit. *Academy of Management Review, 14*, 333–349.

Chatman, J. (1991). Matching people and organizations: Selection and socialization in public accounting firms. *Administrative Science Quarterly, 36*, 459–484.

Cronbach, L. J., & Gleser, G. C. (1953). Assessing similarity between profiles. *Psychological Bulletin, 50*, 456–473.

Denison, D. R. (1990). *Corporate culture and organizational effectiveness.* New York: Wiley.

Edwards, J. R. (1991). Person-job fit: A conceptual integration, literature review, and methodological critique. *International Review of Industrial/Organizational Psychology, 6*, 283–357.

Edwards, J. R. (1994). The study of congruence in organizational behavior research: critique and a proposal alternative. *Organizational Behavior and Human Decision Processes, 58*, 51–100.

Fiedler, F. E. (1967). *A theory of leadership effectiveness.* New York: McGraw-Hill.

Gundry, L. R., & Rousseau, D. M. (1994). Communicating culture to newcomers. *Human Relations, 47*, 1068–1088.

Hackman, J. R., & Oldham, G. R. (1980). *Work Redesign.* Reading, MA: Addison-Wesley.

Herriot, P., & Pemberton, (1995). *Competitive advantage through diversity: Organizational learning from differences.* London: Sage.

Holland, J. L. (1985). *Making vocational choices: A theory of careers.* Englewood Cliffs, NJ: Prentice-Hall.

House, R. J., Rousseau, D. M., & Thomas-Hunt, M. (1995). The meso paradigm: A framework for the integration of micro and macro organizational behavior. In L. L. Cummings & B. M. Staw (Eds.), *Research in organizational behavior* (Vol. 17, pp. 71–114). Greenwich, CT: JAI Press.

Jackson, S. E., Brett, J. F., Sessa, V. I., Cooper, D. M., Julin, J. A., & Peyronin, K. (1991). Some differences make a difference: Individual dissimilarity and group heterogeneity as correlates of recruitment, promotion and turnover. *Journal of Applied Psychology, 76*, 675–689.

Janis, I. L. (1972). *Victims of groupthink.* New York: Houghton-Mifflin.

Jordan, M., Herriot, P., & Chalmers, C. (1991). Testing Schneider's ASA theory. *Applied Psychology: An International Review, 40*, 47–54.

Judge, T. A. (1992). The dispositional perspective in human resources research. In G. R. Ferris & K. M. Rowland (Eds.), *Research in personnel and human resources management*, Vol. 10 (pp. 31–72). Greenwich, CT: JAI Press.

Klein, K. J., Dansereau, F., & Hall, R. J. (1994). Levels issues in theory development, data collection, and analysis. *Academy of Management Review, 19*, 195–229.

Kohn, M. L., & Schooler, C. (1983). *Work and personality: An inquiry into the impact of social stratification.* Norwood, NJ: Ablex.

Kristof, A. L. (1996). Person-organization fit: An integrative review of its conceptualization, measurement, and implications. *Personnel Psychology, 49*, 1–49.

Lofquit, L. H., & Dawis, R. V. (1969). *Adjustment to work.* New York: Appleton-Century-Crofts.

Louis, M. R. (1990). Acculturation in the workplace: Newcomers as lay ethnographers. In, Schneider, B. (Ed.), *Organizational climate and culture.* San Francisco: Jossey-Bass.

McGregor, D. M. (1960). *The human side of enterprise.* New York: McGraw-Hill.

Miller, D. (1990). *The Icarus paradox: How exceptional companies bring about their own downfall.* New York: Harper/Collin.

O'Reilly, C. A., Chatman, J., & Caldwell D. F. (1991). People and organizational culture: A profile comparison approach to assessing person-organization fit. *Academy of Management Journal, 34*, 487–516.

Ostroff, C. (1992). The relationship between satisfaction, attitudes, and performance: An organizational level of analysis. *Journal of Applied Psychology, 77*, 963–974.

Pinfield, L. T. (1995). *The operation of internal labor markets: Staffing practices and vacancy chains.* New York: Plenum.

Schein, E. H. (1992). *Organizational culture and leadership* (2nd ed.). San Francisco: Jossey-Bass.

Schneider, B. (1985). Organizational behavior. *Annual Review of Psychology, 36*, 573–611.

Schneider, B. (1987). The people make the place. *Personnel Psychology, 40*, 437–454.

Schneider, B. (1989). E = f(P, B): The road to a radical approach to person–environment fit. *Journal of Vocational Behavior, 31*, 353–361.

Schneider, B. (1996). When individual differences aren't. In Murphy, K. R. (Ed.), *Individual differences in the workplace*. San Francisco: Jossey-Bass.

Schneider, B., Goldstein, H. W., & Smith, D. B. (1995). The ASA framework: An update. *Personnel Psychology, 48*, 747–774.

Schneider, B., Kristof, A. L., Goldstein, H. W., & Smith, D. B. (1997). What is this thing called fit? In N. R. Anderson & P. Herriott (Eds.), *Handbook of selection and appraisal* (2nd ed.). London: Wiley.

Schneider, B., & Schneider, J. L. (1994). Biodata: An organizational focus. In G. S. Stokes, M. D. Mumford, & W. A. Owens (Eds.), *Biodata handbook*. Palo Alto, CA: CPP Books.

Schneider, B., Smith, D. B., Taylor, S., & Fleenor, J. (1998). Personality and organizations: A test of the homogeneity of personality hypothesis. *Journal of Applied Psychology, 83*, 462–470.

Simco, J. L., & Schneider, B. (1997). Biodata predictors of organizational membership. Unpublished manuscript, University of Maryland, College Park.

Staw, B. M. (1991). Dressing up like an organization: When psychological theories can explain organizational action. *Journal of Management, 17*, 805–819.

Tom, V. R. (1971). The role of personality and organizational images in the recruiting process. *Organizational Behavior and Human Performance, 6*, 573–592.

Turban, D. R., & Keon, T. L. (1993). Organizational attractiveness: An interactionist perspective. *Journal of Applied Psychology, 78*, 184–193.

Vroom, V. R. (1966). Organizational choice: A study of pre- and postdecision processes. *Organizational Behavior and Human Performance, 1*, 212–226.

Walsh, W. B., Craik, K. H., & Price, R. H. (Eds.). (1992). *Person–environment psychology: Models and perspectives*, Mahwah, NJ: Erlbaum.

Weick, K. E. (1969). *The social psychology of organizing*. Reading, MA: Addison-Wesley.

17

Employee–Organizational Relationships in Employment Ads

Anat Rafaeli
Technion Institute of Technology, Israel

An assumption of research on employee motivation is that organizations differ in the psycho-social environment they offer employees (cf. Louis,1990; Trice & Beyer, 1993) or the related "implicit employment contract" (Rousseau & McLean-Parks, 1993). The fit between individual employees and such organizational differences has been shown to influence important outcomes (cf. O'Reilly, Chatman, & Caldwell, 1991).

But how do prospective employees learn about such organizational differences? While such information appears critical to individual choice processes, little is known about how it is obtained by job seekers. Research on employee recruiting, on organizational choice, and on person-organization fit has not answered this question (cf. Judge & Cable, 1996; Miller & Jablin, 1991; Tom, 1971). Building on Rafaeli and Oliver (1998), this essay argues that employment ads can be a valuable source of implicit information about organizational employment arrangements, although ads are typically assumed ineffective recruiting vehicles.

The chapter *does not* address the question of ad effectiveness in recruitment, which is problematic (Breaugh, 1992; Decker & Cornelius, 1979; Saks, 1994; Wanous, 1992). Rather, I argue that one of the functions of ads, which appear all over the world, may be to provide job seekers and other ad readers insight into alternative employment relationships. The function of ads is therefore argued here to be not only, and perhaps even not primarily, to recruit employees. Rather, ads are proposed to be a means of helping individuals in the job market learn about available employment relationships and make a choice among these alternatives.

Even superficial scanning of ads reveals significant variation between ads in the type and focus of the information contained and conveyed.[1] The conceptual framework advanced here begins to make sense of this variation. I begin with the assertion that ads should *not* be viewed as merely trivial, technical artifacts. Next, a variable that can be loosely labeled "the implicit motivational agreement between employees and organizations," which is proposed to be conveyed by the text of ads is described. Variations in the text of ads are then argued to represent values of this variable.

EMPLOYMENT ADS ARE MEANINGFUL ARTIFACTS

The text of an employment ad may represent what organizations or their agents *select* to appear in the ad, rather than the objective reality in the organization. But ads clearly vary in their content. This chapter contends that this variation is meaningful. The text of ads, because it is ultimately determined by organizational employees, can be argued to reflect the organizational culture or values (Schneider, Goldstein, & Smith 1995). This is because the design of the ad can be assumed to be what students of organizational culture label "an artifact" of prevailing assumptions in the organization (Trice & Beyer, 1993). Similar to other organizational actions, such as dress, physical arrangements, or behavioral patterns, the text and appearance of ads can be argued to reflect shared assumptions in the organization. Moreover, the message conveyed in ads is likely to influence attraction to the organization (cf. Schneider, 1987). And, if ads are the first impression that job applicants have of an employing organization, their text may in some fashion frame individual sense-making efforts. Such framing may influence experienced or enacted reality in the organization (Weick, 1979). Thus the text of the ad may turn into a prophecy that is ultimately tested in perceptions of an organizational reality. While this prophecy may fail, individual sense-making efforts may nonetheless be tinted by the messages conveyed by ads. Hence, the text of the ad can contribute to employees' perceptions of the

---

[1]There is also significant variation among ads in nonverbal aspects such as priming and attention-grabbing effects, fonts, use of logos, and other devices. But this variation is outside the scope of this paper, since my focus is only on verbal rather than nonverbal communication in ads.

organizational culture and may contribute to organizational sense-making efforts (Weick, 1995).

EMPLOYMENT ADS ARE MORE THAN TECHNICAL LISTS OF VACANCIES

Research on product advertising suggests that advertising may not lead customers to go out and buy a particular product. But advertising can generate a particular image of the product or a family of products (Aaker & Myers, 1987; Ogilvy, 1985). A similar process can be suggested with regard to employment advertising. Since product advertising serves to formulate images of products, then employment advertising is argued to formulate images of organizations and the employment opportunities they offer.

In a survey of ad readership I conducted (Rafaeli, 1997), I learned that *individuals routinely read employment ads whether or not they are looking for a job.* Individuals actively looking for a job reported more frequent and more thorough reading of the ads, but even these people did not see ads as a primary source of referral to a particular job. Rather, the reading of ads was considered a source of information about a variety of employment opportunities and other aspects of the labor market. One respondent, a manager in a civil service organization with many years of experience and no intent to look for a new job, explained to me: "I read ads all the time. It calms me to read them. It is like reading book or movie reviews even if I have not seen the movie. It's a way of being there, and keeping in touch with the world, even though I am still working in the same place. I can see what other places offer and so on."

I therefore propose that ads convey not only which organizations have openings, but also what employment relationships exist in various organizations. The proposition is a part of a broader argument I make elsewhere, that employment ads are neglected by organization scholars although they are recurring elements of the discourse of employment in Western civilization (for more detail see Rafaeli & Oliver, 1998).

EMPLOYMENT ADS AS ORGANIZATIONAL PROJECTIONS

In the discourse of ads, a shared skeleton of *all* employment ads can be identified. The skeleton included the name of the job title, and a technical invitation to apply for the job in the form of "Send your resume to . . ." or "Call telephone number. . . ." (Rafaeli & Oliver, 1998). However, a review of ads around the world finds that ads also include information about the organization (e.g., structure, product, niche, culture, or clients), the job (e.g., duties, skill requirements, tasks, and rewards), and the employment context (e.g., challenges or opportunities). The text of many ads may also be much more emotional than a technical job posting would predict. To illustrate, consider two examples of ads that appeared in Hong Kong, both posting an opening for an accounting clerk:

Ad Number 1 (the complete text of the ad):

We are a U.S. $10 billion multinational, high-technology corporation with a strong global presence in semiconductors, communications, computers, and data communication. We offer advanced technology training and exposure, professional awards, a rewarding career paths, competitive salary and fringe benefits. In line with our expansion, we invite applications for the position of Accounting Clerk. Please contact . . .

Ad Number 2 (the complete text of the ad):

Accounts clerk Urgently required
—LCC inter
—Full set of books
—Working experience preferable
Please write to . . .

The rich difference in information between the two ads led me to distinguish between "skeletal" ads that are only job postings and "rich" ads that communicate additional information (Rafaeli & Oliver, 1998). This difference also suggests that much more is being communicated by ads than a technical announcement of employment opportunities. As will be developed next, I propose that the text of ads can communicate, among other things, information about the nature of the relationship between employees and employers in an advertising organization.

EMPLOYMENT ADS AND EMPLOYEE– ORGANIZATIONAL RELATIONSHIPS

The variable that I argue to be implicitly projected by the text of ads is the *alternative employment relationship (AER)* of the organization (Tsui, Pearce, Porter, & Hite, 1995). In one extreme case of this variable, the relationship between employees and the organization is formal, calculative, and based on an objective transaction of employment for rewards. In the other extreme case, the AER is affective and intrinsic, comprising greater involvement and commitment of employees. Obviously, in between these two extremes a wide range of relationships is plausible.

My analysis of this variable builds on a loose integration of three streams of research: (a) theory and research about employment motivation, (b) theory and research about employee commitment, and (c) theory and research about implicit psychological contracts (Hertzberg, Mausner, & Snyderman, 1959; Meyer & Allen, 1984; Morrow, 1993, p. 74; Rousseau & McLean-Parks, 1993; Rousseau, 1995). These three streams all maintain a distinction between two employment arrangements: Arrangements in which individuals are intrinsically and emotionally involved, and typically also transformed, are contrasted with arrangements maintaining employees' limited, calculated, and rational involvement. The distinction, and the assertion of a range of AERs in between the two extremes, is recurring in organizational psychology. What is still unclear is how prospective employees learn about these arrangements, or about where a particular organization is situated on this continuum. I propose that employment ads provide at least a partial answer to these questions.

Three aspects of ads are proposed in Table 17.1 to convey the AER: (a) the amount of information that ads provide about advertising organizations

TABLE 17.1
Aspects of Employment Ads Conveying Alternative Employment
Relationships (AER)

Aspect of the Text of Ad	Nature of Employment Relationship[2]	
	Highly Transactional	Highly Emotional
Amount of information about advertising organization provided in ad	"Send CV to P.O. Box. . ."[3]	"We are a team work based high tech organization with a growing market"
Personalization of discourse in description of the organization	"We have an immediate opening for"	"World Leader in professional services has opening for. . ."
Personalization of discourse in description of the individual	"Qualified applicants should. . ."	"Are you tired of your current job? Are you looking for a new job?
Motivational needs addressed in the ad	"Competitive salary, excellent benefits. . ."	"Seeking a challenge? Driven to succeed and excellence? Career path includes. . ."

[2] Entries in this table are literal quotes from ads.
[3] Obviously all ads contain some organizational contact information. The reference here is to ads that provide only this information about the advertising organization.

(minimal or extensive); (b) the personalization of the discourse in the ad; and (c) the nature of needs salient in the text of ads (basic existence needs versus growth needs).

THE ORGANIZATION IN EMPLOYMENT ADS

Employment ads vary significantly in the extent to which they provide information about the organization. Many ads do not mention the recruiting organization, focusing only on the position to be filled. In one survey (Rafaeli, Blum-Kulka, & Shkedi, 1997), only 27% of ads in Hong Kong and 65% of ads in the United States described the organization in any fashion, other than the contact address. Ads with minimal organizational description focus on requirements needed to fill, or the tasks that will compose, the advertised position. Perhaps a prototype of an extreme case in terms of the AER are "skeletal" ads. These ads only list the name of an occupation, prerequirements, and an address for application. In such ads, the hiring organization is only implicitly existent. A somewhat less extreme situation may be depicted by ads that announce the name or type of organization (e.g., "a national security organization," "a large retailer"). These two prototypes are in contrast to a third group, in which great detail about the product, market, history, or growth plans of the organization are provided. A simplified comparison among these three prototypes is offered in Table 17.2.

Such differences can be examined from multiple perspectives (cf. Anderson, 1981; Davidson, 1985; Rafaeli & Oliver, 1998; Rafaeli, 1997). I propose here that variations in the amount of information provided about the advertising organization reflect the organizational AER. Specifically, I propose that the extent to which an ad provides *more and more detailed* information about the organization reflects the extent to which the AER is emotional and intrinsically involving. Less or total lack of detail about the organization is consequently proposed to reflect a narrower, more calculative employment relationship. Thus, the comparison of the ads in Table 17.3, assuming that the ads are otherwise similar, reflects an increasingly more emotional and involving employee–organizational relationship.

In this hypothesis, the text of the ad is viewed as a symbol of the AER. As a symbol, an ad in which the organization is not at all described is proposed to symbolize an organization that is not easily visible or available to the employee. By implication, such as ad symbolizes an AER in which the cognitive and emotional distance between the employee and the organization is large. The interaction between the organization and individuals is therefore projected to be distant and constrained. In contrast, 'richer' descriptions of the organization introduce readers to various aspects of the organization that are *not* an obvious part of the advertised job. An ad that includes such text is proposed here to symbolize an

TABLE 17.2
Organizational Descriptions in Employment Ads[4]

		Extent of Organizational Description		
	Nondescription	*Technical Description Without Identification*	*Technical Description With Identification*	*Rich Description*
Quote from ad	No mention of organizational name or identity	"Challenging purchasing position available in a local growing company..."	"Northern Illinois Water Corporation has an immediate opening for..."	"At Barne's & Noble, Inc., the world's largest bookseller, we believe that who you buy your books from is just as important as the books you buy. That's why we've assembled great superstores, with over 100,000 titles with expansive music departments and the ambiance of upscale, cozy cafes to relax and enjoy. We are now hiring..."
Additional text included in ad but not directly quoted here	Name of position, list of requirements from potential employees, and address for application	Name of position, list of requirements from potential employees, and address for application	Name of position, list of requirements from potential employees, and address for application	Name of position, list of requirements from potential employees, and address for application
Nature of AER	Highly rational, formal, calculated	Moderately rational, formal, calculative	Moderately rational, formal, calculative	Highly intrinsically and emotionally involving

[4] For the purpose of illustration, all the ads in the table are from the Champaign Urbane News Gazette, posting positions of maintenance personnel.

TABLE 17.3
Need Fulfillment in Employment Ads

	Need Implied by Text of Ad		
	---	---	---
	Existence	*Relatedness*	*Growth*
Sample text from ads	"$1,500 Per Mo. GUARANTEED! You can make $30,000 to $60,000 Your First Year!!!... (plus we offer) health, dental, 401K plan, weekly cash bonuses, strongest commission plan in the metroplex. Just ask our sales people."	"We're fun-loving, hard-working people who make a difference in the community we serve. And we're looking for experienced people for our new stores. If you like having fun at work, give us a call."	"Would you like an opportunity to express your creativity? Can you be an individual star and perform with the team? Do you have the passion to make a difference? Would others consider you to be the best in the best? Can you dream the impossible and do it? Are you in the top 1% of your profession? Are you an analog thinker in a digital world? Can you consistently deliver on tough, creative, and technical challenges?"

invitation to readers to become familiar with, or even share, a larger set of organizational aspects. Such an invitation is proposed to symbolize an AER that is more emotional and more involving in scope. The employment relationship communicated is more holistic, or what Hackman and Oldham (1980) labeled, more "enriched."

I conducted a pilot study of individual attributions to such differences among ads. Subjects were asked to observe the following two ads:

Ad Number 1:

Wanted
Assistant Manager
Dynamic, capable, with initiative

Interested applicants should send their resume to
P.O. Box 207, Jerusalem

Ad Number 2:

> **For a large and leading pharmaceuticals company,**
> **with new contracts and new markets, providing new opportunities for**
> **employment and progress**
>
> **Wanted**
> **Assistant Manager**
> **Dynamic, capable, with initiative**
>
> **Interested applicants should send their resume to**
> **P.O. Box 207, Jerusalem**

Subject were then asked two questions: What differences between the two advertising organizations do you think you can infer from these two ads? And, how would you describe the employment relationship in the two organizations in terms of motivation, involvement, or commitment of the employees? The data are qualitative, hence not allowing significance tests. Yet, as expected, descriptions of the AER in response to ads providing greater detail about the organization comprised recurring references to an organization in which employment is more involving, interesting, and committing. While additional scientific (and experimentally controlled) evidence is essential, this preliminary evidence is supportive of my thesis.

Interestingly, the involving and stimulating AER references were not prevalent in a second study in which subjects were also presented with text about the organization, but in which the longer set of text (Ad Number 2) described extrinsic rewards for employment rather than organizational information. A lengthy description of extrinsic rewards led to attributions of a less (rather than more) enriched AER.

THE DISCOURSE PERSPECTIVE
IN EMPLOYMENT ADS

A second aspect that I propose reflects the AER is the nature of discourse the ad maintains. Ads combine a reference to two conceptually distinct perspectives: an "organizational perspective" and an "individual perspective." The organizational perspective is maintained in statements such as "Our product...," or "We are looking for...." The individual perspective is evident in statements such as "Do you have the following skills?" or "Are you looking for a great career opportunity?" A nonpersonalized, yet clearly individual-level perspective is obvious in terms such as "College Educated," or "Fluent English Speaker."

That ads include the multiple perspective (individual and organizational) re- inforces my proposition that ads are potential representations of the relationship between employees and employers, or the AER. Similar to other descriptions of relationships, ads at least symbolically refer to both parties to the relationship. With respect to both the organization and the individual, however, ads vary in the extent to which they maintain a personal or impersonal discourse. I propose that the choice of narrative can symbolize different AERs. Specifically, both descrip- tions of individuals and descriptions of organizations in ads can adopt either a personal or an impersonal perspective ("We" versus "a large organization", and "you" versus "the required employee"). My basic proposition here is that *the de- gree to which personalized discourse ("we" or "you") is engaged in an ad reflects variations in the AER*. This proposition draws on research in social psychology and in discourse analysis that has documented that individual involvement in a situation is enhanced with the use of more personalized interactions (cf. Goffman, 1967).

I conducted an exploratory study that examined readers' reactions to the two types of discourse. The results of this study supported the proposition. In this study, subjects were shown ads with identical text, but in one case the narrative was clearly personal while in the other it was impersonal. Personal text was in first person ("we" or "you"), and impersonal text was in the formal form ("the organization" or "the applicant"). Subjects' reactions to personalized ads consistently included attributions of an employment opportunity that is more emotionally involving than the one portrayed in nonpersonalized terms. Thus, the AER that subjects read in ads that use personal text is less formal and more emotionally involving that the AER read in ads that use impersonal text.

NEED STRUCTURES IN
EMPLOYMENT ADS

A third variation in the narrative of ads that I propose to be an indicator of the AER is the nature of employee needs the ad addresses (see Table 17.1). My qualitative survey revealed that employment ads vary in the extent to which the elements of existence versus growth are emphasized as core to the posted employment opportunity (Ronen, 1994; Alderfer, 1972). Some ads mention both needs, but most ads focus on one set of needs. To illustrate, consider the sets of text quoted in Table 17.3, all appearing in ads for sales positions:

The "existence" ad makes existence needs, or the pay and benefits of employ- ment in the organization, salient (Alderfer, 1972). In contrast, an ad that emphasizes the pleasant interpersonal context of employment may be proposed to make the fulfillment of social or relatedness needs salient. Ads can emphasize the social aspects of employment, in statements such as "Join the Elite" or "Come Be a Player Coach." In ads that emphasize fulfillment of growth needs, individualized opportunities for challenge, promotion, or autonomy are advocated. I propose that when "growth" is the focus of the ad, a more "actualizing" AER is implied, whereas when salary and benefits are emphasized a formal, calculative AER is represented.

In a study that repeated the design described above, subjects were asked to react to ads in which the technical descriptions of the job were held constant. The description of the needs fulfilled by the position was manipulated. "Existence" ads contained emphasized extrinsic rewards such as salary and benefits. "Relatedness" ads emphasized the social atmosphere, with statements such as "have fun in a family environment, with great coworkers." "Growth" ads contained text such as "self-fulfillment" and "autonomy."

The qualitative responses to these three ads supported my thesis above, and also contained support for the idea of a hierarchy among these needs (Ronen, 1994). The condition of the "a relatedness ad" was interpreted by subjects to be indicative of an employment relationship that provides fulfillment of *both* relatedness and existence needs. Similarly, the condition emphasizing growth needs was associated with an AER that would fulfill existence and relatedness needs as well. However, in reacting to ads focusing on basic, existence needs, individuals *did not* assume that there would also be fulfillment of relatedness or growth needs and assumed a calculative AER.

In short, the higher the order of the need emphasized in an ad, the more the implied relationship is emotional—and self-actualizing. Lower-order, existence needs addressed by ads are proposed to represent AERs that are more rational and calculative. As summarized in Table 17.1, higher-order needs, more personalized discourse, and more detail about the advertising organization are proposed to represent an employment relationship that is more enriched and involving. In contrast, the emphasis of lower-order (existence) needs, the use of impersonal discourse, and the failure to provide insight into the organization is proposed to reflect an employment relationship that is constrained, calculated, and formal.

SUMMARY AND CONCLUSIONS

My goal in this essay is to encourage more serious consideration of the value of employment advertising in understanding employment links. The conceptual framework described suggests that the study of the text and structure of employment ads may reveal expectations that job applicants or newly hired employees hold regarding their employee–organizational relationships.

The premise of my analysis is that ads can and should be viewed as potential representations of reality in an organization. Although there is an impression management element inherent to any form of public advertising, I argue that the unique location of employment ads in the interface between prospective employees and the organization makes them a relatively realistic projection of organizational reality.

There are three core implications to my analysis. First, I attempt to advance the notion that employment ads are interesting and important artifacts that are worthy of closer academic scrutiny. Employment ads were shown here to be more than technical lists or job postings. The impact of the specific structure or text of ads needs to be empirically studied in future research. One interesting implication may be that employment ads are public forums in which a collective sharing of information about alternative employment relationships in a given society takes place. In aggregate, the set of ads appearing in a given newspaper or a given society may offer information about employment in the society.

Second, my analysis begins to answer previously unanswered questions about ads. For example, why do ads continue to appear, even though they have been shown to be ineffective means of finding a job? Ads are proposed here to be a form of a public declaration by the organization of the AER that this organization espouses. Building on Weick's (1995) analyses, such declarations can help organizations and their representatives comprehend the very relationships by which they are employed.

The proposed framework may offer an answer as to why ads have been found to be ineffective recruitment vehicles. Perhaps the typical question previously asked: How effective are ads as compared to other recruitment vehicles? is inappropriate. A more appropriate question may be: What employment relationship does an ad convey? or, How effective is this relationship in attracting or recruiting desirable applicants? Previous research considered all ads to be one phenomenon, and considered only how many applicants responded to an ad, ignoring differences between ads. Such research therefore ignored implicit messages that employees may read in the ad. The present analysis builds on the fact that ads are *not* identical in their text and proposes that ads do not all convey the same messages. Future research may decipher the effectiveness of ads in conveying alternative employment relationships.

Third, this essay contributes to emerging research on the important question of implicit psychological relationships between employees and organizations (Rousseau & McLean-Parks, 1993; Shanteau & Harrison, 1991). Ads are positioned here as one medium that may contribute to these relationship. If the thesis advanced here is correct, then relationships between employers and employees may begin to form before an individual formally applies for, or accepts a position of employment. Thus, expectations and assumptions regarding an employment relationship in an organization may precede actual employment. Theories and findings in social psychology about the need for cognitive consistency suggest that such assumptions will ultimately shape the behavior of employees.

In closing, it is important to note that this essay leaves a host of questions open: Are the identified elements mutually exclusive? Or do they operate in tandem? What additional elements in ads contribute to a message regarding the employment relationship? Clearly, this analysis should trigger a broad research agenda regarding employment advertisements, their text, and their message.

REFERENCES

Aaker, D. A., & Myers, J. G. (1987). *Advertising management*. New York: Prentice-Hall.

Alderfer, C. P. (1972). *Existence, relatedness and growth: Human needs in organizational settings*. New York: Free Press.

Anderson, A. (1981). *Foundations of information integration*. New York: Academic Press.

Breaugh, J. A. (1992). *Recruitment: Science and practice*. Boston: PWS Kent.

Davidson, J. 1985. Amount of information and the attitude object and attitude behavior consistency. *Journal of Personality and Social Psychology, 49*, 1184–1198.

Decker, P. J., & Cornelius, E. T. (1979). A note on recruiting sources and job survival rates. *Journal of Applied Psychology, 64*, 463–464.

Goffman, E. (1967). *Interaction ritual*. Garden City, NJ: Doubleday.

Hackman, R. J., & Oldham, G. (1980). *Work redesign*. Menlo Park, CA: Addison-Wesley.

Hertzberg, F., Mausner, B., & Snyderman, B. (1959). *The motivation to work*. New York: Wiley.

Judge, T. A., & Cable, D. M. (1996). Person–organization fit, job choice, and organization entry. *Organizational Behavior and Human Decision Processes, 67*(3), 204–213.

Louis, M. R. (1990). Acculturation in the workplace. Newcomers as ethnographers. In B. Schneider (Ed.), *Organizational climate and culture* (pp. 85–129). San Francisco: Jossey-Bass.

Meyer, J. P., & Allen, N. J. (1984). Testing the side-bet theory of organizational commitment: Some theoretical considerations. *Journal of Applied Psychology, 69*(2), 372–378.

Miller, V. D., & Jablin, F. M. (1991). Information seeking during organization entry. *Academy of Management Review, 16*(1), 92–120.

Morrow, P. (1993). *The theory and measurement of work commitment*. London: JAI Press.

Ogilvy, D. (1985). *Ogilvy on advertising*. New York: Vintage Books.

O'Reilly, C. A. I., Chatman, J., & Caldwell, D. F. (1991). People and organizational culture: A profile comparison approach to assessing person–organization fit. *Academy of Management Journal, 34*(3), 487–517.

Rafaeli, A. (1997). *Employment advertising and employee socialization*. Unpublished manuscript, Hebrew University of Jerusalem.

Rafaeli, A. (2000). *Projecting an organizational identity lesson from employment advertising*. Corporate Reputation Review, 3, 3, 218–2.

Rafaeli, A., Blum-Kulka, S., & Shkedi, S. (1997). *Genre and culture in employment advertising: Cultural and occupational comparisons*. Unpublished manuscript, Hebrew University of Jerusalem.

Rafaeli, A., & Oliver, A. (1998). *Employment ads: A configurational research agenda*. Journal of Management Inquiry, 7, 4, 342–358.

Ronen, S. (1994). An underlying structure of motivational need taxonomies: A cross-cultural confirmation. In H. C. Triandis, M. Dunnette, D. & L. Hough, M. (Eds.), *Handbook of industrial and organizational psychology* (pp. 649–688). Palo Alto, CA: Consulting Psychology Press.

Rousseau, D. (1995). *Psychological contracts in organizations*. London: Sage.

Rousseau, D. M., & McLean-Parks, J. (1993). The contracts of individuals and organizations. In L. L. Cummings & B. M. Staw (Eds.), *Research in organizational behavior* (pp. 1–45). Greenwich, CT: JAI Press.

Saks, A. M. (1994). A psychological process investigation for the effects of recruitment source and organizational information on job survival. *Journal of Organizational Behavior, 15*, 225–244.

Schneider, B. (1987). The people make the place. *Personnel Psychology, 40*, 437–453.

Schneider, B., Goldstein, H. W., & Smith, D. B. (1995). The ASA framework: An update. *Personnel Psychology, 48*, 747–773.

Shanteau, J., & Harrison, P. (1991). The perceived strength of an implied contract. *Organizational Behavior and Human Decision Processes, 49*, 1–21.

Tom, V. R. (1971). The role of personality and organizational image in the recruiting process. *Organizational Behavior and Human Performance, 6*, 573–592.

Trice, H. M., & Beyer, J. M. (1993). *The cultures of work organizations*. Englewood Cliffs, NJ: Prentice-Hall.

Tsui, A. S., Pearce, J. L., Porter, L. W., & Hite, J. P. (1995). Choice of employee–organization relationship: Influence of external and internal organizational factors. In G. R. Ferris (Eds.), *Research in personnel and human resources management* (pp. 117–153). Greenwich, CT: JAI Press.

Wanous, J. P. (1992). *Organizational entry*. New York: Addison-Wesley.

Weick, K. E. (1979). Cognitive processes in organizations. In B. Staw. (Ed.), *Research in organizational behavior* (pp. 41–74). Greenwich, CT: JAI Press.

Weick, K. E. (1995). *Sensemaking in organizations*. Thousand Oaks, CA: Sage.

18

Creating a Strong, Positive Climate for Technology Implementation: Organizations Should, but Often Don't ... Why?

Katherine J. Klein
University of Maryland, College Park, MD

In the past decade, both popular-press and academic commentators have stated, with increasing insistency, that planned large-scale organizational change is critical for long term organizational survival (Kilman & Covin, 1989; Mohrman, Mohrman, Lec Cummings, Lawler, & Associates, 1989). And yet, such change remains enormously difficult. Were there a great, summary ledger of organizational change, it would not balance. The ratio of innovations adopted to benefits obtained would prove top heavy; organizational investments in new programs and technologies would outnumber organizational benefits gained (cf. Harris, 1994).

Perhaps organizations achieve fewer benefits than anticipated from the innovations adopt because these innovations are ineffective. Perhaps the innovations are ill suited for adopting organization, or perhaps they are ill-conceived products of hype and fad. Alternatively, the root of many organizations' failure to achieve the full benefits of the innovations they adopt may lie not in the failure of the innovations per se, but in the failure of their implementation. That is, organizations may fail to benefit fully from the innovations they adopt because the organizations do not implement these innovations optimally; they do not motivate and gain targeted employees' consistent, committed, and skilled use of the innovations in question (Klein & Sorra, 1996).

A growing literature suggests that implementation is in fact a common stumbling block along the path of innovation. Quality circles, total quality management, statistical process control, and computerized technologies often yield relatively little benefit to adopting organizations not because these innovations are ineffective, analysts suggest, but because their implementation is flawed (see, for example, Bushe, 1988; Hackman & Wageman, 1995; Klein & Ralls, 1995; Reger, Gustafson, DeMarie, & Mullane, 1994).

In a recent article (Klein & Sorra, 1996), Joann Sorra and I proposed that the effectiveness with which an organization implements a given innovation is determined by the organization's climate for implementation and by targeted organizational members' perceptions of the fit of the innovation to their values. In our article, we explored the consequences of implementation climate and innovation–values fit. Here, I take a step backward to explore the antecedents of implementation climate. Focusing specifically on the implementation of computerized technologies, I address the question: Why do many organizations fail to develop a strong, positive climate for the implementation of the major new computerized technologies that they adopt, often at considerable expense? My answer highlights the perhaps inevitable tensions between the three organizational groups involved in many organizations' adoption and implementation of major new computerized technologies: managers, computer technicians, and targeted technology users. These three groups differ, I show, in power, expertise, values, and roles. Too often, I suggest, the three groups are unable to transcend these differences. The result is a weak climate for technology implementation, inadequate technology use, and few organizational gains from technology adoption.

To make my argument, I draw on diverse literatures, in multiple steps. I begin, below, with a brief review of the implementation model presented in Klein and Sorra (1996), highlighting the relevance of the model to computerized technology implementation. I then turn to a discussion of Alderfer's (1983) analysis of organizational intergroup dynamics and of Trice's (1993) analysis of occupational subcultures. These authors' models lay the groundwork for my exploration, in the next section of the chapter, of the differing power, expertise, values, and roles held by managers, computer technicians, and targeted users. In the final sections of the chapter, I show how these differences may lead to the creation of poor implementation climates, and I note the implications of my argument for the conceptualization and study of employee motivation during major organizational change.

THE INFLUENCE OF IMPLEMENTATION
CLIMATE AND INNOVATION–VALUES FIT
ON IMPLEMENTATION

In our 1996 article, Joanna Sorra and I defined *implementation effectiveness* as the consistency and quality of targeted organizational members' use of a specific innovation. We conceptualized innovation use as a continuum, ranging from avoidance of the innovation (nonuse) to skilled, enthusiastic and consistent use (committed use). Because we focused on innovations (e.g., TQM, computer-aided design and manufacturing, and manufacturing resource planning) that require the active and coordinated use of multiple organizational members to benefit the organization, we conceptualized implementation effectiveness as an organizational-level variable, describing the overall, pooled, or aggregate consistency and quality of targeted organizational members' innovation use. We thus sought to explain between-organization differences in implementation processes and outcomes, not within-organization individual differences in motivation and innovation use.

Qualitative case studies dominate the literature on the implementation of computerized technologies and other innovations. These studies (e.g., Klein, Hall, & Laliberte, 1990; Markus, 1987; Reger, Gustafson, DeMarie, & Mullane, 1994; Rousseau, 1989) highlight the array of organizational policies and practices and technological characteristics that may shape implementation effectiveness. These include: training in innovation use, user support services, time to experiment with the innovation, rewards for technology use, and the quality and availability of the technology itself (see Klein & Ralls, 1995, for a review). For simplicity, I refer to these innovation, implementation, organizational, and technological policies, practices, and characteristics simply as "implementation policies and practices."

The available literature suggests that while an organization surely requires a critical mass of forceful and constructive implementation policies and practices to inspire employee use of an innovation, no single implementation policy or practice is critical (Klein & Sorra, 1996). Rather, the influence of implementation policies and practices on innovation use is cumulative and compensatory. In one organization, an excellent training program and strong user support may engender employee skill and enthusiasm in using the innovation. But, in an other organization, the provision of time to experiment with the innovation and rewards for innovation use may lead to the same level of employee skill and enthusiasm in using the same innovation.

To conceptualize the collective influence of an organization's multiple implementation policies and practices, Sorra and I drew on Schneider's work on organizational climate (e.g., Schneider, 1975, 1990). Schneider (1990, p. 384) defined climate as employees' "perceptions of the events, practices, and procedures and the kinds of behaviors that are rewarded, supported, and expected in a setting." Following Schneider, we defined an organization's climate for the implementation of a given innovation as "targeted employees' shared summary perceptions of the extent to which their use of a specific innovation is rewarded, supported, and expected within their organization" (Klein & Sorra, 1996, p. 1060). Employees' perceptions of their organization's climate for the implementation of a given innovation, we explained (Klein & Sorra, 1996, p. 1060), are the result of employees' shared experiences and observations of, and their information and discussions about, their organization's implementation policies and procedures. Further, we argued that a strong implementation climate (a) ensures employee

264

KLEIN

skill in innovation use, (b) provides incentives for innovation use and disincentives for innovation avoidance, and (c) removes obstacles to innovation use.

Although we predicted a positive relationship between the strength of an organization's implementation climate and the organization's implementation effectiveness, we noted that a strong implementation climate might only lead to compliant innovation use not to internalized or committed innovation use. Psychological theories and research on conformity and commit (Kelman, 1958; O'Reilly & Chatman, 1986; Sussman & Vecchio, 1991) distinguish between compliance, "the acceptance of influence in order to gain specific rewards and to avoid punishments," (Sussmann & vecchio, 1982, p. 181) and internalization, "the acceptance of influence because it is congruent with a worker's value system and/or because it is intrinsically rewarding" (Sussmann & Vecchio, 1982, p. 182). Applied to the study of innovation implementation, these works suggest that employees who perceive innovation use to be congruent with their values are likely to be internalized—committed, enthusiastic, and self-directed—in their innovation use, whereas individuals who perceive innovation use merely as a means to "gain specific rewards and to avoid punishments" are likely to be compliant—proforma and uninvested—in their innovation use.

Thus, we predicted that innovation use is most likely to be most committed, consistent, and creative when an organization's climate for implementation is strong *and* employees perceive that the innovation represents a good fit with their values. Under these circumstances, employees are skilled in and enthusiastic about innovation use, incentives for innovation use and disincentives for innovation avoidance are ample, and obstacles to innovation use are few. When an organization's climate for implementation is strong but employees perceive that the innovation is a poor fit with their values, employee resistance to innovation use is likely, we predicted, and innovation use is at best compliant. Pressured to use the innovation, employees are likely to do so unenthusiastically and, unless they fear retribution, inconsistently. When an organization's climate for implementation is weak, yet employees perceive that the innovation represents a good fit with their values, employees are committed to innovation use, but—given the weak climate for implementation—lack skills in, and experience few incentives for, and many obstacles to, innovation use. They are likely to be frustrated by the their organization's weak implementation climate and by their own and their fellow employees' poor use of the innovation. When implementation climate is weak and employees find the innovation a poor fit with their values, employees are likely to be pleased that they experience little pressure to use the innovation. Targeted users will happily, if quietly and cynically, let the idea of innovation use fade away.

The Implementation of Computerized Technologies

The model that Sorra and I presented was designed to be broadly applicable to both technological innovations (e.g., computer-aided manufacturing systems) and nontechnological innovations (e.g., total quality management). In developing the model, we drew heavily on numerous studies, including my own, of the implementation of computerized technologies (e.g., Klein, Hall, & Laliberte, 1990; Fleischer, Liker, & Arnsdorf, 1988; Zuboff, 1988). The largely qualitative literature on computerized technology implementation describes in detail the challenges and frequent failures of organizations' implementation of computerized technologies.

A growing literature describes, as well, the failure of many organizations to achieve the expected returns from their investments in computerized technologies (see Attewell, 1994, for a review). Surely, the sources of this "productivity paradox" are many. But, one key factor, I argue, is the failure of many organizations to ensure their employees' skilled, committed, and consistent use of the new computerized systems that the organizations adopt (Schneider & Klein, 1994). This, in turn, reflects the failure of many organizations to build strong, positive climates for technology implementation.

And yet, the insight that an organization must actively and strenuously encourage and support its employees' use of a new technologies if the organization is to gain the intended benefits of technology adoption is not a profound revelation. Indeed, it is merely common sense. Why, then, does the available literature suggest that so many organizations build only weak climates for technology implementation?

I argue below that the development of a strong, positive climate for technology implementation requires the close and active collaboration of managers and computer technicians and the involvement and input of targeted technology users. When collaboration falters, as it so often does, and employee involvement and input are minimal, an organization's climate for technology implementation is likely to be quite weak.

MANAGERS, COMPUTER TECHNICIANS, AND USERS: INSIGHTS FROM ALDERFER'S INTERGROUP THEORY AND TRICE'S ANALYSIS OF OCCUPATIONAL SUBCULTURES

The three key players in the adoption and implementation of computerized technologies are managers, technicians, and users. Managers, of course, make the decision to purchase new computerized systems and bear ultimate responsibility for the performance of the organizations. Computer technicians play an advisory role, typically encouraging managers to approve the purchase of new computerized systems. Computer technicians, in turn, are often called upon, by management, to facilitate and guide the purchase and implementation of new systems. And the users are just that: the individuals targeted by managers and technicians to use the technology on a regular—typically daily—basis.

As this brief introduction suggests, managers, technicians, and users differ greatly in the power, expertise, values, and roles they hold. The quality of their collaboration determines in large measure the strength of an organization's development climate for the implementation of a new technology.

Few organizational theoreticians focus on the effects of intergroup interactions on organizational outcomes. More common are analyses of organizational groups qua groups, that is, of the influence of group-level properties on group-level outcomes (e.g., group performance and group cohesiveness). However, two authors, Alderfer (1983) and Trice (1993), shed light on the interplay among groups within organizations and the influence of this interplay on organization-level outcomes, including the character, culture, and climate of the organization. I turn to a brief review of their work.

Alderfer's Intergroup Theory

Alderfer's (1983) intergroup theory describes the influence of, and interactions among, identity groups and organizational groups. An *identity group* is a "group" within an organization whose members share common biological characteristics (e.g., sex and race), have participated in equivalent historical experiences, are subjected to certain social forces, and thus hold similar worldviews (Alderfer, 1983, p. 410). An *organizational group* is a group whose members hold similar organizational positions, participate in similar work experiences, and thus have similar organizational views (Alderfer, 1983, p. 410). Managers, technicians, and users are organizational groups. But, as Alderfer (1983) has noted, organizational group membership and identity group membership are often highly related. In this case, for example, managers are likely to be older than technicians. Further, technicians and managers are perhaps somewhat more likely than users to be male and white.

Organizational groups are distinguished by their tasks and by their position in the organizational hierarchy. Alderfer (1983, p. 412) suggests that as a function of their distinctive tasks, task group members "develop a perspective on their own group, other groups, and the organization-as-a-whole, which in turn shapes their behavior and attitudes." This insight anticipates a dominant theme in my analysis: Managers, technicians, and users often hold quite distinctive views of computerized technology and its benefits to their group and the organization.

The position of an organizational group in the organizational hierarchy determines group members' "legitimate authority, decision-making autonomy, and scope of responsibility" (Alderfer, 1983, p. 412). "No one who belongs to an organization escapes the effects of hierarchy," Alderfer (1983, p. 413) suggests. Managers, of course, have greater authority, autonomy, and scope of responsibility than do either technicians or users. And yet, as Alderfer (1983, p. 413) notes, "higher-ranking people [managers] tend to be seen by lower-ranking members as possessing more power than they experience themselves as being able to use effectively." This dynamic is often in evidence during technology implementation: Although users and technicians may look to managers for leadership, managers may well perceive that they have less influence than technicians and users imagine. Alderfer (1983, p. 413) notes, too, that "because there are hazards to bearing bad news, lower-ranking people tend to censor information flowing upward so that is has a positive flavor." Thus, during technology implementation, managers may be uninformed of problems in gaining employees' use and acceptance of a new technology.

People in the middle of the organizational hierarchy, Alderfer (1983, p. 413) suggests,"are more in touch with the concrete day-to-day events than those above them, and they have more power, authority, and autonomy than those below them." Middle-level people must "exercise some control over those below them in the system, and they must satisfy those above them if they are to retain their positions" (Alderfer, 1983, p. 413). During computerized technology implementation, technicians are often asked to assume this role—to "exercise some control over" users and to satisfy managers "if they are to retain their positions." Delegation of such responsibility to technicians is often problematic, however. Because technicians typically hold staff positions, not line positions, they may lack important "power, authority, and autonomy" over the users whom they are expected to guide, supervise, and control. Finally, Alderfer suggests:

> the people at the bottom of the organizational system: have fewer material resources and, as individuals working alone, wield less power than any other class of individuals in the system. . . . They withhold some of their potential involvement in objectives set for them by middles in order to retain a modicum of control over their lives. They may also covertly undermine vulnerable parts of the system. (Alderfer, 1983, p. 413)

Here, Alderfer anticipates lower-level employees' possible antipathy and resistance towards innovation use.

Trice's Analysis
of Occupational Subcultures

In his recent book on occupational subcultures, Trice (1993) extends past research and theory regarding organizational culture, suggesting that an organization's culture is rarely entirely monolithic and homogeneous. Rather, Trice argues, most organizations have subcultures, which like organizational cultures have distinctive ideologies and cultural forms. Trice's analysis, like Alderfer's, underscores the distinctive beliefs, values, expertise, skills, and daily activities that may distinguish key organizational groups or subcultures, including managers, technicians, and users. Like Alderfer, Trice (1993) highlights the tensions and conflicts that may occur between subcultures or groups.

"One of the most powerful subcultures," Trice (1993, p. xii) suggests, "is made up of the higher echelons of management. One set of beliefs among members is that they dictate how to organize work and arrange the division of labor among employees." A common second subculture in organizations emerges among the members of an occupational group:

> Such groups include persons who have mastered and applied specialized knowledge about the performance of a set of specialized tasks. Because of this esoteric capacity, they believe that certain workers have rights to perform certain work, to control training for the access to doing such work, and to control the way it is performed and evaluated.... There is a clear possibility that these ideologies will clash with the upper-management subculture and, in effect, deviate significantly at times from the organizational culture. (Trice, 1993, p. xii)

In many organizations, computer technicians represent such an occupational group. Computer technicians share distinctive knowledge and specialized tasks, which may lead them to clash with upper management.

Trice's (1993) analysis also sheds light on the tensions that may emerge between computer technicians and production managers and supervisors. The former are typically staff personnel, while the latter are line personnel. Describing staff units as subcultures, Trice (1993, p. 221) notes that "line managers are inclined to be skeptical and are often resistant to staff recommendations because they view staff as impractical and as representing a threat to their own power and control." Trice's comments anticipate the conflicts that may arise between technicians, admonished by upper management to ensure production employees' use of a new technology, and middle-level line managers, the immediate supervisors of the employees designated to use the new technology.

MANAGERS, COMPUTER TECHNICIANS, AND USERS: DISTINCTIVE VALUES AND AREAS OF EXPERTISE

Alderfer's (1983) and Trice's (1993) analyses suggest that managers, computer technicians, and users may differ in their attitudes toward and knowledge of computerized technologies. In this section, I examine managers', computer technicians', and users' distinctive views and expertise.

Management Values and Expertise Regarding Information Technology

The available, albeit limited, literature on management values and attitudes towards information technology suggests that senior managers may question the merits of both their own use of new computerized technologies and their companies' use of these technologies. Both March and Sproull (1990) and Schein (1992) have written persuasively on this topic.

March and Sproull (1990) suggest that many computerized decision technologies are based on principles and assumptions that are fundamentally at odds with management values:

> Decision technologies "generally ask managers to state their premises or their rules, and then the technologies provide the conclusions. In some cases, they automatically implement them as decisions. But managers often do not want to give up control over their conclusions. Often they already know the answers and are looking for justifications. (p. 151)

Further, although a company's use of computer technologies may serve as a symbol of the company's modernity and competitiveness, the symbolic consequences of managers use of computer technologies may be more ambiguous. Decision technologies, particularly, may arouse "images of managerial routinization that seem to demean managerial functions" (March & Sproull, 1990, p. 155). March and Sproull (1990, p. 156) suggest that "information technology designed to support executive communication or the monitoring of events is likely to spread more quickly among executives than is technology linked directly to decision making." But even electronic mail systems, while useful for communication and monitoring, may clash with managers' preferences for face-to-face, verbal communication (Mintzberg, 1990) and exacerbate already heavy demands for managers' time and attention.

Commenting that "the problems of implementing [information] technology have been horrendous," Schein (1992, p. 277) suggests that the values and assumptions on which information technology (IT) rests clash with managers' assumptions about information and the organization of work. Schein (1992, p. 290) reports, for example, that managers believe that "information is intrinsically dynamic, holistic, and imprecise; therefore it cannot be packaged and transmitted electronically." Schein (1992, pp. 290–291) suggests that managers assume that "the computer limits and distorts thinking by focusing the user on only those kinds of data that can be packaged and transmitted" and that "communication requires face-to-face contact so that one can, at any given moment, assess the full range of cues such as tone of voice, timing, and body language to determine how one's message is being received." Further, Schein (1990, p. 291) argues that managers believe that "IT is too expensive, too complicated, and too unreliable to be a useful tool in spite of its potential strategic advantages in many companies," and that "IT threatens the security and orderliness of the present organizational structures and processes and, thereby, the welfare of present members."

Together, March and Sproull's (1990) portrait of managerial attitudes toward computer technologies and Schein's (1990) portrait suggest that managers are deeply suspicious of computer technologies. Perhaps managers' suspicions and doubts regarding the benefits of computer technologies have abated somewhat in recent years as computerized technologies have grown more and more ubiquitous.

And yet, with the spread of computerized technologies have come more and more frequent stories of implementation failures and of poor payoffs as a result of information technology investments (Attewell, 1994). These may well reinforce managers' latent suspicions and doubts. Further, given that the pace of the development of information technology is both enormous and unremitting, there can be no doubt that managers' knowledge of information technology lags far behind computer technicians'.

Computer Technicians' Values and Expertise Regarding Information Technology

Computer technicians' values and assumptions regarding computerized technologies run counter, of course, to the management values and assumptions just described. Schein (1992, p. 280) reports, for example, that computer technology specialists believe that "it is possible to package and transmit information accurately in an electronic medium" and that "more information is always better than less." Further, Schein (1992, p. 282) suggests that technology specialists believe that "all people can and should learn whatever is required to use the technology" and that if a computerized system "facilitates task performance and efficiency, people will adopt it."

Zabusky and Barley (1996) give voice to the love of computerized technology implicit in Schein's analysis above. Describing the results of their ethnographic studies of technicians, Zabusky and Barley (1996) report that

> the stories technicians told about why they entered their occupations always centered on their attraction to the technical content of the work, an attraction they often referred to as "love." Computer technicians were particularly eloquent on this score. . . . Early fascination with computers and the experience of quickly learning more than a mentor were common themes in the stories computer technicians told about themselves. . . . So powerful was the excitement of technology for these technicians, that several had shirked their studies and even quit college to work for minimum wages in a computer lab. (pp. 9, 197–198)

Users' Values and Expertise Regarding Information Technology

Technology users' values and expertise regarding computerized technologies are not easily typified. While managers and computer technicians usually form relatively small and cohesive groups within an organization, the targeted users of a computerized system may be quite large in number and diverse in tasks and skills. Further, across organizations, managers play relatively similar roles and occupy relatively similar positions within the organizational hierarchy. This is true, as well, of computer technicians. But, across organizations, targeted users do not show such uniformity. The targeted users of a manufacturing resource planning system, for example, may differ greatly from the targeted users of a computer-aided design and manufacturing system. For these reasons, few authors have attempted to summarize "the" values that technology users hold towards new computerized technologies. Indeed, far more common are attempts to analyze and predict differences among users' perceptions of technologies adopted by their organizations.

Targeted technology users are, however, united across organizations in their desire to "make sense" of new technologies that they are expected by their managers and supervisors to use (Goodman & Griffith, 1991; Klein & Ralls, 1997). Invariably, users within an organization that has adopted a new technology seek to understand what a given technology will mean for them—for the quality of their work lives, for the ease of their tasks, and for the extrinsic and intrinsic rewards of their work. The sense that users make of a new system is influenced by the characteristics of the technology itself, of course, but also by the messages about the technology that managers and computer technicians send to users through their words and actions.

Next, I explore the very different roles and managers, technicians, and users typically play during decision making to adopt a new technology.

THE DECISION TO ADOPT A NEW COMPUTERIZED TECHNOLOGY: MANAGERS', COMPUTER TECHNICIANS', AND USERS' ROLES

Dean (1987) conducted intensive case studies of the adoption of advanced manufacturing technologies (AMT; e.g., computer-assisted design, engineering, and manufacturing and manufacturing resources planning) in five manufacturing companies. His findings highlight the roles that managers and computer technicians play during the decision to adopt new technologies. These roles both enact and reflect the differences in managers' and technicians' power, expertise, and values, and, I suggest, too often lay the groundwork for the creation of a weak organizational climate for technology implementation.

"The dynamics of the [AMT adoption] process," Dean (1987, p. 39) suggests, "consist of the lower level participants (proponents or 'champions') attempting to convince the upper level participants to approve the project." The challenge for lower-level participants (the technicians), however, is that

> calculating a level of return for most AMT projects is an extremely difficult undertaking . . . No one really knows what the return will be in any exact sense. Furthermore, if the technology is adopted, it is virtually impossible to tell if the expected level of return has, in fact, been achieved, due to changes in demand and production rates, responses of competitors, and so on. (Dean, 1987, pp. 42–43)

Accordingly, technicians are likely to exaggerate the certainty and magnitude of the financial benefits of AMT adoption. To convince managers of the value of AMT, technicians may also highlight the strategic benefits of AMT adoption, arguing "that competitors will be adopting this technology, customers' perceptions of the firm will be enhanced, this is how things will be done in the future, and so on" (Dean, 1987, pp. 43–44).

Managers are aware that the financial and strategic benefits of AMT adoption are uncertain, Dean (1987) reports. Managers thus base their decisions to adopt AMT not only on proponents' projections, but also on proponents' credibility and commitment:

> Senior managers are very reluctant to approve risky projects, especially those with big price tags. The main way in which the perception of risk is overcome was for the proponents to "swear" or "promise" that the innovation will work and to take responsibility for making it work. . . . [Proponents] know they need to be very confident about the technology in their discussions with management. If the innovation is a failure, however, their credibility is destroyed. On the other hand, they can be more realistic about the risks involved with the technology, thus maintaining their credibility in case of failure. Given this more accurate information about risks, however, most senior managers would simply kill the project. (Dean, 1987, pp. 47–48)

Notably missing from Dean's analysis is any discussion of the role of targeted technology users in the decision to adopt AMT. The reason is clear: In the organizations Dean studied, users were either uninvolved or very little involved in the adoption decision-making process. This is typical. Lacking technicians' computer expertise and managers' decision-making authority, users often play no role in the decision to purchase a new computerized system. Their involvement with the new system begins, instead, when the system arrives at the organization and must be installed, programmed, and customized for the organization and/or when the new system is actually ready for use.

CREATING A CLIMATE FOR TECHNOLOGY IMPLEMENTATION: THE CONSEQUENCES OF MANAGERS', TECHNICIANS' AND USERS' DIFFERING EXPERTISE, VALUES, POWER, AND ROLES

An organization's climate is the message employees get about what is important in the organization. Employees get this message from the experiences they have as they go about their work. These experiences come from HRM (human resources management), OM (operations management), and marketing practices and procedures under which (employees) work and (employees') perceptions of the kinds of behavior management rewards, expects, and supports. (Schneider & Bowen, 1995, p. 239)

Clearly, the direct and indirect verbal and behavioral expressions of *managers'* beliefs, values, and priorities play a critical role in creating an organization's climate. Managers engender a strong climate for the implementation of a new computerized technology by, for example:

- Making extensive, high-quality training in use of the technology readily available (even mandatory) for a broad cross-section of targeted technology users
- Providing employees ample time to use and experiment with the new technology, even if that means that employees' performance of their conventional duties suffers temporarily
- Providing user support services, so that employees' questions about and problems in using the new technology are answered and resolved quickly
- Praising employees' for their use of the new technology
- Communicating to the entire organization the benefits resulting from employees' use of the new technology
- Asking users for their suggestions about what could be done to make technology use more highly skilled, more consistent, and of greater benefit to the organization—and implementing users' suggestions

As I have previously reviewed, senior managers often question the benefits of new technologies for themselves and their organizations. Further, they often lack substantive knowledge and interest in the new technologies. Convinced by computer technicians to approve the purchase of a new computer system, managers often assign computer technicians the task of getting the new technology up and running. "You asked for it, now make it work" is many managers' implicit or explicit message to their computer technicians.

Can computer technicians create the conditions necessary to foster a strong climate for computerized technology implementation without the substantial and active involvement of management? The answer, I believe, is no. Rarely, for example, do computer technicians have the authority to require technology training and to excuse a decrease in production as users master the new technology. Rarely do technicians have the credibility to inspire, through their praises or reprimands, employees' conscientious and consistent technology use. Technicians' standing within the organizational hierarchy does not afford them such power and influence, as Alderfer (1983) might note. Further, technicians are staff members and often mistrusted by line managers and line personnel—that is, by users and their immediate supervisors—as Trice (1993) might note. And finally, technicians may not have the inclination nor the managerial values and skills to manage and motivate employee use, as Zabusky and Barley (1996) might comment.

A strong climate for technology implementation is most likely, I conclude, when managers are strongly and actively committed to creating the conditions necessary for consistent, high-quality technology use, that is, when managers lead and manage and technicians assume primary responsibility for technical, not managerial tasks. Through their formal and informal actions—through their resource allocations, their speeches, and even through the questions that they ask during informal interactions with employees—managers must demonstrate repeatedly their commitment to the full implementation of the new technology. To do much less than this is to send employees a message: "Use of the new technology is not a priority. If you do not use the technology consistently and well, it doesn't really matter."

This admonition to managers is easy, obvious, even platitudinous. But, the realization of the statement—that is, the active, committed management of technology implementation by management, not technicians—runs counter to conventional organizational group values, expertise, and roles. The realization of active, committed management of technology implementation *by management*—and thus the creation of an optimal climate for implementation—is difficult and rare.

Moderating Conditions: Factors that May Facilitate or Inhibit the Creation of a Strong Climate for Technology Implementation

I have painted this chapter in broad brushstrokes, paying little attention to the organizational characteristics that may either facilitate or inhibit the creation of a climate for technology implementation and employees' subsequent use of the technology. I consider some of these organizational characteristics in this section.

Technological Sophistication of the Workforce

In some organizations—particularly those within high-technology industries—the entire workforce is likely to be relatively technologically sophisticated. In these organizations, managers, technicians, and users may differ relatively little in their technical expertise, experience, and values. Managers in these organizations are thus likely to be more active and more credible in supporting and inspiring the implementation of computerized technologies than are less computer-literate managers working in relatively low-tech industries. Accordingly, the more technologically sophisticated the entire workforce of an organization, and especially the more technologically sophisticated an organization's management, the stronger and more positive the organization's climate for technology implementation is likely to be.

Organizational Innovativeness

Organizations differ, of course, in the frequency and success with which they have implemented both technological and nontechnological innovations. By definition, highly innovative organizations have successfully implemented a number of innovations (e.g., statistical process control, leadership training, TQM, telecommuting, etc.). The managers in highly innovative organizations are thus likely to be skilled in the creation of climates for innovation implementation. Further, employees in such organizations have experienced the successful implementation of innovations. They are thus unlikely to greet new attempts at organizational innovation with cynicism and distrust. Conversely, in organizations that have implemented few innovations successfully, employees are likely to be far more skeptical of the promises of technological change. Thus, the more innovative an organization, the more likely it is to create a strong climate for the implementation of new technologies.

Financial Resource Availability

The creation of a strong climate for the implementation of computerized technologies is expensive. It takes substantial financial resources to provide high-quality technology training and user support services while allowing employees time to experiment with the technology—time when they might otherwise be producing the organization's goods and services. Further, an organization's financial resources may be strapped by the purchase of the major new computerized system it now seeks to implement. Thus, the greater an organization's financial resources, the stronger its climate for implementation—provided organizational managers strongly and actively support implementation of the new technology.

The Involvement of Local Managers in the Decision to Adopt Computerized Technology

Often the decision to adopt and implement a major new computerized technology is made at corporate headquarters with little or no involvement of local (e.g., plant or store) management (Guth & MacMillan, 1986; Klein, 1984). The implications are obvious. If the decision to adopt and implement a major computerized system is made far above the local management level, local managers are unlikely to be strong advocates for technology implementation, and the organization's ensuing climate for technology implementation is likely to be relatively weak.

Upward Communication

Technology implementation is an iterative process (Leonard-Barton, 1988). The implementation policies and practices that an organization establishes as it begins to implement a new technology are likely to be flawed. The software may have bugs. The hardware may be overloaded or difficult to access. The training may be more or less technically sophisticated than users need. User support personnel may be overwhelmed by requests and thus slow to respond to employee's questions. Problems of this kind are to be expected during technology implementation. They are to be expected and recognized and resolved. When they are not—either because managers are inattentive and uninterested or because users and technicians fear carrying "bad news" upward to their supervisors and beyond—then the climate for technology implementation necessarily suffers. In sum, the more employees engage in upward communication of problems and concerns, and the more managers are responsive to employee problems and concerns, the stronger an organization's climate for technology implementation is likely to be.

CONCLUSION

Why do many organizations fail to develop strong, positive climates for the implementation of the major new computerized technologies that they have adopted, often at considerable expense? The short answer, I believe, is that many managers know relatively little about computerized technologies and—correctly or incorrectly—question the value of many computerized technologies for their organization. Accordingly, many managers delegate the task of implementing new computerized technologies to the organization's computer technicians, who are expert in the technology but may lack the power, authority, managerial expertise, and values to manage the transition to the new technology. Further, many managers and technicians fail to involve targeted users in planning and realizing the adoption and implementation of computerized systems. The result, quite often, is the underutilization of computerized technologies and the failure of technology adoption to yield intended productivity and performance benefits.

My analysis, in this chapter, has focused not on individual differences in employee motivation, but on organizational differences in creating the conditions—the climate—necessary to motivate employees' use of a major new computerized system. To explain organizational differences in the creation of a climate for technology implementation, I have examined intergroup dynamics within organizations, highlighting the differences in the power, expertise, values, and roles held by the key players during technology adoption and implementation: managers, technicians, and users. I have thus eschewed the traditional individual-level focus of motivation theories and research to consider the higher-level group and organizational context that creates the conditions that motivate individual employees. My focus in this chapter on levels of theory and analysis above the individual complements and extends approaches more focused on individual differences. A multilevel approach may enrich our understanding not only of employee motivation to use new technologies but employee motivation to engage in a broad array of workplace behaviors.

REFERENCES

Alderfer, C. P. (1983). Intergroup relations and organizations. In J. R. Hackman, E. E. Lawler, & L. W. Porter (Eds.), *Perspectives on behavior in organizations* (pp. 408–416). New York: McGraw-Hill.

Attewell, P. (1994). Information technology and the productivity paradox. In D. H. Harris (Ed.), *Organizational linkages: Understanding the productivity paradox* (pp. 13–53). Washington, DC: National Academy Press.

Bushe, G. R. (1988). Cultural contradictions of statistical process control in American manufacturing organizations. *Journal of Management, 14*, 19–31.

Dean, J. W., Jr. (1987). Building the future: The justification process for new technology. In J. M. Pennings & A. Buitendam (Eds.), *New technology as organizational innovation* (pp. 35–58). Cambridge, MA: Ballinger Publishing Company.

Fleischer, M., Liker, J., & Arnsdorf, D. (1988). *Effective use of computer-aided design and computer aided engineering in manufacturing.* Ann Arbor, MI: Industrial Technology Institute.

Goodman, P. S., & Griffith, T. L. (1991). A process approach to the implementation of new technology. *Journal of Engineering Technology and Management, 8*, 261–285.

Guth, W. D., & MacMillan, I. C. (1986). Strategy implementation versus middle management self-interest. *Strategic Management Journal, 7*, 313–327.

Hackman, J. R., & Wageman, R. (1995). Total quality management: Empirical, conceptual and practical issues. *Administrative Science Quarterly, 40*, 309–342.

Harris, D. H. (Ed.). (1994). *Organizational linkages: Understanding the productivity paradox.* Washington, DC: National Academy Press.

Kelman, H. C. (1958). Compliance, identification, and internalization: Three processes of attitude change. *Journal of Conflict Resolution, 2*, 51–60.

Kilman, R. H., & Covin, T. J. (Eds.). (1989). *Corporate transformation.* San Francisco: Jossey-Bass.

Klein, J. A. (1984). Why supervisors resist employee involvement. *Harvard Business Review, 84*(5), 87–95.

Klein, K. J., Hall, R. J., & Laliberte, M. (1990). Training and the organizational consequences of technological change: A case study of computer aided design and drafting. In U. E. Gattiker & L. Larwood (Eds.), *Technological innovation and human resources: End-user training* (pp. 7–36). New York: Walter de Gruyter.

Klein, K. J., & Ralls, R. S. (1995). The organizational dynamics of computerized technology implementation: A review of the empirical literature. In L. R. Gomez-Mejia & M. W. Lawless (Eds.), *Implementation management in high technology* (pp. 31–79). Greenwich, CT: JAI Press.

Klein, K. J., & Ralls, R. S. (1997). The unintended organizational consequences of technology training: Implications for training theory, research, and practice. In J. K. Ford, S. Kozlowski, K. Kraiger, E. Salas, & M. Teachout (Eds.), *Improving training effectiveness in organizations* (pp. 323–354). Hillsdale, NJ: Lawrence Erlbaum Associates.

Klein, K. J. & Sorra, J. S. (1996). The challenge of innovation implementation. *Academy of Management Review, 21*, 1055–1080.

Leonard-Barton, D. (1988). Implementing as mutual adaptation of technology and organization. *Research Policy, 17*, 251–267.

Markus, M. L. (1987). Power, politics, and MIS implementation. In R. M. Becker & W. A. S. Buxton (Eds.), *Readings in human-computer interaction: A multidisciplinary approach* (pp. 68–82). Los Angeles: Morgan Kaufmann.

Mintzberg, H. (1990). The manager's job: Folklore and fact. *Harvard Business Review, 68*(2), 163–176.

Mohrman, A. M., Jr., Mohrman, S. A., Ledford, G. E., Jr., Cummings, G. T., Lawler, E. E., III (Eds.). (1989). *Large-scale organizational transformation.* San Francisco: Jossey-Bass.

O'Reilly, C. & Chatman, J. Organizational commitment and psychological attachment: The effects of compliance, identification and internalization on prosocial behavior. *Journal of Applied Psychology, 71*, 492–499.

Reger, R. K., Gustafson, L. T., DeMarie, S. M., & Mullane, J. V. (1994). Reframing the organization: Why implementing total quality is easier said than done. *Academy of Management Review, 19,* 565–584.

Rousseau, D. M. (1989). Managing the change to an automated office: Lessons from five case studies. *Office: Technology & People, 4,* 31–52. Elsevier Science Publishers Limited.

Schein, E. H. (1992). *Organizational culture and leadership.* San Francisco: Jossey-Bass.

Schneider, B., & Bowen, D. E. (1995). *Winning the Service Game.* Boston: Harvard Business School Press.

Schneider, B., & Klein, K. J. (1994). What is enough? A systems perspective on individual-organizational performance linkages. In D. H. Harris (Ed.), *Organizational linkages: Understanding the productivity paradox* (pp. 81–104). Washington, DC: National Academy Press.

Schneider, B. (1975). Organizational climates: An essay. *Personnel Psychology, 28,* 447–479.

Schneider, B. (1990). The climate for service: An application of the climate construct. In B. Schneider (Ed.), *Organizational climate and culture* (pp. 383–412). San Francisco: Jossey-Bass.

Sussmann M. & Vecchio, R. P. (1982). A social influence interpretation of worker motivation. *Academy of Management Review, 7,* 177–186.

Trice, H. M. (1993). *Occupational subcultures in the workplace.* Ithaca, NY: ILR Press, Cornell University.

Zabusky, S. E. & Barley, S. R. (1996). Redefining success: Ethnographic observations on the careers of technicians. In P. Osterman (ed.), *Broken Ladders: Managerial Careers in Transition,* pp. 185–214. Oxford, Eng: Oxford University Press.

Zuboff, S. (1988). *In the age of the smart machine: The future of work and power.* New York: Basic Books.

19

Motivation and Transformational Leadership: Some Organizational Context Issues

Lyman W. Porter
University of California, Irvine, CA

Gregory A. Bigley
University of Washington, Seattle, WA

The study of motivation and that of leadership progressed relatively independently of one another for decades during the first half of the twentieth century. More recently, however, an intersection of these areas formed and has been expanding at an increasingly rapid rate, as researchers—especially those in the area of leadership—have specifically emphasized the linkage between the two topics. For example, the path-goal theory connected leader behavior to subordinate satisfaction and effort through an expectancy model of follower motivation (House, 1971; House & Dessler, 1974). Additionally, scholars who have investigated the emerging and related topics of transformational and charismatic leadership have, in many cases, discussed motivational constructs as central components in their frameworks (e.g., Bass, 1985, 1990, Shamir, House, & Arthur, 1993). In fact transformational leadership has been explicitly defined in terms of the motivational effects that it has on followers (Bass, 1985).

Even though recent scholarship has enlarged somewhat the conceptual area connecting motivation with leadership, it has done so with relatively little consideration for *organizational context* issues. Conceptual models and empirical studies of transformational leadership have tended to focus narrowly on the leader-follower

relationship. Consequently, motivational effects that are revealed when transformational leadership is viewed as a process embedded within an organization have been
neglected. The purpose of this paper is to demonstrate that the nature and scope of
the linkage between employee motivation and transformational leadership can be
more fully understood through an explicit consideration of organizational context
factors. After a discussion of some of the motivational underpinnings of transformational leadership, the implications of three situations involving such leadership
are explored: (1) the possible effects on followers of multiple transformational
leaders, (2) some likely unintended consequences of transformational leadership
occurring in one part of an organization, and (3) the potential sustainability of
high levels of transformational leadership. The concluding section of this paper
highlights some implications for organizations and sets out several suggestions for
future research.

MOTIVATION AND TRANSFORMATIONAL LEADERSHIP

A new approach to leadership has become increasingly central in the area of
Organizational Behavior over the past two decades. It is characterized by an emphasis on leaders and the leadership processes that appear to have extraordinary
effects on followers and, ultimately, on the groups, organizations, or other collec-
tivities to which both the leader(s) and their followers belong (e.g., Bass, 1985,
1990; Bennis and Nanus, 1985; Berlew, 1974; Bryman, 1992; Burns, 1978; Conger,
1989; Conger & Kanungo, 1987, 1988; House, 1977; House & Baetz, 1979; Howell
& Frost, 1989; Kouzes & Posner, 1987; Nadler & Tushman, 1989, 1990; Sashkin,
1986, 1988; Sashkin & Burke, 1990; Shamir, House, & Arthur, 1993; Tichy &
Devanna, 1990; Trice & Beyer, 1986). Although individual frameworks associated
with this new approach have been given numerous labels—such as "visionary,"
"charismatic," and "transformational" leadership—the expression "transformational leadership" will be used here to refer collectively to these related models,
since it seems to be the most all-encompassing of the existing terms.

At the individual level, transformational leadership purportedly alters the motivational basis of individual action, which, in turn, results in a marked increase in
follower performance (e.g., followers do more than they originally expected to do)
and, possibly, significant personal sacrifices on the part of followers attempting
to pursue the leader's mission or vision (Bass, 1985, 1990; Conger & Kanungo,
1987, 1988; House, 1977; House & Baetz, 1979; Shamir, House, & Arthur, 1993).
Explanations for the motivational effects of such leadership tend to emphasize
how factors within individuals (e.g., needs, values, self-concepts) are activated or
engaged by the leader and then linked to the leader and his or her goals, mission,
or vision.

At least four fundamental and interrelated motivational effects of transformational leadership have been set forth in the literature on this topic. First, transformational leadership raises followers' awareness concerning the importance and value of objectives and goals and about ways to reach them (Bass, 1985, Burns, 1978). Second, such leadership elevates the level of activated needs in followers' psyches from lower to higher orders in Maslow's (or Alderfer's) hierarchy, or it expands followers' needs portfolios at a particular level (Bass, 1985, Burns, 1978). Third, transformational leadership successfully influences followers to transcend their own self-interests for the sake of the team, organization, or larger polity. Finally, it engages particular elements of followers' self-concepts (e.g., values) in pursuit of the leader's vision or mission (Shamir, House, & Arthur, 1993). Supposedly, then, transformational leaders activate certain of their followers' needs or engage particular aspects of their followers' self-concepts, and then present ways for individuals either to fulfill their needs or to express their self-concepts through behaviors that advance the leader's mission or vision.

According to some scholars investigating transformational leadership, the changes in the motivational basis of follower action, such as those described above, are associated with certain types of leader behaviors (Bass, 1985, 1990; Conger & Kanungo, 1987, 1988; House, 1977; House & Baetz, 1979; Shamir, House, & Arthur, 1993). Perhaps the most widely investigated and empirically supported taxonomy of such behaviors is the one presented by Bass (1985, 1990). In his original formulation, Bass introduced three behavioral categories: charisma, intellectual stimulation, and individualized consideration. A fourth, inspirational motivation (which he originally viewed as a subfactor within charismatic leadership behavior) was added later (Bass, 1985, Bass & Avolio, 1990). These four behavior types are described briefly below and employed in several examples in subsequent sections.

Bass (1985, p. 39) defined charisma as "an endowment of an extremely high degree of esteem, value, popularity, and/or celebrity-status attributed to others." Charisma is connected with leaders who instill pride in being associated with them, go beyond their self-interests for the good of the group or organization, act in ways that build followers' respect, and display a sense of power and confidence (Bass & Avolio, 1995). Inspirational motivation is closely associated with charisma (Bryman, 1992). It is characterized as talking optimistically about the future, talking enthusiastically about what needs to be accomplished, articulating a compelling vision of the future, and expressing confidence that goals will be achieved (Bass & Avolio, 1995).

Another category of transformational leadership behavior is intellectual stimulation (Bass, 1985, 1990). This occurs when leaders encourage their followers to rethink "old" ways of doing things. It entails the leader providing a flow of new ideas to followers, shifting their orientation, or raising their level of consciousness so that followers are induced to reformulate problems that require solutions. Finally, individualized consideration (Bass, 1985, 1990) entails the leader showing personal concern for and responding to the needs of individual followers. These four behavior types are purported to directly affect follower motivation. However, we suggest that certain organizational context-related elements may intervene in the leader–follower relationship.

POTENTIAL IMPACTS OF THREE ORGANIZATIONAL CONTEXT FACTORS

In this section, we attempt to demonstrate that the positive motivational effects researchers have attributed to transformational leadership may be enhanced, dampened, or even reversed by organizational context factors. Three examples are provided. First, it is argued that the extent to which transformational leadership behaviors actually result in increased motivation is partly dependent on the distribution of, and coordination among, transformational leaders within the organization's hierarchy. Next, we suggest that transformational leadership taking place in a particular unit may impact the motivation of employees in other units who are neither the intended targets of influence nor the formal subordinates of the transformational leader, and transformational leadership behaviors may trigger group dynamics that could, in turn, have their own (unintended) motivational consequences. Finally, we submit that intense and continuous transformational leadership behaviors may have diminishing motivational effects over time, since individuals cannot be expected to perform at peak levels over extremely prolonged periods.

The Motivational Effects on Organizational Members of Multiple Transformational Leaders

Most of the literature on the topic of transformational leadership deals with cases where individuals are the targets of the influence stemming from only one transformational leader, especially a leader who occupies the highest formal authority position in their followers' group or organization (see Bryman, 1992, for a discussion). As a result, most of the extant research has emphasized situations in which transformational leadership flows in a downward direction in line with the organization's formal authority structure. However, most theoretical frameworks do not restrict transformational leadership to these types of circumstances (e.g., Bass, 1985; 1990). In fact, transformational leadership has been explicitly conceptualized as an influence process that can spring from almost any point in an organization and may flow in almost any direction (downward, laterally, upward); (cf. Bass, 1985; Burns, 1978; Yammarino, 1994). Consequently, transformational leaders may conceivably be dispersed throughout a particular organization, and a certain employee may be, at one particular time, the target of powerful influence attempts from more than one transformational leader within his or her role set.

A role is typically regarded as an expected pattern or set of behaviors attached to a social position or job within an organization (cf. Katz & Kahn, 1978). The expectations connected with a particular role are established and supported primarily by the role occupant and by other people who occupy adjacent organizational roles (e.g., the supervisor, certain peers, subordinates). The extent to which a role may be motivational for employees is partially dependent on the degree to which it is free of ambiguity (i.e., expectations that are not clear to the role occupant) and conflict (e.g., incompatible expectations sent from members of the focal person's role set).

When two or more transformational leaders are present within a focal person's role set, the motivational consequences of transformational leadership are not straightforward. Multiple transformational leaders within a person's role set may increase the focal person's motivation to perform, perhaps even synergistically, if the leaders' behaviors complement or reinforce one another. For example, one such "leader" may establish a direction for a focal person's behavior through the articulation of an appealing vision, another may contribute to helping that individual achieve the vision or mission through compatible intellectual stimulation-type behaviors, and still another may exhibit consistent individualized consideration behaviors toward the focal person. At a more elemental level, transformational leadership behaviors that are consistent with each other will increase motivation by activating the same or complementary needs in employees or by involving the same or complementary aspects of their self-concepts.

In contrast, multiple individuals attempting to exhibit transformational leadership behaviors within an individual's role set may actually *decrease* the focal person's motivation by increasing his or her role ambiguity or conflict, if the leader behaviors work toward cross purposes. For example, the inspirational message of one transformational leader will increase a focal person's role ambiguity and conflict to the extent that it communicates a mission that is inconsistent with that of other transformational leaders or with that of individuals who occupy higher positions of formal authority.

At a basic motivational level, transformational leader behaviors may activate incompatible needs (perhaps needs at different levels in the hierarchy) that result in conflicts when the individual attempts to satisfy them through role behavior. For example, one transformational leader may activate safety needs in a focal person by emphasizing how tenuous job security is at work. Under this circumstance, the focal person may decide that these types of needs can only be satisfied through a narrow focus on routine task accomplishment. However, another transformational leader may activate self-actualization needs by emphasizing the importance of attempting to realize growth potentials. To fulfill self-actualization needs, the focal person may find that engaging in creative and innovative behavior in the performance of his or her tasks is essential. From this focal person's perspective, safety needs and growth needs cannot be satisfied simultaneously, resulting in conflict.

Unintended Motivational Consequences of a Transformational Leader's Behavior

Previous research has typically focused on the *direct* relationship between a transformational leader's behaviors and their effects on the followers within his or her own unit (or within the organization as a whole, as in the case of a CEO; for an exception, see Yammarino, 1994). Here, we will discuss how transformational leadership behaviors exhibited by an individual in one unit (e.g., a department) that is one of several or many such units may affect employees' motivation in other units where the employees are neither the subordinates nor the targets of influence of the transformational leader. In addition, it is suggested that organizational processes—specifically, group conflict—can mediate the relationship between transformational leadership behaviors and the motivation of employees, both within the leader's own unit and within other units of the organization.

The extent to which the effects of transformational leadership behaviors taking place in one unit are actually motivational elsewhere in the organization may depend on a variety of context factors. For example, an inspirational message delivered in one department of an organization but experienced by employees in other departments (through formal or informal communication channels) may activate certain needs in those employees. This situation could result in increased motivation to perform at work if the jobs in those other departments allow people to satisfy their activated needs. On the other hand, individualized consideration occurring in one group may result in a decrease in employee motivation in other groups if employees who are not experiencing direct individualized consideration become jealous of those who are and begin to resent their own supervisors for not treating them similarly.

In addition to the potential "spillover" effects of transformational leadership, such leadership occurring within a given organizational unit can conceivably trigger or intensify certain intra- and intergroup dynamics that may, themselves, either increase or decrease employee motivation throughout the organization. For example, transformational leadership may bring about or exacerbate intergroup conflict within an organization by increasing the cohesion among members of a particular group. Further, the heightened conflict could serve as the catalyst for group dynamics that have various motivational consequences, some of which may augment those typically associated with transformational leadership, and others of which may decrease employee motivation in one or more of the conflicting groups. In addition, intergroup conflict may reduce the potential for certain types of transformational leadership behaviors in subsequent time periods.

To illustrate, the literature investigating transformational leaders suggests that such individuals encourage followers to transcend their own self-interests for the welfare of the group or organization by establishing clear group boundaries, by emphasizing common objectives, and by encouraging social identification through the articulation of vision statements and through inspirational talks and emotional appeals (Bass, 1985; 1990; House, 1977, House & Baetz, 1979; Shamir, et al. 1993). Group members experiencing transformational leadership, then, are likely to become highly cohesive and focused on goals held in common.

However, other research over many years has acknowledged social identification and the consequent group cohesion as potential antecedents to intergroup discrimination and conflict (Sherif, Harvey, White, Hood, & Sherif, 1961, Tajfel, 1974, 1981; Tajfel & Turner, 1979; Turner, 1975, 1987). In fact, intergroup conflict appears to be a natural, though not inevitable, outcome of group member identification and cohesion, and such conflict tends to escalate as cohesion increases. Feelings of solidarity among members within a group can lead to the development of unfavorable attitudes and negative stereotypes of out-group members. Therefore, this research suggests that feelings of hostility and criticism, and subsequent conflict, could exist between two or more groups in an organization, even though the groups may not directly interact or compete with each other for scarce resources.

Any intergroup conflict that is generated appears to have various motivational effects on the employees within the conflicting units (cf. Daft, 1983). On the one hand, it may enhance the impact of transformational leadership. For example, group conflict seems to intensify group cohesion. (This suggests that there is a two-way causal effect between cohesion and conflict.) In addition, members of groups in conflict become focused on their own task performance and committed to their own group objectives . On the other hand, group conflict may result in forces that diminish motivation within the organization as a whole. For instance, it may have negative motivational consequences for members of groups that see themselves as losing. In such groups, member cohesion decreases, members experience increased tension among themselves, and they spend time and energy looking for a scapegoat to blame for their failure.

Further, increasing group conflict may result in intra-group dynamics that could discourage leaders from exhibiting certain types of transformational leadership behaviors as conflict increases. For example, in situations of conflict, particularly extreme conflict, autocratic leadership styles are sometimes preferred by group members (Driskell & Salas, 1991); consequently, certain behaviors associated with transformational leadership (e.g., individualized consideration and intellectual stimulation) may be resisted by followers because they are viewed as ineffective or too time-consuming.

The Sustainability of High Levels of Motivation Resulting from Transformational Leadership Behaviors

Individuals typically cannot be expected to work at their peak levels indefinitely. Further, most organizations, by their nature, bring people into contact with one another for extended periods. Moreover, once an individual has decided to become a member, much of the contact that he or she has with specific others is determined by the structural features (e.g., roles, policies, procedures, norms) of the organization, and employees may not be able to disengage from relationships (at least, short of quitting the organization) that become, in some respects, uncomfortable. Therefore, since employees may not be able to regulate their own contact with the transformational leaders in their organization who encourage them to perform at peak levels, it will be argued that a high level of continuous transformational leadership can be regarded as a stressor that may, over time, exhibit curvilinear effects on employee motivation. In other words, we will suggest that over prolonged periods of time, particular transformational leadership behaviors may actually reduce motivation as employees become "stressed" or "burned out."

Some of the research reported by Beehr (1995) suggests that high levels of stress can negatively impact employee motivation to perform at work. More specifically, stress appears to be accompanied by anger, anxiety, depression, nervousness, irritability, tension, and boredom (e.g., Gaines & Jermier, 1983). High levels of stress experienced at work may lead to what has been termed "burnout," a condition marked by demoralization, frustration, exhaustion, and reduced efficiency (e.g., Beehr, 1995; Golembiewski & Munzenrider, 1988; Schaufeli, Maslach, Marek, 1993). Under conditions of burnout, the individual can no longer cope with the demands of his or her task environment.

Burnout typically contains three components. Employees experiencing burnout (a) feel emotionally exhausted, (b) depersonalize other individuals that they deal with in their work settings, and (c) feel a sense of low personal accomplishment (Jackson, Schwab, & Schuler, 1986; Lee & Ashforth, 1990). The types of psychological problems associated with high levels of stress and burnout, in turn, are related to poor job performance, lowered self-esteem (McGrath, 1976), resentment of supervision, inability to concentrate and make decisions, and job dissatisfaction (Beehr & Newman, 1978). Further, there is some research evidence indicating a positive relationship between stress and absenteeism and turnover (Steers & Rhodes, 1978). In addition, some literature suggests that individuals at risk for burnout have several attributes in common, including a tendency to be idealistic and self-motivating achievers and an inclination to seek unattainable goals (Niehouse, 1984). These characteristics are similar to the qualities of "transformed" followers of transformational leaders (Bass, 1985).

Since transformational leadership can place more of a demand on individuals' psychological and physical capacities to perform than other types of leadership, it potentially represents more of a stressor than other types of leadership. Therefore, although high levels of transformational leadership may lead to higher levels of motivation and performance, this may be only a short-run effect. Such leadership may actually exhibit diminishing (or negative) marginal returns over time. For example, sustained leadership behaviors such as inspirational motivation and intellectual stimulation may have the consequence of increasing motivation and performance initially, but then they may result in diminished motivation and performance as individuals exhaust themselves in their attempts to fulfill the expectations set out by the leader. Although the findings of Seltzer, Numerof, and Bass (1989) suggest that intellectual stimulation is positively associated with charisma and is negatively related to burnout, their study involved a cross-sectional design which could not examine the time dependent nature of the relationships discussed above. It is fair to say that the work to date on transformational leadership has not investigated adequately the effects of high levels of *sustained* transformational leadership behaviors.

IMPLICATIONS FOR ORGANIZATIONS AND SUGGESTIONS FOR FUTURE RESEARCH

Here we suggest both implications for organizations and directions for future research that follow from the discussion presented in the previous section. It is important to note, however, that in either case we do not intend to present a comprehensive list of issues. Rather, we will set out several salient points that seem to be highlighted by an organizational context perspective.

Implications for Organizations

We have attempted to show that within organizations the relationship between transformational leadership behavior and employee motivation may be more complex than has been commonly assumed. One implication of our argument is that, under certain conditions, managers may be able to raise employee motivation through a reduction in transformational leadership behaviors. For example, in situations where the focal person is the target of influence stemming from two or more individuals displaying conflicting transformational leadership behaviors, such behaviors may cancel each other out, and the focal person's motivation to perform at work may be increased if one of the transformational leaders is removed from the focal person's role set. For another example, a decrease in transformational leadership behaviors may increase overall employee motivation over the long run in situations where the leader's behaviors have been causing unusually high stress for employees.

Another implication pertains to the potential indirect and unintended effects of transformational leadership. For example, a transformational leader may have an additional, and often unintended, impact on employees in other units of the organization. Additionally, motivational effects may not be directly related to transformational-type behaviors. Rather, the relationship between transformational leadership behaviors and employee motivation may be mediated by various processes, e.g., an intergroup conflict dynamic, within the organization.

An organizational context perspective is required to ascertain more accurately the effects of transformational leadership on the motivation of an organization's members. The argument presented above suggests that, depending on the circumstances, members' motivation may be heightened through an increase in transformational leadership, through a redistribution of the transformational leaders within the organization (holding the level of transformational leadership behaviors constant), through a reduction in the level of transformational leadership behaviors, or through some combination of these. Thus, the popular idea that low levels of motivation can be remedied by increased transformational leadership behaviors appears to be overly simplistic where organizations are concerned. Indeed, low levels of employee motivation may be caused by too much transformational leadership behavior in the organization.

Suggestions for Future Research

Several directions for future research follow from our discussion. First, researchers investigating the motivational impact of transformational leadership behaviors within an organization should attempt to ascertain the dispersion pattern of such behaviors within that organization. Since transformational leadership behaviors can emanate from almost any point, and since they may interact in either complementary or conflicting ways, the total effects of such behaviors on employees' motivation may not be determinable without an understanding of how those exhibiting significant transformational leadership behaviors are connected to one another within the organization.

Second, future research may be advanced through investigations of how various transformational leadership behaviors, stemming from different individuals, interact to affect the motivation of a particular target person (or persons) within an organizational setting. It has been suggested that such behaviors may be either complementary or conflicting. In addition, they may interact synergistically, or they may have simply an additive effect.

Third, future research may benefit from attempts to identify organizational processes that can be important mediators between transformational leadership behaviors and employees' motivation. As indicated above, these behaviors may serve as catalysts for organizational dynamics that may have their own motivational effects after they have been activated. The case of intergroup conflict was discussed as one potentially important mediating factor. However, there may be other organizational processes that can act as mediators of transformation leadership behaviors.

Fourth, and following Yammarino (1994), researchers should take a broader view of the potential recipients of a transformational leader's influence within an organization. In most studies of transformational leadership, a leader's direct reports or other specifically intended targets are typically the focus of study. This approach may, however, underestimate the motivational effects of a transformational leader's behavior on the members of the larger organization. As discussed in the preceding section, a transformational leader in one unit of an organization may inadvertently affect employee motivation in other units.

Finally, a longitudinal approach to research on transformational leadership may have particularly high payoffs. It has been suggested that in organizations the relationship between certain types of transformational leadership behaviors and the motivation of employees may be curvilinear across time, because these behaviors may be highly stressful and employees may not be able to regulate their own exposure to them. This type of relationship can be investigated most effectively through research designs involving data collection extending over significant time periods. Longitudinal research can help us answer an important but, as of yet, unaddressed question in the area of transformational leadership: From a motivational standpoint, how much transformational leadership behavior can an organization and its members tolerate?

REFERENCES

Bass, B. M. (1985). *Leadership and performance beyond expectations*. New York: Free Press.
Bass, B. M. (1990). From transactional to transformational leadership: Learning to share the vision. *Organizational Dynamics, 18,* 19–31.
Bass, B. M., & Avolio, B. J. (1990). The implications of transactional and transformational leadership for individual, team, and organizational development. *Research in Organizational Change and Development, 4,* 231–272.
Bass, B. M., & Avolio, B. J. (1995). *The multifactor leadership questionnaire 5–45.* Binghamton, NY: Center for Leadership Studies.
Beehr, T. A. (1995). *Psychological stress in the workplace.* New York: Routledge.
Beehr, T. A., & Newman, J. E. (1978). Job stress, employee health, and organizational effectiveness: A facet analysis, model, and literature review. *Personnel Psychology,* Winter, 665–699.
Bennis, W. G., & Nanus, B. (1985). *Leaders: The strategies for taking charge.* New York: Harper & Row.
Berlew, D. E. (1974). Leadership and organizational excitement. In D. A. Kolb, I. M. Rubin, & J. M. McIntyre (Eds.), *Organizational psychology: A book of readings.* Englewood Cliffs, NJ: Prentice-Hall.
Bryman, A. (1992). *Charisma and leadership in organizations.* London: Sage.
Burns, J. M. (1978). *Leadership.* New York: Harper & Row.
Conger, J. A. (1989). *The charismatic leader: Behind the mystique of exceptional leadership.* San Francisco: Jossey-Bass.
Conger, J. A., & Kanungo, R. (1987). Toward a behavioral theory of charismatic leadership in organizational settings. *Academy of Management Review, 12,* 637–647.
Conger, J. A., & Kanungo, R. (1988). Behavioral dimensions of charismatic leadership. In J. A. Conger, & R. N. Kanungo (Eds.), *Charismatic leadership: The elusive factor in organizational effectiveness* (pp. 78–97). San Francisco: Jossey-Bass.
Daft, R. L. (1983). *Organization theory and design.* St. Paul, MN: West.
Driskell, J. E., & Salas, E. (1991). Group decision-making under stress. *Journal of Applied Psychology, 76,* 473–478.
Gaines, J., & Jermier, J. M. (1983). Emotional exhaustion in high stress organization. *Academy of Management Journal,* December, 567–586.

Golembiewski, R. T., & Munzenrider, R. F. (1988). *Phases of burnout: Developments in concepts and applications.* New York: Praeger Publishers.

House, R. J. (1971). A path-goal theory of leader effectiveness. *Administrative Science Quarterly, 16,* 321–339.

House, R. J. (1977). A 1976 theory of charismatic leadership. In J. G. Hunt & L. L. Larson (Eds.), *Leadership: The cutting edge* (pp. 189–207). Carbondale: Southern Illinois University Press.

House, R. J., & Baetz, M. L. (1979). Leadership: Some empirical generalizations and new research directions. *Research in Organizational Behavior, 1,* 341–423.

House, R. J., & Dessler, G. (1974). The path-goal theory of leadership: Some post hoc and a priori tests. In J. Hunt and L. Larson (Eds.), *Contingency approaches to leadership.* Carbondale: Southern Illinois University Press.

Howell, J. M., & Frost, P. J. (1989). A laboratory study of charismatic leadership. *Organizational Behavior and Human Decision Processes, 43,* 243–269.

Jackson, S. E., Schwab, R. L., & Schuler, R. S. (1986). Toward an understanding of the burnout phenomenon. *Journal of Applied Psychology, 71,* 630–640.

Katz, D., & Kahn, R. L. (1978). *The social psychology of organizations* (2nd ed.). New York: John Wiley.

Kouzes, J. M., & Posner, B. Z. (1987). *The leadership challenge.* San Francisco: Jossey-Bass.

Lee, R. T., & Ashforth, B. E. (1990). On the meaning of Maslach's three dimensions of burnout. *Journal of Applied Psychology, 75,* 743–747.

McGrath, J. E. (1976). Stress and behavior in organizations. In M. D. Dunnette (Ed.), *Handbook of industrial and organizational psychology.* Chicago: Rand McNally.

Nadler, D. A., & Tushman, M. L. (1989). What makes for magic leadership? In W. E. Rosenbach and R. L. Taylor (Eds.), *Contemporary issues in leadership.* Boulder, CO: Westview.

Nadler, D. A., & Tushman, M. L. (1990). Beyond the charismatic leader: Leadership and organizational change. *California Management Review, 32,* 77–97.

Niehouse, O. I. (1984). Controlling burnout: A leadership guide for managers. *Business Horizons, 27,* 80–85.

Sashkin, M. (1986). True vision in leadership. *Training and Development Journal, 40,* 58–61.

Sashkin, M. (1988). The visionary leader. In J. A. Conger and R. N. Kanungo (Eds.), *Charismatic leadership: The elusive factor in organizational effectiveness.* San Francisco: Jossey-Bass.

Sashkin, M., & Burke, W. W. (1990). Understanding and assessing organizational leadership. In K. E. Clark and M. B. Clark (Eds.), *Measures of Leadership.* West Orange, NJ: Leadership Library of America.

Schaufeli, W. B., Maslach, C., & Marek, T. (1993). *Professional burnout: Recent developments in theory and research.* Washington, DC: Taylor & Francis.

Seltzer, J., Numerof, R. E., & Bass, B. M. (1989). Transformational leadership: Is it a source of more burnout and stress? *Journal of Health and Human Resources Administration, 12,* 174–185.

Shamir, B., House, R. J., & Arthur, M. B. (1993). The motivational effects of charismatic leadership: A self-concept based theory. *Organization Science, 4,* 1–17.

Sherif, M., Harvey, O. J., White, B. J., Hood, W. R., & Sherif, C. W. (1961). *Intergroup conflict and cooperation: The robber's cave experiment.* Norman, OK: Institute of Group Relations, University of Oklahoma.

Steers, R. M., & Rhodes, S. R. (1978). Major influences on employee attendance: A process model. *Journal of Applied Psychology,* August, 391–407.

Tajfel, H. (1974). *Social identity and intergroup behavior. Social Science Information, 13,* 65–93.

Tajfel, H. (1981). *Human groups and social categories.* Oxford: Blackwell.

Tajfel, H, & Turner, J. C. (1979). An integrative theory of intergroup conflict. In W. Austin & S. Worchel (Eds.), *The social psychology of intergroup relations* (pp. 33–47). Monterey, CA: Brooks/Cole.

Tichy, N. M., & Devanna, M. A. (1990). *The transformational leader.* New York: John Wiley.

Trice, H. M., & Beyer, J. M. (1986). Charisma and its routinization in two social movement organizations. In L. L. Cummings and B. M. Staw (Eds.), *Research in organizational behavior* (vol. 8, pp. 113–164). Greenwich, CT: JAI Press.

Turner, J. C. (1975). Social comparison and social identity: Some prospects for intergroup behavior. *European Journal of Social Psychology, 5*, 5–34.

Turner, J. C. (1987). *Rediscovering the social group: A self-categorization theory.* New York: Basil Blackwell.

Yammarino, F. J. (1994). Indirect leadership: Transformational leadership at a distance. In B. M. Bass & B. J. Avolio (Eds.), *Improving organizational effectiveness through transformational leadership.* Thousand Oaks, CA: Sage Publications.

20

Temporal Dynamics and Emergent Properties of Organizational Withdrawal Models

Kathy A. Hanisch

Iowa State University, Ames, IA

Charles L. Hulin and Steven T. Seitz

*University of Illinois at Urbana-Champaign
Champaign, IL*

A PERSPECTIVE

D. J. Cherrington (1980), on the basis of a two-year observational study of employees in a variety of job categories and job levels, reported that 49% of employees' time was allocated to coffee breaks, late starts, early departures, chatting with coworkers, and other personal activities. Approximately half of an employee's commitment (time and effort) at work was directed at outcomes other than those required role behaviors that are necessary for an organization to survive. Previous results (Fitzgerald, Hulin, & Drasgow,1994; Hanisch & Hulin, 1990, 1991; Roznowski & Hanisch, 1990) from a variety of organizations strongly suggest these behaviors have attitudinal antecedents and, if aggregated into an estimate of work withdrawal (avoidance of dissatisfying work or work tasks, Hanisch, 1995a) would be substantially related to measures of general job attitudes (Hanisch & Hulin, 1990, 1991; Hanisch, Hulin, & Roznowski, 1998; Roznowski & Hulin, 1992).

Researchers need to recognize the possibility that these apparently nonproductive behaviors, freely enacted by employees, are functional for them. They are enacted for a purpose and lead to a desirable outcome or outcomes for the employees or allow them to avoid an aversive condition or activity. A substantial portion of the nonproductive activities observed by Cherrington are likely to be enacted in response to negative job attitudes and stress—to alleviate the stress and negative feelings caused by organizational conditions, work tasks, supervisors, and coworkers. This latter assumption suggests the operation of closed-loop, dynamic models of attitudes and behaviors. If behaviors are functional and rational and are enacted in response to negative job attitudes, there should be a feedback loop from the enacted behaviors to the antecedent attitudes. Without such a feedback loop, employees would enact the behaviors for no rational reasons.

Time is an important but often unacknowledged factor in every study conducted on organizational withdrawal. The very notion of causality implies time's arrow: social and psychological forces produce behavioral and organizational consequences. Temporal patterns are often nonlinear. Certain organizational withdrawal behaviors may demonstrate an aggregate periodicity, just as individual behavior may reflect periods of self-imposed, self-censored rhythms. These substantive issues have immediate research repercussions, such as the appropriate time interval(s) chosen by investigators for observation and analysis.

Any one or two of these features of organizational withdrawal behaviors (their attitudinal antecedents, purposive nature, dynamic feedback, and temporal complexity) would make them difficult to study by means of the two traditional scientific disciplines of psychology (Cronbach, 1957, 1975). The occurrence of all of them within this or any domain of inquiry means that we should explore alternative research methods that have complementary or orthogonal strengths to those of the two traditional research disciplines, strengths that complement the methods that generated our current bases of research knowledge but will allow us to go beyond those foundations and study more, as well as different, important questions in this area.

Employees' behavior is complex and multifaceted. To fully understand the antecedents and effects associated with this complex behavior requires systematic approaches, including the use of general conceptual models. Hanisch (1995b) presented one such model (see Fig. 20.1) specifying the links among attitudes and general behavioral constructs of functionally similar behaviors in the area of employees' attitudes and withdrawal behaviors. This model leads to questions about the effects of organizational interventions on attitudes and behaviors. For example, would organizational interventions designed to influence employees' job attitudes offer an indirect means of control over these nonproductive job behaviors? What are the effects of interventions designed to suppress or block nonproductive behaviors directly without addressing their antecedents? If this latter intervention controlled the primary behavior addressed, what effect, if any, would this have on other withdrawal behaviors? We are interested in this chapter in studying the secondary effects or the effects on nontargeted behaviors if an intervention is imposed on another behavior. The effects will depend on which model or models of the organizational withdrawal process are operating; the environmental and organizational conditions that enhance or block certain of the withdrawal behaviors also need to be considered. Before we describe the computational modeling approach used to

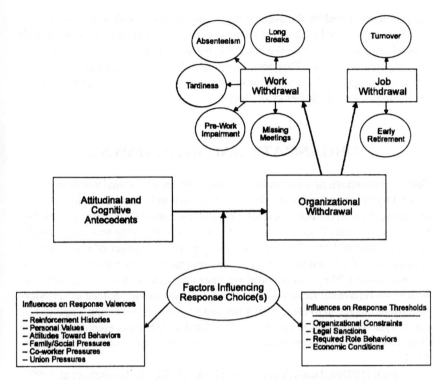

FIG. 20.1. Antecedents, influences on response choices, and behavioral families of organizational withdrawal. Original figure appeared in *Current Directions in Psychological Science*. Copyright 1995 by American Psychological Society. Reprinted with the permission of Cambridge University Press.

address these issues, we present a brief overview of the relations among attitudes and behaviors, and descriptions of the various models hypothesized to explain the relations among organizational withdrawal behaviors.

GENERAL ATTITUDES AND GENERAL BEHAVIORS

General attitudes have been shown to have significant and meaningful relations with aggregated measures or other estimates of an underlying general behavioral construct. Theoretical developments regarding general versus specific attitudes and general behavioral constructs versus specific isolated behaviors began over 45 years ago by Thurstone (1931). He argued that two individuals with the same general attitude toward an object will quite likely behave in different ways; aggregations, composites, or constructs comprised of the different relevant behaviors will, however, accurately reflect their general attitudes. Communality among the behaviors, estimated by the average degree of negativity/positivity, or by the co-variances represented in a sum across many behaviors, will reflect each individual's general attitude and will be predicted by that general attitude. Much conceptual and empirical work since Thurstone's original publication (e.g., Fishbein & Ajzen, 1974) has supported his general propositions and his specific contentions about the inadequacy of single-behavior criteria.

ORGANIZATIONAL WITHDRAWAL

One general behavioral construct of interest is the organizational withdrawal construct. Organizational withdrawal has been defined as behaviors employees enact to remove themselves from their job or avoid their work tasks (Hanisch, 1995a). Hanisch and Hulin (1990, 1991) evaluated the relations among individual specific behaviors assumed to reflect the underlying general construct of organizational withdrawal. They found support for a consistent pattern of behaviors summarized by this construct. They also provided evidence that organizational withdrawal subsumes two behavioral factors they labeled *work withdrawal*, defined as behaviors employees engage in to avoid their work tasks while still remaining employed by one's organization, and *job withdrawal*, defined as behaviors employees engage in to remove themselves from their job with a specific organization (see Hanisch, 1995a).

Hanisch (1995b), Hanisch and Hulin (1990, 1991), and Hanisch, et al. (1998) also argued that attempts to predict and understand organizational withdrawal that focus exclusively on one organizational withdrawal behavior (e.g., absenteeism or turnover) miss several important points. One is the likely substitution of one behavior for another that is blocked by environmental or organizational factors. Another is the possibility that blocking one or two behaviors may change the frequencies of all other withdrawal behaviors in unanticipated ways and degrees. By using a strategy in which patterns of behaviors or the communality among several behaviors are studied, researchers can capitalize on the information contained in the patterns of behaviors. These patterns are influenced by a combination of job attitudes, influences on response valences, and response thresholds (see Fig. 20.1), as well as the specific withdrawal model that usefully describes the withdrawal process in the location of theoretical space being studied.

ORGANIZATIONAL WITHDRAWAL MODELS

Organizational withdrawal models or theories of the withdrawal process describe how individual withdrawal behaviors are related to each other and their different functions given the conditions that precede them. These models either explicitly or implicitly specify the expected structures among withdrawal behaviors, the antecedent psychological processes that control them, and the effects on frequencies of different behaviors. Each of the models is explicit about the between-behavior relationship, but they do not speak to the fact that these between-behavior relationships go on over time. Computational modeling, the research strategy used here, can show some of the implications of the model assumptions over time. Examining the between model effects is also useful in that one can study what some of the differences in implications of the models are over time. There are five distinct models of withdrawal, and they are described in detail in Hanisch, Hulin, and Seitz (1996). Because of space constraints, we focus on three of the models in this paper, including the Independent Forms of Withdrawal model, Spillover Withdrawal model, and Progression of Withdrawal model.

Independent Forms of Withdrawal Model

The Independent Forms of Withdrawal model was developed by March and Simon (1958) and elaborated upon by Porter and Steers (1973). In the original statement of the model by March and Simon (1958), absenteeism and quitting (turnover) were assumed to be unrelated to each other. They argued that absences and turnover are not functionally different because of differences in the factors inducing the initial behavioral impulse; they are different because of differences in their consequences. They argued that dissatisfaction, or motivation to withdraw, is "general and holds for both absences and voluntary turnover" (p. 93). Absences are hypothesized to reduce negative job attitudes by removing the employee temporarily from the stresses of the day-to-day tasks. Quitting reduces stress from a specific job by permanently removing the individual from the organization and associated work tasks. We have expanded the possible withdrawal behaviors to include those demonstrated empirically or logically to be part of the same general behavior set. In the dynamic statement of this model, it is assumed that behaviors enacted have a feedback effect onto the antecedent job attitudes that caused them. We note here that the dynamic versions of this and the other two models evaluated here cannot be derived from the original static statements of the models without additional information or assumptions based on theoretical and empirical work.

Spillover Model of Withdrawal

Beehr and Gupta (1978) argued that withdrawal behaviors should be positively intercorrelated—there should be a nucleus of behaviors, withdrawal events, that occur in concert. They also argued that aversive work situations should generate nonspecific negative attitudes and nonspecific avoidance or withdrawal tendencies. Nonspecific withdrawal tendencies mean that employees enact one or several of the available behaviors that enable them to avoid the aversive work situation.

The nonspecific avoidance tendencies "spillover" from one withdrawal behavior to another in one time period, or across time, or both. Thus, an aversive work situation may generate several different withdrawal behaviors at the same time or several occurrences of the same behavior, depending on the behavior and situational constraints (e.g., unemployment, organizational sanctions) on the behaviors.

There are two antecedents of any withdrawal behavior in the Spillover model: a link from the attitudinal antecedents of the behavior and a second, independent link from any other withdrawal behavior enacted. Psychologically, this withdrawal model accounts for the spread of withdrawal behaviors by mechanisms that function independently of attitudinal antecedents that triggered the initial behavior. This process may reflect habituation or behavioral diffusion. This diffusion can occur nearly simultaneously, in the same behavioral episode, or can occur across several months.

Progression of Withdrawal Model

Several papers contain elements of the Progression of Withdrawal model. Baruch (1944) described absences from work as "short-term quits." Herzberg, Mausner, Peterson, and Capwell (1957) argued that the problems of absenteeism and turnover should be considered jointly because "the small decision which is taken when the worker absents himself is a miniature version of the important decision he makes when he quits his job." Melbin (1961) argued that leaving a job is the outcome of a chain of behaviors leading to a final break with an organization. "High absenteeism (lateness and absence) appears to be an earlier sign, and turnover (quitting and being fired) the dying stage of a long and lively process of leaving" (p. 15).

The Progression of Withdrawal model specifies that individuals, in response to negative job attitudes, enact a stochastically-ordered sequence of withdrawal responses that begins with minor acts, for example, daydreaming or frequent trips to water fountains and restrooms, then progresses to lateness or leaving work early, to absences from meetings and abuse of sick and personal leave, and finally to extreme behaviors such as unexcused absenteeism and quitting or unexpected "early" retirement. The specific ordering of the behaviors, from "mild" to "extreme," will vary based on the characteristics of the organization and the job classifications of employees. The withdrawal behavior most likely to be enacted initially would be one of the mild forms of withdrawal defined with reference to the employees' job classification and organization. If this form of withdrawal reduces job dissatisfaction and job stress to a tolerable level, the employee would either repeat the same or similar withdrawal behavior in the future to maintain the *status quo* and a tolerable level of job dissatisfaction and stress, or would, with a lower probability, enact no withdrawal behaviors. The initial and subsequent behavior(s) enacted by such an employee would be a function of his or her interpretation and reaction to the initial and remaining job dissatisfaction. If the chosen withdrawal behavior was not effective in reducing job dissatisfaction or job stress to tolerable levels, the employee would be expected to increase the extremity of the enacted withdrawal behaviors in the next time period (e.g., the next day, week, or month).

WORKER: A COMPUTATIONAL MODELING PROGRAM

WORKER is a computational modeling software program (Seitz, Hanisch, & Hulin, 1997) that we developed to evaluate the expected relations among withdrawal behaviors. This program can be used to simulate the withdrawal behaviors of individuals in organizational environments.

The initial conditions are set by the user to create a simulated organization of employees with specified age, tenure, gender, and job classification distributions. The user sets the structure of the initial employee attitudes in the organization. In addition to the workforce characteristics, the user can set constant or varying unemployment levels, or can even change the unemployment levels abruptly or gradually in the middle of a simulation run to mimic the effects of a sudden depression or gradual boom in the labor market.

Organizational characteristics that simulate different levels of sanctions or "carrots and sticks" wielded by an organization to influence the frequencies of specific organizational withdrawal behaviors are also user controlled in WORKER. These sanctions can be altered at any point in the simulation by means of the intervention module in the program. This permits the user to simulate an organizational intervention, perhaps in response to one or more behaviors becoming too frequent (e.g., absenteeism) or too infrequent (e.g., retirement).

WORKER is based on fuzzy set theory and fuzzy calculus. These basic mathematical operations are combined with thresholds and feedback dynamics. Negative attitudes that fail to reach the necessary threshold may still be translated into manifest behaviors at a user-defined probability rate. Similarly, attitudes that exceed the necessary threshold may not get translated into manifest behaviors, again based on some user defined rate. This stochastic component of the program essentially allows the probability of translating an attitude into a behavior to vary with the strength of the attitude.

In this chapter, we focus on behaviors that compose the work and job withdrawal behavioral constructs with specific attention to what happens to the work withdrawal behaviors when two job withdrawal behaviors, turnover and retirement, are impacted because of organizational sanctions (i.e., high or low). Specifically, we manipulated sanctions to either decrease or increase the frequency of employees enacting the two job withdrawal behaviors. The potential effect of these manipulations on the frequencies of the other modeled withdrawal behaviors is our major interest. If different patterning is evident as the withdrawal process unfolds across time and across different models, these results would imply that studying isolated behaviors as is typically done may lead to misleading conclusions. By modeling the patterning among withdrawal behaviors we can observe how the withdrawal process will be enacted if our models are correct, and through these observations we can gain a better understanding of how such behaviors may unfold. These results might also suggest that attempts by organizations to control one isolated withdrawal behavior may have many negative unintended consequences.

We are interested specifically in the behavior patterns resulting from the changes in sanctions on some behaviors on the frequencies and dynamics of the other behaviors. The direct and intended effects of sanctions on turnover and retirement are known prior to the simulation. The important question that can be evaluated in this study is the effect these behaviors have on the enactment of other withdrawal behaviors, across time, within each model simulated. Particularly important are the emergent properties of the models on the remaining withdrawal behaviors in the withdrawal set. How do sanctions (positive and negative) on two withdrawal behaviors affect frequencies, equlibria, and the stability of other withdrawal behaviors?

Method

The organization created for the simulations consisted of an employee population of 300 with an equal percentage of male and female employees. Ages of the employees were sampled from a normal distribution with a mean of 31 and a standard deviation of 5; the range was from 18 to 45. Years of service (i.e., organizational tenure) values were sampled from a uniform distribution with a range from 0 to 15 years. Unemployment was set at a constant 6% for the simulation runs completed for this study.

We simulated seven withdrawal behaviors including turnover, early retirement, prework impairment (e.g., drug or alcohol use/abuse before work), absenteeism, tardiness, long breaks, and missing meetings. One parameter set by the user for all behaviors that determines the initial relation between the attitude toward the behavior and the behavior is the loading on the common vector. These loadings control the intercorrelations and structure among the attitudes in the initial simulation period (see Table 20.1 for the initial values used in this study). A second parameter associated with the behaviors is referred to as the threshold. The threshold stochastically imposed for each behavior determines the point at which the attitude is translated into a behavior with a given probability. For the simulations completed here, attitudes above the threshold are translated into behaviors with a probability of .80; the further the attitude is above the threshold, the more likely the behavior is to be enacted. Attitudes below the threshold are translated into behaviors with a probability of .20; the further the attitude is below the threshold, the less likely the behavior is to be enacted. A range of threshold values were set for the behaviors that were consistent with the descriptive labels; they are presented

TABLE 20.1
Parameters of Simulated Behaviors

Behavior	Loading on Common Vector	Thresholds	Degree of Withdrawal
Long Breaks	.35	.10	.30
Tardiness	.40	.15	.25
Missing Meetings	.30	.45	.35
Absenteeism	.50	.50	.50
Prework Impairment	.40	.65	.60
Early Retirement	.85	.70	.70
Turnover	.75	.75	.80

Loading on common vector refers to the loading of the attitude associated with the behavior on an assumed common vector. These loadings control the intercorrelations and structure among the attitudes in the initial time period.

Thresholds refer to the stochastically imposed thresholds at which the attitudes are translated into a behavior with a given probability. Attitudes above the behavior are translated into behaviors with a probability of .80; the further above the threshold the attitude is, the more likely the behavior is to be enacted. Attitudes below the threshold are translated into behaviors with a probability of .20; the further below the threshold the attitude is, the less likely the behavior is to be enacted.

Degree of withdrawal refers to the belongingness of the behavior to the fuzzy set of withdrawal behaviors. This parameter only influences behavioral choice in the Progression of Withdrawal model. The greater the degree of belongingness, the more "severe" the behavior.

in Table 20.1. A final parameter relevant only for one of the models simulated in this study is called the degree of withdrawal and refers to the belongingness of the behavior to the fuzzy set of organizational withdrawal. The greater the degree of belongingness, the more severe or extreme the behavior. This parameter influences stochastically the order of behavioral choice in the Progression of Withdrawal model only.

For the high-sanction condition, the sanctions on turnover and retirement (the two job withdrawal behaviors) were set at .90 (possible values range from 0 to 1.0 with .50 representing a neutral state) to make it unlikely that these behaviors would be enacted. For turnover and early retirement, this could be accomplished operationally by retaining all company contributions to company retirement plans unless the individual had been with the organization more than 20 years, removing health care coverage on the day of termination instead of providing a 30-day grace period or other financial manipulations. To decrease "early" retirement among employees, the organization could have a pension plan that did not provide necessary benefits until after an employee had 20 years of tenure and then provide a steeply rising pension income for employees who stayed beyond 30 years. For the condition of relatively low sanctions on turnover and retirement, the sanctions were set at .30 to make it more likely that these two behaviors would be enacted. In all simulations for all of the remaining work withdrawal behaviors the sanctions were set at .50 to represent neutral sanctions.

For each simulation, using one of the withdrawal models described above, we set the sanctions at low or high for the job withdrawal behaviors and ran the simulation for 25 time periods or rounds. In each time period, each behavior was either enacted or not for each employee depending on the rules of the specific model used (i.e., Independent Forms, Spillover, Progression of Withdrawal) and the attitude of the individual. Attitudes were updated for the next round or time period on the basis of feedback from the behavior(s) enacted in the previous round, stochastics that influence attitudes that do not lead to a behavior, and other conditions imposed by the model being used in the simulation. These dynamic workings of the algorithms in WORKER are described for specific simulations in Hanisch et al. (1996).

In all simulation runs included in this study, the effects of stochastics influence all results and introduce a degree of randomness into the results that adds to verisimilitude; they also make the results less clean than they would be if these stochastics were not included. At the system or organizational level for this study, large sample sizes somewhat ameliorate these effects. At the individual level, a behavior enacted or not enacted because of the stochastically imposed threshold may cause two simulees with identical attitudes to diverge dramatically toward their final states. Both individual and organizational effects were shown in Hanisch et al. (1996). In this chapter we concentrate on the organizational results with all stochastic effects operating.

The output from each round of the simulation consisted of those behaviors enacted during the round and the attitudes at the end of the round. These output variables are available for analysis as the observations of any empirical study would be. We have chosen to display the results of the seven withdrawal behaviors in four separate graphs for each model, with both sanction conditions within behaviors presented on one graph.

Results

Independent Forms of Withdrawal
Model Results

Figure 20.2 presents the frequencies of behaviors generated by the Independent Forms of Withdrawal model across the 25-time-period simulation run. The effects of the sanctions on turnover and retirement can be seen in Fig. 20.2a. Under the high-sanction condition, both early retirement and turnover are infrequently enacted, whereas under relatively neutral sanctions they become, on average, twice as frequent.

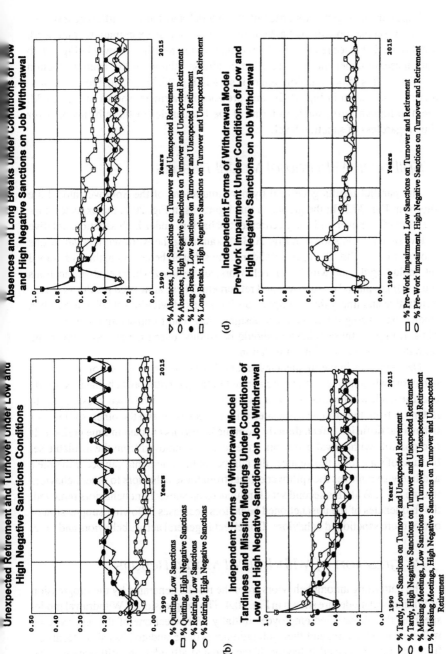

FIG. 20.2. Withdrawal behaviors simulation results for the Independent Forms of Withdrawal model.

Important emergent properties of this model and the two different levels of sanctions on the job withdrawal behaviors are seen in an examination of the work withdrawal behavior results. Tardiness and missing meetings shown in Fig. 20.2b both increase under the high-sanction condition relative to the neutral-sanction condition. This same behavior pattern is seen in Fig. 20.2c for long breaks. Absenteeism, also shown in Fig. 20.2c, and prework impairment, shown in Fig. 20.2d, seem to remain fairly stable in terms of the frequencies of these behaviors over time regardless of sanction level.

Spillover Withdrawal Model Results

The parallel results generated by our simulations of the Spillover model are shown in Fig. 20.3. In the graphs in this figure, as in Fig. 20.2, the expected suppression of turnover and early retirement behaviors under high sanctions relative to low sanctions is shown in Fig. 20.3a. Examining the work withdrawal results shown in Fig. 20.3b, 20.3c, and 20.3d indicates that all behaviors in the withdrawal set, including the job withdrawal behaviors, are *reduced* when negative sanctions (i.e., .90) are placed on turnover and retirement. These simulated results are counterintuitive and imply that multiple manifestations of withdrawal behaviors, when studied only using cross-sectional designs, may lead to misleading conclusions. Thus, it implies these behaviors should be studied over time and as a covarying set rather than one at a time in isolation.

The decreases in the frequencies of all other behaviors in the set of withdrawal behaviors when high sanctions are applied to the job withdrawal behaviors occurs because each withdrawal behavior enacted in time $i + 1$ has two causal paths to it. One is from the attitude associated with the behavior and the other, spillover or behavioral diffusion effect, directly from the behaviors enacted in time period i. If two possible withdrawal behaviors are effectively removed from the available set because of sanctions, this reduces the number of behaviors that can occur in time i and likewise removes the spillover effects from these behaviors to other behaviors in time $i + 1$. With this second set of influences on subsequent behaviors removed, the frequencies of the unsanctioned behaviors decreases following suppression of one or more sanctioned behaviors. This effect is general across behaviors and time.

Progression of Withdrawal Model Results

The patterning among behaviors from the results generated by the Progression of Withdrawal model are shown in Fig. 20.4. The Progression of Withdrawal model specifies that dissatisfied employees initially will select one of the less extreme withdrawal behaviors, and their job attitudes will be updated based on feedback from the initial enacted behavior. If the updated attitudes are still negative, the employee will progress to the next more extreme behavior and enact it on the subsequent round in the simulation. This process continues until the employee

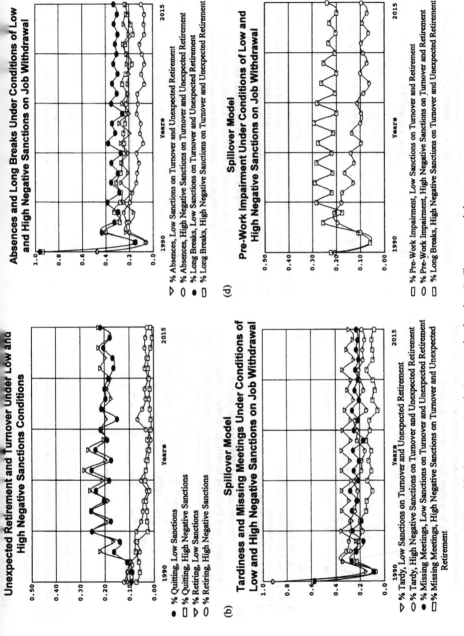

Unexpected Retirement and Turnover Under Low and High Negative Sanctions Conditions

Absences and Long Breaks Under Conditions of Low and High Negative Sanctions on Job Withdrawal

- ● % Quitting, Low Sanctions
- ▢ % Quitting, High Negative Sanctions
- ▽ % Retiring, Low Sanctions
- ○ % Retiring, High Negative Sanctions

(b)

▽ % Absences, Low Sanctions on Turnover and Unexpected Retirement
○ % Absences, High Negative Sanctions on Turnover and Unexpected Retirement
● % Long Breaks, Low Sanctions on Turnover and Unexpected Retirement
▢ % Long Breaks, High Negative Sanctions on Turnover and Unexpected Retirement

(d)

Spillover Model
Tardiness and Missing Meetings Under Conditions of Low and High Negative Sanctions on Job Withdrawal

▽ % Tardy, Low Sanctions on Turnover and Unexpected Retirement
○ % Tardy, High Negative Sanctions on Turnover and Unexpected Retirement
● % Missing Meetings, Low Sanctions on Turnover and Unexpected Retirement
▢ % Missing Meetings, High Negative Sanctions on Turnover and Unexpected Retirement

Spillover Model
Pre-Work Impairment Under Conditions of Low and High Negative Sanctions on Job Withdrawal

▢ % Pre-Work Impairment, Low Sanctions on Turnover and Retirement
○ % Pre-Work Impairment, High Negative Sanctions on Turnover and Retirement
▢ % Long Breaks, High Negative Sanctions on Turnover and Unexpected Retirement

FIG. 20.3. Withdrawal behaviors simulation results for the Spillover model.

(a)

Progression of Withdrawal Model
Unexpected Retirement and Turnover Under Low and
High Negative Sanctions Conditions

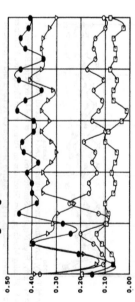

• % Quitting, Low Sanctions
□ % Quitting, High Negative Sanctions
▽ % Retiring, Low Sanctions
○ % Retiring, High Negative Sanctions

(b)

Progression of Withdrawal Model
Tardiness and Missing Meetings Under Conditions of
Low and High Negative Sanctions on Job Withdrawal

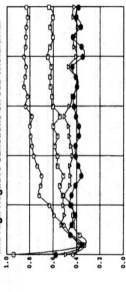

▽ % Tardy, Low Sanctions on Turnover and Unexpected Retirement
○ % Tardy, High Negative Sanctions on Turnover and Unexpected Retirement
• % Missing Meetings, Low Sanctions on Turnover and Unexpected Retirement
□ % Missing Meetings, High Negative Sanctions on Turnover and Unexpected Retirement

(c)

Progression of Withdrawal Model
Absences and Long Breaks Under Conditions of Low
and High Negative Sanctions on Job Withdrawal

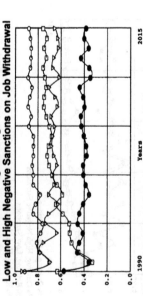

▽ % Absences, Low Sanctions on Turnover and Unexpected Retirement
○ % Absences, High Negative Sanctions on Turnover and Unexpected Retirement
• % Long Breaks, Low Sanctions on Turnover and Unexpected Retirement
□ % Long Breaks, High Negative Sanctions on Turnover and Unexpected Retirement

(d)

Progression of Withdrawal Model
Pre-Work Impairment Under Conditions of Low and
High Negative Sanctions on Job Withdrawal

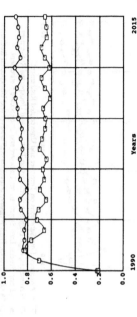

□ % Pre-Work Impairment, Low Sanctions on Turnover and Retirement
○ % Pre-Work Impairment, High Negative Sanctions on Turnover and Retirement

either enacts a job withdrawal behavior and leaves the organization or reaches an equilibrium point and remains at that point enacting the withdrawal behavior that maintains his or her job attitudes at a tolerable level.

Selection of withdrawal behaviors by individual employees, under the assumptions of the Progression of Withdrawal model and our development of WORKER, are influenced by a combination of factors: attitudes of the employee, thresholds at which the attitudes are translated into behaviors, and the degree of withdrawal of the behavior. This latter factor is unique to the Progression of Withdrawal model as discussed earlier. As shown in Table 20.1, turnover and early retirement both have high degrees of belongingness to the fuzzy set; both are extreme behaviors that result in the severing of formal ties between the employee and the organization. These behaviors have higher degrees of belongingness than, say, absenteeism or tardiness; they also have greater dynamic feedback effects onto the antecedent attitudes when they occur. The degree of belongingness can also be conceptualized as the degree to which the behavior is stimulated by, and reflects reasoned desires by, the employee to withdraw from the organization or from the quotidian tasks of one's work role. Behaviors with low degrees of belongingness, such as tardiness or missing a meeting, are likely to reflect both negative job attitudes and minor, temporary, random factors associated with the individual employee or the weather. Behaviors with a high degree of belongingness are more directly influenced by attitudinal antecedents.

In the graphs in Fig. 20.4, the joint effects of thresholds, sanctions, and degrees of belongingness can be seen on the frequencies of turnover and retirement. However, in Fig. 20.4a, the high negative sanctions on these two withdrawal behaviors reduce their frequencies even further. When these suppressing effects of high negative sanctions are imposed, the frequencies of all other behaviors *increase* (see graph b, c, and d in Fig. 20.4). These frequencies show that the individuals are cycling—in only two or three rounds—through the withdrawal behaviors and are quickly reaching the extremes of the available set of withdrawal behaviors. Prework impairment is the most extreme behavior left in the set if turnover and early retirement are not viable alternatives. Prework impairment's high initial threshold (see Table 20.1) coupled with relatively neutral sanctions results in it being selected most frequently after the first three or four rounds in the simulation. Tardiness is selected with approximately equal frequency to that of prework impairment. These two behaviors are followed by the other work withdrawal behaviors.

Comparison of Withdrawal Model Results

The job withdrawal behaviors (turnover and retirement in this study) with high degrees of belongingness and extremity are selected relatively more often under the Progression of Withdrawal model than either of the other two models. After only 15 rounds, only 11 of the original 300 employees were left in the organization under the assumption of the Progression of Withdrawal model with low sanctions;

with high sanctions, 82 of the original 300 employees were left after the complete 25 rounds in the simulation. For comparison purposes, 123 and 172 of the original 300 employees remained after 25 rounds with low and high sanctions, respectively, in the Independent Forms of Withdrawal model. With the Spillover model, the comparable number of the original employees remaining were 116 and 100. These emergent properties of the Progression of Withdrawal model, including very quick progression to the extreme behaviors, relatively higher amounts of job withdrawal, and cleaner separation of the frequencies of the enacted withdrawal behaviors, again illustrate the complexity of patterns of organizational withdrawal. It is further evidence of the risks of studying one or two withdrawal behaviors in isolation because of the behavioral substitution that occurs if the Progression of Withdrawal model or the spillover effects that result if the Spillover model are useful metaphors to describe organizational withdrawal.

Discussion

There are clear distinctions among the three withdrawal models evaluated in this study. The results generated by the simulations suggest the necessity of exploring the entire organizational, employee, environmental, and temporal space to allow meaningful statements about the logical implications and empirical verisimilitude of the different withdrawal models. Depending on which model appears to provide the most accurate representation of the withdrawal process in general, or in delineated regions of the total space, significantly different research procedures will be required if researchers are going to be able to untangle the underlying components of the withdrawal process.

The emergent properties of the withdrawal models evaluated here should alert researchers and managers to the risks inherent in studying or sanctioning one or two withdrawal behaviors and ignoring the dependencies among other withdrawal behaviors. To understand the dynamics and dependencies of the withdrawal process as assumed by any of the models, one must evaluate the information contained in the *pattern* of enacted behaviors rather than that contained in the frequency and antecedents of one or two behaviors.

Things that occur that suppress one or two withdrawal behaviors, in this case, deliberate organizational interventions under the Independent Forms of Withdrawal model, do not suppress *organizational withdrawal*. They suppress those one or two targeted withdrawal behaviors; other withdrawal behaviors increase. With these behaviors suppressed, relationships between them and their antecedents will also be reduced because of the restriction of range, skewed distributions, and reduced variance. Thus, null hypotheses may not be rejected when they should be or hypothesized links in causal models will have misleading parameter estimates. Studies that include several withdrawal behaviors will be sensitive to these patterned responses as well as exploit the psychometric advantages of capitalizing on the communality among responses (see Hanisch, 1995b).

The implications for managers who implement organizational interventions designed to reduce the occurrence of one or two withdrawal behaviors are important. While such interventions may be extremely successful in reducing absenteeism or tardiness, they may not affect the total amount of organizational withdrawal engaged in by employees nor the bottom-line costs of such behaviors if the Independent Forms of Withdrawal model accurately describes the organizational withdrawal process. Only if managers are aware of the complex linkages among attitudes and a set or family of behaviors and attend to these dependencies when they design interventions are they likely to achieve their goals of reducing the total amount of organizational withdrawal and the negative financial implications these behaviors have for an organization (see Hanisch, 2000).

The implications of the results shown in Fig. 20.3 are more complex than the implications of the simulated results generated by the Independent Forms of Withdrawal model. If the Spillover model is a useful description of the withdrawal process, then generally infrequent withdrawal behaviors in any organization may be attributable to generally good working conditions and a workforce with positive attitudes or to the suppression of one or two behaviors because of organizational conditions such as negative sanctions on those behaviors, or temporary factors in an organization or its macro-environment. The effects of suppression on one or two behaviors can be expected to spill over or diffuse to other behaviors in the withdrawal set with the observed general effects. The suppressing, but temporary, effects of changes in organizational factors on one or two behaviors may present a false picture to researchers about the level of negative attitudes or organizational withdrawal in an organization. Further, the generalized suppressing effects may reduce the frequencies of all behaviors below the point at which meaningful correlations can be obtained between the behaviors and their antecedents.

If the Spillover model is a useful summary of the withdrawal process, then the manager's job may be made easier but the researcher's job is more difficult than it might be if the Independent Forms of Withdrawal model were accurate. If management imposes sanctions on one or two behaviors operating under the Spillover model, all behaviors in the set are reduced due to the behavioral diffusion effects. Thus, relative simple organizational interventions in the form, for example, of lotteries based on cards given out each day of the week to form a poker hand by Friday might be expected to reduce all other behaviors in the set. Thus, simple and specific interventions may have complex and general effects. Both contemporary and historical perspectives may need to be adopted to give managers and researchers a complete picture of the state of withdrawal and even job attitudes in their organization.

However, this same behavioral diffusion will also make the results of research studies more difficult to interpret. Studies intended to evaluate the effects of an intervention on, say, absenteeism will be faced with explaining why reducing absenteeism also reduces other behaviors. It is also possible that a research study that targets one specific behavior (e.g., absenteeism) may find a general effect from that behavior to others in the available withdrawal set. These effects, due to the underlying withdrawal process, may lead the researcher to conclude that the intervention was not effective, but that some other event caused the suppression of absenteeism and all other withdrawal behaviors. Based on the Spillover model, the findings would be expected. Empirical research of sufficient complexity that is based on theory or insights necessary to tease apart the dynamics of the Spillover model across time are difficult, rare, and needed.

Simulations based on both the Independent Forms and the Progression of Withdrawal models indicate that substantial behavioral substitution occurs if one or two behaviors are blocked by sanctions. This substitution suggests that the models are treating different withdrawal behaviors in the set as functionally similar or even functionally equivalent. This treatment also has implications for managers concerned about organizational withdrawal by their employees.

Under the assumptions of the Progression of Withdrawal model, the speed with which the employees cycle through the behaviors and progress to the most extreme behavior left in the set, after turnover and early retirement are effectively removed by imposing high negative sanctions, is not specified in the model but not prohibited either. The linkages among the behaviors in this model suggest that managers must act quickly once evidence for negative job attitudes, stress, and organizational withdrawal is seen. If this model is correct, once employees become dissatisfied and embark on a process of organizational withdrawal, they engage in several behaviors and neither the dynamic feedback effects on precipitating job attitudes nor the stochastics in the model are sufficient to break this chain of behaviors once initiated.

CONCLUSIONS

The computational modeling research strategy employed in this study, although not new in general, is unique in industrial and organizational psychology because of its reliance on stochastic, dynamic, nonlinear characteristics. Given our research interests, these are necessary conditions; they approximate the complexity of employees' behavioral responses and their antecedents. The results presented here and in subsequent studies will untangle and evaluate the models of withdrawal under conditions that can be examined in empirical research and situations that a researcher could never study because of several limitations with our other research strategies. Computational modeling overcomes many of these limitations, including, for example, the number of time periods available for study, the effect of relatively extreme changes in macro-organizational variables, and the effects of dynamic feedback versus no feedback from behaviors to attitudes. The goal of computational modeling is to provide results, where possible, that can be evaluated against empirical data, but more importantly to answer questions that are next to impossible to study by any other means. Emergent system properties are one such question and answer. The time for this research strategy to be exploited by organizational researchers has arrived.

ACKNOWLEDGEMENTS

The authors thank Liberty Matt for her time and effort on the setup, runs, and preparation of results presented in this chapter. Address correspondence regarding this chapter to Kathy A. Hanisch, Iowa State University, Department of Psychology, W212 Lagomarcino Hall, Ames, Iowa 50011.

REFERENCES

Baruch, D. W. (1944). Why they terminate. *Journal of Consulting Psychology, 8*, 35–46.

Beehr, T. A., & Gupta, N. (1978). A note on the structure of employee withdrawal. *Organizational Behavior and Human Performance, 21*, 73–79.

Cherrington, D. J. (1980). *The work ethic: Working values and values that work.* New York: Amacom.

Cranny, C. J., Smith, P. C., & Stone, E. (1992). *Job satisfaction: How people feel about their jobs and how it affects their performance.* New York: Lexington.

Cronbach, L. J. (1957). The two disciplines of scientific psychology. *American Psychologist, 12*, 671–684.

Cronbach, L. J. (1975). Beyond the two disciplines of scientific psychology. *American Psychologist, 30*, 116–127.

Fishbein, M. F., & Ajzen, I. (1974). Attitudes towards objects as predictors of single and multiple behavioral criteria. *Psychological Bulletin, 81*, 59–74.

Fitzgerald, L. F., Hulin, C. L., & Drasgow, F. D. (1994). The antecedents and consequences of sexual harassment in organizations: An integrated model. In G. Keita & S. Sauter (Eds.), *Job stress in a changing workforce: Investigating gender, diversity, and family issues.* Washington, DC: American Psychological Association.

Hanisch, K. A. (1995a). Behavioral families and multiple causes. Matching the complexity of responses to the complexity of antecedents. *Current Directions in Psychological Science, 4*, 156–162.

Hanisch, K. A. (1995b). Organizational Withdrawal. In N. N. Nicholson (Ed.), *The blackwell encyclopedic dictionary of organizational behavior* (p. 604). Oxford: Blackwell Publishers.

Hanisch, K. A., (2000). The impact of organizational interventions on behaviors: An examination of different models of withdrawal. In D. R. Ilgen & C. L. Hulin (Eds.), *Computational modeling of behavior in organizations: The third scientific discipline* (pp. 33–60). Washington, DC: American Psychological Association.

Hanisch, K. A., & Hulin, C. L. (1990). Job attitudes and organizational withdrawal: An examination of retirement and other voluntary withdrawal behaviors. *Journal of Vocational Behavior, 37*, 60–78.

Hanisch, K. A., & Hulin, C. L. (1991). General attitudes and organizational withdrawal: An evaluation of a causal model. *Journal of Vocational Behavior, 39*, 110–128.

Hanisch, K. A., Hulin, C. L., & Roznowski, M. (1998). The importance of individuals' repertoires of behaviors: The scientific appropriateness of studying multiple behaviors and general attitudes. *Journal of Organizational Behavior, 19*, 463–480.

Hanisch, K. A., Hulin, C. L., & Seitz, S. T. (1996). Mathematical/computational modeling of organizational withdrawal processes: Benefits, methods, and results. In G. R. Ferris (Ed.), *Research in Personnel and Human Resources Management, 14*, 91–142. Greenwich, CT: JAI Press.

Herzberg, F., Mausner, B., Peterson, B., and Capwell, D. (1957). *Job attitudes: Review of research and opinion.* Pittsburgh: Psychological Services of Pittsburgh.

Hill, J. M., & Trist, E. L. (1955). Changes in accidents and other absences with length of service: A further study of their incidence and relation to each other in an iron and steel works. *Human Relations, 8,* 121–152.

Hulin, C. L. (1991). Adaptation, persistence, and commitment in organization. In M. D. Dunnette and L. M. Hough (Eds.), *Handbook of industrial and organizational psychology.* Vol. 2, (2nd ed., pp. 445–505). Palo Alto, CA: Consulting Psychologists' Press.

March, J. G., & Simon, H. A. (1958). *Organizations.* New York: Wiley.

Melbin, M. (1961). Organizational practice and individual behavior. Absenteeism among psychiatric aids. *American Sociological Review, 26,* 14–23.

Rice, A. K., & Trist, E. L. (1952). Institutional and subinstitutional determinants of change in labor turnover. *Human Relations, 5,* 347–372.

Roznowski, M. A., & Hanisch, K. A. (1990). Building systematic heterogeneity into work attitudes and behavior measures. *Journal of Vocational Behavior, 36,* 361–375.

Roznowski, M. A., & Hulin, C. L. (1992). The scientific merit of valid measures of general constructs with special reference to job satisfaction and job withdrawal. In C. J. Cranny & P. C. Smith (Eds.), *Job satisfaction: How people feel about their jobs and how it affects their performance* (pp. 123–163). New York: Lexington.

Seitz, S. T., Hanisch, K. A., & Hulin, C. (1997). *WORKER: A computer program to simulate employee organizational withdrawal behaviors.* University of Illinois, Urbana–Champaign, Illinois and Iowa State University Ames, Iowa.

Thurstone, L. L. (1931). The measurement of social attitudes. *Journal of Abnormal and Social Psychology, 26,* 249–269.

21

Some New Organizational Perspectives on Moderators and Mediators in the Stress–Strain Process: Time Urgency, Management, and Worker Control

Meni Koslowsky

Bar-Ilan University, Ramat Gan, Israel

In addition to the severity of the objective and subjective stressors, moderators and mediators need to be considered in order to better understand the process that leads to strain reactions or negative outcomes among employees (Edwards, 1988; Kahn & Byosiere, 1991). Many articles in the stress literature include moderators as part of the study hypotheses to explain differences in strain levels among groups or use them as a post hoc explanation for unexpected findings. Mediators are related to both the independent and dependent variables and serve as a link through which the action of the former on the latter must pass (Frese & Zapf, 1988). Recently, two somewhat related concepts, time urgency and time management, have been suggested as important intervening variables in the stress process. The

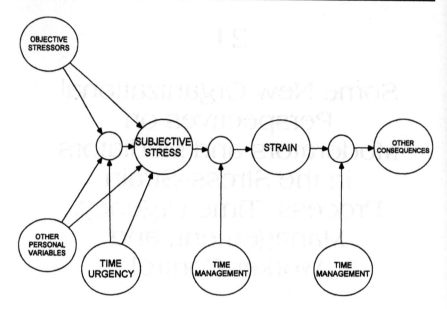

FIG. 21.1.   A model of the stress–strain process.

present article describes the role these intervening variables play in changing the relationship between independent and dependent variables.

Figure 21.1 describes a stress process model that includes time urgency and time management at different locations. The larger ovals represent the antecedent and consequent variables, and the smaller ovals either interactions (small oval on the left) or mediators (two small ovals on the right). Causal linkages are depicted by arrows connecting one oval to another; the interaction oval represents the interaction term between moderators, such as time urgency, and one or more of the first-stage stressors. The "other consequences" oval represents reactions that may occur after the first strain reactions appear. Time management may be effective in preventing or reducing the chances that either the first strain reaction or later consequences will occur.

The model in the figure depicts a stagelike, sequential process. The first stage contains the objective stressors, time urgency, and other personal variables. The placement of time urgency and other personal variables here is quite consistent with other studies; for example, Evans, Palsane, and Carrere (1987) found that Type A personality, from which time urgency is derived, served as a moderator in predicting self-reported occupational strain as well as several other outcomes. Time urgent workers attempt to "control" their environment by being concerned and aware of its passage.

At the second stage, subjective or perceived stress is assumed to be present. The amount of subjective stress is thought to be a function of objective stress, other first-stage variables, and their interaction. In the present formulation, it mediates between the stressors and outcomes. Measurement of the subjective stressor often involves the use of questionnaires that may contain items relating to cognition (e.g., time awareness), appraisals, and perceptions of the stressors (for a more detailed discussion of this variable, see Frese & Zapf, 1988). The next stage, after subjective stress, contains time management as a potential mediator. In the present framework, controlling the effects of the objective and subjective stressor (and their possible interaction with time urgency) can be considered a mediating role. The mediating influence of time management appears again after the strain response has been initiated and breaks the strain–(other or further) consequences link. Accordingly, time management is a technique for stress intervention or coping based on the principle of worker control. The theoretical approach for describing the influence of time management is consistent with models that view coping as a component in a sequential process that is voluntarily activated by workers to minimize or attenuate the negative effects of stressors (Edwards, 1988; Folkman & Lazarus, 1985).

An example of a process model from the world of commuting stress may be appropriate here. A typical objective stressor is the average speed it takes to get from home to work, whereas examples of negative outcomes include anxiety as a first reaction, and poor work performance as a later reaction. Thus, a slow commuting speed may very well lead to anxiety and poor performance, but the subjective stressor or perception of the commute ("It felt like a long commute") is considered as an essential mediator that links the objective stressor (average speed) with outcomes (anxiety and performance). In addition, time urgency can be posited as a personal variable that interacts with average speed to influence perceptions, and time management is another mediator that can reduce anxiety or break the link between anxiety and performance.

In the following sections, some of the theory and findings related to time urgency and time management and its role in the model will be presented.

Time Urgency

Components of personality that relate an individual's perspective about time to a range of potentially meaningful outcomes (Edwards, Baglioni, & Cooper, 1990; Schriber & Gutek, 1987) have been the focus of several investigations in organizational settings. Of particular concern has been the link between time concerns and strain. It is clear that for organizational researchers "the role of time in studies of stress in the workplace is axiomatic" (Landy, Rastegary, Thayer, & Colvin, 1991, p. 655). Its influence can be viewed as double edged. On the one hand, the environment or job demands often require an individual to consider the element of time even when this is not the natural tendency of the employee. On the other hand, an individual's response to this demand is a function of disposition or personality. For present purposes, both aspects of time play a role in an individual's reaction to stress.

Recent work has shown that a specific personality trait, time urgency, may be particularly prone to some of the negative strain effects that result from the lack of worker control (Landy et al., 1991). Time urgency, a major subcomponent of the Type A personality pattern (TABP), may be perceived as a correlate of moderator of various psychological and physical ailments (Price, 1982; Wright, McGurdy, & Rogoll, 1992) and, in many ways, is similar to other personality traits that have recently been identified as significant antecedents of strain (Depue & Monroe, 1986; Kahn & Byosiere, 1991). Moderators, as described by Landy (1985), are so-called third variables in a bivariate correlation that can change the association between antecedents and consequences. Discovery of a significant moderator by examining the interaction term yields new inferences about the relationship among study variables.

Schriber and Gutek (1987) considered the time variable as part of the culture of an organization. The organizational reactions to a late arrival are part of the normative expectations operating within that environment. In turn, job-related stress may be a function of how the organization responds to an individual who arrives late. Furthermore, Schriber and Gutek felt that satisfaction, organizational withdrawal, and productivity may all be related to the match between an individual's use of time and the organization's expectations. In developing the subscales of time urgency, Landy et al. (1991) felt that they could serve as a gauge for assessing the trait in an individual and be considered as a predictor for various organizational outcomes, such as the ones described by Schriber and Gutek.

Measuring Time Urgency

Based on analyses from a combination of self-report measures, Landy et al. (1991) identified a multifaceted construct that includes the following factors: competitiveness, eating behavior, general hurry, task-related hurry, and speech pattern. The third and fourth factors are particularly relevant here. Among the items with high loadings in the general hurry factor were "pressed for time," "in a hurry," and "never in a rush" (reversed scoring). The items with high loadings in the task-related factor were "slow doing things" (must be recoded), "works fast," and "work is slow and deliberate" (must be recoded).

In order to determine whether they had adequately covered the various facets of time urgency, Landy et al. (1991) decided to use an additional procedure, independent of the first one, that would either support the factor analysis described above or yield some new dimensions that should be integrated into the concept. They accomplished this by using the behavioral anchored rating scale (BARS) technique, which uses graphical stimuli and is less prone to some of the common biases found in appraisal instruments. As can be seen from the list below, somewhat different dimensions were generated from the BARS method:

1. Awareness of time—the extent to which an individual is aware of the exact time of day.

2. Eating behavior—the extent to which time is involved in planning or actual eating.
3. Scheduling.
4. Nervous energy—the extent to which the person is in motion.
5. List making—the extent to which a person maintains or keeps lists.
6. Speech patterns—the extent to which a person exhibits rushed speech patterns.
7. Deadline control—the extent to which a person is controlled by deadlines.

In their recent study of the construct validity of the BARS method, Conte, Landy, and Mathieu (1995) found a five-dimension model to fit their data: time awareness, scheduling, list making, eating behavior, and deadline control. Although the relative merits of the different scales still need to be tested empirically, it appears that several inferences from the findings seem reasonable. Time urgency is a multifaceted variable characterized by dispositions that are either associated with or may lead to specific behaviors. Moreover, according to Conte et al. (1995), there may very well be an interaction between external events, such as stressors, and individual difference variables, such as time urgency, which affect individual consequences or organizational outcomes.

Time urgency has both permanent and temporary components associated with it. Thus, some people may feel the pressure of time on all occasions, whereas others choose when to be aware and when not. For some, all activities, including work, recreation, family time, or just relaxing, are attempted only after consulting a watch. Having control, or at least, the perception of control, is fostered and maintained by actively seeking information concerning the hour and minute when a new activity is about to begin. They are always on time for meetings, celebrations such as weddings or going away parties, or at the airplane terminal at the beginning of a vacation. Others for whom time urgency is at a lower level or who are able to pick and choose what to attend to may be forced, nevertheless, to seek time information. For example, a worker in an organization that sets rewards, actual or perceived, as well as performance evaluations on the basis of arrival time at work or meetings, or general punctuality, may have no alternative but to conform. In this case, time urgency is no longer a trait but, rather, a condition imposed on the individual by external stimuli.

Time awareness.   Both Landy et al. (1991) and Conte et al. (1995) found time awareness to be one of the underlying dimensions of time urgency. Unlike the other dimensions of time urgency, time awareness can be considered as the cognitive component of time urgency. Although specific behaviors are associated with this variable, it is the perception that is of interest here. For example, a "time aware" commuter stuck in traffic is likely to notice and experience every minute that passes without vehicle movement. Such a situation can be quite stressful and its appraisal can indeed lead to immediate behaviors such as fidgeting, blowing a horn, or even screaming and, in the long run, to poor performance or organizational withdrawal. In the extreme, time awareness may not even require conscious processes. This can be seen in the behavior of some individuals who just seem to know that it is time to go home from work or school, wake up in the morning, or go out for a lunch break without any visible outside catalyst.

According to Lazarus and Folkman (1984), the cognitive process in stress–strain reactions includes appraisal of environmental stimuli. Although the temporal relationship between appraisal and perception is unclear and each probably could be viewed as a distinct stage (Kahn & Byosiere, 1991), it is sufficient in the present discussion to consider all comparable elements that precede the outcome measure as influencing the subjective stressor.

Time Management

Time management is a related concept that is considered here in the stress–strain model as a mediating variable. Mediators are said to explain (fully or partially) the relationship between antecedents and consequences. Time management is posited as part of the coping process that allows an individual to mitigate or, in some cases, eliminate the negative outcomes associated with stress. In order to understand its theoretical underpinnings in the model, a short digression to the job control literature is needed.

Job Control

Thompson (1981) saw control as the belief that one can influence aversive features in the environment. Common organizational stressors such as role conflict and role ambiguity have been shown to be amenable to participative decision making (PDM), one of the more formalized methods for accomplishing stress intervention (Murphy, 1988; Sagie, Elizur, & Koslowsky, 1995). A more empirical perspective of job control was provided by Karasek (1979), who saw strain responses as a function of both job demands and degree of worker latitude or control. As the amount of the former increased and the latter decreased, negative consequences could be expected. Person–environment (P–E) theory, a popular explanation of the stress–strain process, takes a similar view in that the degree of fit between two variables, objective job demands and subjective worker needs, is suggested as the main determiner of strain (Murphy, 1988). A lack of P–E fit, the difference between perceived workload and workers' desired workload, is a better predictor of strain than either of the two independent variables by themselves. Finally, some approaches, such as the Hackman and Oldham (1980) Job Characteristic model, include control variables as an important component in understanding organizational behavior and attitudes. In the latter model, autonomy, or the opportunity to make the decision by oneself on how to do a specific job, is one of the core job dimensions that is associated with critical psychological states and work outcomes.

Actual and Perceived Control

The beneficial effects from perceived control are expected to be similar to those obtained from actual control. The fact that perceived control is an adequate coping mechanism implies that high levels of perceived control modify or even reduce the negative impact of stressor stimuli (e.g., Glass & Singer, 1972; Thompson, 1981; for exceptions see a review by Burger, 1989). Murphy (1988) argued that the perception of control in a specific situation is one of the critical ingredients in stress reduction, or coping. According to Murphy, control can be viewed either as a method for preventing strain or as a legitimate intervention (i.e., treatment) after negative consequences have already appeared.

Furthermore, based on the available data, Murphy argues that it is probably less stressful never to have had control over a situation than to have had it and lost it (1988, p. 324). For many organizational intervention procedures, this is a cardinal proposition. When increased worker control is introduced, it should not be for a temporary period. Rather the organization that has decided to make changes for the purposes of greater worker control must make a long-term commitment and either give the worker actual control or perceived control. Knowledge that control will remain in the hands of the worker is essential. In practice, perceived control may be enough, as it allows the person to assume that the stressful stimulus can be turned off or at least reduced.

Time and Job Control

What exactly constitutes control? One way of answering the question is to view the individual's reaction to time. Is he or she aware that time is passing? Does this concern him or her? Is the individual reacting to time, or does time "respond" or "bend" to the individual's need? A close examination of some of the scales that have commonly been used to measure coping techniques in studies of stress reveal that time-related items are an integral part of the concept. For example, the Moos, Cronkite, Billings, and Finney (1987) Health and Daily Living coping measure contains several items that are clearly time-oriented: "make a plan and follow it," "take things a day at a time, one step at a time," and "try not to act hastily." In each case, the issue of concern is the extent to which the individual perceives that time is under his or her control.

Control and Time Management

Time management is considered a learned activity and not a personality or innate characteristic. Time management can be considered as a specific coping strategy allowing the individual to control several of the time-related components of the stressor. Koeske, Kirk, and Koeske (1993) argued that both the behavioral and cognitive components are employed in such coping mechanisms. This implies that those who are attempting to actively control time need to plan their strategy and tactics very carefully. In this formulation, time management can be seen as a conscious attempt by the individual to behave in a way so as to reduce the impact of stress.

The literature indicates that time management involves a strategy whereby need and wants are first identified and then ranked in importance. Resources and time are then allocated according to these preferences (Hall & Hursch, 1982; Macan, Shahani, Dipboye, & Phillips, 1990). Several controlled studies have shown that time management can be taught and that it is amenable to intensive training programs. For example, King, Winett, and Lovett (1986) analyzed responses of subjects who had undergone time management instruction. The authors showed that they were better able to cope with stressful stimuli. Such subjects spent more time in stress-reducing and fun-type behaviors. However, the data, although indicative of a relationship between time management and strain, did not show a consistent reduction in the latter after implementing the former.

Realizing that time management was important in stress, Macan et al. (1990) tried to identify the factor that has the largest impact. Their work showed that the largest impact of time management was on perceived control of time. Students who perceived greater control of their time reported performance and psychological benefits. In particular, their level of academic achievement was higher, and somatic symptoms decreased as time control increased. The authors argued that an individual who works efficiently has the ability to control time rather than the other way around.

Measuring Time Management

Macan (1994) presented a model that shows a relationship between time management behaviors, perceived control of time, and stress outcomes. In particular, time management behaviors were significantly linked, by path coefficients, to perceived control of time and, in turn, to negative consequences. A time management scale was constructed, with 33 items grouped into three factors: goal setting or prioritizing, mechanics of time management, and preference for organization. The path model linking the variables showed that the largest coefficient was the one between the latter factor and perceived control of time.

Interestingly, Macan could not explain why, in her model, some respondents who practiced time management activities did not perceive any control over time. She suggested the consideration of personal variables that identify the individual who is more likely to benefit from making lists and scheduling activities. It is suggested here that time urgency is just such a variable. Thus, an individual with a high score on time urgency who practices time management activities is likely to experience less strain or, alternatively, the largest absolute decrease in negative consequences. Conversely, low-time-urgency people who engage in time-management behaviors may not show much of a decrease in strain response.

General Considerations
of a Stress–Strain Model

A theoretical framework that describes the link between independent and dependent variables must define clearly the stressors, strain measures, mediators, and moderators. The latter two are essential, as the relationships reported in the literature are often inconsistent or even nonexistent (see Evans & Carrere, 1991). Furthermore, using the terminology from structural equation modeling, it is suggested that only if the model includes both time urgency and time management will the fit between hypothesized linkages of the process and the observed data be maximized. Although models usually contain distinct moderator and mediator variables, it is possible that different aspects of the same domain may play both roles within the same model. For example, G. W. Evans (personal communication, October 26, 1995) has made this argument in discussing the effects of stress. He indicated that it is quite possible for one type of control indicator (e.g., predictability, or the certainty with which an individual can predict the appearance of a stressor) to function as a moderator at the same time that another aspect of control (perceived control) functions as a mediator. This is particularly relevant here, as the model described in the article includes two related measures, time urgency and time management.

Moreover, it is the researcher's perspective that determines whether a specific variable is considered an antecedent or a moderator. For example, personality, self-esteem, and locus of control can be considered a main effect, or a moderator variable. Thus, an organizational psychologist analyzing the influence of objective stressors on subjective stress may consider personality as a moderator. Another researcher who is interested in the impact of personality differences on strain may perceive the objective stressors as moderators. In either case, the interaction term (objective stressor X personality) may explain significant variance beyond that explained by the sum of the main effects/moderators.

The present model has not described all the linkages possible, and not all stress processes, of course, need include these moderator and mediator variables. Yet, the formulation here describes one approach of understanding the relationship between time urgency, time management, and stress. Many issues often considered in testing stress models, such as reverse causation and feedback loops, were not examined. Nevertheless, several clear advantages in using the suggested model can be indentified. First, it has potential theoretical and practical significance for understanding the role of time-related indicators in stress models. Second, testing hypotheses generated here, perhaps with longitudinal designs, allows for purposive data collection that may help in further refining the model and deciding which links should be included and which ones dropped. Finally, if the role of time management as a mediator can be confirmed, then its practial importance as a technique of intervention in the stress–strain process within an organizational context can be ascertained. As many aspects of time management can be learned, individuals can develop coping skills to mitigate and control strain and enhance well-being.

REFERENCES

Burger, J. M. (1989). Negative reactions to increases in perceived personal control. *Journal of Personality and Social Psychology, 56*, 246–256.

Conte, J. M., Landy, F. J., & Mathieu, J. E. (1995). Time urgency: Conceptual and construct development. *Journal of Applied Psychology, 80*, 178–185.

Depue, R. A., & Monroe, S. M. (1986). Conceptualization and measurement of human disorders in life stress research: The problem of chronic disturbance. *Psychological Bulletin, 99*, 36–51.

Edwards, J. R. (1988). The determinants and consequences of coping with stress. In C. Copper & R. Payne (Eds.), *Causes, coping, and consequences at work* (pp. 233–263). Chischester, England: Wiley.

Edwards, J. R., Baglioni, A. J., Jr., & Cooper, C. L. (1990). Job demands and worker health: Three-dimensional reexamination of the relationship between person–environment fit and strain. *Journal of Applied Psychology, 78*, 628–648.

Evans, G. W., & Carrere, S. (1991). Traffic congestion, perceived control, and psychophysiological stress among urban bus drivers. *Journal of Applied Psychology, 76*, 658–663.

Evans, G. W., Palsane, M. N., & Carrere, S. (1987). Type A behavior and occupational stress: A cross-cultural study of blue-collar workers. *Journal of Personality and Social Psychology, 52*, 10002–10007.

Folkman, S., & Lazarus, R. S. (1985). If it changes, it must be a process: A study of emotion and coping during three stages of a college examination. *Journal of Personality and Social Psychology, 48*, 150–170.

Frese, M., & Zapf, D. (1988). Methodological issues in the study of work stress: Objective vs. subjective measurement of work stress and the question of longitudinal studies. In C. L. Cooper and R. Payne (Eds.), *Causes, coping, and consequences of stress at work*. New York: Wiley.

Glass, D. G., & Singer, J. E. (1972). *Urban stress: Experiments on noise and social stressors*. New York: Academic Press.

Hackman, J. R., & Oldham, G. R. (1980). *Work redesign*. New York: Addison-Wesley.

Hall, B. L., & Hursch D. E. (1982). An evaluation of the effects of a time management training program. *Journal of Organizational Behavior Management, 3*, 73–96.

Kahn, R. L., & Byosiere, M. (1991). Stress in organizations. In M. Dunnette (Ed.), *Handbook of industrial and organizational psychology* (pp. 571–650). Palo Alto, CA: Consulting Psychologists Press.

Karasek, R. A. (1979). Job demands, job decision latitude, and mental strain: Implications for job redesign. *Administrative Science Quarterly, 24*, 285–307.

King, A. C., Winett, R. A., & Lovett, S. B. (1986). Enhancing coping behaviors in at-risk populations: The effects of time management instruction and social support in women from dual-earner families. *Behavior Therapy, 17*, 57–66.

Koeske, G. F., Kirk, S. A., & Koeske, R. D. (1993). Coping with job stress: Which strategies work best? *Journal of Occupational and Organizational Psychology, 66*, 319–355.

Landy, F. J. (1985). *Psychology of work behavior*. Homewood, IL: Dorsey Press.

Landy, F. J, Rastegary, H., Thayer, J., & Colvin, C. (1991). Time urgency: The construct and its measurement. *Journal of Applied Psychology, 76*, 644–657.

Lazarus, R. S., & Folkman, S. (1984). *Stress, appraisal, and coping*. New York: Springer.

Macan, T. H. (1994). Time management: Test of a process model. *Journal of Applied Psychology, 79*, 381–391 .

Macan, T. M., Shahani, C., Dipboye, R. L., & Phillips, A. P. (1990). College students' time management: Correlations with academic performance and stress. *Journal of Educational Psychology, 82*, 760–768.

Moos, R. H., Cronkite, R. C., Billings, A. G., & Finney, J. W. (1987). *Health and daily living form manual* (Rev. ver.). Stanford, CA: Social Ecology Laboratory

Murphy, L. R. (1988). Workplace intervention for stress reduction and prevention. In C. L. Cooper & R. Payne (Eds.), *Causes, coping, and consequences of stress at work* (pp. 301–339). Chichester, UK: Wiley.

Price, V. A. (1982). *Type A behavior pattern: A model for research and practice.* New York: Academic Press.

Sagie, A., Elizur D., & Koslowsky, M. (1995). Decision type, participative decision making (PDM), and organizational behavior. An experimental simulation. *Human Performance, 8*, 81–94.

Schriber, J. B., & Gutek, B. A. (1987). Some time dimensions of work: Measurement of an underlying aspect of organizational culture. *Journal of Applied Physchology, 72*, 642–650.

Thompson, S. C. (1981). Will it hurt less if I can control it? A complex answer to a simple question. *Psychological Bulletin, 90*, 89–101.

Wright, L., McGurdy, S., & Rogoll, G. (1992). The TUPA scale: A self-report measure for the type A subcomponent of time urgency and perceptual activation. *Psychological Assessment, 4*, 352–356.

IV

The Cultural Level

INTRODUCTION—*MIRIAM EREZ*

The internal and external forces that motivate individual behavior were the focus of attention of the classical theories of motivation. However, over the years, researchers have realized that these individual-level variables do not fully explain the motivated behavior. Rather, motivational variables at the group and organizational levels further enhance our understanding of work motivation. More recently, attention has been shifted to the more macro-level of culture as an explanatory variable of work motivation. All four chapters in part 4 focus on the cultural level of analysis.

Kwok Leung in his chapter on *"Different Carrots for Different Rabbits: Effects of Individualism—Collectivism and Power Distance on Work Motivation,"* demonstrates how the two cultural values of individualism and collectivism, and power distance help understand the differential effect of motivational approaches. Four propositions serve for explaining the causal links between collectivism and individualism and group behavior, and between power distance and adherence to the goals initiated and implemented by supervisors. Three areas of work motivation are then discussed in light of these propositions: merit-based incentive schemes, role theory, and goal-setting theory. A number of suggestions for extending the universality of several motivation theories are proposed.

Simcha Ronen explores *"Self-Actualization Versus Collectualization: Implications for Motivation Theories."* He lays out the major dilemmas of individualistic motivational theories as they try to account for behavior associated with a collective identity and attempts to offer a partial solution to some of these dilemmas.

Ronen recognized that efforts to subsume collective phenomena under individualistic theories have been quite futile. He then proposes to modify the need theory
originally proposed for understanding individualists' need structure so that it can
explain the collectivists' need structure. In doing so, Ronen coined a new concept
collectualization, parallel to the concept of self-actualization. His chapter further
discusses the two need hierarchies.

   P. Christopher Earley focuses on *understanding social motivation from an
interpersonal perspective*. His chapter specifically discusses face as a key concept
in understanding how employees interact and conduct themselves in the workplace.
Earley proposes that the emphasis on motivation in a social context is rooted in a
person's desire for self-definition in a given social context, or what has been called
"face" by various researchers. He distinguishes between two forms of face—*lian*
and *mianzi*. The former refers to a general attachment formed by individuals to
society; the later reflects a person's position in a social hierarchy. Earley further
examines the mechanisms of social exchange as a means of predicting the impact
of cultural orientation on face.

   Nigel Nicholson presents *an evolutionary perspective on change and stability
in personality, culture, and organization*. The conceptual framework of evolutionary psychology serves to understand processes of change across levels-individuals,
groups, and cultures. Essential to this perspective is that human psychological
functioning is posited on a common genetic platform, adapted to our ancestral
environment. From this vantage point, structures and processes of personality,
organization, and culture are discussed. Although Nicholson touches on many different issues, he raises some important questions regarding motivation, suggesting
for example, that there are limits regarding the range of stimuli that will motivate
individuals. Additionally, culture has deeply rooted and enduring structural properties, it is the organization that has a more transient structure. This poses perhaps
more strict limits to organizational change than is usually believed nowadays.

   Finally, **Michael Bond**'s chapter focuses on *approaches to measuring group,
organizational, and national variation*. Bond struggles with the conceptual and
methodological challenges that the multilevel of analysis posits to researchers.
Psychologists focus on understanding the behavior of individuals, yet, at any moment an individual is a member of groups, organizations, cultures, and a society.
Each of these social entities may constrain, inhibit, guide, and reward the behavior of individuals. The standard procedure for psychologists is to use individual
perceivers to rate a given entity (the self, the group, the organization, the nation)
and then to process the ratings in a way that reveals characteristics of the entity
in question. These characteristics may then be related to nonpsychological outcome measures of the entity, such as group productivity, organizational turnover,
or national health. The use of ratings derived from individuals poses a number of
questions. For example, the extent to which individuals are biased in their evaluation of the higher-level entity; the extent to which a selected group of individuals
is representative of the higher-level entity; the best methodological approach for

combining individuals' scores to the entity in question; and what statistical techniques can be legitimately used in this process. Bond's chapter attempts to answer these questions.

In conclusion, this book proposes a multilevel framework for studying work motivation. It goes beyond the traditional theories of motivation, which focused on motivation at the individual level, to examine macro-level effects on individual motivation. Furthermore, it examines motivation at the group, organization, and social levels. These higher levels of analysis pose new theoretical and methodological challenges to the field of work motivation.

22

Different Carrots for Different Rabbits: Effects of Individualism–Collectivism and Power Distance on Work Motivation

Kwok Leung
Chinese University, Hong Kong

The globalization of businesses and migration patterns have led to increasing workplace diversity. To maintain the effectiveness of multicultural work teams, it is crucial that the motivational strategies employed are cross-culturally valid. The purpose of this paper is to analyze work motivation from the perspective of individualism–collectivism and power distance, two of the four cultural dimensions identified by Hofstede (1980).

According to Hofstede (1980), individualism refers to a tendency to put a stronger emphasis on one's interests and goals, whereas collectivism refers to a stronger emphasis on the interests and goals of ingroup members. The distinction between ingroups and outgroups is also sharper for collectivists than for individualists. Power distance refers to the extent to which the centralization of power in organizations and society is regarded as legitimate. Compared with low-power-distance societies, social institutions are more hierarchical, and power holders are granted more privileges in high-power-distance societies. These two dimensions are highly correlated, but Hofstede (1980) maintains that they are distinct conceptually. With Hofstede, I also argue in this chapter that the effects of these two dimensions on work motivation are different and distinct.

INDIVIDUALISM–COLLECTIVISM AND
WORK MOTIVATION

The framework of individualism–collectivism has been used to explain a variety of cross-cultural differences in social and organizational behaviors (Erez & Earley, 1992; Triandis, 1995). In the following, several propositions that may prove fruitful for future exploration are discussed.

When Do Collectivists Regard Their Work Group as an In-group?

The rise of Japan as an industrial power and its group-oriented approach to productivity enhancement may sometimes lead to the belief that in collectivist societies, workers usually work selflessly and single-mindedly for their work groups. However, it is widely known that collectivists are willing to work hard and make sacrifices for a work group only if they regard it as their in-group (Leung & Bond, 1984; Triandis, 1995). If they see the group as an outgroup, there is no reason why they will be more committed to the group than individualists. For instance, staff turnover has now become a serious problem in major cities in China. Sensenbrenner and Sensenbrenner (1994) reported that approximately 15% of employees changed jobs in Shanghai from 1992 to 1993. In Hong Kong, the figure is even worse, and an annual turnover rate of 50% is common for many industries (Farh, Leung, & Tse, 1995). Obviously, for those employees who are ready to switch jobs anytime, it is unlikely that they regard their work group as an in-group. Another example is provided by Tomita (1983), who reported that Filipino workers in Japanese companies in the Philippines usually showed a low involvement with their company. It is not likely that these workers regarded their companies as their ingroup. Finally, in a simulation with MBA students, Chatman and Barsade (1995) found that the cooperative behavior of individualists was less affected by whether the company culture was individualistic or collectivistic. In contrast, collectivists behaved in a cooperative manner in a collectivist organizational culture but individualistically in an individualist culture. Furthermore, when the organizational culture was collectivistic, collectivists behaved more cooperatively than did individualists. The finding that collectivists behaved differently as a function of the organizational culture is consistent with the argument that collectivists are more likely to differentiate between outgroups and ingroups. A collectivistic work culture is conducive to the emergence of ingroup involvement, which explains why collectivists were more cooperative than individualists in this work culture. When collectivists are placed in an individualistic culture emphasizing interdependence, there is no reason to expect collectivists to be more cooperative than individualists.

Despite the importance of in-groups to collectivists, we do not know much about the factors that lead collectivists to regard their work group as an ingroup. Current theorizing on individualism–collectivism suggests that a crucial characteristic of collectivists is their conceptualization of the self as interdependent (Markus & Kitayama, 1991; Triandis, 1995). Based on this framework, I propose that factors that promote a sense of interdependence between a member and his or her work group will facilitate the acceptance of the work group as an in-group. Two clusters of factors are hypothesized to be instrumental to the development of an in-group relationship: unconditional benevolence and social identify.

Unconditional Benevolence

A sense of interdependence can be established if people, when in need, can expect the ingroup to help them unconditionally. In other words, if a work group is able to help an individual unconditionally, the group is likely to be seen as an ingroup. The form of help may be tangible, such as the provision of resources, or it may be emotional and social support. For instance, in Japan supervisors sometimes play the role of a matchmaker and help subordinates to seek a suitable spouse (Smith & Misumi, 1989). Unconditionality is important because if the help provided is conditional, it may be seen as a form of social exchange. Conditionality may prompt a sense of calculative involvement, which emphasizes the calculation of costs and benefits (Etzioni, 1975). On the other hand, unconditionality is likely to trigger a sense of moral obligation in the recipients. For instance, in China, the concept of *bao* requires that individuals should not owe others any favors, both tangible and intangible, and should make an effort to repay them (e.g., Hsu, 1981; Hwang, 1987). There are many traditional sayings in China that urge people to repay those who help them, such as "whatever favors you receive from others, remember them for a thousand years" and "He who repays not a favor is no gentleman" (Chen, 1975, pp. 53–54.). In Japan, there is a similar concept of *giri*, which refers to the moral obligation of repaying others for their favors. It is interesting to note that the Chinese have actually developed elaborate strategies to avoid owing others favors so that they will not be obliged to return them (King, 1991). Broadly speaking, this moral obligation may be interpreted as a norm of reciprocity (Gouldner, 1960) but with a much stronger moral and affective tone. In sum, unconditional benevolence will promote an ingroup involvement with a work group.

Social Identity

The social identity theory developed by Tajfel (1981) posits that people's identity and self-esteem is partly derived from the groups to which they belong. Many studies have found that people identify more strongly with groups that are higher in social status. For instance, high-caste Hindus and Muslims reported a more positive social identity than scheduled castes (Majeed & Ghosh, 1982). In a laboratory experiment, participants who were assigned to a high-status group reported a higher level of ingroup identification than participants from low-status groups (Ellemers, Van Knippenberg, deVries, & Wilke, 1988). Based on these results, I propose that if a group constitutes a source of pride and social status for a member, a strong sense of identification with the group will result. An ingroup relationship with the group will develop, which will motivate members to work hard and make sacrifices for the group. Consistent with this argument, Mael and Ashforth (1992) found that alumni of a college were more willing to make financial contributions to their alma mater if they identified with it more strongly.

The reasoning just presented is summarized in the following proposition:

Proposition 1: Unconditional benevolence and positive social identify will lead to an in-group involvement with a work group.

Are Work Groups in Collectivist Societies More Motivated?

Because of the prominence of Japan as a prototype of a collectivist society, one may be tempted to conclude that collectivistic work groups are more motivated. However, it is well-known that collectivism correlates highly with poverty, and hence with low productivity at the national level (Hofstede, 1980). Take China as an example. Work motivation and productivity among factory workers were low before the 1980s, and this problem is still serious (Jin, 1993). Japan and the four "tigers" (Hong Kong, Singapore, Taiwan, and Korea) are probably the only exceptions to this pattern. While there are numerous reasons why collectivist societies tend to be poor, it is clear that work groups in collectivist societies are not necessarily motivated. In fact, Erez and Somech (1996) argued that work teams made up of individualists can also be set up in a certain way to achieve a high level of productivity.

Based on the individualism–collectivism framework, Earley (1989, 1993) proposed and confirmed that collectivists are less likely to display social loafing than individualists. Social loafing refers to the tendency for people to work less hard when they work in a group than when they work alone. However, these results do not imply that work groups in collectivist societies are more motivated than those in individualist societies. They actually suggest that collectivism may show a homogenizing effect on the productivity of group members. Collectivists are sensitive to whether they are accepted by the group and hence are sensitive to their performance in relation to other members. Their primary motive is to be accepted by the group rather than the enhancement of group performance. A typical way to achieve this goal is to perform at a level that is similar to the performance of most members and to avoid outperforming others in the group. The famous Japanese saying that a nail that sticks out must be hammered in provides a vivid illustration of this logic. In contrast, individualists are less concerned with the acceptance by the group, and as a result their performance should vary more from the group average.

The above discussion is reminiscent of the literature on group cohesiveness and productivity. Cohesiveness in a work group does not always lead to a higher level of productivity, but it reduces the difference in the productivity of the workers (Seashore, 1954). The effect of collectivism is thus similar to the effect of cohesiveness, which is summarized in the following proposition:

Proposition 2 (the homogenizing effect): Productivity and work performance in work groups are more homogenous in collectivist than in individualist societies.

POWER DISTANCE AND WORK MOTIVATION

Compliance With Authority Figures

One direct consequence of a high-power-distance-orientation is the tendency for people to comply with the demands of authority and accept its disciplinary actions if they fail to reach an expected performance level (Hofstede, 1980). For instance, Bond, Wan, Leung, and Giacalone (1985) found that while both American and Chinese participants regarded an insult as more legitimate when the insulter was a superior than when he was a subordinate, this tendency was stronger for Chinese. Chinese participants also evaluated the superior less negatively than did American participants. In a recent study with Chinese and American MBA students, Leung, Su, and Morris (in press) found that after being criticized by a superior, Chinese regarded the criticism as less unfair and were less likely to attribute negative traits to the supervisor than did Americans.

If the organizational goal is to outperform competitors, the willingness to comply with supervisory demand by high-power-distance employees may constitute a competitive advantage. For instance, Smith and Misumi (1989) have concluded that the superior–subordinate relationship in Japan is similar to a parent–child relationship. Subordinates are expected to show deference and loyalty to superiors through commitment and hard work. In a similar vein, Redding and Wong (1986) concluded that one reason for the diligence of Hong Kong workers is due to their willingness to accept the autocratic demands of their superiors. Kim (1994) also noted that paternalism is a salient feature of superior–subordinate relationships in South Korea. For instance, Kim (1994) reported that in a survey of personnel or general managers from over 900 firms, 81% of the respondents agreed that the relationship between employers and employees are similar to the relationship between father and son. Employees are expected to be committed and loyal to their firms.

The above analysis suggests that authority figures may be able to motivate subordinates more successfully in high-power-distance than in low-power-distance societies. In high-power-distance societies, motivational strategies that are initiated and implemented by high-status superiors should be more effective. In contrast, in low-power-distance societies, the effectiveness of motivational strategies should be less dependent on the status of the superior who initiates and implements them. This idea is summarized in the following proposition:

> *Proposition 3 (the compliance effect):* Motivational strategies are more effective if they are initiated and implemented by superiors with a high status, and this pattern is stronger in high-power-distance than in low-power-distance societies.

The Overshadowing Effect of Authority

Although members of high-power-distance societies may be more likely to comply with supervisory demand, their concern with the relationship to authority figures may distract them from focusing on their tasks. As explained before, in highly centralized, paternalistic organizations, the relationship of an employee to the superior is often discussed in terms of cardinal relationships of filial piety (Redding & Wong, 1986). Because of this tradition, subordinates regard their interactions with superiors as highly significant events and monitor them very carefully. The nature of their relationship with superiors is often read as a signal of their social standing in the organization. The tendency to assess one's standing, or face (*mianzi*) from the characteristics of social interactions with superiors may create an overshadowing effect of authority, and lead them to overreact to negative feedback from superiors. Earley (Earley, 1986; Earley & Stubblebine, 1989) found that direct feedback from superiors heightened the performance of American workers but had a less positive effect on British workers. Earley explained his results in terms of the difference in power distance between American and British workers. Because of the high power distance of British workers, they were less comfortable with receiving direct feedback from superiors and preferred a more distant relationship with them. As a result, British workers were less responsive to supervisory feedback, which explains why such feedback showed a less positive effect on their performance. In a recent study with Chinese and American MBA students, Leung et al. (in press) found that the Chinese were so less willing to accept the responsibility for criticism received from a high-status superior than Americans. This cultural difference may reflect a stronger fear of the Chinese for the negative consequences of reprimands from superiors because of their high power distance. This fear may have been a source of defensiveness, which explains why supervisory criticism led to a stronger denial of the criticism among the Chinese subjects. In sum, negative supervisory feedback may show a stronger overshadowing effect on subordinates in high-power-distance than in low-power-distance societies.

> *Proposition 4 (the overshadowing effect):* Negative supervisory reactions toward subordinates are more demoralizing and trigger stronger defensive reactions in high-power-distance than in low-power-distance societies.

INDIVIDUALISM–COLLECTIVISM, POWER DISTANCE, AND MOTIVATION THEORIES

Many people have observed that management research is dominated by American academics, and consequently current management theories may be laden with individualistic and low-power-distance biases (e.g., Hofstede, 1980). Motivation theories are no exception to this challenge. In the following, three areas of work motivation are discussed in light of the four propositions proposed. The universality of several motivation theories is also explored.

Merit-Based Pay Schemes

Merit-based pay schemes, such as piece-rate incentives and year end bonuses, are widely adopted in organizations. The underlying principle of these schemes is reinforcement theories (Skinner, 1969). Contingent reinforcement of behaviors that are regarded as desirable will enhance the occurrence of these behaviors. In organizational settings, contingent reinforcement schedules have been found to lead to a higher level of productivity in the United States (e.g., Luthans, Paul, & Baker, 1981; Pritchard, Leonard, Von Bergen, & Kirk, 1976). Merit-based pay schemes are by definition conditional, and as argued before, they should hinder the development of ingroup involvement of members and extinguish their fervor to strive for the group. Observers of Japanese management practices are often surprised by the emphasis on non-merit-based pay schemes in Japan, such as the *nenko* system (a seniority-based system for pay increment). However, overpaying the underperformers, while violating the principle of contingent reinforcement, is a form of unconditional benevolence. As argued before, it should induce a strong sense of moral obligation and in-group involvement among collectivists. In time, this moral debt will propel the members to work hard for the group and improve their performance.

Role Theories

In the American literature, roles are usually not discussed in association with work motivation but with work stress. Role conflict and role ambiguity are often regarded as major stressors (e.g., Rizzo, House, & Lirtzman, 1970). However, when people are put in a role that they accept, role prescriptions function to guide them to comply with the requirements set by the organization (e.g., Graen, 1976). From this angle, it may be argued that roles also serve a motivational function. Role prescriptions legitimize task requirements, and it is well-known that people are more motivated to comply with legitimate than illegitimate demands (e.g., Tyler, 1990).

It is interesting to note that in the United States, while roles are seldom linked to work motivation, fairness issues have long been regarded as crucial to work motivation (e.g., Greenberg, 1990). It is instructive at this point to examine the literature on morality before we further examine the relation between roles and work motivation. In Kohlberg's (1981) approach to moral reasoning, justice is seen as an issue of morality, whereas interpersonal responsibilities are assumed to subordinate to justice obligations in case of conflict. In line with this argument, research in the United States has shown that interpersonal responsibilities are often seen as personal decisions (e.g., Higgins, Power, & Kohlberg, 1984). Cross-cultural research with Indians, however, has shown that moral breaches of interpersonal responsibilities are seen as moral issues (Miller, Bersoff, & Harwood, 1990; Shweder, Mahapahtra, & Miller, 1987). Compared with Americans, Indians were more likely to yield to interpersonal responsibilities than to justice concerns because of role obligations to help others (Miller & Bersoff, 1992). Likewise, Japanese were also found to give more weight to role considerations in judgments of responsibility than did Americans (Hamilton & Sanders, 1983; Hagiwara, 1992). In light of these findings, Miller (1994) concluded that the moral codes of interpersonal responsibilities should be considered individual oriented in the United States, whereas as such moral codes should be considered as duty based for Indians, who emphasize interpersonal obligations and regulation of social order.

Miller's (1994) analysis perhaps explains why fairness is considered relevant to work motivation in the United States and roles are usually not. In the United States, role prescriptions are likely to be evaluated in terms of justice principles, and the focus on justice and the inattention to roles are consistent with the construel of the self as independent. In collectivist societies, however, the moral significance of role prescriptions are distinct from that of justice, and the motivational effects of role prescriptions should be independent of those of justice as well.

The above analysis suggests that role prescriptions should be more motivational in collectivist than in individualist societies. Furthermore, compliance with role prescriptions should be higher in high-power-distance than in low-power-distance societies. One corollary of this argument is that it is more effective for high-status superiors to be role-senders in high-power-distance than in low-power-distance societies.

Goal-Setting Theory

Goal-setting theory is one of the most robust theories in work motivation. In a review of the literature, Locke, Shaw, Saari, & Latham (1981) reported that 90% of the studies reviewed provide support for the central tenet of goal setting theory: performance increases with goal difficulty. However, the great majority of these studies were conducted in North America, and it is unclear how well this result will replicate in other cultures. It is possible that the overshadowing effect of authority discussed before may weaken or nullify this effect in high-power-distance societies. Suppose a high-status superior in a high-power-distance society assigns a difficult goal to a subordinate, and by definition the subordinate is unlikely to meet the goal. In the first instance, the typical goal-setting effect should be observed, and perhaps the effect will even be stronger because of the compliance effect in high-power-distance societies. However, after the task is completed, the failure to meet the difficult goal set by the high-status superior may trigger the overshadowing effect of authority. The subordinate may worry that because of his or her failure, the relationship between him or her and the superior is at risk, and their future interactions may be problematic. One likely possibility is that the subordinate may be demoralized and become defensive in future interactions with the superior. This tendency will be accentuated If this goal-setting principle is used repeatedly and the subordinate usually fails to meet the goal set by the superior.

CONCLUSIONS

Based on the constructs of individualism–collectivism and power distance, four propositions relevant to theories of work motivation are advanced. Three areas of work motivation are then discussed in light of these propositions. A number of suggestions for extending the universality of several motivation theories are proposed. Hopefully, the ideas propounded in this paper will stimulate more cross-national research on work motivation and lead to the development of pan-cultural theories of work motivation.

REFERENCES

Bond, M. H., Wan, K. C., Leung, K., & Giacalone, R. (1985). How are responses to verbal insults related to cultural collectivism and power distance? *Journal of Cross-Cultural Phychology, 16,* 111–127.

Chatman, J. A., & Barsade, S. G. (1995). Personality, organizational culture, and cooperation: Evidence from a business simulation. *Administrative Science Quarterly, 40,* 423–443.

Chen, J. T. S. (1975). *1001 Chinese sayings.* Hong Kong: Chung Chi College, Chinese University of Hong Kong.

Earley, P. C. (1986). Trust, perceived importance of praise and criticism, and work performance: An examination of feedback in the United States and England. *Journal of Management, 12,* 457–473.

Earley, P. C. (1989). Social loafing and collectivism: A comparison of the United States and the People's Republic of China. *Administrative Science Quarterly, 34,* 565–581.

Earley, P. C. (1993). East meets West meets Mideast: Further explorations of collectivistic and indivi-sualistic work groups. *Academy of Management Journal, 36,* 319–348.

Earley, P. C., & Stubblebine, P. (1989). Intercultural assessment of performance feedback. *Group and Organization Studies, 14,* 161–181.

Ellemers, N., Van Knippenberg, A., deVries, N., & Wilke, H. (1988). Social identification and perme-ability of group boundaries. *European Journal of Social Psychology, 18,* 497–513.

Erez, M., & Earley, P. C. (1992). *Culture, self-identity, and work.* New York: Oxford University Press.

Erez, M., & Somech, A. (1996). Is group productivity loss the rule or the exception? Effects of culture and group-based motivation. *Academy of Management Journal, 39,* 1513–1537.

Etzioni, A. (1975). *A comparative analysis of complex organizations: On power, involvement, and their correlates.* New York: Free Press.

Farh, J. L., Leung, K., & Tse, D. K. (1995). Managing human resources in Hong Kong: 1997 and beyond. *Columbia Journal of World Business, 30*, 42–49.

Gouldner, A. W. (1960). The norm of reciprocity: A preliminary statement. *American Sociological Review, 25*, 161–178.

Graen, G. B. (1976). Role making processes within complex organizations. In M. D. Dunnette (Ed.). *Handbook of industrial and organizational psychology* (pp. 1201–1246). Chicago: Rand McNally.

Greenberg, J. (1990). Organizational justice: Yesterday, today, and tomorrow. *Journal of Management, 16*, 399–432.

Hagiwara, S. (1992). The concept of responsibility and determinants of responsibility judgment in the Japanese context. *International Journal of Psychology, 27*, 143–156.

Hamilton, V. L., & Sanders, J. (1983). Universals in judging wrongdoing: Japanese and Americans compared. *American Sociological Review, 48*, 199–211.

Higgins, A., Power, C., & Kohlberg, L. (1984). The relationship of moral atmosphere to judgments of responsibility. In W. M. Kurtines & J. L. Gewirtz, (Eds.), *Morality, moral behavior and moral development* (pp. 74–106). New York: Wiley.

Hofstede, G. (1980). *Culture's consequences: International differences in work-related values.* Beverly Hills, CA: Sage.

Hsu, F. L. K. (1981). *Americans and Chinese: Passages to differences.* Honolulu: University of Hawaii Press.

Hwang, K. K. (1987). Face and favor: The Chinese power game. *American Journal of Sociology, 92*, 944–974.

Jin, P. (1993). Work motivation and productivity in voluntarily formed work teams: A field study in China. *Organizational Behavior and Human Decision Processes, 54*, 133–155.

Kim, U. M. (1994). Significance of paternalism and communalism in the occupational welfare system of Korean firms: A national survey. In U. Kim, H. C. Triandis, C. Kagitcibasi, S. C. Choi, & G. Yoon (Eds.), *Individualism and collectivism: Theory, method, and applications.* Thousand Oaks, CA: Sage.

King, A. Y. C. (1991). Kuan-hsi and network building: A sociological interpretation. *Daedalus, 120*, 63–84.

Kohlberg, L. (1981). *The philosophy of moral development: Moral stages and the idea of justice: Vol. 1. Essays on moral development.* New York: Harper & Row.

Leung, K., & Bond, M. H. (1984). The impact of cultural collectivism on reward allocation. *Journal of Personality and Social Psychology, 47*, 793–804.

Leung, K., Su, S. K., & Morris, M. W. (in press). When is criticism *not* constructive? The role of fairness perceptions and dispositional attributions in employee acceptance of critical supervisory feedback. *Human Relations.*

Locke, E. A., Shaw, K., Saari, L., & Latham, G. (1981). Goal setting and task performance: 1969–1980. *Psychology Bulletin, 90*, 125–152.

Luthans, F., Paul, R., & Baker, D. (1981). An experimental analysis of the impact of contingent reinforcement on sales persons' performance behavior. *Journal of Applied Psychology, 66*, 314–323.

Mael, F., & Ashforth, B. E. (1992). Alumni and their alma mater: A partial test of the reformulated model of organizational identification. *Journal of Organizational Behavior, 13*, 103–123.

Majeed, A., & Ghosh, E. S. (1982). A study of social identity in three ethnic groups in India. *International Journal of Psychology, 17*, 455–463.

Markus, H., & Kitayama, S. (1991). Culture and self: Implications for cognition, emotion, and motivation. *Phychological Review, 98*, 224–253.

Miller, J. G. (1994). Cultural diversity in the morality of caring: Individually oriented versus duty-based interpersonal moral codes. *Cross-Cultural Research, 28*, 3–39.

Miller, J. G., & Bersoff, D. M. (1992). Culture and moral judgment: How are conflicts between justice and friendship resolved. *Journal of Personality and Social Psychology, 62*, 541–554.

Miller, J. G., Bersoff, D. M., & Harwood, R. L. (1990). Perceptions of social responsibilities in India and in the United States: Moral imperatives or personal decisions? *Journal of Personality and Social Psychology, 58*, 33–47.

Pritchard, R., Leonard, D., Von Bergen, C., & Kirk, R. (1976). The effects of varying schedules of reinforcement on human task performance. *Organizational Behavior and Human Performance, 16*, 205–230.

Redding, S. G., & Wong, G. Y. Y. (1986). The psychology of Chinese organizationl behavior. In M. H. Bond (Ed.), *The psychology of the Chinese people* (pp. 267–295). Hong Kong: Oxford University Press.

Rizzo, J. R., House, R., & Lirtzman, S. (1970). Role conflict and role ambiguity in complex organizations. *Administrative Science Quarterly, 15*, 150–163.

Seashore, S. E. (1954). *Group cohesiveness in the industrial work group.* Ann Arbor, MI: University of Michigan Press.

Sensenbrenner, J., & Sensenbrenner, J. (1994, November–December). Personnel priorities. *The Chinese Business Review*, 40–45.

Shweder, R. A., Mahapahtra, M., & Miller, J. G. (1987). Cultural and moral development in India and the United States. In J. Kagan & S. Lamb (Eds.), *The emergence of morality in young children* (pp. 1–89). Chicago: University of Chicago Press.

Skinner, B. F. (1969). *Contingencies of reinforcement: A theoretical analysis.* New York: Appleton-Century-Crofts.

Smith P. B., & Misumi, J. (1989). Japanese management–A sun rising in the West? In C. L. Copper & I. T. Robertson (Eds.), *International review of industrial and organizational psychology* (Vol. 4). Chichester, England: Wiley.

Tajfel, H. (1981). *Human groups and social categories.* Cambridge: Cambridge University Press.

Tomita, T. (1983). Responses to Japanese affiliated enterprises. *Philippine Economic Journal, 22*, 52–81.

Triandis, H. C. (1995). *Individualism amd collectivism.* Boulder, CO: Westview Press.

Tyler, T. R. (1990). *Why people obey the law.* New Haven, CT: Yale University Press.

23

Self-actualization versus Collectualization: Implications for Motivation Theories

Simcha Ronen
Tel Aviv University, Israel

A PERSONAL PERSPECTIVE

Twenty-five years ago, I conducted a study comparing work values and job attitudes of two distinct populations of industrial workers in Israel: those employed in kibbutz factories and similar employees in the private sector. The study's basic hypotheses concerned the cultural differences between the two populations, one presumed to be individualistic, the other collectivistic. The expected differences were indeed confirmed (Ronen, 1977, 1978). Having been part of the social milieu of the kibbutz in the past, I was not surprised by these results.

However, 25 years later, cultural and ideological transitions in the kibbutz movement have altered one of the major bastions of collectivist social organization in the individualistic West. Although the kibbutz movement has undergone a number of fascinating adaptation processes, the focus here is mainly on transformations of its cultural value system. The seamless collectivist values that were part of these communities have begun to give way to certain individualistic notions, which allow much more room for individual differences in material rewards.

These changes prompted me to investigate the collectivist–individualist dimension of teamwork with a newfound curiosity. My questions were based on the

341

conflict to which each individual in a Western society is continuously subjected: between an individual-oriented value system and the inevitability of membership in various groups. These group affiliations and the general phenomenon of "belongingness" are the subject of the following discussion.

A basic axiom that is presumed is that each individual in the Western world is simultaneously operating as a self-controlled optimizing system and as a member of some collectivity, and furthermore that each system has the potential of having different values and norms. For example, if we return to the case cited, we may ask why members of the kibbutz movement were so attuned to a collectivist value system even while living within a Western country. The answer has to do with the presence of some of the necessary elements that mediate between values of individualism and collectivism:

1. The founding members of the collectives shared a high level of social and cultural homogeneity: Most came from eastern Europe, and all were committed to a distinct social and national ideology.
2. Work values were shared by all. Work was the means to achieve social goals: a just society, national identity, community security, and finally, the in-gathering of all Jews of the Diaspora.
3. For the followers, these values were congruent across all social subsystems: family, organization, community, nation.

The collectivist culture of this advanced community became a model for social scientists. The main attraction for members of the movement, as well as for the social scientists who observed it, was the fact that the group's spirit and daily behavior seemed to provide the simultaneous fulfillment of the full range of Maslow's (1954) hierarchy, namely, basic needs (existence and security), social needs (love, belongingness, recognition), as well as higher-order needs (accomplishment, growth, and self-identity). In addition, the research on the kibbutz provided a vital methodological lesson: By examining the values and motives of members of collective communities through the prism of Western research tools and theoretical models, I fell victim to the trap of ignoring the etic–emic distinction (Triandis & Martin, 1983). The efforts to make cross-cultural and cross-national comparisons prevented us from a thorough emic analysis that would have been more sensitive to the perceptions of the kibbutz members themselves.

In retrospect, it seems to me that in spite of increased sensitivity and sophistication to cultural variations, and the models and assumptions used to research such social phenomena, Western societies have, and in many cases still are, tied to the notion that group membership is mainly an *instrumental* strategy in the pursuit of more important individualistic goals. It is important to resolve the conflicting results and conclusions on issues associated with motivational paradigms associated with team membership.

The purpose of this chapter is: to survey the major dilemmas of individualistic motivational theories as they try to account for behavior associated with a collective identity, and to offer a partial solution to some of these dilemmas. Our theories, and therefore our research and applications, are at best confused and at worst plagued by incompatible assumptions and conflicting messages about individual and group behavior. I shall thus attempt to delineate some of the reasons for this state of affairs. Finally, I shall introduce a conceptual paradigm based on cultural anthropological grounds and supported by preliminary field data that may account for some of these dilemmas. This paradigm refers to higher-order needs aimed at the welfare of a team. But first I shall review some dilemmas that introduce inconsistancies to motivational claims related to team membership.

TEAMWORK—DILEMMAS
AND CONFLICTING MESSAGES

Groups in Industrial-Organizational Psychology as Viewed Through a Western Prism

We in the West have recently witnessed a renewed interest in teams and group processes as evidence in the frequency of these topics in professional meetings (e.g., The Society of Industrial and Organizational Psychology and the Academy of Management academic annual meetings) and in the research literature (e.g., Guzzo & Salas, 1995; Hackman, 1990). The reasons most often given for this attention to groups include global economic competition and the introduction of Japanese managerial style; the growing awareness of the need for cooperation in decision making; and a continuation of the 1960s and 1970s romanticization of team work in the form of interpersonal communication training and the human relations movement.

But this fascination with group phenomena itself needs to be further explained. Why has Western organizational thought become so preoccupied with the task of comparing team effectiveness to individual performances? There seems to be a need to justify the use of groups and perhaps an ideological bias within industrial-organizational psychology that compels us to sell (to the executive board and management) the notion that teams are a good tool to achieve organizational goals.

The enthusiasm for work teams also seems to overlook some limitations in our knowledge of group phenomena. For instance, it is not clear whether the existence of effective teams in organizations is even a question of choice. In addition, the construct team itself may obscure differences between short-term and long-term groups, and between, for example, results of lab research and field observations of decision-making teams, producing inappropriate generalizations.

Methodologically, there has not been sufficient recognition of the limitations of individual-level analyses for understanding the "team" as a collective entity.

Some of the most basic axioms of scientific psychology actually exclude the notion of a team as an identifiable entity. These include the principle that the individual is the unit of analysis, the insistence that individuals have the freedom to be deviants, and the scientific difficulty in attributing any observable individual effect to random chance (McIntyre & Salas, 1995). These assumptions diminish our ability to account for group phenomena such as the formation of teams during crises or the response to risks that requires a cooperative decision-making process. Our individualistic framework renders unintelligible the efforts of individuals to increase their interdependence and vulnerability and to reduce their very individuality. In cases such as the above, we should probably consider whether individuality is sufficiently reduced to allow us to abandon the usual unit of analysis in favor of group theories and models. We cannot afford to ignore the old dilemma that was expressed most succinctly a century ago by Comte, who asked, "How can the individual be at once cause and consequence of society?"

A partial solution to the above challenge has been advanced within the philosophy of science: It suggests that the research question should determine the appropriate unit of analysis, whether the individual or the group. This is the question of level of analysis (e.g., Ilgen, Major, Hollenbeck, & Sego, 1995; Yammarino & Dubinsky, 1994; Yammarino & Bass, 1990; Klein, Dansereau, & Hall, 1994; and Klein & House, 1995). Still, it seems that improvements in research methodology has not advanced motivational theories to incorporate new aspects associated with team membership. Moreover, some of the conclusions and applications of team paradigms tend to act as demotivations; following are examples.

Task Structure and the Conflicting Reward Systems

The contradiction between demands for team loyalty and the search for individual gains is a daily occurrence in the Western world. Employees in all types of organizations are regularly told simultaneously to strive to better themselves and to sacrifice for the group.

Patterns of employee responses to these multiple and contradictory reward systems indicate a failure to implement genuine team-based motivation. Indeed, it seems likely that individualistic considerations supersede any collectivistic affiliation to teamwork when financial rewards are concerned. Park, Oforr-Dankwa and Bishop (1994) found that low performers were more likely to leave the organization under individual incentives, whereas high-performing individuals were more likely to leave under group incentive systems. This finding, when interpreted in light of perceptions of distributive justice (Adams, 1965), suggests that teams in these organizations were unsuccesful in creating a kind of motivation that could offset material considerations.

It is suggested that when an individual employee's rational analysis of job contingencies perceives high congruency between task structure (e.g., interdependence), reward systems, and feedback, it will result in the highest effective group performance (Shea & Guzzo, 1987a, 1987b; Saavendra, Early, & Van Dyne, 1993). Such needed congruency among various group characteristics are rarely available.

The key factor here is congruency; the ideal optimal congruency should include norms and values from various domains of life—social, material, and perceived preferences of how to reach self-realization.

What Is a Group?

A question that I have never heard raised in the East has and still does preoccupy Western social scientists (e.g., Ilgen et al. 1995): "What is a (small) group?" The continuous need for a precise definition of something so intuitive and experientially obvious is quite astonishing. Members of collective cultures or teams do not have to wonder whether they have fulfilled the usual requirements of consisting of two or more individuals, interacting among themselves, perceiving their interdependence, and having a shared purpose (vague as it may be).[1] Work teams are formed in the context of Western organizations, usually to carry out a specific and temporary assignment. We then typically observe and analyze the "collective" characteristics of such groups. However, the self-identity of members of such a team can rarely be defined by the collective. Thus our attributions of continuous and meaningful group membership under these conditions seem naive. I shall give some examples later. The literature, however, provides advice in order to form effective groups.

Various recommendations have been advanced for producing successful teams within Western organizations (e.g., Guzzo & Salas, 1995):

(a) An organizational culture or climate that can nurture a value system that will reinforce team work. It has been suggested that this can be achieved by various techniques: electing the right people; designing appropriate reward systems; assigning team accountability.

(b) Within the organization, training members to be effective in teams. The operating assumption, we presume, is that teams are desirable from the organizational viewpoint(?)! Let's examine some of these assumptions.

Teams as Instrumental for Achieving Individual Intrinsic Goals

The social psychology literature has offered explanations for why people join and participate in groups, while (Industrial/Organizational) psychology has offered

---

[1] Definition of a team: Teams are "Distinguishable sets of [more than two] individuals who interact interdependently and adaptively achieve specific, shared and valued objectives" (Morgan, Glickman, Woodrad, Blaiwes, and Salas, 1986, p. 3).

complimentary rationales for why people want to work in teams (Guzzo, 1986, 1995). These approaches treat group membership as a means to fulfill needs associated with individualistic models of motivation. For example: A work team will enable rotation that can provide *job variety*; a task team enables the understanding of a whole task, and as a result a better understanding of the final product, which can make a job more meaningful; discovering problems and troubleshooting in teams can provide novelty, identity, and self-worth.

The analysis of team processes as instrumental to the achievement of individualistic goals is reasonable. However, it overlooks the team's potential, as perceived by members of collectivist societies, to provide meaningfulness at all levels of the need hierarchy. Indeed, as Shamir (1990) has pointed out, individualistic models of human motivation in organizations are utilitarian and rational and leave moral considerations mainly to members of religious or voluntary organizations. Motives of individuals working in borderline institutions like hospitals and schools are difficult to identify within this framework. In short, there is hardly a theoretical justification for individuals achieving intinsic fulfillment in economically oriented organization through team participations.

Crisis Task Force

When team research is done, what can we expect from the results? Of the many types of work teams, researchers have reserved a privileged place for the ad hoc "crisis task force." These groups consist of individuals who are interdependent (during the assigned hours) and have common goals, and it seems entirely unwarranted to equate this working group to teams found within collectivist cultures. Even if no such equation is intended, the differences between work teams and groups that occur outside of Western society must be clearly spelled out and conclusions carefully generalized.

The individuals assigned to such teams in the West are usually successful individual achievers who have proven themselves in times of crisis and are willing to invest in a team effort temporarily. It is usually the potential for individual recognition that stimulates the contribution to the team, rather than devotion to the group. The fact that recognized "stars" are selected to the team introduces values and norms that may promote effective solutions but may also underline the fact that the team is ephemeral. Such teams may focus their efforts on solving problems, while group maintenance issues receive low priority. Granted, individuals in such groups may act as good team members and at times may even share values and draw prestige from the affiliation, but it would be an overstatement to suggest that these individuals have made a complete transition to a new self-identity.

It is not my intention to question the evidence that groups have the potential to solve complex problems effectively. Rather, it is the individual's perception of his or her association with the group and the extent to which the collective norms have been shaped by individual needs that are in question. By simply raising the issue of the objective effectiveness of a crisis task force, we have already provided part of the answer. By evaluating the objective effectiveness of these groups, we reaffirm the self-evidence of individualistic norms in Western societies in which teams must be justified in terms of instrumental results. But by transmitting such a message in our research and in practice, we may be undermining the chances for individuals to commit themselves to a team. When we call for "full"—temporary—commitment, and insist that "it's through cooperation and teamwork that we shall achieve our goals," we are sending a double message and the process and the results are evaluated from different perspectives.

It seems pathetic and at times even hypocritical when evaluations of team decision making combine external, objective measures of outcomes with measures of internal criteria like feelings and group process (e.g., Ilgen et al., 1995). Is there any reason to expect a wide range on the various internal criteria? Do these ratings really matter for such teams? And furthermore, what about the composition of such teams? The familiar research finding that consensus can be more easily achieved by homogeneous rather than heterogeneous groups is far from surprising. It borders on tautology, and what more, defies the recent calls for increased openness in terms of gender, sexual orientation, age, race, and ethnic origin.

Although we might all agree that improving team decision making processes is desirable in both the West and the East, it seems that Southeast Asians are less pre-occupied with March's and Simon's (1958) notion of satisfying VS optimizing or with Kahaneman and Tversky's (1973) identification of biases in desicion-making, (D.M.), which gives rise to the heuristics, or simplifying strategies of D.M. Once more, this raises the question of why Western scientists using assumptions of individualistic rationality invest so much effort in proving or justifying the importance of groups (Ilgen et al., 1995; Guzzo, 1995). Justifying the existence of effective teams seems to require all the analytic skills we can muster. By comparison, collectivist societies seem to devote much less research to this issue (Hui, 1988; Hui & Triandis, 1986; Triandis, 1994). Let's turn now to some of the dilemmas and contradicting conclusions one may encounter when research deals with teams' composition and membership.

Characteristics of Team Members

Trust. Research on group norms within an individualistic culture, as opposed to a collectivist society, tends to focus on individual characteristics of the group members. One essential component of effective teams is trust. To the collectivists, this is self-evident. To the West it is a challenge, especially when a team is formed for an assigned temporary task. In these settings, numerous questions arise that are rarely asked in the non-Western context: Is trust easily acquired or is it a natural tendency? Is it a socially learned attitude, and, once acquired, can it be maintained in crisis situations? And how can trust stand up to competing individualistic tendencies like suspicion and competition? How can management promote trust and commitment to the group when other competing individualistic values are so deeply ingrained? And finally, what implications do some of these have on motivational forces?

Accountability. It took three decades of management paradigms to develop an awareness of the values of delegation, decentralization, and empowerment with the objective of endowing the individual with responsibility, autonomy, and the power to make decisions. But these innovations raised new problems of accountability. This difficulty occurred in spite of our understanding that the D.M. process necessitates team contribution because information is distributed, information processing is complicated, and level of ambiguity varies among individuals (Guzzo, 1986). Are these contradicting trends and practices? Under the requirements of dual accountability, can we hope to achieve an effective team process? A valuable team product?

Homogeneity vs. diversity dilemma (an argument against collectivistic identity). There is a traditional hostility to conformity and homogeneity implied by the Western liberal principle of openness and tolerance to human diversity (Goldstein, 1986; Jackson & Alvarez, 1992). Taken further, the same hostility can be directed toward the collectivist culture of conformity and consensus, which seems to subdue all diversity beneath sweeping generalizations. In Southeast Asia, in comparison to other cultures, the quest for harmony is subordinated much more to the need for individualized achievements.

However, the effects of various sources of human diversity—gender, ethnic affiliation, age differences—on group effectiveness are not straightforward. On one hand, such diversity may provide a climate for group productivity, while on the other hand research shows that team effectiveness is associated with shared stereotyping about the self and others. This is simply another way of describing the effects of homogeneity, which in collectivist societies becomes the major catalyst for communication, shared values, common goals, and a source of self-identity; for example, many Westerners interpret "saving face" as no more then a form of prestige.

The "Nonsucker" syndrome—to be avoided. The relentless emphasis in the West on individual freedom of choice, territorial integrity, and privacy has reached a level that alarms any person when s/he is requested to surrender any of these rights to a nebulous collectivity. Nothing is as detestable (or threatening) to a Westerner as having to sacrifice individuality for an ambiguous team identity. This distrust and suspicion has incapacitated us when the opportunity arises to form "effective" teams. The "Sucker Syndrome" makes an outcast of anyone who is exploited by any overarching authority. On the other hand, Americans and Europeans crowded the volunteer lists to join kibbutzim, where the ideals of cooperation and mutual care really seemed to work. The fascination with the luxury of fearless vulnerability is compelling. This observation, like others, promotes the present discussion (and self-search) appearing in this chapter.

The Neurotic Rationale (Teams as Instrumental for Management Goals), or: How to Exploit Legitimately

Any discussion in the search for promoting teamwork should not dismiss the following point: Management and consultants are not free of exploitative motivation when promoting team work. Many potential gains ensue from the formation of working teams on the shop floor. The promotion of team spirit, from this viewpoint, is attractive to management, as it potentially increases cooperation, encourages loyalty, and, in short, increases conformity and assures industrial acquiescence. Personal goals and demands may thereby be reduced, and the tendency toward peer interdependence can nurture amiability and cooperation. These benefits may be realized whether the process is a deliberately manipulative strategy or a by-product of a collectivist well-intended environment. The only difference is in the resiliency and the persistence of such an attitude over time.

The Entrepreneurial Dilemma

While in Japan learning and researching managerial styles (using, in retrospect, Western theoretical paradigms and employing individualistic evaluation schema that turned out to be almost completely useless), I was relieved to find a flaw in this otherwise legendary collectivist organizational culture: lack of creativity. This apparent finding was a saving grace that allowed me to reaffirm the values of individualistic organizational culture despite all the achievements of collectivist culture in Japanese production and service organizations.

Creativity, according to common wisdom, is a characteristic of the individual employee. Any advances made by entrepreneurial activity can only emerge from free-floating individuals and would be blocked in a team culture. While organizations in the West preached this principle and have taken measures to encourage risk-taking and experimentation, the Japanese, concerned about the lack of creativity in their organizational culture, seem to have taken it to heart. Indeed, the Japanese government has formed a special interministrial committee to fight off this debilitating danger and to promote creativity. They have been busy developing educational and training methods to achieve this goal.

But the theory of a Japanese creativity deficit does not stand up well in the face of the flood of new products from Japan and the rate of improvement in existing products. I am doubtful whether a collectivist culture and committed group membership truly weakens creativity. Two points need to be raised when individually associated characteristics are praised. First, when we attribute motivational preferences to individuals, we must remember that individualism and collectivism are not extremes of a single continuum such as the one once drawn for national comparative ratings (Hofstede, 1980). People in the West and in the East may simultaneously hold individualistic and collectivist values, norms, and motives. The relationship between these two orientations is an empirical question. Second, increasing team effectiveness in the West can create an organizational climate that legitimizes team membership and thus enhances the effectiveness of such teams (Guzzo, 1995). When teams are legitimized, individuals are more likely to draw their identity from collective behavior such as contribution to group goals and achievements and development of relevant skills that enhance team effectiveness.

But the question of how creativity can be promoted in a team setting remains. Rather than providing immediate and organization-wide recognition as a reward, it may be more effective and practical for team members to provide it in the short term. This is typical of collectivist settings and is becoming prevalent in the West as well. But the adoption of this approach in an individualistic culture is unlikely to produce all the benefits it has on its home ground. A task-based interdependence is less powerful in providing rewards and reinforcement for desirable behavior than the enduring collectivist team environment, where task interdependence and social Interdependence are combined.

The discussion so far highlited the biases, within the Western world, concerning the individual prism of evaluating the environment and the futile efforts to find anchors for implementing or prefering teams in work organizations. The following sections will expand the traditional motivational need paradigms within which collectivistic goals and values can coexist with individualistic needs of the same hierarchial importance.

MOTIVATIONAL MODELS
AND NEED HIERARCHY

One of the challenges of cross-cultural comparative management research concerns the question of the universality of models developed in the West. The research and reviews of the universality of work motivational theories have been equivocal at best (Ronen, 1986a; Bhagat & McQuaid, 1982; Ronen & Shenkar, 1985). More recently, the proliferation of literature on the issue of collectivism versus individualism (Holfstede, 1980; Triandis, 1985; 1994) has raised the question of whether individualistic motivation theories can predict or even explain group behavior.

In the preceding pages, I have pointed out ambiguities and contradictions in work on the motivational implications of group behavior. The following discussion will offer an alternative conceptualization that will allow us to consider motivational predispositions of behavior directed toward group welfare. This alternative can be framed as a response to three theoretical challenges:

1. Is it possible to define collectivist motives in terms of predispositions of behavior?
2. Can categories of collectivist motives and needs be conceptualized in terms parallel to the more traditional individual motivational models?
3. If the above two questions were to be answered affirmatively, can the categories of collectivist motivation be hierarchically ordered from basic needs to higher-order needs that parallel those suggested by various Western need-motivational theories?

In answering these questions, it will be necessary to formulate an alternative to existing individualistic models that we know do not address the challenges raised earlier in this chapter. It will also be occasionally necessary to make propositions that have not yet been confirmed by research as long as they do not contradict available data.

Collectivist Motives for Joining Groups

As discussed earlier, social psychology has delineated various reasons for individuals to join groups. Most of these involve individual needs that can be fulfilled through means other than participation in groups. But there may be other considerations for joining groups that have to do with perceived characteristics of the group and the interrelationship between the individual and his or her peers. For example, although individuals join groups for the potential to gain prestige, security, and other valued benefits, they may also be attracted by the intrinsic benefits of intragroup processes and experiences. The traditional distinction between the energy expended to reach goals versus the effort required for group maintenance is relevant here, since the existence of a group can become a goal of its own. Recent writings have even defined collectivist behavior as motivated by the wish to contribute to the group's welfare (e.g., Kim, 1994). Such a conceptualization makes it meaningless to talk about collective motivations unless the group's welfare is in the service of the individual and can be conceptualized in terms of purely hedonistic individual motivations.

However, theoretical discussions have found it difficult to relinquish the individualist conceptualization of motivation, considering the observable fact that the behaving homeostatic system is the individual person. It may therefore be necessary to move to another level of analysis when considering a collectivist act, though these notions are still in the experimental stages (e.g., Dansereau, Yammarino, & Markham, 1995). Shamir (1990) have provided a rationale for distinguishing between frames of reference for acts aimed at the collective entity and acts traditionally identified as calculative and hedonistic. This direction of research is worth pursuing, because it is clear that the traditional hedonistic and calculative logic of behavior provides a poor explanation for ideological commitment and identity established through the collective.

Defining Individualist and Collectivist Constructs

The individualism–collectivism dimension (I–C) has proven to be a concise, coherent, integrated, and empirically testable dimension of cultural variation. It has also allowed for a fruitful integration of knowledge within the discipline of psychology (such as cognitive, developmental, social, organizational, and clinical psychology) across disciplines (such as anthropology, sociology, economics, and management) and methodologies (such as ethnography, surveys, and experiments; Kim, Triandis, Kagitcibasi, Choi, & Yoon, 1994). Hofstede (1991) defines individualism and collectivism as follows:

> *Individualism* pertains to societies in which the ties between individuals are loose: everyone is expected to look after himself or herself and his or immediate family. *Collectivism* as its opposite pertains to societies in which people from birth onwards are integrated into strong, cohesive ingroups, which throughout people's lifetime continue to protect them in exchange for unquestioning loyalty. (p. 51)

According to Hofstede (1980), individualist societies emphasize "I" consciousness, autonomy, emotional independence, individual initiative, right to privacy, pleasure seeking, financial security, need for specific friendship, and universalism. Collectivist societies, on the other hand, stress "we" consciousness, collective identity, emotional dependence, group solidarity, sharing, duties and obligations, the need for stable and predetermined friendship, group decisions, and particularism. Triandis, Leung, Villareal, and Clark (1985) propose that at the psychological level, the personality dimensions of *idiocentrism* and *allocentrism* are parallel to the I–C dimension at the cultural level. Idiocentrics place their personal goals above the goals of others, while allocentrics place more weight on the goals of their in-groups than to their own personal goals.

Teams in Individualist vs. Collectivist Cultures

As shown earlier, much lip service has been devoted to team-based systems in the Western business community. But the realization of such systems in the West is limited for the reasons I have mentioned: naïvete, the tension between group processes and instrumental goals, and contradictions between the host culture and the group. In order to employ teams effectively, we need to recognize some basic shortcomings of our system, obstacles that prevent Western managers from achieving what Avolio (1995) calls "highly developed teams."

To identify the limitations of the Western setting, we need to understand the cultural conditions that shape the team's spirit, resiliency, and collectivist identity. What conditions allow a team in the East to have an identity of its own, to constitute a whole that is greater than the sum of its members? These conditions can be understood in terms of the extent to which they contribute to the following set of special features of groups in collectivist cultures, which I propose constitute the difference from a Western individualistic environment:

1. **The psychological contract.** This is the acceptance of a long-term shared fate and the expectation of an extended interaction and interdependence create the basis for a mutually compelling contract. Once the contract is made, there is no need to reevaluate its fairness relative to other possible arrangements. There is no need to continuously monitor the contributions of others and the distribution of rewards. The positive implications of this contract compensate group members for giving up the kind of freedom of choice that is so cherished in the West.

2. **Equity considerations.** Another factor of the collectivist setting in unifying the group is that individuals do not have to concentrate on results when judging the contributions of others. It is enough to evaluate others simply on the basis of effort, or intention to contribute, for two reasons: First, rewards are distributed over an extended period and therefore short-term performance is an irrelevant criteria; and second, investment of effort has a positive effect on team maintenance independent of results.

3. **Time reference.** Long-term commitments, and the more diverse kinds of contributions required by the group, lend themselves to an atmosphere of tolerance and permissiveness within the group.

4. **Diverse environments.** Evaluating the contributions of members to the group are not confined to the work setting but extend to community and cultural activities.

5. **Variety of roles.** The extended range of team life, like the analogy of a family, allows for a more flexible differentiation of tasks and roles and greatly reduces the need to continuously monitor the equity of rewards.

6. **Group identity.** In such cases, group members are much more likely to assume an identity derived from the group and its activities than is possible in the short-lived and task-oriented teams found in the West.

7. **Contribution to the team.** Contributions to the collective need not be justified in terms of any individualistic pleasure principle. At times they may even contradict such principles, as in the case of altruistic motivation.

These seven points are part of the elements of a psychological contract between the individual and the organization. In a collectivist culture, due to the stability of this kind of arrangement, this contract is likely to become a normative one shared by all members of the society (Rousseau, 1995; Robinson, Kaalz, & Rousseau,

1994). The emphasis on fluidity and adaptability of economic institutions in the West makes it much more difficult to realize the perceived contractual conditions that lead to stability, commitment, and loyalty.

The analysis of these conditions requires a revision of motivational theory in order to take collectivist motivations into account. In the next section, I will begin to develop such an approach, starting with the innovation in need theories proposed in an earlier publication (Ronen, 1994) and then defining need categories that include collectivist values.

Taxonomy and Hierarchy of Need Categories

Notwithstanding the collectivistic issues, need motivational theories have been a subject of dispute in the absence of decisive empirical evidence for either the claimed need categories or the prepotency principle of these needs. Based on a review of this literature and an analysis of cross-cultural data, I have suggested (Ronen, 1994)[2] that need categories indeed exist, but that they should be understood in terms of a two-dimensional structure rather than the unidimensional level of prepotency (or importance) suggested by Maslow (1954, 1959). I have summarized the available data pertaining to taxonomies of need, concentrating on those theories that have been developed primarily in the United States but which have been found to be valid in other cultures. The review allowed for the identification of a multidimensional structure that is discernible through multivariate techniques. From this structure it is possible to derive valence categories of job characteristics that can serve as universal dimensions for understanding specific culturally bound organizational reward systems.

Before describing the proposed model in detail, a brief review of some basic principles of this type of model is in order. Need–satisfaction models of job attitudes consist of two types of theory: expectancy theory and need theory (Alderfer, 1969, 1972, 1977). The two can be viewed as complementary (Campbell, Dunnette, Lawler, & Weick, 1970; Hackman & Oldham, 1976; Porter & Lawler, 1968). This is possible because expectancy models contain a process theory of motivation, whereas need models depict a content theory concerned with features of the individual or the environment that energize and sustain behavior (Alderfer, 1977; Campbell & Pritchard, 1976). The two theories converge in their mutual concern, with the valence associated with the outcomes of a specific act. Need theory considers the type and level of the valence associated with an act, whereas expectancy theory adds the perceived probability of the outcomes.

There have been a number of need theories that have stimulated research in the field of work motivation, of which Maslow's has been without doubt the most popular. Maslow's formulation (Maslow, 1954, 1959) begins with a few basic

---

[2]The following section relies heavily on this source.

assumptions:

- A person may experience five distinct need categories: physiological needs, safety needs, belongingness needs, esteem needs, and self-actualization needs.
- These needs are arranged in a hierarchy of declining importance, from basic needs to self-actualization needs.
- This hierarchy is manifested in the prepotency principle, by which a lower-level need—higher in importance—must be satisfied before the next need becomes the source of motivational forces.
- The fifth need, self-actualization, is not satiable—it is never fully fulfilled.
- These needs can be considered universal.

The goal of the research cited was to establish the basic tenens of need theories, usually using Maslow's as the exemplar, as his research offers the most detailed and general conceptualization. These tenets are the basis for the following research and the proposed new model for motivational need theories. It will also enable a preliminary investigation of collectivistic elements in individualistic motivational paradigms.

Work Values

The analyses reviewed were based on data gathered by means of questionaire items designed to elicit work values. Certain assumptions are implicit in this kind of methodology. First, it is assumed that if one can indeed identify values associated with the work domain, they can be regarded as specific forms of more general values that are presumed to transcend various life domains (see Kluckhohn, 1951; Rokeach, 1973, 1979). This is consistent with Kluckhohn's (1961) definition of a value as "a conception, explicit or implicit, distinctive of an individual or characteristic of a group, of the desirable which influences the selection from available modes, means and ends of action" (p. 395). The features of these values, therefore, incorporate concepts of beliefs, pertain to desirable end states or behaviors, guide selection or evaluation of behavior and events, and may be ordered in terms of relative importance (Schwartz & Bilsky, 1987, 1990).

Second, the psychometric approach assumes that these features of basic values may be associated with the more specific work values proposed by Kalleberg (1977) in terms of the range of gratification available from work and its environment. This assumption implies the possibility of assessing basic value preferences by means of individual priorities regarding characteristics of jobs and their rewards.

Third, it must be assumed that these kinds of items are applicable cross-culturally (Bass & Burger, 1979; MOW, 1987; Ronen, 1986). The problem of comparability of items across cultures is relevant here and has been pointed out by others (Poortinga, 1989). However, the purpose of this research was not to compare rankings of values across national populations, but to analyze the data

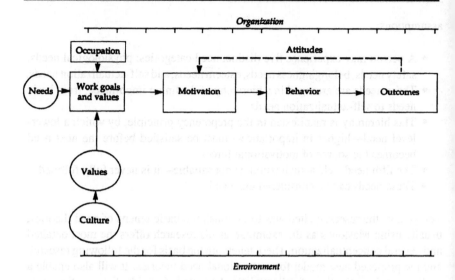

FIG. 23.1. Needs, values, and motivation: individual, organiza-
tional, and environmental antecedents. From *Comparative and
Multinational Management* (p. 137), by S. Ronen, 1986, New York:
Wiley. Copyright 1986 by Wiley. Reprinted by permission.

separately for each sample, thus somewhat reducing the hazards of insensitivity to
the emic–etic dilemma (Ronen, 1986a; Ronen & Shenkar, 1989). Fig. 23.1 depicts
my basic approach to the cultural and organizational environment as it relates to
the established work values of an individual.

Multidimensionality of Work Values

The geometric representations of data produced by Ronen and associates
(Ronen, 1979; Ronen & Barkan, 1985; Ronen & Kraut, 1980; Ronen Kraut,
Lingoes, & Aranya, 1979; Shenkar & Ronen, 1987b) and which appeared in the
original articles are reanalyzed in Ronen (1994). The original papers all used a
specific multivariate analysis technique and shared the goal of identifying need
taxonomies, particularly Maslow's categorization. Maps were produced that included the geometric representation of the intercorrelation matrices in the form of
the work values location on a two-dimensional computer printout (Guttman, 1959,
1968; Lingoes, 1965, 1977). Table 23.1 summarizes the items used and their relationship to well-known motivational taxonomies. An example of the geometrical
display is presented in Fig. 23.2. and 23.3.

A close examination of the actual items' location in the maps reveals some
structural information. For example, most of the items contained in the lower right
half of the maps, below one of the diagonals, are associated with characteristics

TABLE 23.1
Questionnaire Wording of 14 Work Values and Assignment
to Various Motivational Taxonomies

Work Goal	Questionnaire Wording How Important Is It for You to:	Category of Various Taxonomies Maslow's	Alderfer's	Herzberg's
Physical	Have good physical working conditions (good ventilation and lighting, adequate work space, etc.)			
Area	Live in an area desirable to you and your family			
Time	Have a job which leaves you sufficient time for your personal for family life	Physiological and Security	Existence	
Security	Have the security that you will be able to work for your company as long as you want to			Hygienes
Benefits	Have good fringe benefits			
Earnings	Have an opportunity for high earnings			
Coworkers	Work with people who cooperate well with one another	Social		
Manager	Have a good working relationship with your manager		Relatedness	
Recognition	Get the recognition you deserve when you do a good job			
Advancement	Have the opportunity for advancement to higher-level jobs	Self-esteem		
Training	Have training opportunities (to improve your skills or to learn new skills)			
Autonomy	Have considerable freedom to adopt your own approach to the job		Growth	Motivators
Skills	Fully use your skills and abilities on the job	Self-actualization		
Challenge	Have challenging work to do—work from which you get a personal sense of accomplishment			

Note. From "A Nonmetric Scaling Approach to Taxonomies of Employee Work Motivation," by S. Ronen, A. I. Kraut, J. C. Lingoes, and N. Aranya, 1979, *Multivariate Behavioral Research, 14*, p. 392. Copyright 1979 by *Multivariate Behavioral Research.* Reprinted by permission.

of the collectivity or groups of employees, such as social benefits, tenure, and interpersonal relations. In contrast, the upper left half of the maps, above the same diagonal, contains items associated primarily with the individual employee, such as promotion, autonomy, and challenge. Using the other diagonal as a boundary, the lower left half of the maps seem to contain items that are by and large material

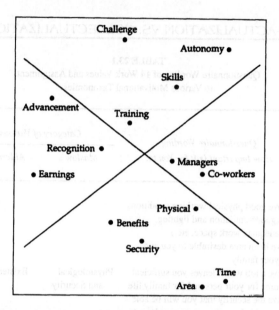

FIG. 23.2. A smallest-space analysis map of U.K. sample, with diagonals inserted (*n* = 1,535). From "Cross-national Study of Employee Work Goals," by S. Ronen, 1979, *International Review of Applied Psychology, 28*, p. 7. Copyright 1979 by *International Review of Applied Psychology*. Reprinted by permission.

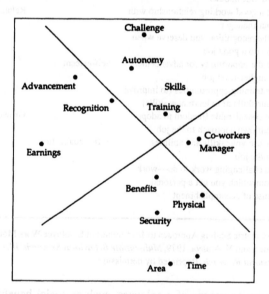

FIG. 23.3. A smallest-space analysis map of German (I) sample, with diagonals inserted (*n* = 800). From "An Experimental Examination of Work Motivation Taxonomies," by S. Ronen, and A. I. Kraut, 1980, *Human Relations, 33*. Copyright 1980 by Plenum. Reprinted by permission.

in nature, such as pay, tenure, and promotion. In contrast, the items contained in the upper right half of the maps are nonmaterial by nature, such as relations with coworkers, autonomy, and challenge. This interpretation of the data in terms of a *two-dimensional configuration* is not surprising in view of published research in other psychological areas (e.g., Wiggins, 1979; Bengston, 1975).

The Resulting Quadrants and Need Taxonomies

The two dimensions and the composition of the content area of each quadrant are presented in Fig. 23.3. They seem to define the cluster of values in each quadrant in terms of Maslow's needs taxonomy, as depicted in the diagrams for the different countries. The lower-level needs (physiological and security), which signify orientations to both materialism and collectivism, appear in the bottom quadrant. These are job characteristics that are financially quantifiable and are usually allotted to employees because they belong to a group (e.g., having the same organizational level, similar tasks, or similar seniority). The lefthand quadrant is associated with the ego, or self-esteem; it is inherently materialistic and based on individual differences and contains job features such as recognition and promotion. The righthand quadrant consists primarily of interpersonal relations and is therefore primarily nonmaterialistic and group-oriented. The top quadrant (self-actualization) is defined by individualism and nonmaterialism, and contains such job aspects as challenge and autonomy. Fig. 23.4 and 23.5 illustrate the quadrants.

From the available data, we seem to be faced with a pair of dichotomies: collectivist versus individualistic items, and materialistic versus nonmaterialistic items. Furthermore, these dimensions are well anchored in previous research on the dimensionality of social values. Thus, the need taxonomies offered by various motivation theories actually have a two-dimensional structure. The fact that these findings were based on data from many countries, including mostly Western societies but also China and Japan, lends partial support for the universality of these taxonomies.

In their review of work motivation theory and practice, Katzell and Thompson (1990) wrote that "the motivational imperative inherent in motive/need theory is that it is important to ensure that workers have motives and values relevant to the type of organization and to jobs on which they are placed" (p. 146). The two-dimensional structure of employee needs proposed by Ronen (1994) may assist us in more effectively matching workers' motives and work values with the organizational and cultural environment. It reaffirms the validity of various taxonomies of needs—particularly Maslow's—but also offers an explanation for the difficulty of empirically establishing a unidimensional hierarchy of needs.

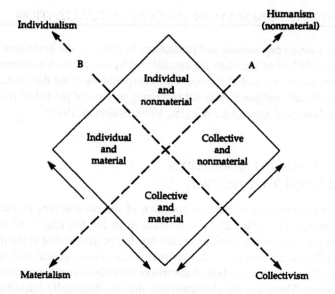

FIG. 23.4. The dimensions and their combined contribution in forming need categories.

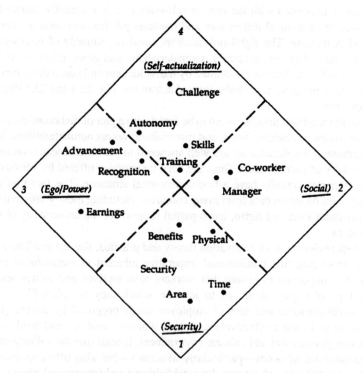

FIG. 23.5. Representation of Fig. 23.3 with Maslow's Needs inserted into the appropriate quadrons presented in Fig. 23.4.

EXPANDING NEED CATEGORIES TO INCLUDE ACTUALIZING COLLECTIVISTIC MOTIVES—THE COLLECTUALIZATION

An initial acceptance of the universality of the two-dimensional taxonomy of need categories and their hierarchy would support the following propositions concerning needs associated with team affiliation:

> *Proposition 1:* Collectivist needs are fairly basic needs, and prepotency requirements demand their fulfillment before the need for self-actualization is activated.

However, it seemed that the map of the Chinese sample, presented in Fig. 23.6, included two values that were collective in nature and that appeared in the upper quadrant of the map. Thus, in order to compensate for the possible Western bias of our original cross-cultural comparisons (Shenkar & Ronen, 1987b, 1990), we returned to the People's Republic of China to collect additional data that would

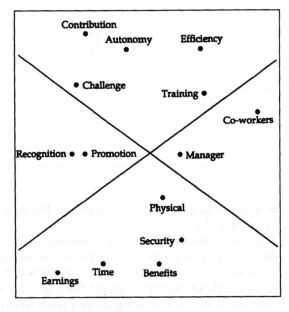

FIG. 23.6. A smallest-space analysis map of Chinese sample, with diagonals inserted (*n* = 163). From "The Structure and Importance of Work Goals Among Managers in the People's Republic of China," by O. Shenkar and S. Ronen, 1987, *Academy of Management Journal, 30*(3), p. 569. Copyright 1987 by *Academy of Management Journal.* Reprinted by permission.

TABLE 23.2
Factor Analysis—Varimax Rotation of Four Factors
in the People's Republic of China

Work Values	Factors			
	1	2	3	4
Stress	.44			
Physical Conditions	.45			
Security of Employment	.49			
Successful Company	.48			
Area	.40			
Defined Job	.42			
Security in Job	.58			
Effificent Department	.52			
Time	.34			
Help Others	.41			
Challenge		.60		
Autonomy		.46		
Contribution		.64		
Consultation by Loss		.43		
Serve Country		.51		
Variety in Job		.49		
Relationship with Boss			.48	
Relationship with Coworkers			.42	
Training			.56	
Recognition			.55	
Earnings				.64
Advancement				.54

reflect some of the unique features of the collectivist culture. The analyses of these data are presented in Table 23.2.

The factor analysis of the new sample contains a surprising result: Certain collectivist work values were located in a cluster corresponding to the individualistic category of Self-Actualization. These values were associated with the altruistic wish to contribute to the collective welfare. It appears that collectivist values were associated with basic needs as well as with higher-order needs (contribution and serving country). And indeed, Nevis (1983), in a pioneering review of collectivist culture, offered a needs pyramid locating collectivist values both at the bottom of the scale (belonging) and at the top of the pyramid (self-actualization in the service of society). Similarly, Schwartz (1990), in an extensive cross-cultural research project, includes both conformity and benevolence as collectivist values.

In order to provide a theoretical synthesis of these findings, Ronen and Shenkar have suggested the concept of *collectualization*, which they defined as the "realization of self through behavior aimed at enhancing in-group's welfare" (Ronen and Shenkar, 1990). Clearly, this realization is parallel to the individualist notion of self-actualization, which refers to the employment and development of one's own unique and valued attributes. Thus, Proposition 1 must be supplemented by two additional propositions that recognize the existence of higher-order collectivist needs:

Proposition 2: Some of the collectivist needs, such as collectualization, may be as high in the hierarchy as the highest individualistic needs of self-actualization.

Proposition 3: Higher-order collectivist needs, such as collectualization, may coexist with higher-order individualistic needs such as self-actualization.

If such a modification to the traditional motivational need theory is acceple, and furthermore, that it is applicable to Western societies and cultures, the next challenge is to build such teams and a supportive organizational climate that nurtures and reinforces such values.

SUMMARY

In this chapter, I have tried to point out some of the blind spots in existing paradigms for understanding collectivist motivations and to suggest a way of revising our conceptual tools in order to account for unexplained human behavior in a social context. It seems that efforts to subsume collective phenomena under individualistic theories have been quite futile. Therefore, an approach to motivation that remains anchored in the homeostatic–hedonistic approach, with occasional assistance from social psychological paradigms such as equity theory, will only deprive us of the theoretical tools and conceptual means necessary to explain a broad range of social behavior.

The approach recommended here should be considered a preliminary effort at bridging the two levels of analysis—the individual and the group—in order to account for behavior aimed at group welfare.[3] We have found that such behavior can be motivated by either low-level needs or by higher-order needs associated with accomplishment and self-realization. With the growing interest of organizations in team reward systems (Sundrom, et al.1990; Guzzo & Shea, 1992), recognition of the distinct structure of collectivist motivations could help make these innovations more effective.

---

[3]For example, see two special issues of *The Leadership Quarterly*, guest editor: Fred Dansereau, 1995, vol. 6, nos. 2 and 3.

364 RONEN

REFERENCES

Adams, J. S. (1965). Injustice in social exchange. In L. Berkowitz (Ed.), *Advances in experimental social psychology* (Vol. 2). New York: Academic Press.

Alderfer, C. P. (1969). An empirical test of a new theory of human needs. *Organizational Behavior and Human Performance, 4*, 142–175.

Alderfer, C. P. (1972). *Existence, relatedness and growth: Human needs in organizational settings.* New York: Free Press.

Alderfer, C. P. (1977). A critique of Salancik and Pfeffer's examination of need-satisfaction theories. *Administrative Science Quarterly, 22*, 658–669.

Avolio, B. J. (1995). Leadership: Building vital forces into highly developed teams. *Human Resource Management, 11*(7), 10–15.

Avolio, B. J, & Howell, J. M. (1992). The impact of leader behavior and leader-follower personality match on satisfaction and unit performance. In K. E. Clark, M. B. Clark, & D. R. Campbell (Eds.), *Impact of leadership.* Greensboro, NC: Center for Creative Leadership.

Avolio, B. J., Yammarino, F. J., & Bass, B. M. (1991). Identifying common methods variance with data collected from a single source: An unresolved sticky issue. *Journal of Management, 173*, 571–587.

Bandura, A. (1986). *Social foundations of thought and action: A social cognitive theory.* Englewood Cliffs, NJ: Prentice-Hall.

Bass, B. M. (1985). *Leadership and performance beyond expectations.* New York: Free Press.

Bass, B. M. (1990). *Bass & Stodgill's handbook of leadership: Theory, research and management applications.* New York: Free Press.

Bass, B. M., & Avolio, B. J. (1993). Transformational leadership: A response to critiques. In M. M. Chemers & R. Ayman (Eds.), *Leadership theory and research: Perspectives and directions.* San Diego, CA: Academic Press.

Bass, B. M., & Burger, P. C. (1979). *Assessments of managers: An international comparison.* New York: Free Press.

Bengston, V. L. (1975). Generation and family effects in value socialization. *American Sociological Review, 40*, 358–371.

Bhagat, R. S., & McQuaid, S. J. (1982). Role of subjective culture in organizations: A review and direction for future research. *Journal of Applied Psychology Monograph, 67*(5), 635–685.

Campbell, J. P., Dunnette, M. D., Lawler, E. E., & Weick, K. E. (1970). *Managerial behavior, performance, and effectiveness.* New York: McGraw-Hill.

Campbell, J. P., & Pritchard, R. D. (1976). Motivation theory in industrial and organizational psychology. In M. D. Dunnette (Ed.), *Handbook of industrial and organizational psychology.* Chicago: Rand McNally.

Dansereau, F. (Guest Ed.) (1995). *The Leadership Quarterly, 6*, (2–3).

Dansereau, F., Yammarino, F. J., & Markham, S. E. (1995). Leadership: The multiple approaches. *Leadership Quarterly, 6*(2), 97–109.

Eden, D. (1990). *Pygmalion in management: Productivity as a self-fulfilling prophecy.* Lexington, MA: Lexington Books.

Eden, D. (1995, August). *From self-efficacy to means-efficacy: Internal and external sources of general and specific efficacy.* Paper submitted to the Academy of Management for the meeting in Cincinnati, OH.

Gist, M. E. (1987). Self-efficacy: Implications for organizational behavior and human resource management. *Academy of Management Review, 12*(3), 472–485.

Glickman, A. S., Zimmer, S., Montero, R. C., Guerette, P. J., Campbell, W. J., Morgan, B. B., Jr., & Salas, E. (1987). *The evolution of teamwork skills: An empirical assessment with implications for training.* (NTSC Technical Report No. 87-016). Orlando, FL: Naval Training Systems Center.

Goldstein, I. L. (1986). *Training in organizations: Needs assessment, development, and evaluation.* Pacific Grove, CA: Brooks/Cole.

Guttman, L. (1959). A structural theory for intergroup beliefs and action. *American Sociological Review, 24,* 318–328.

Guttman, L. (1968). A general nometric technique for finding the smallest coordinate space for a configuration of points. *Psychometrika, 33,* 461–469.

Guzzo, R. A. (1986). Group decision making and group effectiveness in organizations. In P. S. Goodman (Ed.), *Designing effective work groups* (pp. 34–71). San Francisco: Jossey-Bass.

Guzzo, R. A. (1995). Introduction: At the intersection of team effectiveness and decision making. In R. A. Guzzo, & E. Salas (Eds.), *Team effectiveness and decision making in organizations* (pp.1–8). San Francisco: Jossey-Bass.

Guzzo, R. A., & Berman, L. M. (1995). At what level of generality is psychological contract fulfillment best measured? Paper presented at the annual meeting of the Academy of Management, Vancouver, Canada.

Guzzo, R. A., Salas, E., & Associates. (1995). *Team effectiveness and decision making in organizations.* San Francisco: Jossey-Bass.

Guzzo, R. A., & Shea, G. P. (1992). Group performance and intergroup relations in organizations. In M. D. Dunnette, & L. M. Hough (Eds.), *Handbook of industrial and organizational psychology* (Vol. 3, pp. 269–313). Palo Alto, CA: Consulting Psychologists Press.

Guzzo, R. A., Yost, P. R., Campbell, R. J., & Shea, G. P. (1993). Potency in groups: Articulating a construct. *British Journal of Social Psychology, 32,* 87–106.

Hackman, J. R. (1987). The design of work teams. In J. W. Lorsch (Ed.), *Handbook of organizational behavior* (pp. 315–342). Englewood Cliffs, NJ: Prentice-Hall.

Hackman, J. R. (Ed.). (1990). *Groups that work (and those that don't): Creating conditions for effective teamwork.* San Francisco: Jossey-Bass.

Hackman, J. R., & Oldham, G. R. (1976). Motivation through the design of work: Test of a theory. *Organizational Behavior and Human Performance, 16,* 250–279.

Hackman, J. R., & Porter, L. W. (1968). Expectancy theory predictions of work effectiveness. *Organizational Behavior and Human Performance, 3,* 417–426.

Haire, M., Ghiselli, E. E., & Porter, L. W. (1966). *Managerial thinking: An international study.* New York: Wiley.

Hall, E. T. (1959). The silent language. Greenwich, CT: Fawcett.

Hall, E. T. (1976). *Beyond Culture.* New York: Doubleday.

Hofstede, G. (1980). *Culture's consequences: International differences in work-related values.* Beverly Hills, CA: Sage.

Hofstede, G. (1991). *Cultures and organizations: Software of the mind.* London: McGraw-Hill.

Hofstede, G. (1994). Foreword. In R. A. Guzzo, & E. Salas (Eds.), *Team effectiveness and decision making in organizations* (pp. 9–15). San Francisco: Jossey-Bass.

Hofstede, G., & Bond, M. M. (1984). Hofstede's cultural dimensions: An independent validation using Rokeach's value survey. *Journal of Cross-Cultural Psychology, 15,* 417–433.

Hui, C. H. (1988). Measurement of individualism–collectivism. *Journal of Research in Personality, 22,* 17–36.

Hui, C. H., & Triandis, H. C. (1986). Individualism–collectivism: A study of cross-cultural researchers. *Journal of Cross-Cultural Psychology, 17,* 225–248.

Ilgen, D. R., Major, D. A., Hollenbeck, J. R., & Sego, D. J. (1995). Raising an individual decision-making model to the team level: A new research model and paradigm. In R. A. Guzzo, & E. Salas (Eds.), *Team effectiveness and decision making in organizations* (pp. 113–148). San Francisco: Jossey-Bass.

Jackson, S. E., & Alvarez, E. B. (1992). Working through diversity as a strategic imperative. In S. E. Jackson and Associates (Eds.), *Diversity in the workplace: Human resources initiatives* (pp. 13–15). New York: Guilford Press.

Jackson, S. E., Brett, J. F., Sessa, V. I., Cooper, D. M., Julia, J. A., & Peyronnin, K. (1991). Some differences make a difference: Individual dissimilarity and group heterogeneity as correlates of recruitment, promotions, and turnover. *Journal of Applied Psychology, 76,* 675–689.

Janis, I. L. (1989). *Crucial decisions: Leadership in policy-making and management.* New York: Free Press.

Kahneman, D., & Tversky, A. (1973). On the psychology of prediction. *Psychology, 18,* 183–245.

Kalleberg, A. L. (1977). Work values and job rewards: A theory of job satisfaction. *American Sociological Review, 42,* 124–143.

Kanfer, R. (1991). Motivation theory and industrial and organizational psychology. In M. D. Dunnette, & L. M. Hough (Eds.), *Handbook of industrial and organizational psychology* (Vol. 1, pp. 75–170). Palo Alto, CA: Consulting Psychologists Press.

Katzell, R. A., & Thompson, D. E. (1990). Work motivation: Theory and practice. *American Psychologist, 45,* 144–153.

Kim, U. (1994). Individualism and collectivism: Conceptualism clarification and elaboration. In U. Kim, H. C. Triandis, & G. Yoon (Eds.), *Individualism and collectivism: Theoretical and methodological issues.* Newbury Park, CA: Sage, 19–41.

Kim, U., Triandis, H. C., Kagitcibasi, C., Choi, S. C., & Yoon, G. (1994). Introduction. In U. Kim, H. C. Triandis, & G. Yoon (Eds.), *Individualism and collectivism: Theoretical and methodological issues* (pp. 1–16). Newbury Park, CA: Sage.

Klein, K. J., Dansereau, F., & Hall, R. J. (1994). Levels, issues in theory development, data collections, and analysis. *Academy of Management Review, 19*(2), 195–229.

Klein, K. J., & House, R. J. (1995). On fire: Charismatic leadership and levels of analysis. *Leadership Quarterly, 6*(2), 183–198.

Kluckhohn, C. (1951). Values and value-orientations in the theory of action: An exploration in definition and classification. In T. Parsons, & E. Shils (Eds.), *Toward a general theory of action* (pp. 388–433). Cambridge, MA: Harvard University Press.

Kluckholn, C. (1961). The study of values. In D. N. Barrett (Ed.), *Values in transition.* Notre Dame, IN: University of Notre Dame Press.

Kraut, A.I., & Ronen, S. (1975). Validity of job facet importance: A multinational multicriteria study. *Journal of Applied Psychology, 60*(6), 671–677.

Lingoes, J. C. (1965). An IBM-7090 program for Guttman–Lingoes smallest space analysis. *Behavioral Science, 10,* 183–184.

Lingoes, J. C. (1977). Identifying regions in the space for interpretation. In J. C. Lingoes (Ed.), *Geometric representations of relation data.* Ann Arbor, MI: Mathesis Press.

Locke, E. A. (1975). Personnel attitudes and motivation. *Annual Review of Psychology, 26,* 457–480.

Locke, E. A. (1976). The nature and causes of job satisfaction. In M. D. Dunnette (Ed.), *Handbook of industrial and organizational psychology* (pp. 1297–1349). Chicago: Rand McNally.

March, J. G., & Simon, H. A. (1958). *Organizations.* New York: Wiley.

Maslow, A. H. (1954). *Motivation and personality.* New York: Harper & Row.

Maslow, A. H. (Ed.). (1959). *New knowledge in human values.* New York: Harper & Row.

McIntyre, R. M., & Salas, E. (1995). Measuring and managing for team performance: Lessons from a complex environment. In R. A. Guzzo, & E. Salas (Eds.), *Team effectiveness and decision making in organizations* (pp. 9–45). San Francisco: Jossey-Bass.

Morgan, B. B., Jr., Glickman, A. S., Woodard, E. A., Blaiwes, A., & Salas, E. (1986). *Measurement of team behaviors in a Navy environment* (NTSC Report No. 86-014). Orlando, FL: Naval Training Systems Center.

MOW. Meaning of Work International Research Team. (1987). *The meaning of work.* London: Academic Press.

Park, H. Y., Ofori-Dankawa, J., & Bishop, D. R. (1994). Organizational and environmental determinants of functional and dysfunctional turnover: Practical and research implications. *Human Relations, 47,* 353–366.

Pearce, J. A., & Ravlin, E. C. (1987). The design and activation of self-regulating work groups. *Human Relations, 40*(11), 751–782.

Porter, L. W., & Lawler, E. E. (1968). *Managerial attitudes and performance.* Homewood, IL: Irwin-Dorsey.

Poortinga, Y. H. (1989). Equivalence of cross-cultural data: An overview of basic issues. *International Journal of Psychology, 24,* 737–756.

Rokeach, M. (1973). *The nature of human values.* New York: Free Press.

Rokeach, M. (Ed.). (1979). *Understanding human values.* New York: Free Press.

Ronen, S. (1977). A comparison of job facet satisfaction between paid and unpaid industrial workers. *Journal of Applied Psychology, 62*(5), 582–588.

Ronen, S. (1978). Personal values: A basis for work motivational set and work attitudes. *Organizational Behavior and Human Performance, 21,* 80–107.

Ronen, S. (1979). Cross-national study of employees' work goals. *International Review of Applied Psychology, 28*(1), 1–12.

Ronen, S. (1986a). *Comparative and multinational management.* New York: Wiley.

Ronen, S. (1986b). Equity perceptions in multiple comparisons: A field study. *Human Relations, 39,* 333–346.

Ronen, S., & Barkan, S. (1985). *A multivariate approach to work values: A two facets analysis* [Working Paper]. Israel Research Institute, Tel Aviv University.

Ronen, S., & Kraut, A. I. (1977). Similarities among countries based on employee work values and attitudes. *Columbia Journal of World Business, 12*(2), 89–96.

Ronen, S., & Kraut, A. I. (1980). An experimental examination of work motivation taxonomies. *Human Relations, 33*(7), 565–516.

Ronen, S., Kraut, A. I., Lingoes, J. C., & Aranya, N. (1979). A nonmetric scaling approach to taxonomies of employees' work motivation. *Multivariate Behavioral Research, 14,* 387–401.

Ronen, S., & Punnett, B. J. (1982, Spring). Nation or culture: The appropriate unit of analysis in cross-cultural research. Paper presented at the Northeast Meeting of the Academy of International Business, NY.

Ronen, S., & Shenkar, O. (1985). Clustering countries on attitudinal dimensions: A review and synthesis. *Academy of Management Review, 10*(3), 435–454.

Ronen, S., & Shenkar, O. (1989). Clustering variables: The application of non-metric multivariate analysis techniques in comparative management [Special Issue: Strategic Management Research]. *International Studies of Management and Organization, 28*(3), 72–87.

Rousseau, D. M. (1995). Issues of level in organizational research: Multi-level and cross-level perspectives. In L. L. Cummings & B. M. Staw (Eds.), *Research in organizational behavior* (Vol. 7, pp. 1–37). Greenwich, CT: JAI Press.

Saavedra, R., Earley, P. C., & Van Dyne, L. (1993). Complex interdependence in task-performing groups. *Journal of Applied Psychology, 78,* 61–72.

Schwartz, S. H. (1990). Individualism–collectivism: Critique and proposed refinements. *Journal of Cross-Cultural Psychology, 21,* 139–157.

Schwartz, S. H. (1994). Beyond individualism/collectivism: New cultural dimensions of values. In U. Kim, H. C. Triandis, & G. Yoon (Eds.), *Individualism and collectivism: Theoretical and methodological issues.* Newbury Park, CA: Sage.

Schwartz, S. H., & Bilsky, W. (1987). Toward a universal psychological structure of human values. *Journal of Personality and Social Psychology, 53*(3), 550–562.

Schwartz, S. H., & Bilsky, W. (1990). Toward a theory of the universal content and structure of values: Extensions and cross-cultural replications. *Journal of Personality and Social Psychology, 58,* 878–891.

Shamir, B. (1990). Calculations, values, and identities: The sources of collective work motivation. *Human Relations, 43*(4), 313–332.

Shamir, B. (1991). The charismatic relationship: Alternative explanations and predictions. *Leadership Quarterly, 2*(2), 81–104.

Shamir, B., House, R. J., & Arthur, M. B. (1993). The motivational effects of charismatic leadership: A self-concept based theory. *Organizational Science, 4*(2), 1–17.

Shea, G. P., & Guzzo, R. A. (1987a). Group effectiveness: What really matters? *Sloan Management Review, 28,* 25–31.

Shea, G. P., & Guzzo, R. A. (1987b). Groups as human resources. In K.M. Rowland, & G. R. Ferris (Eds.), *Research in personnel and human resources* (Vol. 2, pp. 323–356). Greenwich, CT: JAI Press.

Shenkar, O., & Ronen, S. (1987a). The cultural context of negotiation: The implications of Chinese interpersonal norms. *Journal of Applied Behavioral Science, 23,* 163–275.

Shenkar, O., & Ronen, S. (1987b). The structure and importance of work goals among managers in the People's Republic of China. *Academy of Management Journal, 30*(3), 564–576.

Shenkar, O., & Ronen, S. (1990). Culture, ideology, or economy: A comparative exploration of work-goals importance among managers in Chinese societies. In S. B. Prasad (Ed.), *Advances in international comparative management* (Vol. 5, pp. 117–134). Greenwich, CT: JAI Press.

Sundstrom, E., DeMeuse, K. P., & Futrell, D. (1990). Work teams: Applications and effectiveness. *American Psychologist, 45,* 120–133.

Triandis, H. C. (1972). *The analysis of subjective culture.* New York: Wiley.

Triandis, H. C. (1975). Subjective culture and interpersonal behavior. In J. W. Berry, & W. J. Lonner (Eds.), *Applied Cross-Cultural Psychology.* Amsterdam: Swets and Zeitlinger.

Triandis, H. C. (1982–1983). Dimensions of cultural variations as parameters of organizational theories. *International Studies of Management and Organization, 12*(4), 139–169.

Triandis, H. C. (1985). Collectivism vs. individualism: A reconceptualization of a basic construct in cross-cultural psychology. In C. Bagley, & G. R. Vermal (Eds.), *Personality, cognition and value: Cross-cultural perspectives of childhood and adolescence.* London: McMillan.

Triandis, H. C. (1994). Theoretical and methodological approaches in the study of collectivism and individualism. In U. Kim, H. C. Triandis, & G. Yoon (Eds.), *Individualism and collectivism: Theoretical and methodological issues.* Newbury Park, CA: Sage.

Triandis, H. C., Leung, K., Villareal, M. V., & Clark, F. L. (1985). Allocentric versus idiocentric tendencies: Convergent and discriminant validation. *Journal of Research in Personality, 19,* 395–415.

Triandis, H. C., & Martin, G. (1983). Etic plus emic versus pseudo etic. *Journal of Cross-Cultural Psychology, 14*(4), 489–500.

Triandis, H. C., & Vassiliou, V. (1972). A comparative analysis of subjective cultures. In H. C. Triandis (Eds.), *The Analysis of Subjective Culture* (pp. 299–335). New York Wiley.

Tversky, A., & Kahneman, D. (1974). Judgments under uncertainty: Heuristics and biases. *Science, 185,* 1124–1131.

Vroom, V. H. (1964). *Work and motivation.* New York: Wiley.

Wiggins, J. S. (1979). A psychological taxonomy of trait-descriptive terms: The interpersonal domain. *Journal of Personality and Social Psychology, 37,* 395–412.

Yammarino, F. J., & Dubinsky, A. J. (1994). Transformational leadership theory: Using levels of analysis to determine boundary conditions. *Personnel Psychology, 47,* 787–811.

Yammarino, F. J., & Bass, B. M. (1990). Transformational leadership and multiple levels of analysis. *Human Relations, 43,* 975–995.

24

Understanding Social Motivation From an Interpersonal Perspective: Organizational Face Theory

P. Christopher Earley
Indiana University, Bloomington

A fundamental aspect of human activity is that we interact in a given social context for a variety of symbolic, utilitarian, and pragmatic purposes (Etzioni, 1968). Critical in this context of interaction is the way that we present ourselves and how others judge our actions and self-worth. Self-worth and impression conveyed are at the heart of the concept of face. Face refers to a universal aspect of interaction concerning how we present ourselves to others as well as how they perceive us. Within an organizational context, face regulates social exchange and individual action, and it varies systematically according to individual differences as well as societal value orientations (Redding & Ng, 1982; Ting-Toomey & Cocroft, 1994).

In this chapter, I draw from my work on Organizational Face Theory (Earley, 1997), and I present a model of face and culture in which I describe two general categories of face, *lian* and *mianzi*, and describe their relations to the social exchange practices observed in various societies. Next, these two aspects of face are explored using two key aspects of cultural variation, individualism and power distance, in order to better understand face across cultural boundaries.

DEFINITION OF FACE

A person's face has both internal and external sources that are evidenced, directly and implicitly, in social settings. The internal component refers to an inner voice or reflection, much like a person's conscience, and the external component refers to an attributed aspect of a person's self-presentation. For example, an employee who steals company materials supplies information to both his conscience as well as to potential observers. From Goffman's (1959) perspective, a critical external aspect of face is the symbolic nature of a person's actions within a given social context. Thus, an employee may lose face in a company having high moral standards of conduct, but he may not lose face in a company for which such actions are ignored or reinforced by peers. Face, then, captures those aspects of self externally presented to one's peers and community as well as those aspects of self assessed by internal standards shaped by important referent others. In this sense, I define *face* as *the evaluation of self based on internal and external (to the individual) judgments concerning a person's adherence to moral rules of conduct and position within a given social structure* (Earley, 1997). This definition captures two general facets of self, namely, assessments of moral conduct and position in a social setting. Further, it posits that these facets are based on judgments of self and others in combination. Thus, face is not simply a product of self-perceptions, nor is it a result of external evaluators' perceptions alone.

Face has several defining characteristics. First, it represents the evaluated aspects of self, as defined by society and internalized by an individual, self-perceived and projected toward others. The internalized standards of society concerning moral conduct are referred to by Hu (1944) as *lian*, and the status and prestige a person holds is *mianzi* (both using the Chinese words for *face*). Second, it has both internal and external bases. Face captures the positive and negative aspects of self with the assumption that a person's self-perceptions are dominated by positive characteristics that may only correspond weakly with others' perceptions of those characteristics. Third, face results from rules of moral conduct and righteousness as well as status or position in a social structure.

General Categories of Face

As I mentioned, face consists of two general parts. First, there is a distinction between face tied to rules of conduct versus face as position in a social hierarchy. Second, there is the source of these perceptions, namely, internally—versus externally—referenced. In addition, there is a distinction among qualitatively different forms of face. I discuss a two-factor categorization of face. According to this typology, two dimensions and two referent sources of face can be combined to form four general groups of face characteristics. The first dimension refers to the type of face under discussion, namely, *lian* versus *mianzi*. The basic logic of this distinction stems from the linguistic guidance provided by Hu (1944), among others, but my use of these constructs differs from the existing literature. Whereas the existing discussions of *lian* and *mianzi* treat the constructs as a judgment of self from external sources (e.g., Hu, 1944) or overlapping versions of self as derived from a social interaction (e.g., Ho, 1976), I define *lian* as a product of one's behavior as compared with a set of rules for moral conduct, and *mianzi* as an person's position within a social structure. In this general sense, *lian* is a resultant of a person's "correct" behavior (and values/beliefs/norms underlying those behaviors) whereas *mianzi* reflects an outcome state of social interaction. Both *lian* and *mianzi* are a product of self and external evaluations. *Lian* reflects the legitimacy that an individual has within a given society. Lacking regard for *lian*, a person is viewed as a sociopath, or outsider. Mianzi refers to face as a person's characteristic reflecting his standing in a social hierarchy, such as position, status, or role. A CEO of a large multinational corporation has much *mianzi*, whereas an administrative clerk has relatively little. Likewise, an employee who is relied on by others as the "local expert" for computer networking information has *mianzi* attributable to her knowledge. Power and *mianzi*, however, should not be confused. Whereas power is the capacity to influence the actions of others, *mianzi* refers to the evaluations of a person's position in a hierarchy relative to others.

To some extent, *lian* and *mianzi* are interdependent constructs. For example, a subordinate who gives his superior proper respect (*mianzi*) at a business meeting with new clients will receive both *mianzi* and *lian*. He reaffirms his lian by adhering to the social expectations of paying respect to his superior, and this enhances the superior's *mianzi* in front of the new clients. At the same time, he receives status from the respected superior, who acknowledges the respectful act and gains *mianzi*.

As I suggested, if one were to posit the primary versus secondary sources of face, the general origins of each would depend largely on the societal context in which face is operating. I will return to this point in more detail later but, ceteris paribus, *lian* is most directly derived through internal sources, whereas *mianzi* is derived from external sources. Why is this? *Lian* reflects the rules of conduct for behavior that are taught through early socialization experiences in childhood, school, and other stages. It forms the basis for normal interaction within society, and it is ingrained into each person at a very early age. These rules are relatively fundamental to functioning in a society (e.g., Thou shalt not commit adultery), and they guide behavior in a general fashion. These are general rules for behavior that generalize across settings and time. Just as we are taught as children not to steal from our parents, we endorse rules that punish those who steal as adults in their company. These rules of conduct reflect deeply embedded values of a society that do not easily change within a single generation (Hofstede, 1980).

Mianzi, in contrast, is transient in many ways. Not only does a person's *mianzi* increase or decrease with various social encounters, what constitutes a basis for *mianzi* changes as well. For example, prior to the 1970s, an expatriate assignment often reflected poorly on an employee suggesting that she would "never be heard from again" and that she had been sidetracked by her company. More recently, such assignments have become highly desirable in American multinational companies, reflecting the grooming process whereby a manager is prepared for executive levels in a company. Clearly, the *mianzi* gained or lost attributable to an expatriate work assignment has changed in the last 20 years. Actions and outcomes associated with *mianzi* can be highly transient as well. For instance, the proper style of dress, car to drive, bars to frequent, and other behaviors denote who is "in" or "out" each season in some social circles.

This discussion reflects a difference between *lian* and *mianzi*. Lian reflects an adherence to *rules of conduct* within a social structure whereas *mianzi* reflects possession of resources that *position oneself* within that structure. Both types of face are derived from an interaction of self and other perceptions and social behavior.

Sources of Face

The second dimension concerning face refers to the locus from which it is derived. Face is derived from both internal and external (to the person) sources. That is to say, face reflects an interaction of self and others' perceptions and attributions. There are at least two useful ways to address the nature of person perception as it relates to face. First, the content of person perception can be discussed from a cross-cultural viewpoint. That is to say, What characteristic(s) are used by people as a basis for their personal and social perceptions? Just as researchers have sought to define the general nature of values and beliefs that underlie social culture (e.g., Kluckhohn & Strodtbeck, 1961), others have focused on the constituent elements of person schema and perception (e.g., Bond & Forgas, 1984). Second, the source of these perceptions constitutes an additional element of social perception of face. I employ a basic dichotomy in characterizing referent source, namely, internal versus external.

An internal referent reflects a person's own intrinsic system for evaluating face. For instance, an employee working for a prestigious company may derive *mianzi* from knowing that she works for a famous company. This form of *mianzi* is not dependent on others' social constructions concerning of the company, even though it can be influenced by it. *Lian* also can be derived internally. A person who commits an immoral act (loses *lian*) does not need an external referent to witness the deed in order to experience guilt. A great deal of social behavior in a collectivist society such as China relies on such internalized regulation of moral behavior (Redding & Ng, 1981). In fact, citizenship behavior is generally predicated on the assumption that behavior is voluntary, not contingent upon reward, and regulated internally. *Lian* is most directly tied to internal referents. A person's perceptions of his adherence to society's rules of conduct is often a very personal and internal aspect of social behavior.

Mianzi is most directly affected by the actions and reactions of others. An employee who gets a promotion, a company car, key to the executive washroom, and other benefits will likely gain *mianzi* from her peers. The respect that a senior executive receives from her junior managers signals a bolstering of *mianzi*. Behavior in an organizational context reflects the giving and exchanging of *mianzi* in a dynamic fashion. During important negotiations over a joint venture, the decision of who attends the negotiations, where the negotiations are held, and who sets the agenda all reflect the relative status of the parties.

Lian can be derived from external sources as well. In a typical American organization, an employee who continually engages in sexual misconduct (e.g., harassment of women coworkers) will be labeled as lewd, perverted, and/or immoral. A moral judgment has been made concerning his conduct by others, and his *lian* reflects such conclusions. Work colleagues will treat him with suspicion or disdain, and his subsequent actions will be influenced by their reactions.

Face is not merely the by-product, or perception and attribution, of observers, as argued by several researchers in the communications field (e.g., Ho, 1976; Ting-Toomey & Cocroft, 1994); it is both personal possession and interactional property. Indeed, it is the interactional aspect that gives rise to an individual's self-conception of face. I view the sources of face as reciprocally interdependent. Just as a person's self-perceptions of face will influence her actions in the midst of others, a social context will impact her self-perceptions. (Admittedly, the congruence of self and other perceptions may differ; see Bond, 1991; Yik & Bond, 1993).

Clearly, there is face associated with status and position quite separate from observers, although it may have been shaped by them at an earlier point in time, and this face can be lost or gained by an individual who occupies that position or who has legitimate power. To the institutionalist (e.g., Scott, 1994), this face is derived from the institutional rules surrounding a particular role occupied by the person. Constitutive rules are especially relevant to the nature of face derived from the role an individual occupies and my discussion. It is the constitutive rules that determine the nature of an actor's authority and power within a given institutional structure; such authority is independent of the other actors' observations.

FACE REGULATION IN SOCIETY

The importance of social context is evident because a person's face varies as a function of a particular setting. In some instances, an employee has much face, whereas in other circumstances she has little face. However, this variability is primarily in reference to *mianzi* rather than *lian*. As described earlier, *lian* is primarily an internally derived aspect of face, and so it is much less malleable due to the social setting. Returning to the employee theft example, the extent to which honesty is an internalized aspect of a person's value system will determine the impact of such an action on *lian*. In other words, the impact of theft on a person's *lian* occurs even if fellow employees endorse such an action. What suffers from the theft, as a social phenomenon, is *mianzi*. An employee not only loses personal status, he may weaken the bond between himself and others. However, if the employee has not internalized a strong value of honesty or has encoded that employee theft is not a dishonest practice, then he will not lose *lian*. This is tempered somewhat by the external aspect of *lian*. Recall that lian has an interpersonal aspect as well as the internalized referent. In this case, the employee's lian may be reduced through subsequent feedback that he receives from important social others (friends).

In trying to map out culture's influence on face, a large number of levels must be crossed. Ultimately, interpersonal behaviors related to face regulation are tied to cultural context (e.g., values, beliefs, norms) through the forms of exchange endorsed within a given culture, organizational and institutional practices, political system, and other structures. In describing and predicting interpersonal motivations within a given society, institution, organization, and work group, an important "translation" mechanism; that is to say, a way of mapping the effects of culture and society on individual-level behavior refers to the social exchange practices operating in a given society and organization context.

Although there are a number of models describing social exchange practices in societies, a recent formulation by Fiske (1991) provides an interesting perspective on exchange in social interaction. Fiske identified four basic forms of social behavior, arguing that these are universal aspects of social exchange. The first form, *communal sharing*, refers to the behavior observed in a family context. Resources in such a circumstance are shared according to need, and people monitor their consumption of community resources themselves. The second form is *authority ranking*, and it refers to resource allocations based on status differentials. For example, in traditional Chinese society, the eldest son receives command over the family's resources after the death of a father. In nearly all organizations, the CEO receives more attention and respect than a shop-floor employee. The third form is *equality matching*, which refers to a distribution of resources based on an equality principle. In other words, each person (by virtue of their humanity) is equally deserving of a comparable share of resources as each other person in a community. In this form of exchange, there is an emphasis on reciprocity and fairness, and it is characteristic of Western systems of justice. Further, exchanges are made on a relatively comparable basis such that resources exchanged are similar (e.g., friendship is traded for friendship). Finally, the fourth form is *market pricing*, which refers to an equity-based distribution of resources using general market principles. In this case, if someone spends twice as long working in a company, she should receive twice as much in terms of reward.

According to Fiske, social behavior is based on these four universal resource exchange principles, but the specific form generally endorsed varies within and across societies. As a result, a common institution such as marriage occurs as an etic, but its underlying impetus may differ. For example, in certain cultures people may marry for love (e.g., communal sharing), but in other cultures they may marry for position and status (e.g., authority ranking; Triandis & Bhawuk, 1997). An important aspect of Fiske's argument is that all four principles exist within each society but that they vary in relative magnitude of importance as well as specific manifestation. Thus, market pricing may be very important in the United States, but less so in Sweden. Furthermore, in the United States it may manifest itself as individual achievement over others in a business context (e.g., the corporate "rat race") but as a social achievement in Sweden (e.g., individual achievement in an environmental cause). However, it is present in both countries. A useful aspect of Fiske's analysis and model is that these four exchange principles are acting in a quasi-independent fashion within any given culture. This suggests that social relationships may be governed by principles that are, at times, complementary, independent, or even conflicting.

I adapt the four forms of social exchange described by Fiske and map them on a grid composed of two general, cultural orientations—individualism and power distance—along with their hypothesized relation to *lian* and *mianzi*. Briefly, individualism refers to a cultural orientation concerning the role of self in relation to others (Erez & Earley, 1993). People from an individualistic culture place a strong emphasis on their personal needs and goals over those of others around them, and they rely on internal cues and references for the judgments they make in life. In contrast, collectivists place an emphasis on in-group (e.g., family) needs and goals over their own, and they rely on cues and references from in-group members for the judgments they make in life. Power distance refers to the hierarchical nature of a society and a distribution of power across social strata. Hofstede (1980) defined power distance as the acceptability within a society of more powerful members being able to influence the actions and outcomes of those less powerful. In a high-power-distance culture, it is acceptable for powerful people to influence those who are less powerful—acceptable from both parties' perspectives.

My focus on these two cultural dimensions is based on a number of considerations. First, these two dimensions capture a great deal of variance in social behavior within organizations (Hofstede, 1980) and a great deal of research has been conducted on them.

Second, these dimensions are core to organizational functioning (Triandis & Bhawuk, 1997). Although I present just two cultural dimensions in Fig. 24.1, the logic of my analysis can be applied to other clusters of cultural dimensions. Before discussing the specifics of the figure, some clarification of my nomenclature is in order. Specifically, I adopt two conventions in representing the relative strength of *lian* and *mianzi* in a given quadrant. First, face, represented by uppercase characters denotes relative importance in a given society. For instance, in the upper right quadrant, mianzi is represented as "MIANZI," meaning that it is salient in this quadrant, and *lian* is represented as "lian," meaning that it is relatively less salient. Second, the types of face are presented in relative order of importance. For instance, in the lower right quadrant, *mianzi* is listed before *lian*, suggesting its relative

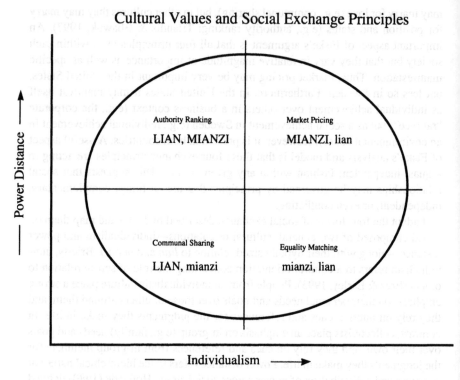

Cultural Values and Social Exchange Principles

Power Distance →

Authority Ranking	Market Pricing
LIAN, MIANZI	MIANZI, lian
Communal Sharing	Equality Matching
LIAN, mianzi	mianzi, lian

Individualism →

FIG. 24.1. Cultural values and social exchange.

importance. Note, however, that in this quadrant both constructs are represented in lowercase, suggesting that they are relatively less salient than for a society in the upper left quadrant. Although I propose relative differences in salience, this does not suggest that face does exist in a given quadrant. Additionally, a society with *lian* in uppercase versus one with *lian* in lowercase does not imply that the former is higher in moral character than the latter. This simply suggests that *lian* is relatively more salient to people within the culture.

The significance of these forms of social ties or interdependencies to face lies in the nature of how face is maintained, gained, or lost. *Mianzi* can be traded or exchanged, analogous to a physical product in a variety of interdependence structures. Although *mianzi* can be exchanged in any of the four models, it is most heavily emphasized in an authority-ranking or market-pricing context because it can provide individuals with desired material or status gains.

Lian is most likely the relevant domain of authority ranking and communal exchanges. Why is this? In exchanges among strangers, the only rules needed to be endorsed are those that impact and regulate exchange. Questions of moral character are minimized through an emphasis and dependence on rules of exchange (e.g., equity or reciprocity), and the market becomes a surrogate for moral character (Fiske, 1991; Wilson, 1993). In such a case, the rules of exchange are the defining characteristics of social goodness, and *lian* becomes less critical to successful exchange (except for those instances in which people not having *lian* are not trusted to follow the market rules). However, given the relative stability of authority ranking and communal exchanges, a question of lian becomes of tantamount importance. There are at least two reasons for this: First, people in these exchanges are concerned with maintaining and promoting this relationship as an end rather than for personal gain. Second, individuals in authority ranking and communal exchanges are most highly concerned with the moral character of their compatriots because a violation of moral principles threatens the existence and stability of the collective. An authority ranking exchange and communal form is regulated through personal integrity and devotion to the good of the relationship. The success of the family depends on maintenance of the relationship itself.

In a market-pricing relationship people designate value in a single universal metric, typically price (or "utility"), by which they can compare any two persons or associated commodities. In a market relationship, individuals seek to influence others through various means, and although some trust and mutual support exists, individuals do not view the relationship itself as an end. People share common characteristics (e.g., come from the same town or region) and some common goals, but each person views himself as the central point of an interaction.

Finally, an equality matching form of social exchange represents an exchange in-kind. Each person (by virtue of their humanity) is deserving of a comparable share of resources, but members do not necessarily form long-term bonds or ties. In this form of exchange there is an emphasis on reciprocity and fairness, and it is characteristic of Western systems of justice. Exchanges reinforce existing relationships, and they are enjoyed to this end.

The importance of these exchanges becomes increasingly important as a cultural context is imposed on the model of face. In Fig. 24.1, the dominant forms of exchange found in an individualistic culture are market, pricing and equality matching, whereas the dominant forms of a collectivistic culture are authority ranking and communal sharing. The reason for this polarization is that the strong focus on individual freedom and achievement stressed in an individualistic culture is best demonstrated in market forms of relationships (Triandis & Bhawuk, 1997). In these relationships, people are able to maximize their personal gains through effort and work, and enhance their *mianzi*. For collectivists, the relationship is an important outcome because people identify with their in-group and not as autonomous actors. Thus, *lian* becomes critical given the high degree of trust that is placed in one another (e.g., given that gifts cannot be immediately reciprocated, it is essential that in-group members trust that one another will contribute fairly to group success and responsibilities).

The dominate form of relationship in a high-power-distance culture is that of authority ranking and market pricing relying on *mianzi* and, to a lessor extent, *lian*.

EARLEY

In this form of exchange, a social hierarchy is maintained by the extent to which participants acknowledge and reinforce status differentials among members. For instance, in an organization from a high-power-distance culture, a CEO's position is reinforced through a large office, fancy car, private secretary, company jet, and other benefits. These physical manifestations of *mianzi* emphasize to all members of the company that the CEO is powerful and in charge of things. Additionally, there is likely to be an important contribution of *lian* in a high-power-distance culture in as much as charismatic leaders must show significant, personal integrity in order to be effective. In contrast, an organization in a low-power-distance culture emphasizes equality and social memberships over personal gain and differentiation. Given that status and material differentials are less significant in this type of society, an effective CEO is denoted by someone who garners the personal respect of organizational members as having a strong moral character and vision (emphasis on *lian*).

SUMMARY

In this paper I have outlined a number of aspects of social motives based on a general construct of self-presentation and evaluation, namely, face. There are two general forms of face, *lian* and *mianzi*, and they are derived from both internal as well as external sources. *Lian* refers to a general attachment formed by individual to society based on an endorsement and enactment of social norms and morals. After this attachment is affirmed, a key aspect of face becomes that of *mianzi*, or social status. *Mianzi* reflects a person's position in a social hierarchy based on a variety of characteristics such as work position held, education, wealth and possessions, and family heritage. Mianzi can be given to others as well as possessed by a given individual, and it operates as a social exchange currency.

Additionally, this paper has focused on the translation mechanism of social exchange as a means of predicting the impact of cultural orientation on face. Four facets of social exchange described by Fiske (1991), were used as a means of mapping out the influence of cultural context (individualism and power distance) on face-related behavior. My argument is that the meso-level effect of social exchange practices provides a means of connecting culture to individual-level behavior.

REFERENCES

Bond, M. H. (1991). Cultural influences on modes of impression management: Implications for culturally diverse organizations. In R. A. Giacalone & P. Rosenfeld (Eds.), *Applied impression management: How image-making affects managerial decisions.* Newbury Park, CA: Sage Publications.
Bond, M. H. (1994). Trait theory and cross-cultural studies of person perception. *Psychological Inquiry,* 5, 114–117.

Bond, M. H., & Forgas, J. P. (1984). Linking person perception to behavioral intention across cultures: The role of cultural collectivism. *Journal of Cross-cultural Psychology, 15*, 337–352.

Brown, P. & Levinson, S. (1978). Universals in language use. In E. N. Goody (Ed.), *Questions and Politeness* (56–289). Cambridge, England: Cambridge University Press.

Earley, P. C. (1997). *Face, harmony, and social structure: An analysis of organizational behavior across cultures*. New York: Oxford University Press.

Erez, M. & Earley, P. C. (1993). *Culture, self-identity, and work*. New York: Oxford University Press.

Etzioni, A. (1968). *The active society*. New York: Free Press.

Fiske, A. (1991). *The four structures of social life*. New York: Bantam Books.

Goffman, E. (1959). *The presentation of self in everyday life*. Garden City N. J.: Doubleday.

Ho, D. Y-F. (1976). On the concept of face. *American Journal of Sociology, 81*, 867–884.

Hofstede, G. (1980). *Culture's consequences: International differences in work related values*. Newbury Park, CA: Sage.

Hu, H. C. (1944). The Chinese concepts of 'face'. *American Anthropologist, 46* (January–March), 45–64.

Hwang, K. (1987). Face and favor: The Chinese power game. *American Journal of Sociology, 92*, 944–974.

Kluckhohn, F. Strodtbeck, F. (1961). *Variations in value orientation*. Westport, CT: Greenwood Press.

Lim, T. (1994). Facework and interpersonal relationships. In S. Ting-Toomey (Ed.), *The challenge of facework* (pp. 209–230). Albany: State University of New York Press.

Markus, H. & Kitayama, S. (1991). Culture and the self: Implications for cognition, emotion, and motivation. *Psychological Review, 98*, 224–253.

Redding, S. G. & Ng, M. (1981). The role of face in the organizational perceptions of Chinese managers. *Organization Studies, 3*(3), 201–219.

Scott, W. R. (1994). Institutions and organizations: Toward a theoretical synthesis. In W. R. Scott & J. W. Meyer (Eds.), *Institutional environments and organizations* (pp. 55–80). Thousand Oaks, CA: Sage Publications.

Ting-Toomey, S. (1988). A face negotiation theory. In Y. Kim and W. Gudykunst (Eds.), *Theory and intercultural communication*. Newbury Park, CA: Sage.

Ting-Toomey, S. & Cocroft, B.-A. (1994). Face and facework: Theoretical and research issues. In S. Ting-Toomey (Ed.), *The challenge of facework* (pp. 307–340). Albany: State University of New York Press.

Triandis, H. C. (1989). The self and social behavior differing cultural contexts. *Psychological Review, 96*, 506–520.

Triandis, H. C., & Bhawuk, D. P. S. (1997). Culture theory and the meaning of relatedness. In P. C. Earley & M. Erez (Eds.), *New perspectives on international industrial/organizational psychology*. San Francisco: Jossey-Bass.

Wilson, J. Q. (1993). *The Moral Sense*. New York: Free Press.

Yik, M. S. M., & Bond, M. H. (1993). Exploring the dimensions of Chinese person perception with indigenous and imported constructs: Creating a culturally balanced scale. *International Journal of Psychology, 28*, 75–95.

25

An Evolutionary Perspective on Change and Stability in Personality, Culture, and Organization

Nigel Nicholson

London Business School, Centre for Organizational Research, England

THE EVOLUTIONARY IMPERATIVE

Biological approaches to human behavior got themselves a bad name from the excesses of naked ape and territorial-imperative theorising in the 1960s. Since then, palaeontology and genetics have made major advances in our understanding of the mechanisms of evolution, while neuropsychology and biological sciences have been rapidly expanding knowledge of human functioning. Parallel to these developments, evolutionary psychology has emerged as a substantially new field (Barkow, Cosmides, & Tooby, 1992 Crawford & Krebs, 1998) seeking to escape the taints of its populist forebears by serious scholarship into the functionality of human behavior and, by implication, the subject of this paper, the processes and constraints on human action.

The core idea is that human psychological functioning is built on a common genetic platform whose design is adapted to our origins. These origins are those of the ancestral environments of hunter-gatherers (Wright, 1994). Although still the subject of new discovery and debate, it is generally accepted that these stretch back some four million years to our bipedal hunter-gatherer ancestors, with modern man, *Homo sapiens sapiens*, emerging around a quarter of a million years ago. From this

382 NICHOLSON

lineage, it was a mere 10,000 years ago that we walked out of the Eden of hunter-gathering to till the soil and build the agrarian communities on which our modern institutional life is founded (Cohen & Armelagos, 1991). There is no evidence that this was caused by any genetic change in our constitutions, though the evolution of language was clearly an essential precursor (Diamond, 1991). A key point here is that the innovation of language took place in the context of our hunter-gatherer existence, which it adaptively served (Dunbar, 1996). The process of speciation, it is now generally accepted, is dominated by stasis—species do not evolve in their own lifetime, apart from minor genetic drift (Eldredge, 1995). Species faced with radical environmental change are most likely to face extinction or survive by habitat tracking, i.e., successfully locating new environments congruent with their gifts. Continuous evolutionary change via adaptive mutations to catch up with environmental change is the most improbable outcome due to the norming effect of population genetics in established species (most mutations are harmful). Rapid evolution through adaptive mutation tends only to occur when small interbreeding subpopulations become reproductively separated from the parent population, as seems to have occurred with the origin of the human species in Africa.

The genetic result in humans is a very tightly specified profile of species identity (Wills, 1995), which has barely altered since the time of our origination. The astonishing changes we have undergone in our very recent past, i.e., the last 10,000 years, are of two kinds. One is the selection adaptations of the human species through recombination of genes in the current pool, which creates the genetic drift that results in subgroup differences (e.g., in pigmentation and physiognomy). The other is what has been called "exaptation" (Gould & Vrba, 1982), the utilization of capabilities for purposes other than those for which they evolved, e.g., our manual dexterity for picking berries turns out to be useful for making stone axes, embroidery, and word processing.

Language, of all our gifts, is perhaps most creatively subject to this process. And it is on language that many modern motivational theories rest—the manipulation of meanings and symbols to create new sets of social arrangements and adjustments. Our power to do this is astonishingly varied, and it is entirely understandable that we tend to believe that our god-like powers of conceptual dexterity confer on us an ability to create whatever motivational arrangements we choose. It is true that through symbol manipulation we are capable of believing almost anything about ourselves and our situations, and certainly this is an enormous source of power on the principle of the dictum that what is perceived as real is real in its consequences. But that does not make perceptions real in substance, and from time to time we are puzzled and dismayed when confronted by our own primitivism, as has been recorded daily in news reports of recent years from Bosnia, Rwanda, Chechnya, and the like, or when we witness the special peculiarity of our own "irrational" impulses, emotions, and desires. The point here is that language is a tool, used to serve our purposes in our current environment, and it is our purposes that are the source of the limits of change.

The crux of the evolutionary-psychology argument is that human purposes have at root a genetically based structure, adapted to our ancestral environment (see Nicholson, 1997b, for an analysis of these). Because we uniquely have the power to socially construct our own environments, we run up against the limits to change and dysfunctional outcomes when we attempt to inhabit environments that violate the principles of human nature. What we actually do, as Tooby and Cosmides (1992) have pointed out, is construct environments with design features and processes that bear the imprint of our persistent ancient goals, or else we subvert incongruent environments so they can give expression to our impulses and wants.

A SELECTIONIST VIEW OF PERSONALITY, GROUPS, AND CULTURE

Table 25.1 provides some starting points at three levels: individual psychology, collective living, and culture. The left column illustrates some structural universals at these three levels; the right column some core processes that mediate their appearance and impact. This is not akin to a nature–nurture division, a dichotomy that evolutionary psychology rejects. The processes are as much a part our nature as the structures and purposes they are designed to serve.

The debate about the structure and process of personality is by no means resolved, but there is an emerging consensus around three propositions. First is the

TABLE 25.1
Structure and Process in Personality, Organization, and Culture

	Structure	*Process*
Personality	Emotionality	Self-esteem
	Sociality	Self-efficacy
	Curiosity	Consistency
	Nurturance	
	Order	
Organization	Hierarchy	Values
	Functions	Norms
	Systems	Self-image
	Diversity	Community
Culture	Kinship	Worldview
	Stratification	Exchange
	Resource-based Power	Meaning

idea that human dispositions exhibit five main dimensions, the so-called Big Five factor model (Digman, 1990). Each has clear evolutionary functionality (Buss, 1991): emotionality (or Neuroticism in some measures) as the radar necessary for social adjustment, sociality (or Surgency) as the drive towards group living, curiosity (or Openness to Experience) as an essential need for physically weak organisms to explore and adapt to varied environmental conditions, nurturance (or Agreeableness) for bonding and reciprocal altruism, and order (or Conscientiousness) to strive to regulate and dominate complex and changing circumstances. The fact that individuals vary in the strength or weakness of these drives is a sign that there is and has been no consistent selective environmental pressure to favor one profile over another, and, indeed, that there are advantages in being different from others, serving the purposes of assortative mating and complementary functioning in social exchange.

Second, evidence is mounting from genetic investigations and twin studies that there is a strong genetically inherited component to individual personality profiles (Bates & Wachs, 1994; Bouchard, 1997). This probably applies more clearly to some dimensions (e.g., Surgency) than others, where the neonatal environment may also be an early determinant. This is an area where rapid advances in knowledge can be expected in coming years.

Third, whether inborn or shaped by early experience, by late adolescence the profile has achieved a high degree of stability. Longitudinal studies show that the basic structure remains intact for most people over adulthood (Alwin, 1994). However, it is also true that for a sizeable minority, possibly up to 30% of people, personality does change over adulthood. Why and how this occurs is little understood, though it seems that radical change that entails prolonged exposure to new experiences (migration, bereavements, major life transitions) are likely to be significant agents (Kohn & Schooler, 1983). Yet it is also true that many people experience such changes without them altering their core profiles as much as their self-concepts.

What does change more continually, and is highly instrumental in our orientation to relationships, tasks, and environments, is our idea of ourselves: self-identity. The distinction between personality as an inborn set of temperamental propensities, and self-identity as a set of socially and linguistically mediated frames for interpreting one's place in the world, is important (Nicholson, 1996). Unlike trait theory, which seeks parsimony in explanatory concepts, identity theory is properly concerned with exploring the variety of ways in which individuals are stimulated to conceive of themselves. Erez and Earley (1993) have identified three important ways in which self-identity concepts function: self-esteem (belief in one's own worth, attractiveness, etc.), self-efficacy (belief in one's own goal-achievement capacities), and self-consistency (integrity and harmony of perceived elements of the self).

However, the foregoing analysis suggests there are limits to the range of self-conceptions individuals may entertain. The genetically anchored structure of personality can be conceived as a set of primary goals (Cropanzano, James, & Citera, 1993) from which a range of possible selves may be derived and environmentally tuned (Yost, Strube, & Bailey, 1992). Subidentities, motives, and behavior patterns are developed as compromises between the structures of temperament and the demands of local environments. This model would be falsified if, for example, adopted social identity were able to modify trait structure. Although he claims to argue from an evolutionary perspective, Sulloway's (1996) argument that birth order fundamentally shapes personality advances just such a proposition. Analyses from the author's personality data bank disconfirm the birth order hypothesis (Nicholson, 1997b). The core structures of personality are immune to these influences and much more evidently linked to biogenetic themes, such as gender. It seems likely that the birth order effects that Sulloway notes are the enacted strategies of children in the family environment before they find the postfamilial freedom to realize and act out their own uniqueness. In adult life these effects represent more malleable social values than personality traits.

The implications of this perspective for work motivation theory are threefold. First, it suggests that there are limits in general as to the range of stimuli that will motivate individuals. Second, the stability of individual differences in dispositions means that within this range outcomes that will motivate are nonequivalent in their relevance and impact, e.g., a given kind of payment system will motivate members of a workforce unevenly (see Thierry, Chap. 10, this volume). Third, it suggests that the process mechanisms of motivation management, such as feedback and resources, can achieve maximum impact if they assist the retuning of self-identity toward root structures.

The evolutionary perspective gives unequivocal primacy to individual psychology, albeit within the frame of our identity as profoundly social animals. All social forms are adapted expressions and outcomes of how individuals strive to protect and promote the transmission of their genes to subsequent generations (Dennett, 1995). So when we look at the structures of organizations and cultures, as illustrated in the left column of Table 25.1, we are identifying features of human societies created by human agency (Staw, 1991). These have been repeatedly found in anthropological investigations and remain universal in industrialized society as forms that promote control and order, which maximize adaptive diversity.

Hierarchical stratification, functional division of labor, kinship and quasi-kinship groupings, systems, and resource-based power are all socially evolved means to promote assortative sexual selection, role differentiation, and cooperative living, and are universal features of every enduring social form (Murdock, 1945; Foley, 1987). However, it is also clear that some societies work better than others in terms of the fulfilment they bestow upon their members and in what they are able to achieve collectively. This is largely through the process mechanisms of transacted meanings and identities listed on the right of Table 25.1, which evolve socially to satisfy structural imperatives. The anthropologist Sperber (1996) has argued along similar lines for an epidemiology of meaning founded on materialist and naturalistic premises. Meanings take hold and spread through social networks to the degree that they achieve the same sort of successful compromise between our nature and our environment, as I have argued for self-identity concepts.

This spells failure for attempts, as in the case of the great communist experiment, to engineer norms of exchange, community, belief, and value through ideology and institutional design that run up hard against persistent dispositions of the society's members to follow more ancient impulses (self-interest, primary group identification, and informal exchange relations). The triumph of the liberal market political economy is not the right answer to the problem of how to create societies that are consistent with human nature—we are still very far removed from our ancestral social order—but within it we may analyze the functions and dysfunctions of the many experiments in group living (e.g., subcultures, economies, organisations) we have created in terms of the reconciliations they are able to achieve with our inherited human nature. Archaeological and anthropological evidence about the kind of social system in which we attained our adapted natures conveys an image quite unlike the modern state in most of its forms. Our hunter-gatherer society would have been marked by status differentiation and sexual division of labor, but with extreme fluidity of roles and functions under strong communitarian network ties through kinship (Megarry, 1995). One may speculate that the contemporary organizations that come closest to these conditions are the small family firm and some of the new professional service organisations. The forced labor camps of capitalism and communism, and the Fordist factories and corporate bureaucracies have survived so long because of their abilitiy to generate wealth and because their structures and political processes do partially feed our ancient impulses. But throughout society we have been witnessing the ills of social maladjustment created by the distance they stand from the ancestral model, themes that have largely absorbed applied social science during this century. Evolutionary psychology offers both hope and guidance for how new forms of organization, under the liberating influence of information technology, might bring us closer to our psychological home. To do so means embracing radical change. Let us consider what barriers stand between us and change.

CHANGE—LIMITS AND OPPORTUNITIES

We long to believe in the limitless possibilities of change. It is, and has been, one of the greatest selling hooks for media throughout history. Occasional dark notes have been sounded about the illusory nature of progress (e.g., Steiner, 1971), but this is not a generally popular theme, as the burgeoning literature on the management of change testifies. Much writing on the subject does contain sage advice, but our capacity to follow it seems to be uneven at best. To understand why this should be so, we need to consider the primary mechanisms of stability and change and how they operate. Four are illustrated in Table 25.2.

TABLE 25.2
Change and Stability Dynamics in Individuals, Organizations and Cultures

		Change	*Stability*
Emotion	Failure	....	Success
Cognition	Dissonance	....	Identification
Action	Innovation	....	Investment
Systemic	Evolution	....	Homogeneity

The traditional tripartite division of human functioning: affect, cognition, and action, can be loosely adopted to distinguish these, plus the category of "systemic" to represent conjunctive relations.

The first mechanism is the success–failure dynamic. It has long been understood that success is a powerful reinforcer—especially when intermittent and irregular—embedding patterns of action and belief (Hantula & Crowell, 1994). What was once called effectance motivation (White, 1959) drives us in pursuit of feelings of efficacy, self-esteem and internal consistency, to use again the Erez–Earley framework. The same is true at the organizational level. Cyert and March (1963) argue that slack as well as pain should be a stimulus for change, but it is apparent that the erroneous lesson that recipes of past success will serve for the future is a powerful enemy of change (Audia et al., 2000). It is not hard to understand why success ill equips individuals and organizations to contemplate the need for radical change. This is a particular problem when the need for change precedes awareness of it. One needs reliable radar about an approaching storm to be motivated to batten down the hatches when the sky is blue and sea is calm. Organizations seem to lack this, and many corporate disasters have been due to awareness of the need for change coming only when it is too late, at the point of crisis.

This has been much written about, as has the important principle that negative feedback provides uniquely valuable opportunities for learning. The principle applies in science through the notion of falsification (Popper, 1979), and in management through the idealized system dynamic of the learning organization (Senge, 1990). Less discussed is why individuals and organizations continue to respond inappropriately when presented with negative information (see also Kluger, Chap. 7, this volume). Indeed, it is interesting and perhaps indicative of the preeminence of optimism as a theme in theory and research that this issue has been so neglected in the literature, despite some telling indications. For example, a well-known problem in management is the tendency to persist with projects well beyond the point at which it is productive to do so.

Kernis and colleagues (1982) demonstrated the effect experimentally in a series of studies. Their work takes care to depend on sunk costs effects, i.e., persistence is not merely due to an unrecoverable material investment. There are sunk costs, but these are psychological—the escalating commitment of the emotions to success (see also Staw & Ross, 1987). Moreover—and this is of special interest and importance in the context of motivation theory—the effect is most strong under conditions of high self-esteem. Subjects persist with failing causes even when experimenters present messages and cues to indicate that they should desist rather than persist.

So pervasive is this phenomenon that the word *failure* has become one of the great taboo concepts of corporate culture. Two recent doctoral theses have begun to shed light on this neglected area. Joel Kahn (1994), a student of Karl Weick, argues that failure can be a source of learning when conceived as a performance gap. This requires a climate that includes norms of failure acceptance, necessary to trigger a search for and treatment of causes. Without this, rationalization and external attribution block learning. More recently, the research of David Cannon at the London Business School (Cannon, 1995, 1999) has explored the psychology of processing failure experiences at the individual level. His study finds that individuals typically had not adequately come to terms with their failures at the time of their occurrence, in the sense of having achieved a rational integration of them with a consistent problem-solving worldview. As a consequence, when recollected in interviews, almost all members of his sample reexperienced powerful negative emotions, and from these constructed a variety of dysfunctional interpretive frames. These involve a mix of self-derogation and "magical" thinking about the causes of failure and what can be learned from it. Individuals typically self-blame via reasoning that they should have been perfect and omniscient, even when it was clear that the failure and the circumstances producing it were beyond their control. The lessons learned from this kind of thinking are unproductive, e.g., simple avoidance generalizations ("I will never go to x again") rather than any more genuinely heuristic or analytical insights.

Cannon draws upon control theory to explain these results. These cognitions are emotionally driven from a powerful need-for-control to a degree that overwhelms reason and prevents learning. Langer's (1983) work on the control illusion is clearly relevant in this context. Further studies are exploring the generality of the phenomenon, but it is evident that the emotional impact of failure is a major barrier to change emanating from it. Cannon's (1995) sample including some sports people and artists. They were not immune from the process, though at the same time in their working lives there is a range of everyday negative experiences (e.g., losing a race) which their professional value/appraisal systems can help to frame as "normal" failures and enable incremental learning to take place. But when events fall beyond these accustomed boundaries (e.g., a singer fouling up an audition) the same unproductive self-attribution processes occur as are found among high-achievement-motivated managers.

The implication is that we are hardwired for achievement and to experience extreme negative emotions to failure (Karniol & Ross, 1996; Nicholson, 2000). Constructive change in response to these emotions—shame and its relatives—requires subcultures of acceptance and redemption, such as have featured in preindustrial cultures (Turner, 1992). Failure has a unique capacity to yield analytical insights and behavioral lessons, but to do so requires the creation of failure-accepting climates (Kahn, 1994).

The second set of issues around change dynamics are those to do with how people construe social reality. The key process here is how concepts of social reality are sustained and modified. Probably the most powerful mechanism for this is conflict, or dissonance, between competing ideas, and the context in which it can work most strongly is the group. One of the most replicated and well-researched phenomena of social psychology is the group polarization effect, as summarized in a monograph by Moscovici and Doise (1995). When individuals freely exchange ideas and views in a group context, they arrive at a new social representation of reality. This occurs because each individual is forced to examine the reasoning underlying his or her own beliefs, is exposed to the reasoning of others, and acquires a new awareness of the diversity of opinion and belief among peers. The resulting consensus forges a new and more articulated belief system, that is not only more extreme than individual starting points, but is also a source of enduring change to individual attitudes, lasting well after the group event. Moscovici and Doise are sanguine about this process as a force for change in society, but are they right to be so? The preconditions that they summarize from experimental studies seem much more readily created in the psychological laboratory than in organizations. They include lack of procedural formality, absence of status divisions, diversity in other attitudinal dimensions, no time limits, a consensus rather than a majority voting decisional requirement, no formal leadership, external competitive threat, belief in the importance of their group objectives, and individuals acting as fully participating and immersed group members rather than holding reserved positions as representatives of any external body or interest group. These are the characteristics of the organic communities described earlier—ancestral contexts which are rarely replicated in corporate life.

What we see all too often in organizational settings is, on the one hand, "groupthink," i.e., excessive group homogeneity and conformity around a leading position, or dissensus between individual or factions constellated around outside interests. The problem in either event is that investment, either in a single position represented within the group or with a position outside the group, blocks the kind of creative tension out of which new meanings can emerge. The inabilities of organizations to engineer strategic change seem frequently to stem from the problems of executive teams encompassing insufficient diversity, overformalized processes of decision-making, and overidentification with cognitive anchor points (Hambrick & Mason, 1984).

The third level of Table 25.2 extends this logic to the realm of action. Much so-called innovation in organizations is incremental. Radical challenge to orthodoxy is hard to achieve because of investment in current knowledge, structures, and behaviour patterns. The essence of radical innovation is the evolutionary logic of punctuated equilibrium (Gersick, 1991)—the necessity to dissolve old assumptions, habits, and practices before genuinely new forms can be implemented. But organizations are built on logics of investment. Let us illustrate one way in which this happens. In organizations, as in arts and sciences, innovation often comes about from the migration of one set of ideas into a new unaccustomed domain. Mobile individuals are often the key carriers of these perspectives (Nicholson, 1984), and it can often be observed that it is the individual who comes as an immigrant into one setting from another quite different one who is able to see the environment with a fresh pair of eyes and import new ways of tackling its problems. Chief executives recruited externally from different businesses are more likely to innovate than same-industry-bred leaders (Helmich & Brown, 1972).

The implication is that cross-functional mobility, external recruitment to leadership positions, and other mechanisms of cross-fertilization can stimulate an innovation dynamic. The difficulty here is that this has costs—costs of the learning curve for the new individual and costs of risk for the new approaches they may import. Companies often prefer the investment of breeding their own leaders, allowing what have been called fortresses (Sonnenfeld & Peiperl, 1988) to accrete around products, functions, and divisions. Again we see what in effect is the triumph of the control dynamic over the diversity and change dynamic.

If we look at these processes systemically, one can see parallels in evolutionary theory. A premise of this set of ideas is that diversity and opportunities for heterogeneous recombination are necessary preconditions for evolutionary change, more through the extinction of redundant variants than the creation of new ones (Cziko, 1995). It has been through population movements, wars, and revolutionary challenges mounted by subcultures to central authority that many of the most valued forms of social change have come about (Diamond, 1997). But our evolutionary instincts lie in an opposite direction: to secure group membership and identity, highly selective association, and defense of tradition. These are what promote our narrow self-interest of genetic reproduction. One could argue that it is only through organization, where we can be farsighted enough to look beyond this self-interest, that we can create conditions that override it. But even the most venturesome businesses, after initial exploratory growth, generally seek the stabilizing internal order required for consistent niche exploitation and habitat tracking. In most cases, organizations seem to act like self-interested and self-deceptive individuals (Brunsson, 1995). The list of stability drivers in the right column of Table 25.2 is much more in tune with the cost-effectiveness, security-oriented, success-obsessed ethos of businesses in a threateningly competitive environment, than is the change list in the left column. As with species, organizations become extinct more readily than they evolve, for the elements of the right column follow the selectionist logic of past imperatives more than future requirements.

In the context of a globalizing economy, one might wish and expect diversity dynamics to assume greater significance. Yet it seems that these same forces apply pressures to business with a stability-reinforcing dynamic, whether they intend it or not.

IMPLICATIONS FOR PRACTICE

This analysis suggests that there are important limitations in our ability to motivate through different forms of organization and contains a warning about the consequences of current trends in organizational change. If we accept the reasoning of evolutionary theory, individuality and culture have deeply rooted and enduring structural properties. Organizations are more transient structures, sitting between individuals and their culture, and achieve effective integrated functioning to the degree that they are adaptive to these forces. For organizations to achieve an effective motivational order, they need to be consistent with the needs and interests of their members and capable of integrating them. Evolutionary psychology would encourage us especially to assess their qualities as *communities* in which fundamental human interests, mediated by cultural expression, can be acted out. The adaptive mechanisms by which organization as community are shaped are: selection (and self-selection), socialization, transition, social representation, structuration, and leadership, some of which we have looked at here.

Under the influence of information technology, business globalization, and new ideologies of strategic management we are witnessing far-reaching upheavals in the structures, functions, and management practices of organizations, both commercial and public. Some of these have beneficial and enlightened objectives but they are nonetheless creating some significant dysfunctions, many of which are predictable from the foregoing analysis (Nicholson, 2000). The implication is that traditional forms and functions, such as hierarchy, family, and bureaucracy, will persist as preferred design principles in many areas of business and society. Yet at the same time we can continue to expect to see wide-ranging experimentation with new organizational forms, mediated by the flexibility that new information technology permits. The net result, already visible, will be a more diverse array of employment conditions and acted-out motivational models than we have previously witnessed. This presents new opportunities for social evolution through the mobility of people and ideas across sectors of the economy. It also offers interesting and important new challenges for scholarship and management practice, especially to do with career development, self-identity, group behavior, job design, and leadership.

However, the selectionist model and evolutionary psychology also imply that the evolution of new ways of managing and organizing will resolve around the ancient and familiar centers of gravity in human nature.

REFERENCES

Alwin, D. F. (1994). Aging, personality and social change: The stability of individual differences over the adult life-span. In D. L. Featherman, R. M. Lerner, & M. Perlmutter (Eds.), *Life-span development and behavior* (Vol.12). Hillsdale, NJ: Erlbaum.

Audia, P. G., Locke, E. A., & Smith, K. G. (2000). The paradox of success: An archival and a Laboratory study of strategic persistence following a radical environmental change. *Academy of Management Journal*, 43:837–853.

Barkow, J. H, Cosmides, L., & Tooby, J. (Eds.). (1992). *The adapted mind: Evolutionary psychology and the generation of culture*. Oxford, England: Oxford University Press.

Bates, J. E., & Wachs, L. D. (Eds.). (1994). *Temperament: Individual differences of the interface of biology and behavior*. Washington, DC: APA Press.

Bouchard, T. J. (1987). Genetic influence on mental abilities, personality, vocational interests and work attitudes. In C. L. Cooper & I. T. Robertson (Eds.), *International review of industrial and organizational psychology, 1997* (Vol.12.) Chichester, England: Wiley.

Brunsson, N. (1995). *The Organization of Hypocrisy*. New York: Wiley.

Buss, D. M. (1991). Evolutionary personality psychology. *Annual Review of Psychology, 42*, 459–492.

Cannon, D. C. (1995). *Making sense of failure: Learning or defence?* Unpublished doctoral thesis, London Business School.

Cannon, D. C. (1999). Cause or control? The temporal dimension in failure sense-making. *Journal of Applied Behaviorol Science*, Vol. 35, pp. 416–438.

Cohen, M. N., & Armelagos, G. J. (1991). *Paleopathology and origins of agriculture*. London: Academic Press.

Crawford, C., & Krebs, D. L. (Eds.). (1998). *Handbook of evolutionary psychology*. London: Erlbaum.

Cropanzano, R., James, K., & Citera, M. (1993). A goal hierarchy model of personality, motivation, and leadership. *Research in Organizational Behavior* (Vol. 15, pp. 267–322). Greenwich, CT: JAI Press.

Cyert, R., & March, J. (1963). *A behavioral theory of the firm*. Englewood Cliffs, NJ: Prentice-Hall.

Cziko, G. (1995). *Without miracles: Universal selection theory and the second Darwinian revolution*. Cambridge, MA: MIT Press.

Dennett, D. C. (1995). *Darwin's dangerous idea: Evolution and the meanings of life*. New York: Simon & Schuster.

Diamond, J. (1991). *The rise and fall of the third chimpanzee*. London: Radius.

Diamond, J. (1997). *Guns, germs, and steel: The fate of human societies*. New York: Norton.

Digman, J. M. (1990). Personality structure: Emergence of the five-factor model. *Annual Review of Psychology, 41*, 417–440.

Dunbar, R. (1996). *Gossip, grooming and evolution of language*. London; Faber & Faber.

Eldredge, N. (1995). *Reinventing Darwin: The great evolutionary debate*. New York: Wiley.

Erez, M., & Earley, P. C. (1993). *Culture, self-identity, and work*. Oxford, England: Oxford University Press.

Foley, R. A. (1987). *Another unique species*. London: Longman.

Gersick, C. J. C. (1991). Revolutionary change theories: A multilevel exploration of the punctuated equilibrium paradigm. *Academy of Management Review, 16*, 10–36.

Gould, S. J., & Vrba, E. S. (1982). Exaptation—A missing term in the science of form. *Paleobiology*, *8*, 4–15.

Hambrick, D. C., & Mason, P. A. (1984). Upper echelons: The organization as a reflection of its top managers. *Academy of Management Review, 9*, 195–206.

Hantula, D. A., & Crowell, C. R. (1994). Intermittent reinforcement and escalation processes in sequential decision making: A replication and theoretical analysis. *Journal of Organizational Behavior Management, 14*, 7–36.

Helmich, D. L., & Brown, W. B. (1972). Successor type and organizational change in the corporate enterprise. *Administrative Science Quarterly, 17*, 371–381.

Kahn, J. A. (1994). *Failure construction in organizations: Exploring the effects of failure norms.* Unpublished doctoral dissertation, University of Michigan.

Karniol, R., & Ross, M. (1996). The motivational impact of temporal focus: Thinking about the future and the past. *Annual Review of Psychology, 47*, 593–620.

Kernis, M. H., Zuckerman, M., Cohen, A., & Spadafora, S. (1982). Persistence following failure: The interactive role of self-awareness and the attributional basis for negative expectancies. *Journal of Personality and Social Psychology, 43*, 1184–1191.

Kohn, M., & Schooler, C. (1983). *Work and personality: An inquiry into social stratification.* Newark, NJ: Ablex.

Langer, E. J. (1983). *The psychology of control.* Beverley Hills, CA: Sage.

Megarry, T. (1995). *Society in prehistory: The origins of human culture.* London: Macmillan.

Moscovici, S., & Doise, S. (1995). *Conflict and consensus: A general theory of collective decisions.* London: Sage.

Murdock, G. P. (1945). The common denominator of cultures. In G. P. Murdock (Ed.), *Culture and society.* Pittsburgh, PA: University of Pittsburgh Press, 1965.

Nicholson, N. (1984). A theory of work role transitions. *Administrative Science Quarterly, 29*, 172–191.

Nicholson, N. (1996). Towards a new agenda for work and personality: Traits, self-identity, "strong" interactionism and change. *Applied Psychology: An International Review, 45*, 189–205.

Nicholson, N. (2000). *Executive instinct: Managing the human animal in the information age.* New York: Crown.

Nicholson, N. (1997a). Birth order and personality [Working Paper, Centre for Organisational Research, London Business School].

Nicholson, N. (1997b). Evolutionary psychology: Towards a new view of human nature and organizational society. *Human Relations*, Vol. 50, pp. 1053–1078.

Popper, K. R. (1979). *Objective knowledge: An evolutionary approach* (Rev. ed.). Oxford, England: Clarendon Press.

Senge, P. (1990). *The fifth discipline: The art and practice of the learning organization.* New York: Doubleday.

Sperber, D. (1996). *Explaining culture: A naturalistic approach.* Oxford, England: Blackwell.

Sonnenfeld, J. A. & Peiperl, M. A. (1988). Staffing policy as a strategic response: A typology of career systems. *Academy of Management Review, 13*, 588–600.

Staw, B. M. (1991). Dressing up like an organization: When psychological theories can explain organizational action. *Journal of Management, 17*, 805–819.

Staw, B. M., & Ross, J. (1987). Behavior in escalation situations: Antecedents, prototypes, and situations. *Research in Organizational Behavior* (Vol. 9, pp. 39–78). Greenwich, CT: JAI Press.

Steiner, G. (1971). *In Bluebeard's castle.* London: Faber & Faber.

Sulloway, F. (1996). *Born to rebel.* New York: Little, Brown.

Tooby, J., & Cosmides, L. (1992). The psychological foundations of culture. In J. H. Barkow, L. Cosmides, & J. Tooby (Ed.), *The Adapted mind: Evolutionary psychology and the generation of culture.* Oxford: Oxford University Press.

Turner, F. (1992). Shame, beauty and the tragic view of history. *American Behavioral Scientist, 38,* 1060–1075.

White, R.W. (1959). Motivation reconsidered: The concept of competence. *Psychological Review, 66,* 297–333.

Wills, C. (1995). *The runaway brain: The evolution of human uniqueness.* London: HarperCollins.

Wright, R. (1994). *The moral animal: Evolutionary psychology and everyday life.* New York: Little, Brown.

Yost, J. H., Strube, M. J., & Bailey, J. R. (1992). The construction of self: An evolutionary view. *Current Psychology: Research and Reviews, 11,* 110–121.

26

Surveying the Foundations: Approaches to Measuring Group, Organizational, and National Variation

Michael Harris Bond
Chinese University of Hong Kong
Hong Kong

> *Soft things are easy to melt.*
> *Small particles scatter easily.*
> *The time to take care is before it is done.*
> *Establish order before confusion sets in.*
>
> —Lao Tzu, *The Way of Virtue*, poem 64

An individual person has a "suchness" for us as observers, created in large measure by his or her physical presence. As psychologists, we can take measures from people, associate the variables measured with other individual behaviors, and feel comfortable that we are doing something real.

When groups, organizations, or nations become our target of interest, matters become less sure. These phenomena exist not as physical but as social constructions, defined by their articles of association, symbols, discourses, products, and interactions. As people, we parcelate the social world into groups, the institutional world into organizations, and the political world into nations because we believe these entities to be important (e.g., Berger & Luckman, 1966). As psychologists, we likewise parcelate because we believe that these social constructions influence people's behavior. It then becomes important to characterize groups, institutions, and nations so that we may factor in their influence when we wish to understand differences in behavior that occur across groups, institutions, or nations.

However, how have we gone about constructing these characterizations? Over time we have developed a number of strategies whose products are commonly used in our professional discourse. These products, such as Hofstede's (1991) five-factor model of cultures, have quickly become reified, as diversity issues gain prominence and social scientists are pressed to address the issues involved. Perhaps it may now be judicious to examine these strategies we have developed, exercising due diligence in these early stages. At very least we will become more aware of our procedures; perhaps we will also avoid becoming entrapped by our past and thereby facilitate the emergence of new procedures. "Reculer pour mieux sauter," as the French would advise.

PERSONS AS MEASURING TOOLS

> Man is the measure of all things
> Of what is, that it is
> Of what is not, that it is not.
>
> —Protagoras

As psychologists, we are familiar and comfortable with the practice of using individual persons to assess our phenomena of interest. The phenomenon then becomes characterized in terms of the dimensions teased out of the descriptions given by people using the rating scales provided by psychologists. Of course, the resulting dimensions are constrained in their potential usefulness by the characteristics of the raters and the useability of the rating scales—their precision, reliability, comprehensiveness, and statistical treatment. Debates circulate around these issues. Nonetheless, the procedure of using "insiders" to measure and characterize the phenomenon of interest is basic to our discipline.

Measuring the Individual

The Self

People are "socialized into selfhood" so that society may function by integrating the inputs of distinctive, responsible, accountable actors. To this end, individuals come to conceptualize themselves as having moods, traits, values, beliefs, attitudes, opinions, and so forth. Each of these aspects of the self may be instrumented, measured, and dimensionalized. So, for example, Schwartz (1992) developed from theory and reading what he believed to be a comprehensive measure of human values and showed that 45 of his values could be grouped into 10 metrically equivalent domains by people in 20 countries. Similarly, those in the lexical tradition of person perception (e.g., Goldberg, 1980) have used the natural language to adduce a five-factor lay model of personality variation found in many cultures (Bond, 1994). The literature of social cognition is rich, indeed, with such analyses of self-ratings.

The Other

Just as people develop a conception of themselves (Epstein, 1973), they also develop a conception of the other. The same instruments may be used to rate the other's temperament, traits, and so forth as are used to rate the self. Indeed, it appears as if the categories or schema used to assess the other are the same as those used to assess the self (Goldberg, 1980), although their functions may differ (Hogan, 1992).

A variation in the use of other-ratings is worth mentioning in passing. Respondents may be asked to rate the psychological characteristics of the "typical" member of a particular group, organization, or nation. Such a request is made in stereotype research and requires an act of generalization on the part of the respondent. Respondents are capable of generating distinct profiles for a large set of such typical others (e.g., Weinreich, Luk, & Bond, 1994) and agreement on the features of these profiles may be high even when respondents from different cultures are asked to rate the same set of typical others, e.g., Russians, Americans, and Japanese (see Stephan et al., 1996)

Ratings of typical members of the subject's own group may be solicited in such stereotype surveys. It is important, however, not to presume that respondents would rate themselves in the same ways they rate typical in-group members. People may distinguish their own characters (Weinreich et al., 1994), values (Bond & Mak, 1996), beliefs, and practices from those of typical in-group members. This difference will have consequences when the researcher uses averaged self-ratings (as in Hofstede, 1980) to measure an entity as opposed to using averaged ratings of typical in-group members to measure that same entity.

These stereotypes of the "typical" other become significant in understanding intergroup, interorganizational, and international interactions whenever these types of identity become salient (Tajfel, 1974). When members of different groups, organizations, or nations hold different conceptions of one another, each member's identity becomes an important factor in understanding each member's behavior toward the other. Research measuring the stereotypes of *all* the parties to such an interaction are rare (see Everett & Stening, 1987, for an exception), given the labor required, the statistical sophistication necessary, and the potential sensitivity of the subject matter. Such research is, however, necessary if psychologists are to apply their knowledge about group, organizational, and national differences to occasions when people from different groups, organizations, and nations interact. And increasing diversification will lead to more such occasions.

The Group

Members of a group can be asked to rate their group as an entity (its character, norms, and outcomes) or to rate aspects of their group's functioning. So, for example, Watson and Michaelson (1988) interviewed groups' members on their group dynamics and their group members' behaviors *in general*. These responses were used to construct a 51-item Group Style Description. Bond and Shiu (1997) borrowed this scale along with others and administered it twice to members of 17 task groups in the first author's class of social psychology. As they were interested in characterizing the group (and not individual understanding of group process), each item was scored in each group by averaging each member's rating of his or her group on that item.

This approach to measuring the group might be termed "reality by democracy." It is full democracy, since all members "vote." An alternative, albeit costly, approach would be to train observers to a similar system and standard, and then have them observe the group meetings and rate aspects of the group (e.g., Bales, 1950). This approach might be termed "reality by expertocracy." In both cases, the focus of the analysis is the group and not the individual group member, even though the source of the rating was an individual observer.

Avoiding "Group Shift"

Surprisingly, psychologists rarely shift to this group level of analysis when examining group process. A number of interrelated reasons may be suggested to explain this avoidance. I believe that the basic reason is what Sampson (1981) termed the individualistic bias, i.e., the cultural tendency to focus exclusively on the reality of individuals and to ignore the reality and importance of larger units. According to this perspective, individuals are the fundamental, autonomous realities; each person's behavior is mediated by his or her perceptions; a group is simply another context like any other social setting to be transmuted by the individual's perceptions. A group is not a viable, influential entity in its own right, merely background to the individual foreground.

Statistical considerations reinforce this individualistic bias. When the group becomes the unit of analysis, one's crucial n falls. Attaining statistical significance is thereby believed to be more difficult. This, of course, is not necessarily the case, because one's error term may well also fall due to the increased stability of group scores; the capacity to detect differences among the groups may thereby increase.

Higher reliabilities occur when mean scores are derived from multiple observers of the group, as in Bond and Shiu (1997). There, a factor analysis was run using the average scores that a group's five members gave to each of the 51 items of the GSD. There were "only" 17 groups, so only 17 observations per item. This low observation to item ratio is anathema to psychometricians socialized with less reliable individual ratings. Even Guilford (1954), the most liberal guide to factor analysis, prescribed a 2 to 1 ratio. These concerns may, however, be eliminated when more reliable averages are used as input.

In the Bond and Shiu (1997) factor analyses of the group process scores, two factors emerged. Considerable confidence may be placed in these two factors, as the saturation of items to factor was very high (Guadagnoli & Velicer, 1988). These factors, labelled Performance Focus and Shared Exchange, bear a striking resemblance to Bales' (1950) task and maintenance functions of leadership, derived from considering individual-level data. Such parallelism is encouraging but is not a necessary outcome when individual-level and group-level phenomena are compared (Leung, 1989).

Presuming such fallacious parallelism is natural for psychologists whose whole disciplinary training focusses them onto individual-level processes. Groups are merely "individuals writ large" so that anthropomorphic extrapolations into theorizing about groups are readily accepted by other psychologists (but not by some alert sociologists, e.g., Scheuch, 1967). Most of us are simply not experienced in thinking at the level of groups (or organizations, or nations) and must "discipline" ourselves anew to treat each level on its own terms. Such careful treatment involves labeling group-level constructs in nonpsychological terms and establishing the construct validity of these constructs in their own right.

Staying at the Individual Level

It is, of course, quite legitimate to remain at the individual level. So, for example, in the Bond and Shiu (1997) study, one may work with the 102 individual members (of the 17 groups). One could factor analyze their responses to the 51-item GSD, identify factors, and give each individual a score for each factor obtained. These factors could then be related to variables of possible interest. So, for example, one could ask whether those higher in interpersonal agreeableness (Costa & McCrae, 1992) are more likely to perceive their groups as higher in some maintenance-type factor.

A basic assumption must first be made, however. One must assume that the processes occurring in each of the 17 groups are similar and do not interact in some way with the variables being related to one another. Otherwise, one cannot regard all the group members as if they are sampled from a universe of "group members." This issue is typically not checked, even though recent advances in structural equation modelling (e.g., Bentler, 1992; Joreskog & Sorbom, 1993) permit such an assessment to be made.

Another needed assumption relates to the independence requirement. All subjects whose data are pooled into an analysis of any sort are presumed to be independent of one another in the statistical sense that measurement error is uncorrelated across individuals. This caveat is usually observed in the process of data collection and so need not concern us here.

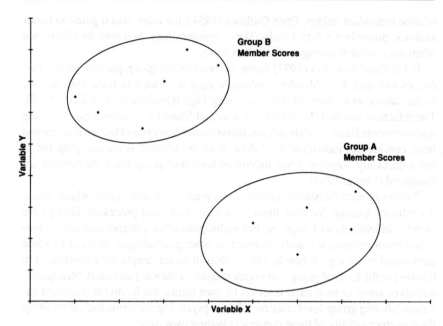

FIG. 26.1. Example of a situation in which the group-positioning effect distorts the individual correlation between variables X and Y.

However, members of a given group are *not* responding in a conceptually independent way; their group and its processes have a reality that its members share and that distinguish their group from others. These different group realities will position each group differently on any grid that locates groups with respect to measured variables. These separate realities will position the group ratings from members of various groups differently on Fig. 26.1.

The outcome of this "group positioning effect" will be to distort the correlation between the variables at the individual level (see Klein, Dausereau, & Hall, 1994; Ostroff, 1993). If one wishes to explore these individual correlations, then the group positioning effect must first be eliminated before all the groups' members data are pooled for analysis (see Bond, 1988, for an example of this procedure).

Group-Level and Individual-Level Analyses Combined

It is conceivable that one wants to know both the individual-level relationship between two variables and also the group-level relationship between the same two variables. As Leung (1989) and Leung and Bond (1989) have shown, these relationships are not the same. To presume one from another commits "the fallacy of transposed levels" (Hofstede, 1980, pp. 28–31; Robinson, 1950; Tannenbaum & Bachman, 1964). Fortunately, statistical techniques are now available to examine the relationships among a set of variables at two (or more) levels simultaneously in the same data set using hierarchical linear modelling (Bryk & Raudenbush, 1992; Goldstein, 1987).

The results of such bi-level analyses provide behavioral scientists with the empirical inputs for two types of theories: (a) theories about individual perceptions of a group and its processes, and (b) theories about groups as measured by averaged perceptions of the group and its processes by a group's members. These are different orders of theory and must be carefully, ploddingly distinguished from one another in our writing about groups (see especially Klein et al., 1994).

The Organization

Organizations differ from groups in that they are usually legal entities, composed of identifiable groups called departments, are work or task-focused, and constituted by larger numbers of persons. This last point is important when an organization's members are asked to assess aspects of their organization, as is done in some studies of organizational culture (e.g., Hofstede, Neuyen, Ohayv, and Sanders, 1990). With a larger population of members, logistical considerations make it impractical to sample all members in rating a given organization. Stratified random sampling may then be used to ensure broad representation and to avoid bias in the outcome.

As with groups, the ratings of organizations by its members may be analyzed at the individual level or at the organizational level (by averaging members' ratings of their organization). Factor analyses of organization ratings at these two levels can yield different numbers of factors, each differently constituted (e.g., Hofstede, Bond, and Luk, 1993).

When ratings of organizations are factor analyzed at the individual level, the "organizational positioning effect" must first be eliminated, say, by standardization procedures or by averaging the correlation matrix from respondents in each of the organizations (Leung and Bond, 1989). Then, each respondent may be given factor scores on each of the resulting factors. These scores may finally be related to subject characteristics by regression analysis. So, for example, Hofstede et al., 1993, found that the perception of organizational "orderliness" was related to an organization member culture, gender, age, seniority, and education.

When ratings of organizations are factor analyzed at the organizational level (e.g., Hofstede et al., 1990), such individual-level conclusions may *not* be drawn. Factor scores may be assigned to organizations, however, and these factor scores can then be related to characteristics of the organization, such as its size, type, and age. The resulting relationships can then be used to construct a theory of perceived organizations (see, e.g., Hofstede et al., 1990).

402   BOND

The Nation

Nations are perceptual entities for their citizens, as indeed are other countries of which one is not a citizen. Techniques like multidimensional scaling may be used to elicit the dimensions that people use to perceive nations, and these solutions may be compared across citizens from different countries (e.g., Forgas and O'Driscoll, 1984; Wish, Deutsch, and Biener, 1970). Alternatively, bipolar adjective scales may be used to have citizens from various countries assess one another's countries (e.g., Stephan et al., 1996). Such research on "nations as perceptual targets" faces a number of challenges: (a) nations are constituted by *many* citizens—how representative is the sample of informants used to perceive nations in this research? If a specific type of citizen is used in the sample (e.g., university students), how might their position in the nation bias the results? (b) citizens can hardly be said to experience their nations (or other nations) with the same immediacy and expertise as they experience their own groups or other groups. So, to what realm of behavior might such perceptions, analyzed at the individual level, be usefully related? Political behavior, such as voting, perhaps? If the data were analyzed at the level of nations (i.e., each nation represented by an average score taken from its citizens on each of the measured perceptions), how would one understand the groupings of these perceptions? To what other variables might these nation scores be related? Gross national product/capital? Human rights observance (Humana, 1986)? Status of women (Population Crisis Committee, 1988)? Degree of industrial unrest?

The above questions have a speculative, "iffy" quality. That is a consequence of the observable fact that there is at present scant research aimed at the nation as perceptual target (see Lissen and Hagendoorn, 1994, for an exception). The emergence of supranational political units like the European Community will, however, drive an interest in the kinds of question that can be addressed by such research (e.g., Hewstone, 1986). So, its frequency will increase, and I suggest that we prepare ourselves intellectually for its emergence.

USING SELF-RATINGS OF UNIT MEMBERS TO DEFINE THE UNIT

> Individual man is all things—
> Of what is, how it is;
> Of what he is not, that it is naught
>
> —With apologies to Protagoras

In this approach to the study of groups, organizations, or nations, self-ratings of those constituting the units are averaged. The unit is then characterized by its members' average scores on self-ratings of their personality, values, beliefs, and other attributes. These measures of, say, values may themselves be interrelated, with simplification techniques like factor analysis (Chinese Culture Connection, 1987) or smallest space analysis (Schwartz, 1994) used to dimensionalize the set of variables. Regardless of the technique, it is the *average* score of the unit's members on a given measure that is used as input in the analysis and transformation of the data. So, one is then dealing with dimensions derived from group-level, organization-level, or nation-level data. But, it must be borne in mind that these data are themselves derived from psychological measures of individuals in the unit. One is reminded of Louis XIV's assertion, "L'etat, c'est moi!" In the present approach, one might instead assert, "L'etat, c'est nous!"

This approach may be another reflection of the individualistic bias (Sampson, 1977) in that an entity is conceptualized as the sum of its individual, psychological components. No sense of a broader Gestalt is usually built into the conceptualization of the unit. Such need not be the case, however, even when using individual data. One may, for example, also characterize the unit in terms of the range of individuals in the unit on a given variable. So, for example, Bond and Shiu (1997) characterized a group's personality resources in terms of the variance of group members' scores on various dimensions of personality (see also Jackson et al., 1991). This variance score represents a distinctive configuration of a group. Such a group measure allows one to develop empirically grounded theories about the impact of differences among the individuals constituting the unit (see also Triandis, Bontempo, Leung, and Hui, 1990, for another example).

There is nothing wrong with the use of individually based measures, however combined, to define a unit. It simply yields psychologically based constructs to define the unit. A unit may alternatively be conceptualized in terms of its features, processes or products (see Measures of the Unit Itself, below) and such unit-based approaches will yield constructs and theories of their own. The psychologically based constructs may then be related to the unit-based constructs (e.g., Bond & Shiu, 1997, at the group level; Hofstede et al., 1990, at the organizational level; Hofstede, 1980, at the national level). But, the source of the constructs being interrelated must be kept clearly in mind at all stages in our scientific work (Klein et al., 1994).

The Group

With a group, one is usually able to sample all its members on a given psychological measure, thereby eliminating concerns about representativeness.Furthermore, group processes may be readily conceptualized as emerging out of the interaction among the members. In consequence, it may be felt as appropriate to relate group phenomena to the measured attributes of its members. So, for example, averaged beliefs of a group's members about another group (e.g., Staub's, 1988 "ideologies of antagonism," or Esses,' Haddock's, & Zanna's, 1993, symbolic beliefs) can be related to that group's intergroup behavior. Or, a group members, averaged personality may be related to measures of its group process (Bond & Shiu, 1997;

404   BOND

Gersick, 1989; Weingart, Bennett, & Brett, 1993) or to group outcomes like absenteeism (George, 1990, 1992) or attrition (Schneider, Smith, & Paul, chap. 15,
this volume).

The possibilities are endless. Surprisingly, however, there is little research
within this schema (Hoyle & Crawford, 1994; Moreland, Levine, and Wingert,
1995). One suspects that researchers in the group area are *social* social psychologists, sceptical about the usefulness of personality-type measures (Mischel, 1968)
and dismissive of individually based approaches to wholistic phenomena.

The Organization

The sampling issue becomes particularly salient in this approach, because one is
using averaged self-ratings to characterize a whole organization. Because sampling
all members is logistically difficult, a subset must be used to represent the whole.
Stratified random sampling (e.g., Hofstede et al., 1990) maximizes the represen-
tativeness of the resulting measures.

There are even fewer studies using this psychologically based approach with
organizations than with groups. The reason is probably much the same: Organizations tend to be studied by sociologists who have even less familiarity and
sympathy with individually based measures than do group psychologists. The
Marxian tradition in sociology also tends to dismiss individually derived measures
of organizations as epiphenomena, mere reflections of the means of production,
having no generative capacity of their own. I expect, then, that psychologists will
have to make the running in this demanding approach to organizations.

The Nation

Hofstede (1980) chose to represent a nation by the average score on 32 self-
rated "values" provided by a stratified sample of IBM employees in 40 countries.
The Chinese Culture Connection (1987), Schwartz (1994) and Smith, Dugan,
and Trompennaars (1996) have subsequently proceeded with a similar approach
to examining national variation. The use of this approach has the considerable
advantage of side-stepping the need to establish metric equivalence among the
values at the individual level *within* each of the national samples included. Such
equivalence may be impossible to establish using previous traditional approaches
(Bosland, 1985), although Schwartz's (1992) value survey has shown remarkable
cross-cultural equivalence using Smallest Space Analysis.

The problems associated with using this self-rating approach for measuring
groups and for organizations is writ even larger when considering nations: How
well matched are the samples? How representative are the samples? How can psychologically based measures represent such a complex, higher-order phenomenon
as a nation? This latter concern has been moderated somewhat by the frequent
assertion that cultures (nations) are defined by their values and that individuals can
and do reflect these cultural values (e.g., Kluckhohn, 1951; Schwartz, 1994).

Hofstede's (1980) work has been vigorously challenged on these points, amongst others (e.g., Triandis, 1982). Nonetheless, the hunger for a psychologically based theory of "cultural" variation was so great in social science that the Hofstede system has become the gold standard for over the last 20 years of cultural research and diversity training (Hofstede, 1995). Refinements of the Hofstede (1980) approach, e.g., Schwartz (1994), may supplant it, or replicas of his pioneering work may be extended to other psychological variables like beliefs (Leung, 1996), but the need for such a psychologically based theory of culture will remain.

MEASURES OF THE UNIT ITSELF

Horses for courses . . .

—British admonition

The two previous approaches to assessing a unit have either used persons to report their perceptions of the unit or persons' averages as measures of the unit. The final approach attempts to develop measures of the unit that reflect features, processes, or outcomes of the unit independent of the individuals constituting it. Many would argue that such "unit measures" are the appropriate measures when one is developing theories about the functioning of such units. Not surprisingly, fewer psychologists involve themselves in such intellectual work.

Once concepts, measures and theories have been judiciously developed at the individual, group, organization, and nation levels, it will become possible to link these levels (Klein et al., 1994). So, for example, individual-level analyses of values can yield average value scores for persons of various nations (Bond, 1988). These *individually based* nation averages may then be related to nation-based scores like rate of coronary heart disease or the relative status of women (Bond, 1991). Theorizing then follows about how effects at one level may interact with those at another level (e.g., Bond, 1991; Lytle, Brett, Barnsness, Tinsley, & Janssens, 1995; Schwartz, 1994; Triandis, 1984).

The Group

Bales (1950) developed the Interaction Process Analysis, a system for categorizing verbal inputs to a group discussion by its individual members. The results enabled Bales to identify, for example, which individuals assumed the roles of task and maintenance leaders. It was a system for profiling an individual's functioning within groups but not for profiling the group itself.

Profiling the group would require the use of measures that reflect group-level processes rather than individual-level behavior. Some of these group-level processes may be teased out of the individual measures already taken. One could examine the *distribution* of various types of inputs across the various group members, e.g., the variance for task-related suggestions made by group members.

Additionally, one could develop new, group-level verbal measures, like the proportion of total simultaneous speech, interruptions, or silence. Also, one could examine nonverbal, group-level processes, like amount of shared laughter or average seating proximity, and so forth to supplement the group-level, verbal processes.

All these measures could then be combined into a group-level factor analysis that would yield dimensions of group process. These, in turn, could be related to group features like size, composition, and type of task, or to group outcome measures like productivity or turnover. Additionally, they could be related to alternative approaches for measuring group process, such as by averaging members' ratings of their group (Bond & Shiu, 1997).

The Organization

This same logic may be extended to organizations. Given the longer life, internal complexity, and greater external connections of most organizations, the potential number of measures is even greater and may have to be limited by the purpose of a given study, e.g., to explore internal communication patterns.

A groundbreaking start in this area was made by the Aston studies (Pugh & Hickson, 1976). These researchers identified a two-factor taxonomy of organizational structure, viz., "structuring of activities" and "concentration of authority." These two dimensions of organizational structure were then related to "organizational context," including organization size and type of technology.

As with groups, so may these dimensions of organizations be related to organizational outcomes like measures of creativity (Woodman, Sawyer, & Griffin, 1993), inertia (Dean & Snell, 1991) labor unrest, productivity, diversification, interorganizational relationships (Smith Ring & Van den Ven, 1994), and so forth. They may also be linked to average-member perceptions of organizational practice. So, for example, Hofstede et al. (1990) showed that organizations perceived by their members to be more process oriented (as opposed to more results oriented) in their practices were higher in both their degree of specialization and formalization; those perceived as more professional (rather than more parochial) in their practices tend to be larger in size.

The Nation

Nations may be characterized with respect to many observable, nation-level variables—economic, social, political, and health related (e.g., Dogan & Pelassy, 1990; Taylor & Jodice, 1983). Additionally, nations' ecological "inputs," e.g., proportion of arable land, exposure to natural disaster, and humidity may be used to distinguish one nation from another. These inputs (Georgas & Berry, 1995) and outputs (Rummel, 1972; Sawyer, 1967) may be factor analyzed to reveal dimensions. In turn, these dimensions can be used to cluster nations into similar groups, often revealing unsuspected results (Georgas & Berry, 1995).

The first factor in such output analyses is typically an economic modernization factor. However, there are always additional factors, an outcome used by anticonvergence thinkers to counter the claim that modernization must lead to homogenization of national variation (Smith & Bond, 1998, chap. 12). The dimensions of nations may be related to the results of other approaches characterizing nations. So, for example, Forgas and O'Driscoll (1984) linked their three perceptual dimensions of nations held by citizens to the nation's degree of Western cultural heritage, its type of political system, and level of economic development. Similarly, Hofstede (1980) used correlations between nation outputs, like GNP per capita or maximum driving speed, to validate his four dimensions of nations derived from averaging citizens' value scores. Likewise, Whiting and Whiting (1975) related social structural properties of nations to the characteristics of children's typical behavior in those countries.

It should be mentioned here that the Marxian tradition in social science accords a primacy to this "national indicators" approach for defining and dimensionalizing nations (see, e.g., Harris, 1979). In this tradition, the means of production and other material forces play a determining role, and psychological processes, such as self-ratings of value or perceptions of a nation, are epiphenomena, mere reflections of these basic forces. Such debates can now be addressed by the results of studies linking the psychological and the material approaches to defining a nation. As a result, psychologists may come to identify some distinct domains of psychological jurisdiction.

FURTHER CONSTRUCTIONS

> . . . as if it was self-evident that a particular
> content is real, whereas some other possible
> content is not part of normal science.
>
> —H. P. Dachler (1995)

In this essay I have stood back to take stock of the various empirical strategies behavioral scientists have taken to construct variables to understand groups, organizations, and nations. I have also pointed out our tentative explorations to link approaches at the same level (e.g., Bond's & Shiu's, 1997, linking of group personality resources to group members' ratings of their group's process) and across levels (Leung, 1989), using either the same (e.g., Schwartz, 1994) or different (e.g., Bond, 1991) approaches to conceptualizing a given entity.

Some of these approaches are better explored than others, perhaps because they are more compatible with our implicit disciplinary epistemologies, themselves derived from our basic cultural assumptions (Gergen, 1993; Sampson, 1977). Dachler (1995) and others have been exorting us professionals to broaden these epistemological perspectives used to construct the contents of work and organizational psychology. As this discipline and others "go cross-cultural," there will be both opportunities and demands to broaden our cultural assumptions, including those that shape our epistemology. This extension is important, "as critic after critic has pointed out, it is in the context of discovery that culture-wise assumptions, or at least culturally preferred ones, shape the very statement and design of the research project, and therefore select the 'methods'." (Harding, 1993, p. 17)

Disciplined self-consciousness about potential cultural variation in constructing the person, group, organization, and nation becomes a fundamental tool for us to promote throughout this process of expansion. Let us listen carefully to the cultures whose variation we are trying to understand.

SURVEYING THE SURVEY

I used the writing of this paper as a way to help me clarify and organize the various approaches I have experienced as a social scientist exposed to theorizing about persons, groups, organizations, and nations. What I have identified are the various building blocks currently at our disciplinary disposal. This overview seems essential for those beginning to examine the many and various influences impinging on organizational behavior. For, as Klein et al. (1994) assert:

> By their very nature, organizations are multilevel. Individuals work in dyads, groups, and teams within organizations that interact with other organizations both inside and outside the industry. Accordingly, levels issues pervade organizational theory and research. No construct is level-free. Every construct is tied to one or more organizational levels or entities, that is, individuals, dyads, groups, organizations, industries, markets, and so on. To examine organizational phenomena is thus to encounter levels issues. (p. 198)

In meeting this demanding challenge, we will need considerable statistical (e.g., Hannan, 1991), conceptual (Klein et al. 1994), and theoretical (Lytle et al., 1995) sophistication. I hope that this essay contributes to the growth of our competence in approaching this challenge.

> For is and is-not come together;
> Hard and easy are complementary;
> Long and short are relative;
> High and low are comparative;
> Pitch and sound are in hormony;
> Before and after are a sequence.
>
> —Lao Tzu, *The way of harmony*, poem 2

ACKNOWLEDGEMENTS

I wish to acknowledge the contributions of the following scholars who made helpful inputs to previous versions of this paper: Chris Earley, Geert Hofstede, Virginia Kwan, Kwok Leung, Michael Morris, Ben Schneider, Catherine Tinsley, Harry Triandis, and Fons Van de Vijver. "Nemo dat quis non habet."

REFERENCES

Bales, R. F. (1950). *Interaction process analysis: A method for the study of small groups.* Cambridge, MA: Addison-Wesley.

Bentler, P. M. (1992). *EQS structural equation program manual.* Los Angeles: BMDP Statistical Software.

Berger, P. L., & Luckman, T. (1966). *The social construction of reality: A treatise in the sociology of knowledge.* New York: Doubleday.

Bond, M. H. (1988). Finding universal dimensions of individual variation in multi-cultural studies of values: The Rokeach and Chinese value surveys. *Journal of Personality and Social Psychology, 55,* 1009–1015.

Bond, M. H. (1991). Chinese values and health: A cultural-level examination. *Psychology and Health, 5,* 137–152.

Bond, M. H. (1994). Trait theory and cross-cultural studies of person perception. *Psychological Inquiry, 5,* 114–117.

Bond, M. H., & Mak, A. L. P. (1996, June). *Deriving an intergroup topography from perceived values: Forging an identity in Hong Kong out of Chinese tradition.* Invited paper prepared for the Korean Psychological Association's 50th Anniversary Conference, Seoul.

Bond, M. H., & Shiu, W. Y. F. (1997). A group's personality resources and its group process. *Small Group Research, 28,* 194–217.

Bosland, N. (1985). *The cross-cultural equivalence of the power distance–, uncertainty avoidance–, individualism–, and masculinity-measurement scales* [Working Paper, Institute for Research on Intercultural Cooperation].

Bryk, A. S., & Randenbash, S. W. (1992). *Hierarachical linear models: Application and data analysis methods.* Newbury Park, CA: Sage.

Chinese Culture Connection. (1987). Chinese values and the search for culture-free dimensions of culture. *Journal of Cross-Cultural Psychology, 18,* 143–164.

Costa, P. T., Jr., & McCrae, R. R. (1992). *Revised NEO personality inventory (NEOPI-R) and NEO five-factor inventory (NEO-FFI).* Odessa, FL: Psychological Assessment Resources.

Dachler, H. P. (1995). Crucial issues in the field of work and organizational psychology: Overlooked, forgotten, neglected? *International Association of Applied Psychology Newsletter, 7*(2), 4–12.

Dean, J. W., & Snell, S. A. (1991). Integrated manufacturing and job design: Moderating effects of organizational inertia. *Academy of Management Journal, 34,* 776–804.

Dogan, M., & Pelassy, D. (1990). *How to compare nations: Strategies in comparative politics* (2nd ed.). Chatham, NJ: Chatham House.

Epstein, S. (1973). The self-concept revisited or a theory of a theory. *American Psychologist, 28,* 404–416.

Esses, V. M., Haddock, G., & Zanna, M. P. (1993). Values, stereotypes, and emotions as determinants of intergroup attitudes. In D. M. Mackie and D. L. Hamilton (Eds.), *Affect, cognition and stereotyping: Interactive processes in group perception* (pp. 137–166). New York: Academic Press.

Everett, J. E., & Stening, B. W. (1987). Stereotyping in American, British and Japanese corporations in Hong Kong and Singapore. *Journal of Social Psychology, 127*, 445–460.

Forgas, J. P., & O'Driscoll, M. (1984). Cross-cultural and demographic differences in the perception of nations. *Journal of Cross-Cultural Psychology, 15*, 199.

Georgas, J., & Berry, J. W. (1995). An ecocultural taxonomy for cross-cultural psychology. *Cross-Cultural Research, 29*(2), 121–157.

George, J. M. (1990). Personality, affect, and behavior in groups. *Journal of Applied Psychology, 75*(2), 107–116.

George, J. M. (1992). The role of personality in organizational life: Issues and evidence. *Journal of Management, 18*(2), 185–213.

Gergen, K. J. (1993). *Toward transformation of social knowledge* (2nd ed.). New York, Berlin: Springer.

Gersick, C. J. G. (1989). Marking time: Predictable transitions in task groups. *Academy of Management Journal, 32*, 274–309.

Goldberg, L. R. (1980, May). *Some ruminations about the structure of individual differences: Developing a common lexicon for the major characteristics of human personality.* Paper presented at the meeting of the Western Psychological Association, Honolulu, HI.

Goldstein, H. (1987). *Multilevel models in education and social research.* New York: Oxford University Press.

Guadagnoli, E., & Velicer, W. F. (1988). Relation of sample size to the stability of component patterns. *Psychological Bulletin, 103*, 265–275.

Guilford, J. P. (1954). *Psychometric methods.* New York: Mcgraw Hill.

Hannan, M. T. (1991). *Aggregation and disaggregation in the social sciences.* Toronto: Lexington Books.

Harding, S. (1993, June). *Feminist philosophy of science: The objectivity question.* Paper presented at the international conference "Out of Margin, Feminist Perspectives on Economic Theory," Amsterdam, The Netherlands.

Harris, M. (1979). *Cultural materialism: The struggle for a science of culture.* New York: Vintage.

Hewstone, M. (1986). *Understanding attitudes to the European Community: A social-psychological study in four member states.* Cambridge, England: Cambridge University Press.

Hofstede, G. (1980). *Culture's consequences: International differences in work-related values.* Beverly Hills, CA: Sage.

Hofstede, G. (1991). *Cultures and organizations: Software of the mind.* London: McGraw-Hill.

Hofstede, G. (1995, July). *An american in paris.* Keynote speech for 12th EGOS colloquium Istanbul, Turkey.

Hofstede, G., Bond, M. H., & Luk, C. L. (1993). Individual perceptions of organizational cultures: A methodological treatise on levels of analysis. *Organization Studies, 14*, 483–583.

Hofstede, G., Neuyen, B., Ohayv, D. D., & Sanders, G. (1990). Measuring organizational cultures: A qualitative and quantitative study across twenty cases. *Administrative Science Quarterly, 35*, 286–316.

Hogan, R. (1992). Personality and personality measurement. In M. D. Dunnette & L. Hough (Eds.), *Handbok of Industrial/Organizational Psychology* (pp. 1–47). Palo Alto, CA: Consulting Psychologists Press.

Hoyle, R. H., & Crawford, A. M. (1994). Use of individual-level data to investigate group phenomena: Issues and strategies. *Small Group Research, 25*(4), 464–485.

Humana, C. (1986). *World human rights guide.* London: Pan Books.

Jackson, S. E., Brett, J. F., Sessa, V. I., Cooper, D. M., Julin, J. A., & Peyronnin, K. (1991). Some differences make a difference: Individual dissimilarity and group heterogeneity as correlates of recruitment, promotions, and turnover. *Journal of Applied Psychology, 76*, 675–689.

Joreskog, K. G., & Sorbom, D. (1993). *Lisrel 8: Structural equation modeling with the SUMPLIS command language.* Chicago: Scientific Software Interventional, Inc.

Klein, K. J., Dansereau, F., & Hall, R. J. (1994). Levels issues in theory development, data collection, and analysis. *Academy of Management Review, 19,* 195–229.

Kluckhohn, C. (1951). Values and value-orientations in the theory of action: An exploration in definition and classification. In T. Parsons and E. A. Shils (Eds.), *Toward a general theory of action* (pp. 388–433). Cambridge, MA: Harvard University Press.

Leung, K. (1989). Cross-cultural differences: Individual-level vs cultural-level analysis. *International Journal of Psychology, 24,* 703–719.

Leung K. (1996). The role of beliefs in Chinese culture. In M. H. Bond (Ed.), *The handbook of Chinese psychology* (pp. 233–248). Hong Kong: Oxford University Press.

Leung, K., and Bond, M. H. (1989). On the empirical identification of dimensions for cross-cultural comparisons. *Journal of Cross-cultural Psychology, 20,* 133–151.

Lissen, H., & Hagendoorn, L. (1994). Social and geographic factors in the explanation of the content of European nationality stereotypes. *British Journal of Social Psychology, 33,* 165–82.

Lytle, A. L., Brett, J. M., Barnsness, Z. I., Tinsley, C. H., & Janssens, M. (1995). A paradigm for confirmatory cross-cultural research in organizational behavior. In B. M. Staw & L. L. Cummings (Eds.), *Research in organizational behavior* (Vol. 17, pp. 167–214). Greenwich, CT: JAI Press.

Mischel, W. (1968). *Personality and assessment.* New York: Wiley.

Moreland, R. L., Levine, J. M., & Wingert, M. L. (1995). *Creating the ideal group: Composition effects at work.* Unpublished manuscript, University of Pittsburgh.

Olmstead, R. E., & Bentler, P. M. (1992). Structural equations modeling: A new friend? In F. B. Bryant, J. Edwards, R. S. Tindale, E. J. Posavac, L. Heath, E. Henderson, & Y. Suarez-Balcazar (Eds.), *Methodological issues in applied psychology* (pp. 135–158). Chicago: Loyola University.

Ostroff, C. (1993). Comparing correlations based on individual-level and aggregated data. *Journal of Applied Psychology, 78,* 569–582.

Population Crisis Committee. (1988, June). *Country rankings of the status of women: Poor, powerless, and pregnant.* Population Briefing Paper, No. 20.

Pugh, D. S., & Hickson, D. J. (1976). *Organizational structure in its context: The Aston programme I.* London: Saxon House.

Robinson, W. S. (1950). Ecological correlations and the behavior of individuals. *American Sociological Review, 15,* 351–357.

Rummel, R. J. (1972). *The dimensions of nations.* Beverley Hills, CA: Sage.

Sampson, E. E. (1977). Psychology and the American ideal. *Journal of Personality and Social Psychology, 35,* 767–782.

Sampson, E. E. (1981). Cognitive psychology as ideology. *American Psychologist, 36,* 730–743.

Sawyer, J. (1967). Dimensions of nations: Size, wealth and politics. *American Journal of Sociology, 72,* 145–172.

Scheuch, E. (1967). Society as a context in cross-national comparisons. *Social Science Information, 6,* 7–23.

Schwartz, S. H. (1992). Universals in the content and structure of values. Theoretical advances and empirical tests in 20 countries. In M. Zanna (Ed.), *Advances in experimental social psychology* (Vol. 25, pp. 1–65). Orlando, FL: Academic Press.

Schwartz, S. H. (1994). Beyond individualism/collectivism. New cultural dimensions of values. In U. Kim, H. C. Triandis, C. Kagiteibasi, S. C. Choi, & G. Yoon (Eds.), *Individualism and collectivism: Theory, method, and applications* (pp. 85–119), Newbury Park, CA: Sage.

Smith, P. B., & Bond, M. H. (1998). *Social psychology across cultures.* (2nd edition). London, England: Prentice Hall.

Smith, P. B., Dugan, S., & Trompenaars, F. (1996). National culture and the values of organizational employees. *Journal of Cross-Cultural Psychology, 27,* 231–264.

Smith Ring, P., & Van den Ven, A. H. (1994). Developmental processes of cooperative interorganizational relationships. *Academy of Management Review, 19,* 90–118.

Staub, E. (1988). The evolution of caring and nonaggressive persons and societies. *Journal of Social Issues, 44*, 81–100.

Stephan, W. G., Stephan, C. W., Abalakina, M., Ageyev, V., Blanco, A., Bond, M. H., Saito, I., Turcinovic, P., & Wenzel, B. (1996). Distinctiveness effects in intergroup perceptions: An international study. In H. Grad, A. Blanco & J. Georgas (Eds.), *Key issues in cross-cultural psychology* (pp. 298–308). Lisse, Netherlands: Swets and Zeitlinger.

Tajfel, H. (1974). Social identity and inter-group behavior. *Social Science Information, 13*, 65–93.

Tannenbaum, A. S., & Bachman, J. G. (1964). Structural versus individual effects. *American Journal of Sociology, 69*, 585–595.

Taylor, C. L., & Jodice, D. A. (1983). *Handbook of political and social indicators* (2nd ed.). New Haven, CT: Yale University Press.

Triandis, H. C. (1982). Review of *Culture's consequences*. *Human Organization, 41*, 86–90.

Triandis, H. C. (1984). Toward a psychological theory of economic growth. *International Journal of Psychology, 19*, 79–95.

Triandis, H. C., Bontempo, R., Leung, K., & Hui, C. C. H. (1990). A method for determining cultural, societal, and personal constructs. *Journal of Cross-Cultural Psychology, 21*, 302–318.

Watson, W. E., & Michaelson, L. K. (1988). Group interaction behaviors that affect group performance on an intellective task. *Group and Organization Studies, 13*(4), 495–516.

Weingart, L. R., Bennett, R. J., & Brett, J. M. (1993). The impact of consideration of issues and motivational orientation on group negotiation process and outcome. *Journal of Applied Psychology, 78*, 504–517.

Weinreich, P., Luk, C. L., & Bond, M. H. (1994, June). *Ethnic identity: Identification with other cultures, self-esteem, and identity confusion.* Paper presented at the International Conference on Immigration, Language Acquisition, and Patterns of Social Integration, Jerusalem.

Whiting, B. B., & Whiting, J. W. M. (1975). *Children of six cultures: A psycho-cultural analysis.* Cambridge, MA: Harvard University Press.

Wish, M., Deutsch, M., & Biener, L. (1970). Differences in conceptual structures of nations: An exploratory study. *Journal of Personality and Social Psychology, 16*, 361–373.

Woodman, R. W., Sawyer, J. E., & Griffin, R. W. (1993). Toward a theory of organizational creativity. *Academy of Management Review, 18*, 293–321.

Author Index

Numbers followed by the letter |f| indicates a figure; |n| denotes a footnote; and |t| indicates tabular material.

A

Aaker, D.A., 249, *259*
Abalakina, M., 397, 402, *412*
Abraham, L.M., *xvii*
Ackerman, P.L., 29, 30, 31, 33, 35, 36, *46*, *47*, *48*, 50, 52, 69, *71*, 170, *179*
Adams, J.A., 112, *119*
Adams, J.C., 155, *163*
Adams, J.S., 344, *364*
Ageyev, V., 397, 402, *412*
Aiello, J., 113, 115, 116, 118, *119*
Ajzen, I., 104, *108*, 157, *164*
Alavi, M., 18, 19, *25*
Alderfer, C.P., 256, *259*, 262, 266, 267, 268, 273, *277*, 354, *364*
Algera, J.A., 186, *195*, 199, *209*, 209, *209*
Allen, N.J., 251, *259*
Alvarez, E.B., 348, *365*
Alwin, D.F., 384, *392*
Anderson, A., 252, *259*
Anderson, B., 156, *163*
Anderson, J.R., 33, *46*
Andriessen, J.H.T.H., 141, 142, *145*
Antoni, C.H., 181, *195*
Aranya, N., 356, 357*t*, *367*
Argote, L., 177, *178*
Argyris, C., 237, 239, *244*
Armelagos, G.J., 382, *392*
Arnold, H.J., 132, *145*
Arnsdorf, D., 265, *277*
Arthur, M.B., 151, *165*, 279, 280, 281, 285, *290*
Arvey, R.D., *xvii*
Ash, R.A., 239, *244*

Ashforth, B., 123, *129*
Ashforth, B.E., 286, *290*, 332, *338*
Atchison, T.A., 155, *163*
Atkinson, J.W., 122, *129*, 170, 171, 174, *178*, 184, *195*
Attewell, P., 265, 270, *277*
Audia, G., 50, 52, *70*
Austin, G.A., 34, 35, 37, *47*
Austin, W., 151, *163*
Aviram, A., 83, *84*, 96, *97*
Avolio, B.J., 281, *289*, 352, *364*

B

Bachman, J.G., 401, *412*
Baddeley, A.D., 54, 68, 68*n*, *70*
Baetz, M.L., 219, *224*, 280, 281, 285, *290*
Baglioni, A.J., Jr., 315, *322*
Bailey, J.R., 385, *394*
Bailey, T., 29, *48*
Baker, D., 335, *338*
Baker, D.D., 22, *25*
Balcazar, F., 111, *119*
Bales, R.F., 398, 399, 405, *409*
Balkin, D.B., 150, 154, 158, *163*, *164*
Bandura, A., 14, 15, 16, 17, 19, *24*, 26, 27, 28, 29, 34, 41, 42, *46*, *48*, 74, 75, *84*, 87, 88, 91, 94, *97*, 103, *107*, 112, *119*, 141, *145*, 189, *195*, 198, *209*
Bannister, B.D., 154, 158, *163*
Bargh, J.A., 69, *70*
Barkan, S., 356, *367*
Barkow, J.H., 381, *392*

413

Subject Index

Numbers followed by the letter |f| indicates a figure; |n| denotes a footnote; and |t| indicates tabular material.

A

Accountability, in team members, 348
Achievement in work motivation, 185, 185f
Achievement-oriented relation, in group work, 183
Action, change dynamics and, 390
Action theory, personality constructs within, 104
Advanced manufacturing technologies (AMT), 271–272
AER. *See* Alternative employment relationships
Affiliation
in group work, 183
in work motivation, 185, 185f
Air Traffic Control (ATC) task, 33, 33n
Alderfer's intergroup theory, 266–267
Allocentrism, 352
Alternative employment relationships (AER), in employment ads, 250–252, 251t
AMT. *See* Advanced manufacturing technologies
Arousal, 115, 115t, 117f
ASA. *See* Attraction-selection-attrition theory
Assigned goals, for mediation-linking model, 16–17
ATC. *See* Air Traffic Control
Attitudes, organizational withdrawal and, 295
Attraction-selection-attrition (ASA) theory, 237–240, 243
logic of, 238
model of, 232–233
Authority figures, compliance with, 333–334
Authority ranking, 374, 377

B

Automaticity, as personality factor, 104
Autonomy, compensation and, 158–159

BARS. *See* Behavioral anchored rating scale
Behavioral anchored rating scale (BARS), in measuring time urgency, 316–317
Behavioral measures, reemployment and, 92–93
Behaviors, organizational withdrawal and, 295
Benefectance, 123
Between-subjects independent variables, 134–135
experiment results, 136–137, 137t
Biodata study of homogeneity, 240–241
Burnout, components of, 286

C

Characteristics, of team members, 347–349
Charismatic leadership, 281. *See also* Leadership, charismatic
Cognitive effort, definition of, 30–32
Cognitive evaluation theory, compensation and, 158
Cognitive performance theories, assumptions of, 68–69
Collective efficacy
definition of, 79–80
importance of, 81
peers as source of, 79–81
See also Efficacy; Means efficacy

427